NEW AGENDAS IN IRISH PREHISTORY

New agendas in Irish prehistory

Papers in commemoration of Liz Anderson

Edited by
Angela Desmond, Gina Johnson, Margaret McCarthy,
John Sheehan and Elizabeth Shee Twohig

Wordwell

First published in 2000
Wordwell Ltd
PO Box 69, Bray, Co. Wicklow

ISBN 1 869857 34 8

British Library Cataloguing-in-Publication Data.
A catalogue record for this book is available from the British Library.

This publication has received support from the Heritage Council under the 2000 Publications Grant Scheme, from the National Museum and from *Dúchas.*

Original conference sponsored by the Discovery Programme; the Heritage Council; Faculty of Arts, UCC; the British Council; the Archaeological Society, UCC; Bank of Ireland, UCC.

Cover design: Rachel Dunne.
Cover includes photographs of Newgrange kerbstone and Liz's oak tree at UCC (both by Elizabeth Shee Twohig).

Typeset in Ireland by Wordwell Ltd.
Origination by Wordwell Ltd and the Type Bureau.

Printed by Brookfield Printing Co.

Contents

Preface

The papers published in this volume were presented at a conference held in memory of Liz Anderson at University College Cork in February 1999.

The conference took its general theme from a third-year course, 'Problems in Irish Prehistory', which Liz had helped to shape over several years.

The publication of the conference papers provides an opportunity to identify and review a range of current problems in Irish prehistory. We present them as a tribute to Liz.

List of contributors

Ms Rose Cleary, Department of Archaeology, University College, Cork.

Professor Gabriel Cooney, Department of Archaeology, University College, Belfield, Dublin 4.

Professor John Coles, Fursdon Mill Cottage, Thorverton, Devon, FX5 5JS, England.

Mr Martin Doody, Discovery Programme, 34 Fitzwilliam Place, Dublin 2.

Dr Mike Kimball, 1313 Farwell Drive, Madison, Wisconsin 53704, USA.

Ms Sinéad McCartan, Department of Archaeology and Ethnography, Ulster Museum, Botanic Gardens, Belfast BT9 5AB.

Ms Margaret McCarthy, Archaeological Services Unit, Department of Archaeology, University College, Cork.

Ms Denise Maher and Mr John Sheehan, Department of Archaeology, University College, Cork.

Mr Michael Monk, Department of Archaeology, University College, Cork.

Dr William O'Brien, Department of Archaeology, National University of Ireland, Galway.

Mr Denis Power, Archaeological Survey of Ireland, National Monuments Depot, Greenmount, Mallow, Co. Cork.

Dr Elizabeth Shee Twohig, Department of Archaeology, University College, Cork.

Dr Caroline Wickham-Jones, 21 Dudley Gardens, Edinburgh EH6 4PU, Scotland.

Professor Peter Woodman, Department of Archaeology, University College, Cork.

Acknowledgements

The editors wish to thank all those who helped in the production of this volume, from the moment when the conference was first proposed to the appearance of the final bound conference proceedings. It was an easy task in many ways, owing to the level of commitment of those involved.

The conference was generously sponsored by the Discovery Programme, UCC's Arts Faculty Conference Fund, the Heritage Council, the British Council, UCC's Archaeological Society and the Bank of Ireland, UCC, to whom we are very grateful. The organisation of the conference was mainly looked after by Angela Desmond and John Sheehan, ably assisted by Abigail Brewer, Elizabeth Byrne, Noelle Guinane, Denise Maher, Carol Martin and Diana Reynolds. The organisers would like to thank the following for their help during the conference and in arranging a tree-planting ceremony in the President's Garden at University College Cork: the General Services Office; Frank O'Donovan of Audio-Visual Services; and the Buildings and Estates Office, in particular Michael McCormack.

The editorial work was very much a Departmental effort, with help from some friends. Papers were checked by an army of volunteers—Rose Cleary, Angela Desmond, Gina Johnson, Denise Maher, Margaret McCarthy, Mick Monk, Barra Ó Donnabháin, Mary O'Donnell, John Sheehan, Elizabeth Shee Twohig, Peter Woodman—along with Sinéad McCartan and Caroline Wickham-Jones. Gina Johnson looked after the standardisation of formatting and text-editing, and Rhoda Cronin produced many of the illustrations for the publication.

The conference speakers deserve special thanks as the quality of the presentations contributed enormously to the success of the event. Their subsequent efforts in producing papers for the volume and their prompt response to any queries from the editors made the task of editing the volume very easy and pleasant. One person deserves special mention for doing a difficult job very well. Professor John Coles took on the task of acting as Discussant at the conference. He presented a very constructive summation of the issues addressed in the conference papers, offering a very useful outside view of possible new agendas in Irish prehistory. What really impressed, however, was the very personal note he struck in his paper, which was appropriate in view of the commemorative nature of the conference and admirable in that he had not known Liz personally. We are all very grateful for his thoughtful contribution to the event and to the subsequent publication, and we are very glad that we made such an inspired choice as Discussant.

The publication was generously sponsored by the Heritage Council, the National Museum of Ireland and *Dúchas*. Finally the editors wish to thank Wordwell, in particular Nick Maxwell, for all the help received during the course of production. Advice was always provided when sought on any aspect of the work and for this we are very grateful.

Elizabeth Anderson, MA
30 November 1961–22 February 1997

Elizabeth Anderson, or 'Liz A', as she was affectionately known, died in Cork on 22 February 1997 at the age of 35.

She graduated from University College Cork in 1984 with an Honours BA in Archaeology and Greek and Roman Civilisation, and was subsequently awarded a First Class Honours MA for her thesis entitled 'Flint technology in the Later Mesolithic'. This work has since influenced the course of lithic studies in Ireland.

Liz loved archaeology with a passion that is rarely seen these days. Her contribution to the subject as a researcher cannot be underestimated and goes beyond the list of her publications included in this volume. Perhaps her greatest strength was her ability to communicate her exceptional enthusiasm to students at all levels—undergraduate, postgraduate or, very importantly to Liz, simply those who shared her interest in 'the past'. Liz taught in UCC's Archaeology Department from 1984 up to the time of her death, and was particularly appreciated by her students for the fact that she 'got down and did it'. She took as much pleasure from her flint-knapping sessions as her students did.

While UCC played a significant role in her career, Liz also shared her knowledge of and enthusiasm for archaeology outside the campus grounds. Her clear style of lecturing and her open personality resulted in many invitations to speak to schoolchildren. She was also involved with Adult Education courses and travelled to various locations in Munster to give classes. When it came to archaeology, the word 'no' didn't exist in Liz's vocabulary.

Outside of the lecture hall, Liz readily indulged in other aspects of archaeology. She contributed to the development of a new generation of field archaeologists by supervising on four training excavations. Although she worked on numerous 'later' sites, her particular *grá* for coastal locations took her on excavations from the Orkney

Islands to her beloved Dingle Peninsula, where she fine-tuned her interest in the Mesolithic period. In 1990 she was enticed inland to excavate a site at Kilcummer, Co. Cork, in the ongoing search for the Early Mesolithic along the Blackwater.

Liz specialised in lithic studies, and her talents in this area were acknowledged by the many excavators who sought her out to analyse assemblages from their sites. She was also a very accomplished illustrator, especially of lithic artefacts, and her distinctive drawings appear in many publications. In her 'spare' time, Liz also served as a production assistant for the Cork Archaeological Survey, inputting data on sites in preparation for publication. From 1991 Liz worked on the Keiller–Knowles Project, which involved the computerised cataloguing of *c.* 15,000 lithic artefacts that formed part of a large antiquarian collection housed in the National Museum of Ireland. She also worked as a research archaeologist with the Discovery Programme, undertaking post-excavation analysis for the Ballyhoura Hills Project between 1995 and 1996.

The above is only a sketch of Liz's involvement with archaeology, an involvement that brought her into contact with a large number of people in the profession and won her many friends. For those who knew her well, it was not what she did but how she did it that is most remembered. She was *always* available when needed, whatever the request, and would happily drop what she was doing to give someone her full attention—either to assist or often just to listen (the memory of the ever-open office door is much quoted). It is for that quality that she is most missed.

When the conference was first proposed, no coaxing was required to find organisers and speakers. Their deep affection for Liz meant that all her friends and colleagues were eager to be involved in achieving the ultimate goal—to produce a book in her honour. The theme of the conference related to a course, 'Problems in Irish Prehistory', that Liz was involved in teaching. The success of the conference was due as much to the high esteem in which Liz was held as to the quality of the conference programme. While some of the 250 attendees had never met Liz, most of the participants saw the conference as an opportunity to celebrate and share personal memories of her all-too-short life.

Liz's contribution to archaeology is at least in part documented in her publications. However, her personal qualities—her energy, her inquisitive mind, her sense of fun, her courage in facing her illness, and most of all her friendship—will live long in the memories of those who knew her.

'In small proportions we just beauties see;
And in short measures life may perfect be.'
(Ben Jonson)

PUBLICATIONS OF ELIZABETH (LIZ) ANDERSON

Anderson, E. 1990 Flint and stone tools. In M. Ryan (ed.), *An illustrated guide to Irish archaeology*, 35–7. Dublin. Town House.

Anderson, E. 1991 Kilcummer Lower, Co. Cork—flint scatter. In I. Bennett (ed.), *Excavations 1990: summary accounts of archaeological excavations in Ireland*, 3–4. Bray. Wordwell.

Anderson, E. 1993 The Mesolithic in Munster: fishing for answers. In E. Shee Twohig and M. Ronayne (eds), *Past perceptions: the prehistoric archaeology of south-west Ireland*, 16–24. Cork University Press.

Anderson, E. 1993 Appendix 2: Lithic report. In A.M. Lennon, 'Excavation of a ringfort, Raheens 1, Carrigaline, Co. Cork'. *Journal of the Cork Historical and Archaeological Society* **98**, 87–9.

Anderson, E. 1995 Report on the lithics. In G. Walsh, B.E. Beirne and P.J. Tobin, *Archaeological excavations on the Ballinrobe Sewerage and Sewage Disposal Scheme 1994*, 33–6. Mayo County Council Archaeological Series 3.

Anderson, E. 1996 The lithic assemblage. In R.M. Cleary, 'Later Bronze Age settlement and prehistoric burials, Lough Gur, Co. Limerick'. *Proceedings of the Royal Irish Academy* **95**C, 68–71.

Anderson, E. 1996 Use wear analysis. In P.C. Woodman and G. Johnson, 'Excavations at Bay Farm 1, Carnlough, Co. Antrim, and the study of the "Larnian" technology'. *Proceedings of the Royal Irish Academy* **96**C, 232–5.

Anderson, E. 1996 The lithics. In E. Shee Twohig, 'Excavations at St Saviour's Dominican Priory, Limerick, Part II'. *North Munster Antiquarian Journal* **37**, 81–2.

Anderson, E. and Johnson, G. 1993 A refitting and use-wear analysis of a Later Mesolithic flint assemblage from Bay Farm, Co. Antrim. *Archeomaterials* **7** (1), 83–100.

Anderson, E. and Johnson, G. 1995 Irish Later Mesolithic flint technology: further developments. In E. Grogan and C. Mount (eds), *Annus Archaeologiae. Proceedings of the OIA Winter Conference 1993*, 7–22. Organisation of Irish Archaeologists.

Anderson, E. and McCartan, S. 1991 Caught knapping—lithic studies in archaeology. *Archaeology Ireland* **5** (4), 23–6.

Anderson, E. and McCarthy, M. 1991 Report on an excavation at Robber's Den Cave, Ballynahown, Co. Clare. *Irish Speleology: the Journal of Irish Caving* **14** (May 1991), 11–13.

Anderson, E. and Woodman, P. 1995 Computers in archaeology: coping with museum collections. In T. Stevens and V. James (eds), *The future for Europe's past. Proceedings of COMETT Workshops, September 1995*, 23–36. Swansea Institute of Higher Education.

McCartan, S. and Anderson, E. 1992 Irish lithic bibliography. *Lithics: the newsletter*

of the Lithic Studies Society **13**, 69–75.
Woodman, P.C. and Anderson, E. 1990 The Irish Late Mesolithic: a partial picture. In P. Vermeersch and P. van Peer (eds), *Contributions to the Mesolithic in Europe*, 377–87. Leuven University Press.
Woodman, P.C., Anderson, E. and Finlay, N. 1999 *Excavations at Ferriter's Cove 1983–95: last foragers, first farmers in the Dingle Peninsula.* Bray. Wordwell.

Liz

By Connie Kelleher, for the memorial service, May 1997, on behalf of the MA classes of the Department of Archaeology, UCC

There is a room within that has her presence there,
among the drawings and artefacts, the boxes and the chair.
There is a place where she will be
remembered constantly—
But it is not limited to that room
or the space that you can see.

For her spirit is within our minds
and in all that we were shown;
From the knapping of a flint core
to the shape of a hammerstone.
Her knowledge was to us divulged
in such a pleasant way,
That the learning was made easy
by what she had to say.

Her pragmatic way of teaching
was by humour interspersed,
Which gained our full attention
and ensured our interest.
The ease with which she taught us
was as if a friend were there—
A frankness and an eagerness
with her willingness to share.

It is that special quality
which now leaves such a void,
In the field of archaeology
and in our personal lives.
We grieve at the passing
of our lecturer and friend,
But her resilience was evident
right to the end.

We remember with fondness,
with respect and privilege,
Being given the chance
to have known someone like Liz.

HAMMERS AND SHOEBOXES: NEW AGENDAS FOR PREHISTORY

Peter Woodman

The word hammer in my title comes from a line in *Timescape* (Benford 1992, 197): 'The man who has only a hammer to work with finds that every new problem needs a nail'. I am also sure that it was based on a memory of Moore and Keene's introduction to *Archaeological hammers and theories* (Moore and Keene 1983), where they quote Kaplan (1964, 28):

> Give a small boy a hammer and he will find that everything he encounters needs pounding. It comes as no particular surprise that a scientist formulates problems in a way which requires for their solution just those techniques in which he himself is skilled.

The 'shoeboxes' come from an analogy proposed by Stephen J. Gould in *Wonderful life* (1989), where he discusses the major shift in the description and understanding of the Pre-Cambrian Burgess shale faunas, from an assumption that this Pre-Cambrian fauna could be categorised as variants of trilobites (the study area of Charles Doolittle Walcott, who carried out the original research) to Whittington's realisation that the fauna was unique and different, consisting mostly of life-forms that did not exist within traditional geological classifications. This change illustrates the constraints of the intellectual shoeboxes we create for ourselves. I would like to suggest that we in Ireland have been using the same archaeological shoeboxes for so long that we have begun to forget that our systems of classification are little more than mental constructions that were created for our convenience. In our case we have also chosen to store ideas and shoeboxes in a large tea chest which we call '*Irish* prehistory', and in many cases we have been using hammers to ensure that our ideas fit in these shoeboxes.

Some years ago a Scottish colleague and I were asked to speak on 'What's new in Irish/Scottish prehistory'. The question was raised as to whether we should look at the *archaeology* of a country rather than identifying more general problems. At the time I felt that we should place the archaeology of Ireland before more general issues. However, in retrospect I feel that I was wrong, because by looking at the Irish archaeological record as it existed we missed the obvious—namely the gaps.

Recently I have proposed that the most likely period during which Ireland could have been colonised, the Lower Palaeolithic, was Oxygen Isotope Stage 7, i.e. approximately 200,000 years ago (Woodman 1998). Unfortunately there is a real problem; Coxon (1993) has noted that there are as yet no known OIS7 deposits in Ireland! In one way it could be argued that this rendered my discussion irrelevant, if not ludicrous, but only if we accept that archaeology must always start from the position of examining and interpreting the extant record. Surely, even in Ireland, we can pose questions and try to make a contribution to some of the larger issues associated with the origin and development of human society. A realistic assessment of a Palaeolithic presence in Ireland can raise issues beyond Ireland and can contribute to a much wider debate; thus a discussion on OIS7 and Ireland is far from meaningless as it places Ireland in a broader discourse. As I noted (Woodman 1998), Gamble (1996) has rightly pointed to a crisis of confidence in the types of issues which scholars working on the Lower/Middle Palaeolithic of north-west Europe are prepared to tackle. In this case the potential for early forms of modern humans, such as *H. heidelbergensis*, to colonise difficult environments is an issue in which Ireland could play a role. Obviously this is even more true of the Middle Palaeolithic and earlier phases of the Upper Palaeolithic, when time was available (perhaps 20,000 years) for other forms of mammals to reach Ireland and when settlement is also known to have occurred quite close to Ireland (Woodman *et al.* 1997; Woodman 1998). If there was a marine element in Palaeolithic economies at the time of lower sea-levels which only survived as now-inundated coastal settlements, this could be signalled by the presence of early settlement on islands such as Ireland.

Many would still feel that looking at gaps in our archaeological record is pointless because we regard the existing record as the national record of our past. This is not necessarily a *nationalist* record. We have all learned to recognise our ethnic and nationalist biases and are aware of the danger of using the archaeological record to underpin a particular perspective in contemporary politics here in Ireland—we all know of examples, such as the 1970s debate on the origins of Irish Bronze Age gold objects. However, a national past is something different. It is not an attitude confined to Ireland but can be found elsewhere, particularly in smaller countries, where there was a need for national self-identification. Even the creation of chairs of archaeology can be a product of nationalism. In the nineteenth century, Eugene O'Curry's chair of archaeology was in an establishment created for very definite politico-religious reasons, i.e. the Catholic University of Ireland. Even Bertram Windle's creation of a chair of archaeology in University College Cork, in 1909, can be seen as a product of his ideals of cultural nationalism. Denmark and the Netherlands are also examples of smaller countries where chairs of primarily national archaeology were established early in the last century. Indeed, we all know of the significance of the name change in German archaeology from the *German Society for Prehistory* to the *Society for German Prehistory.* I have heard only one person, a historian, commenting on the fact that we have a *Journal of Irish Archaeology* rather than an *Irish Journal of Archaeology.*

Somewhere along the line we created our National Archaeology. I would put it down to *Antiquities of the Irish countryside* (Ó Ríordáin 1942), which changed from what was originally a useful handbook and guide to field monuments to an attempt to be the definitive set of statements on Irish archaeology. Other textbooks, such as J. Raftery's *Prehistoric Ireland* (1952), did not, nor were ever intended to, serve in that manner. Even Macalister's *Archaeology of Ireland* (1928), ending with its very political aspirations for the well-being of the fledgling Free State, did not attempt to provide that type of definitive statement.

The result was that by the end of the 1960s we had created a sacred canon of Irish archaeology in which we formalised monument types and periods, and interpreted the past through interpreting them. This canon has served us well during the period of archaeological surveys when there was a need for an identification and maintenance of the archaeological resources of the island. We created a useful management tool, but we are inclined to defend it as Holy Writ. As a result our tendency is to make minimal contributions to larger debates in European archaeology. Although our universities teach courses on European archaeology, we appear to be unaware of the broader issues that are being debated and are therefore content to confine ourselves to a provincial descriptive form of archaeology which relies on the excellent quality of our primary data. This contemporary attitude is well-founded in the history of our discipline in Ireland. It is noteworthy that the only papers emanating from Ireland which are quoted in Trigger's (1989) *History of archaeological thought* are one by Monsignor O'Laverty (1857), casting serious doubt on the Three Age System, and another, which Trigger treated more sympathetically, by Eoin MacWhite (1956), someone who left Irish archaeology.

It was, and perhaps still is, more usual to have the archaeological record in Ireland mired in highly personalised local disputes. While geologists saw rocks at Portrush and the Giant's Causeway as contributing to the debate on Diluvianism versus Vulcanism, Irish archaeology has rarely confronted the bigger issues, even when it can make a contribution. On issues such as 'Deep Time' the obvious implications of the extinct giant deer were never drawn upon. In a planned world, where God created all and where evolution of species was still not acceptable to many, strange extinct animals such as the giant deer presented a conundrum. The French traveller to Ireland, de Latocnaye, put it rather well when he commented: 'What was nature thinking of to lodge in an island an animal which must have felt itself imprisoned' (de Latocnaye 1798, 129).

From an Irish perspective it was preferable to solve these problems within the received wisdom of the day. Thus Crofton Croker (*Literary Gazette,* July 1849) wished to see this species as contemporaneous with people—in fact as a domesticated species! By adopting these attitudes it was possible to avoid the issues surrounding the concept of a God who could invent animals that became extinct before he put people on this earth.

Changing attitudes is very difficult. Over 100 years ago Robert Day (1891) complained that the failure to record polished stone axes in Munster was because of an underlying lack of interest in the province! Today the same perspective still exists. Cooney and Mandal (1998) recorded less than 30 polished stone axes from County Kerry, while Cork did not fare much better. Similarly, outside excavations, stone arrowheads of the Neolithic and Bronze Age are virtually non-existent (Woodman and Scannell 1993). Thus there was no relevant database to test the challenge thrown down by Lynch's work indicating a Neolithic presence at Cashelkeelty, Co. Kerry (Lynch 1981). Similarly, the discovery of the Mesolithic of Munster in the 1980s begs the question, 'How was it possible to avoid discovering the obvious for so long?' In this case it was not because of a convergence of natural factors, such as the absence of arable farmland or an interested local population, as in northern Scotland, but because of a respect for our archaeological canon that there was no Mesolithic and possibly no Early Neolithic in many parts of Munster.

The resistance of authors such as O'Laverty, or others such as Clibborn (1859), to the Three Age System and a Palaeolithic seems to be part of a pattern. In spite of the fact that John Evans was in Ireland within a few weeks of his momentous meeting at Abbeville with Boucher de Perthes, few in Ireland were prepared to follow his lead. Three decades later the personalised debate on the age of the flint artefacts in the gravels at Larne showed how a classic opportunity to use Irish data to confirm a suggestion by Hodder Westropp[1] that there was a human presence between Europe's Palaeolithic and Neolithic, i.e. in the Mesolithic, could get bogged down in irrelevant details. In this case William Gray, originally from Cork, and William Knowles, from Ballymena, each had half the truth. Knowles correctly identified the fact that the stone tools found in the raised beach gravels were different from the Neolithic forms found in the overlying sand-dunes. For this reason he proposed that the 'Older Series' should be considered as Palaeolithic in age. In contrast, Gray correctly noted that the extinct Ice Age faunas usually associated with Palaeolithic industries were absent. He therefore considered that the raised beach material post-dated the Palaeolithic. Of course, within a decade Piette was to identify the 'Mesolithic' at the Mas d'Azil (Woodman 1978)!

This conservative trend was not confined to nineteenth-century archaeological thought. Today O'Kelly's pioneering work on *fulachta fiadh* (O'Kelly 1954) is generally recognised, but his early espousal of ^{14}C dating at Killeens is usually forgotten. Even in this paper he was able to make a strong case for a Bronze Age date for many *fulachta fiadh* on the grounds of both archaeological association and ^{14}C dating. However, the received wisdom that they were primarily Iron Age continued through the 1970s (see Herity and Eogan 1977), and it was only at the beginning of the 1980s that the work of one of O'Kelly's students confirmed that they were primarily Bronze Age (Ó Drisceoil 1988).

I wonder sometimes if we are too much in awe of other disciplines which we feel to be more intellectually rigorous or to have more structured research strategies than our own. As a result we are often afraid of being wrong. It is therefore very comforting to read statements of researchers such as the particle physicist Frank Wilczek: 'If you don't make mistakes, you're not working on hard enough problems and that's a big mistake' (taken from the introduction to Benford's *Cosm* (1999)).

Perhaps, therefore, it is time to look at some of the tenets that have underpinned our archaeological canon, tenets that have become implicit founding principles of our archaeological 'self-evident truths'. I would like to examine just two of these, although others would, of course, identify a different set of priorities.

MONUMENT AND ARTEFACT TYPES ARE ALWAYS SPREAD EQUALLY THROUGHOUT AN ARCHAEOLOGICAL PERIOD

This first tenet comes from a time when, for prehistory in particular, we had to live with a fatal flaw—that the chronological framework for our archaeological record relied to a great extent on our grouping of monuments and/or artefacts. This we then used in a self-sustaining set of circular arguments—namely that monuments and artefact types were found in and, it was gradually assumed, characterised particular archaeological periods. The next obvious step was to assume that the period was characterised by the occurrence of a particular package and could only be characterised by it.

The most obvious example of this was the gradual shift in attitudes towards court tombs. It was first suggested, rightly or wrongly, that they were a part of the Early Neolithic in Ireland (de Valera 1960), and then it was assumed that they characterised the Early Neolithic

(Herity and Eogan 1977). As a consequence, it was then logical to assume that any region which did not have court tombs could not have an Early Neolithic. Other theories have since been added, such as the proto-megalith theories (Powell *et al.* 1969). However, again there was an assumption that megalithic tombs were part of the primary Neolithic. In the case of Munster, O'Kelly's (1981) suggestion that the wedge tombs were the Neolithic equivalent of the court tombs was part of the same perspective, i.e. to have an Early Neolithic there had to be Neolithic monuments. Aside from the debate about why court and portal tombs differ from passage tombs, one of the most interesting arguments must centre on the growing evidence for alternative burial rites in south-west Ireland, in particular the use of caves.

The canon dictated that certain monument types were found in certain regions. For example, portal tombs seem to exist uneasily in parts of the south-west. I would suggest that suspicion about the Castle Mary tomb, Co. Cork, is an example. It is treated as a suspect monument in the Cork Archaeological Survey and it has gone missing from the new Discovery Series maps! Yet Sharon Wells (1995, 24, figs 2.12 and 2.13) has shown that there are eighteenth-century sketches of the Castle Mary dolmen already in a state of collapse. It is therefore unlikely to be an antiquarian folly. However, it does not fit the conventional wisdom as to how we distribute our monuments through space and time. Condit and Connolly (1998) have amply demonstrated our capacity to ignore Neolithic monuments in a region where a Neolithic presence was not expected, i.e. the Lee Valley near Tralee, Co. Kerry. In this area there are, of course, the potential indications of distinct forms of Neolithic burial monuments, shown through the excavations at Ballycarty (Connolly 1999). Hopefully the excavation of a less disturbed example of this monument type will help to resolve the issue of the age of these structures.

The occurrence of substantial Neolithic houses at Tankardstown, Co. Limerick (Gowen and Tarbett 1988), or Cloghers, Co. Kerry (Dunne and Kiely 1999), as well as the early domesticated animals from Ferriter's Cove, Co. Kerry, and Kilgreaney Cave, Co. Waterford (Woodman *et al.* 1997), show that farming communities existed in Munster apparently without the relevant visible monuments. Instead of wasting our energies trying to bend the evidence to suit our accepted national canon, we have the opportunity to explore issues such as why the Irish archaeological record can be different, to examine these differences and use them to contribute to the wider European debate. Frankly I feel that we are often far too self-indulgently insular. We have a lot to contribute, and much of that contribution could be based on our differences.

Instead of confining our deliberations to the age of particular monuments, we should have been paying attention to the debates between Zvelebil and Rowley-Conwy (1986) and Thomas (1988), or in Scandinavia between Rowley-Conwy (1985) and Jennbert (1985). What were the triggers that led to the adoption of agriculture and, if the social dimension was important, was it necessary, as Thomas (1988) suggested, to have something such as a communal burial monument as part of the social apparatus for the existence of Neolithic communities? Similarly, was the spread of farming in Scandinavia the result of ecological change, as suggested by Rowley-Conwy (1985), or did it occur through a social vector such as Jennbert's productive gift (1985)?

Certain classes of monuments need not necessarily be distributed throughout a period.

We can take hillforts as an example. We now see them as having been created as a part of social change in the second half of the Irish Bronze Age, i.e. they are typical of our Later Bronze Age. If we accept a military function for them, should we see them as being a creation of the Later Bronze Age? Many military fortifications are, of course, a specific response to a particular need. Perhaps we should draw analogies with Martello towers. They are not a product of the nineteenth century in its totality but initially a response to one perceived threat which left tangible monuments in a landscape—monuments which, of course, continued to be used for the next two centuries (Joyce 1922). In a more recent context, I was struck by the prevalence of World War II German military fortifications in Finnmark, Norway. Axis airfields, barracks buildings and swarms of anti-aircraft battery emplacements dominate parts of the region. These were built in a five-year period but still survive, while the domestic architecture of east Finnmark is a product of rebuilding after the towns were razed during the Axis retreat in 1945. Have we become so afraid of the concept of invasion that we never wish to identify the single important event? We do not have to fully endorse all of Baillie's (1998) correlations of archaeological events and cometary cataclysm to accept that specific significant social or natural events may have had effects on society so as to create major portions of our archaeological record in a very short time. Getting a more precise and accurate estimate of the ages should be our most important priority. Thus the recent revelation (Lynn and Mallory's paper to the Celtic Congress, Cork, 1999) that the ditch at Navan Fort may be close to 1000 years later than that at nearby Haughey's Fort must be food for thought. We can always construct stories and have discourses on the hierarchical nature of later prehistoric society, but without a really rigorous approach to chronology there is little chance that we will have any contact with reality.

So far I have considered monuments, but it is possible that certain prestige objects may not be typical of a full archaeological period. O'Brien (1994) has made the point that, while Ireland's Early Bronze Age is often thought of as a period of export of bronzes, there is really only one phase—that associated with Ballyvalley axes—when there was significant export of Irish bronzes. Perhaps much of our gold production could be associated with short episodes of time. Warner (1993) has shown that different types of objects were made from different sources, and therefore it is probable that much of the gold production came from disjointed pulses of production. In Munster the concentration of lunulae in Kerry, facing west as opposed to the south coast Cork and Wexford distribution of gold discs (Taylor 1980), suggests not only two chronologically distinct phases of production but production to serve two different needs.

Therefore, again, should we not be considering pertinent questions as we go on with our research rather than simply waiting for the next find, excavation or radiocarbon date which we will then seek to trap within the national canon? Did the Discovery Programme's original document (Discovery Programme 1992) set a new agenda? It provided an opportunity for real debate that was not taken up. In particular, are we well served by the assumption that the processes of change in human society can best be studied with traditional classifications and assumptions based on received wisdom?

WE CAN EXPECT A CORRELATION BETWEEN ACTIVITY AND THE CREATION OF OUR ARCHAEOLOGICAL RECORD

The second tenet of our archaeological canon that I would like to consider is based on how we deal with artefacts. Again we seem to have reversed our logic. We expect all sites of a particular period to produce the relevant type fossils, and we also expect to be able to interpret the purpose of an archaeological site from the convenient discarding of a series of distinctive implements. The trouble is that prehistoric communities did not have our optimistic textbooks on bio-archaeology, economic archaeology or computers in archaeology and so were unaware of how *we* expect them to behave.

Some years ago I caused consternation at a Palaeo–Meso meeting in the British Museum by suggesting that certain phases of the British Mesolithic might not have had microliths associated with them. The near-hysteria that this suggestion generated was based on the awful prospect that a phase of human activity might not have a convenient set of signposts associated with it—an 'appalling vista' for archaeologists.

For me, this point can be best illustrated by examining aspects of Ireland's Later Mesolithic. I continue to have an interest in this period mostly because it challenges so many of our convenient self-evident truths as to what a Mesolithic site should look like: it has that appalling vista—it lacks those infamous microliths. Nowhere have these challenges been more evident than in the material from Ferriter's Cove.

In spite of the recognition of the role of curation, which shows that there will not always be convenient '*ad hoc*' production and, perhaps more importantly, discarding of tools at the location of their use, there is still an unspoken expectation that prehistoric settlements are much more interesting if they contain a reasonable selection of artefacts. Yet it is apparent that at Ferriter's Cove (Woodman *et al.* 1999) there are as many locations without the discarding and accumulation of artefacts associated with fireplaces and shell heaps as there are locations where artefacts occur. There is, however, no doubt that as much settlement has taken place around the former as around the latter. Liz and I pointed out nearly ten years ago that there was a group of sites in Munster that produced no convenient concentration of Mesolithic material, yet whose radiocarbon dates suggested that activity took place in the Later Mesolithic (Woodman and Anderson 1990). There is now a significant number of sites of this type throughout Ireland, and their implication is that human settlement is not always marked by convenient scatters of the right type of artefacts.

Many of our Bronze Age settlement sites also fall into this category. At some sites, such as Cullyhanna, Co. Armagh (Hodges 1956), virtually no artefacts were recovered, while the Bronze Age phase from Donegore Hill (Mallory and McNeill 1991) was really only distinguishable through ^{14}C dating. Even at Clonfinlough, Co. Offaly (Moloney 1993), few diagnostic objects were recovered. Perhaps on many prehistoric sites similar lessons can be learnt as have been learnt from Later Mesolithic sites such as Ferriter's Cove.

At Ferriter's Cove, while at one level the Bann Flakes, backed and bar forms, picks and borers challenge the 'conventional wisdom' of the European Mesolithic, there is a danger that we may have developed our own conventional wisdom that the Irish Later Mesolithic is characterised only by these artefacts. However, what can be seen from the assemblage is that many less distinctive forms, such as the thick robust blades, despite the occasional intractability or unsuitability of the raw material, appear to have been deliberately produced. Found on their own or in small numbers, how do we recognise these as indications of Mesolithic settlement? At Ferriter's Cove there are also a series of chipped pebbles and notched pieces that are as common as the classic type fossils. Again, found elsewhere, would we recognise these tools as indicating where Mesolithic settlement had taken place?

I feel, and I have said it elsewhere, that the coastal/inland model which some of us have used for our Mesolithic may need to be challenged (Woodman *et al.* 1999). In Denmark it has been recognised that Mesolithic communities not only had their own territories, which might have been comparatively small, but also that they might not have been only coastal and inland but could have been coastal *or* inland. What happens if some of our distinctive Later Mesolithic tool types were not needed in certain localities? Could there be traces of activity which leave virtually no convenient traces of specific tool types? Are we identifying only particular types of 'hot spots' which we assume are totally representative of a society's activities? Our assumptions that the type fossils *must* be there is just as dangerous as the assumption that our Early Neolithic must have court tombs!

We rarely face up to the fact that certain activities do not require the deposition of a requisite set of artefacts, but it is perhaps even rarer for us to acknowledge that whole phases of our past may be somewhat lacking in distinctive type fossils. At different levels these are the lessons of the Irish Later Mesolithic. It differs from the accepted norms in both Britain and continental mainland Europe, but so does much of Fenno-Scandinavia. Too rarely do we ask, 'Why do these differences exist?' For me, however, one of the most intriguing questions concerns our Early Iron Age.

Barry Raftery (1994), among others, has given up the unequal struggle of trying to create an Irish La Tène of the correct European proportions in terms of pottery, artefacts, art or burial rites. He notes that objects decorated in the La Tène art style are Iron Age, but that does not make them products of European La Tène cultures. If there is a problem in the Iron Age it is that the early Halstatt Iron Age is even harder to identify. Therefore it is not surprising that some would wish to associate major changes in prehistory with La Tène-style metalwork simply because we can see it (Mallory 1984).

This presents us with certain challenges. Excavations, inadvertently rather than by design, have shown us that there is some form of continuity throughout much of the first millennium BC. Some years ago we set ourselves a challenge of identifying how Irish society transformed itself at the beginning of the early medieval period and in the centuries just before it. This was one of the main tasks outlined by the original Discovery Panel (of which I was a member). However, it required tackling one of the most intractable problems in Irish archaeology: a period which effectively lacked pottery, had metal artefacts subject to varying interpretations of age, and lacked really distinctive monuments. Frankly an Irish Palaeolithic would have much clearer criteria.

The result was, I believe, that we funked the challenge. This was not a conscious decision; it was simply safer to continue to excavate more Bronze Age sites because we could see our returns. The Discovery Programme's excavations have made contributions and provided new insights, yet it has always struck me as ironic that Conor Newman's (1997) contribution to the deconstruction of our mythical Tara was accomplished without a spade being put into the ground.

In the Ballyhoura Hills Project I feel that we missed an opportunity when we walked away from the sites at Conva (Doody 1995) and the other sites on the Blackwater. Here was an opportunity to address what was happening in the period before the floruit of ringforts and monasteries. But it lacked artefacts. At heart we are all still antiquarians who need to focus on the obvious range of artefacts. B. Raftery (1981) identified a range of Iron Age burial rituals which we have added to with spectacular sites such as the Ballydavis series of burials (Keeley 1996) or the extensive series of later burials at Knoxspark (Mount 1994). Although many settlement sites have produced groups of Iron Age material, e.g. Rathgall or Haughey's Fort (J. Mallory and C.J. Lynn, pers. comms), or in the case of reuse of monuments at Altar wedge tomb (O'Brien 1999) and Carrowmore passage tombs (Burenhult 1984), the potential never seems to be followed up and Iron Age material is simply seen as a surprise and is regarded as anomalous or intrusive. In the case of the Glencloy Project (Woodman 1983) it was easy to identify the earlier prehistoric periods, but in terms of physical evidence the Iron Age was lacking. However, a consistent series of Iron Age ^{14}C dates from Bay Farm 1, 2 and 3 showed that extensive Iron Age activity had taken place in the glen (e.g. see Woodman and Johnson 1996). This was confirmed by Francis's (1987) suggestion that during the Iron Age extensive deforestation had taken place in Glencloy, resulting in a major phase of soil erosion. In the case of Glencloy there were no objects or monuments like Navan Fort to force us to treat these radiocarbon dates seriously and force us to recognise that they indicated a potentially significant Iron Age presence.

If we can accept that (a) certain Later Mesolithic sites can exist without artefacts, (b) there can be difficulties identifying Iron Age settlement sites, and (c) in fact there may be many Bronze Age settlements which are also difficult to identify, then we need new agendas. Maybe we can learn from the early search for the 'Vikings' in Cork city, where there had been an expectation of the existence of a classic Viking assemblage. As a result it is not surprising that a less diagnostic pre-Anglo-Norman phase of settlement was not recognised until recently (see Hurley 1997).

DISCUSSION

I would like to put down again the challenge I issued some years ago in *Archaeology Ireland* (Woodman 1990). What is our primary concern? Is it to produce lists of monuments and to describe the artefacts we recover from our excavations, or is it to use whatever approach we feel is necessary, within the criteria we feel are relevant, to try to gain insights into earlier societies that lived on this island? In other words, we should not be bound by monument types and artefacts. There are phases from the past that may require other approaches because there are phases that lack a convenient visibility. They are not less important because they are less visible (Bradley 1993).

The work of Brindley and Lanting in their radiocarbon programme and, in a very small way, our own Quaternary Faunas Project (Woodman *et al.* 1997) show us another way.

Renfrew (1973) talked of a 'Radiocarbon Revolution' because ^{14}C dating shattered the assumptions of Montelius and others that everything to the south and east of Europe was earlier. However, I believe that the real radiocarbon revolution was that it freed us from the circularity of our arguments based on typology. It provided an independent check on our hypotheses, and with the introduction of AMS dating we now have an even more powerful checking method. Radiocarbon dating has allowed us to date the less eye-catching aspects of the record—bog bodies (Brindley and Lanting 1995), *fulachta fiadh* (Brindley *et al.* 1990), animal bones (Woodman *et al.* 1997)—and we can see patterns that have nothing to do with our traditional paradigm. We can, provided that we sample properly, begin to treat all periods equally and to look for other changes that have nothing to do with phases of the Three Age System.

The need to seek new directions and to devise new agendas has never been more urgent. In the last decade the exponential increase in excavation has been frightening. The surgical destruction of the archaeological record through excavation is matching the rural destruction of monuments in the 1960s and 1970s and, as in any period when information is being collected without time to consider its implications, the temptation is to hold fast to well-tried principles. We need a breathing space to make considered assessments and judgements. Perhaps that should be one of the research roles of universities. Therefore, at a time when post-modernism and its relativistic attitudes are seducing more and more of Irish archaeology, we should accept its lessons but remember that much of archaeology is about the quality of the ordinary evidence. Perhaps we should keep our infatuation with public monuments and ritual in proportion and consider what we can learn from the fine grain of our ongoing tidal wave of excavations.[2]

Ultimately what we need to do is not just borrow other people's ideas and apply them to the archaeology of this island—something which some, such as Alison Sheridan (1993), suggest we do not do very well. Instead, while we tell our story, we should first recognise that we are still heavily influenced by a national canon of archaeology that leaves us with a set of unconscious biases against change. Secondly we should recognise that there are, at times, differences between the archaeological record of Ireland, including internal regional differences, and other adjacent parts of Europe. As a result we should ask why, at certain times, do we differ from other adjacent regions? It was not pre-ordained simply because we live on an island. Finally, instead of always borrowing other people's intellectual clothes, we should recognise that we can contribute to the larger questions of European archaeology. In fact we should have the confidence to use our own quality material and design a collection to catch the eye of other European colleagues. To do this we need to think about the quality of our questions and ensure that we make a responsible attempt to seek answers, even though we know that our answers will be flawed, partial and probably only valid for a short time.

ACKNOWLEDGEMENTS

I would like to thank Nyree Finlay and the editors for their advice in turning a lecture written in Brussels Airport into a paper written on the beach on the Côte de Rousillon. Thanks are also due to Jim Mallory for reminding me about the quote in *Cosm* and to Angela Desmond for coping with the long process of transition from lecture notes to typescript.

This is not the paper I had intended to write for Liz, but I miss the comments she would have made about it.

REFERENCES

Baillie, M.G.L. 1998 *Exodus to Arthur.* London. Batsford.

Benford, G. 1992 *Timescape.* New York. Bantam.

Benford, G. 1999 *Cosm.* London. Orbit.

Bradley, R. 1993 'For I would ask a question of them all'. Reflections on the prehistory of south-west Ireland. In E. Shee Twohig and M. Ronayne (eds), *Past perceptions: the prehistoric archaeology of south-west Ireland,* 151–4. Cork University Press.

Brindley, A. and Lanting, J.N. 1995 Irish bog bodies: the radiocarbon dates. In R.C. Turner and R.G. Scaife (eds), *Bog bodies: new discoveries and new perspectives,* 133–6. London. British Museum.

Brindley, A., Lanting, J.N. and Mook, W.G. 1990 Radiocarbon dates from Irish *fulachta fiadh* and other burnt mounds. *Journal of Irish Archaeology* **5**, 25–33.

Burenhult, G. 1984 *The archaeology of Carrowmore.* Theses and Papers in North-European Archaeology 14. Stockholm.

Clibborn, E. 1859 On the probable age of flint implements found in gravel beds. *Ulster Journal of Archaeology* (1st series) **7**, 324–33.

Condit, T. and Connolly, M. 1998 Ritual enclosures in the Lee Valley, Co. Kerry. *Archaeology Ireland* **12** (4), 8–12.

Connolly, M. 1999 *Discovering the Neolithic in County Kerry: a passage tomb at Ballycarty.* Tralee. Kerry County Council.

Cooney, G. and Mandal, S. 1998 *The Irish Stone Axe Project Monograph 1.* Bray. Wordwell.

Coxon, P. 1993 Irish Pleistocene. *Irish Journal of Earth Sciences* **12**, 83–106.

Day, R. 1891 Flint axe found near Conna, Co. Cork. *Journal of the Royal Society of Antiquaries of Ireland* **21**, 103.

de Latocnaye, Chevalier 1798 *A Frenchman's walk through Ireland 1796–7.* Cork. M. Harris.

de Valera, R. 1960 The court cairns of Ireland. *Proceedings of the Royal Irish Academy* **60**C, 9–140.

Discovery Programme 1992 *The Discovery Programme: strategies and questions.* Dublin. Discovery Programme.

Doody, M. 1995 Enclosures at Conva. *Discovery Programme Reports* **2**, 24–38. Dublin. Royal Irish Academy.

Dunne, L. and Kiely, J. 1999 Archaeologists discover Neolithic settlement in Tralee.

Archaeology Ireland **13** (1), 14.

Francis, E. 1987 The palynology of the Glencloy area. Unpublished Ph.D thesis submitted to the Queen's University of Belfast.

Gamble, C. 1996 Hominid behaviour in the Middle Pleistocene; an English perspective. In C. Gamble and A.J. Lawson (eds), *The English Palaeolithic reviewed: papers from a day conference held at the Society of Antiquaries of London, 28 October 1994*, 63–72. Salisbury. Wessex Archaeology.

Gould, S.J. 1989 *Wonderful life*. London. Hutchinson Radius.

Gowen, M. and Tarbett, C. 1988 A third season at Tankardstown. *Archaeology Ireland* **2** (4), 156.

Herity, M. and Eogan, G. 1977 *Ireland in prehistory*. London. Routledge Kegan Paul.

Hodges, H.W.M. 1956 A hunting camp at Cullyhanna Lough, near Newtown Hamilton, Co. Armagh. *Ulster Journal of Archaeology* **21**, 7–13.

Hurley, M. 1997 Medieval settlement and architecture: discussion. In R. Cleary, M.F. Hurley and E. Shee Twohig (eds), *Skiddy's Castle and Christ Church, Cork: excavations 1974–77 by D.C. Twohig*, 101–8. Cork Corporation.

Jennbert, C. 1985 Neolithisation—a Scanian perspective. *Journal of Danish Archaeology* **5**, 196–7.

Joyce, J. 1922 *Ulysses*. Paris. Shakespeare.

Kaplan, A. 1964 *The conduct of enquiry*. San Francisco. Chandler.

Keeley, V. 1996 Ballydavis Early Iron Age complex. In I. Bennett (ed.), *Excavations 1995*, 51–2. Bray. Wordwell.

Lynch, A. 1981 *Man and environment in south-west Ireland 4000 BC–AD 800. A study of man's impact on the development of soil and vegetation.* British Archaeological Reports, British Series 85. Oxford.

Macalister, R.A.S. 1928 *The archaeology of Ireland*. London. Methuen.

MacWhite, E. 1956 On the interpretation of archaeological evidence in historical and sociological terms. *American Anthropologist* **58**, 3–25.

Mallory, J. 1984 The origins of the Irish. *Journal of Irish Archaeology* **2**, 65–9.

Mallory, J. and McNeill, T. 1991 *The archaeology of Ulster from colonization to plantation.* Belfast. Institute of Irish Archaeology.

Moloney, A. 1993 *Excavations at Clonfinlough, Co. Offaly.* Irish Archaeological Wetland Unit Transactions 2. Dublin. Crannóg.

Moore, J.A. and Keene, A.S. 1983 Archaeology and the law of the hammer. In J.A. Moore and A.S. Keene (eds), *Archaeological hammers and theories*, 3–13. New York. Academic Press.

Mount, C. 1994 From Knoxspark to Tir na nÓg. *Archaeology Ireland* **8** (3), 22–3.

Newman, C. 1997 *Tara: an archaeological survey.* Discovery Programme Monographs 2. Dublin. Royal Irish Academy.

O'Brien, W. 1994 *Mount Gabriel: Bronze Age copper mining in Ireland.* Galway University Press.

O'Brien, W. 1999 *Sacred ground. Megalithic tombs in coastal south-west Ireland.* Bronze Age Studies 4. Department of Archaeology, National University of Ireland, Galway.

Ó Drisceoil, D. 1988 Burnt mounds: cooking or bathing? *Antiquity* **62**, 671–80.

O'Kelly, M.J. 1954 Excavations and experiments in ancient Irish cooking places. *Journal of the Royal Society of Antiquaries of Ireland* **84**, 105–55.

O'Kelly, M.J. 1981 The megalithic tombs in Ireland. In J.D. Evans, B. Cunliffe and C. Renfrew (eds), *Antiquity and Man: essays in honour of Glyn Daniel*, 177–90. London. Thames and Hudson.

O'Laverty, J. 1857 Relative antiquity of stone and bronze weapons. *Ulster Journal of Archaeology* (1st series) **5**, 122–7.

Ó Ríordáin, S.P. 1942 *Antiquities of the Irish countryside.* Cork University Press.

Powell, T.G.E., Corcoran, J.X.W.P., Lynch, F. and Scott, J.G. 1969 *Megalithic enquiries in the west of Britain.* Liverpool University Press.

Raftery, B. 1981 Iron Age burials in Ireland. In D. Ó Corráin (ed.), *Irish antiquity. Essays presented to Prof. M.J. O'Kelly*, 173–204. Cork. Tower Books.

Raftery, B. 1994 *Pagan Celtic Ireland.* London. Thames and Hudson.

Raftery, J. 1952 *Prehistoric Ireland.* London. Batsford.

Renfrew, A.C. 1973 *Before civilization: the radiocarbon revolution and prehistoric Europe.* London. Cape.

Rowley-Conwy, P. 1985 The origin of agriculture in Denmark: a review of some theories. *Journal of Danish Archaeology* **4**, 188–95.

Sheridan, A. 1993 Review of *Irish prehistory: a social perspective* (G. Cooney and E. Grogan). *Ulster Journal of Archaeology* **56**, 181–2.

Taylor, J.J. 1980 *Bronze Age goldwork of the British Isles.* Cambridge University Press.

Thomas, J. 1988 Neolithic explanations revisited: the Mesolithic–Neolithic transition in Britain and south Scandinavia. *Proceedings of the Prehistoric Society* **54**, 59–66.

Trigger, B.G. 1989 *A history of archaeological thought.* Cambridge University Press.

Warner, R.B. 1993 Irish prehistoric goldwork: a provisional analysis. *Archaeomaterials* **7**, 101–13.

Wells, S. 1995 Antiquarian illustration in Ireland (contributions to a study of archaeology). Unpublished MA thesis, National University of Ireland, University College Cork.

Woodman, P.C. 1978 *The Mesolithic in Ireland.* British Archaeological Reports, British Series 58. Oxford.

Woodman, P.C. 1983 The Glencloy Project in perspective. In T. Reeves-Smyth and F. Hamond (eds), *Landscape archaeology in Ireland*, 25–34. British Archaeological Reports, British Series 116. Oxford.

Woodman, P.C. 1990 Why are we digging anyway? *Archaeology Ireland* **4** (1), 25–6.

Woodman, P.C. 1998 Pushing out the boat for an Irish Palaeolithic. In N. Ashton, F. Healy and P. Pettit (eds), *Stone Age archaeology*, 146–57. Oxbow Monograph 102. Oxford.

Woodman, P.C. and Anderson, E. 1990 The Irish Later Mesolithic: a partial picture. In P.M. Vermeersch and P. van Peer (eds), *Contributions to the Mesolithic in Europe*, 377–87. Leuven University Press.

Woodman, P.C. and Johnson, G. 1996 Excavations at Bay Farm 1, Carnlough, Co. Antrim, and the study of the Larnian technology. *Proceedings of the Royal Irish Academy* **96**C, 137–235.

Woodman, P.C. and Scannell, M. 1993 A context on the Lough Gur lithics. In E. Shee

Twohig and M. Ronayne (eds), *Past perceptions: the prehistoric archaeology of south-west Ireland*, 25–34. Cork University Press.

Woodman, P.C., Anderson, E. and Finlay, N. 1999 *Excavations at Ferriter's Cove 1983–1995. Last foragers/first farmers in the Dingle Peninsula.* Bray. Wordwell.

Woodman, P.C., McCarthy, M. and Monaghan, N. 1997 The Irish Quaternary Faunal Project. *Quaternary Science Review* **16** (2), 129–59.

Zvelebil, M. and Rowley-Conwy, P. 1986 Foragers and farmers in Atlantic Europe. In M. Zvelebil (ed.), *Hunters in transition*, 67–93. Cambridge University Press.

Endnotes

1 Hodder Westropp, originally from Cork, was not himself a great visionary as he contended that Stonehenge could only have been built by a classical civilisation.

2 Hopefully the work of the Oxford Archaeological Unit will lay the foundation for a new process of adequate publication of archaeological excavations.

THE UTILISATION OF ISLAND ENVIRONMENTS IN THE IRISH MESOLITHIC: AGENDAS FOR RATHLIN ISLAND

Sinéad B. McCartan

INTRODUCTION

Islands, by their nature, present well-defined areas of study. They share many characteristics, such as isolation, vulnerability, and limitation in size, resources and biodiversity; some islands also offer unique resources, such as a particular food type or raw material (Evans 1973; Fosberg 1963; Kirch 1986; Renfrew and Wagstaff 1982). The interplay between humans and the island ecosystem has had implications for the evolution and development of island cultures and societies. A detailed discussion of these subjects is unfortunately beyond the scope of this paper, but there is no doubt that coping with and adapting to the combination of shared and unique features of the island ecosystem presented challenges and opportunities for Mesolithic hunter-gatherers, and undoubtedly determined the extent, if any, to which an island was exploited.

This study of the utilisation of island environments in the Irish Mesolithic was prompted by the recent discovery of Mesolithic material on Rathlin Island, Co. Antrim. Subsequently, in an attempt to understand the Rathlin material, the evidence for the Mesolithic exploitation of other Irish islands was examined (Fig. 1). This paper represents an interim statement on the progress of this project. It summarises the evidence for the two types of islands exploited during the Mesolithic period—the land-based 'lake island' and the offshore coastal island. The evidence for settlement on Rathlin Island during the Mesolithic period is then presented, with a discussion of the issues raised about its role in the subsistence strategies, settlement patterns and social organisation of Mesolithic hunter-gatherers.

'LAKE ISLANDS'

In the early post-glacial period areas of open water existed which are today bog, and islands within these areas were exploited by early peoples for a variety of reasons. 'Lake islands' are found within an inland lakeland environment and can be divided into two subtypes—the natural island and the deliberately constructed or artificial island. The function of each was probably very different.

At Lough Derravaragh, Co. Westmeath, the area of Clonava was once an island and was used by Late Mesolithic hunter-gatherers who exploited the island-based chert outcrops, built fires, processed plant foods, hunted, gathered and fished in the surrounding wetlands (Mitchell 1972a, 162; O'Sullivan 1998, 49–50). Mitchell seems to have viewed the Clonava sites as representing 'casual visits', but it has also been suggested that the island could have sustained longer-term settlement (Cooney and Grogan 1994, 19).

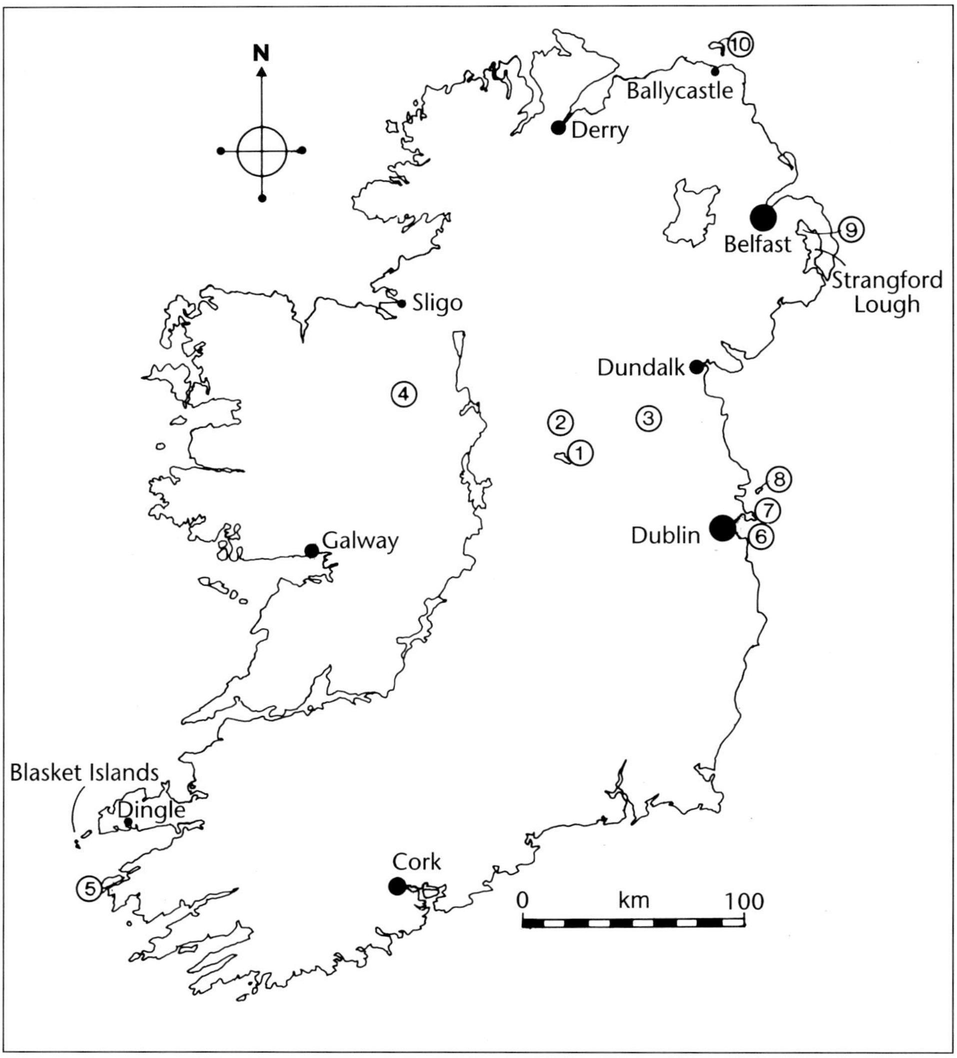

Fig. 1—Map showing principal sites mentioned in the text.
Key to map: (1) Lough Derravaragh, Co. Westmeath; (2) Lough Kinale, Co. Longford; (3) Moynagh Lough, Co. Meath; (4) Lough Gara, Co. Sligo; (5) Coarha Beg, Valencia Island, Co. Kerry; (6) Dalkey Island, Co. Dublin; (7) Howth (Sutton), Co. Dublin; (8) Lambay Island, Co. Dublin; (9) Rough Island, Co. Down; (10) Rathlin, Co. Antrim.

In the similar environmental context of Lough Kinale, Co. Longford, Late Mesolithic hunter-gatherers settled at Derragh, which in earlier times had also been an island within a larger wetland area. Three main flint scatters or 'sites' have been recorded, one of which (Site 1) was of particular interest. Here a natural knoll, or possibly a deliberately constructed mound of clay and wood, was the focus of activity (Mitchell 1970, 7; O'Sullivan 1998, 50–2, 57). O'Sullivan (1998, 51–2) has suggested that the Lough Kinale sites were positioned to exploit the resources of a number of ecological habitats, indicating extended rather than short-term use of the island of Derragh.

At Moynagh Lough, Co. Meath, Late Mesolithic hunter-gatherers also appear to have stabilised and enhanced natural clay knolls with mud, stones and brushwood, which would have formed dry areas, 'platforms' or 'islands' within the former lake. Bradley (1999, 6) has suggested that 'such a position would have been attractive from the point of view of security as well as affording excellent opportunities for fishing and fowling'. A comparison has been made by Bradley (*op. cit.*, 7) with the series of artificial islands, possibly associated with Late Mesolithic artefacts, at Lough Gara, Co. Sligo (Cross 1953; Fredengren 1998).

It would appear, therefore, that both natural and artificial islands, within an extensive inland lakeland environment, were exploited during the Mesolithic period. With the possible exception of some Early Mesolithic microblade cores from one of the Lough Gara sites (N. Finlay, pers. comm.), all the Mesolithic evidence suggests that these 'lake islands' were primarily used during the later part of the period. Both types of island share the characteristics of isolation and potential for protection, to varying degrees. Some, particularly the larger natural islands, offered additional benefits such as a local source of raw material, as at Lough Derravaragh, or an advantageous position from which to exploit food resources from several ecological habitats, for example the Lough Kinale sites. Woodman (1986, 13) has suggested that the Late Mesolithic hunter-gatherers may have moved away from the more sedentary lifestyle of the Early Mesolithic, adopting a highly mobile low-density economy featuring specialised industrial sites. Certainly, the small artificial islands at Moynagh Lough, and possibly at Lough Gara, could be viewed as short-term specialised sites used to exploit a specific resource, although the large natural islands may also have fulfilled this function. Current excavations of the artificial mounds and Mesolithic deposits at Moynagh Lough may provide new insights into the purpose of such mounds and their role within the broader subsistence strategy of late hunter-gatherers. Woodman's proposal, however, has been questioned by Cooney and Grogan (1994, 21–2), who argue that Ireland followed the general European trend towards a more sedentary lifestyle, and it is possible that the larger natural islands such as Clonava and Derragh may have been suitable for long-term settlement.

The two types of island may therefore represent different facets of the economic and settlement activities of late hunter-gatherers. The artificial islands most probably represent very short-term, specialised activity sites, and long-term use is highly unlikely. The larger islands could also have functioned as task-specific sites, but their potential for long-term settlement was much greater, although long-term sustainability of any population would have been dependent on contacts with neighbouring hunter-gatherer groups. O'Sullivan (1998, 59) postulates three explanations, not necessarily mutually exclusive, for the use of 'lake islands', particularly with reference to Derragh and Clonava—that they may have provided views of local wetland territories, afforded protection from competing groups, or acted as 'central places' from which territories could be controlled. The various possibilities, however, will only be clarified through excavation.

THE OFFSHORE ISLANDS

The offshore islands, with their coastal setting, present a different range of opportunities and a more varied set of constraints than islands in the inland lakeland environment. Middens are known from a number of the islands, particularly along the Atlantic west coast, and examples exist for most periods of the past. Some, however, remain undated and these may eventually provide evidence for Mesolithic activity. Middens have been the subject of much interest, especially in the late nineteenth and earlier twentieth centuries, but they have yielded no definitive associated Mesolithic material (Atkinson 1872–3; Brunicardi 1914; Knowles 1889–91a; 1889–91b; 1893–6; 1900–2; Leonard 1868; Lymbery 1864; Windle 1911). In recent years a number of the coastal islands and their middens have been surveyed (Cuppage *et al.* 1986; Gosling 1993; Lacy 1983; O'Kelly and Shee 1976; O'Sullivan and Sheehan 1996; Power *et al.* 1992; 1994), but again no Mesolithic associations have been discerned. In addition, Peter Woodman (pers. comm.) has surveyed the Blasket Islands for evidence of both middens and Mesolithic activity, but with little success.

The most tangible evidence for Mesolithic activity from the west coast islands is to be found at Coarha Beg on Valencia Island, Co. Kerry. Mitchell (1989, 78–9) described a 6m spread of stone slabs, laid on a bog surface which has been dated to 6560 ± 120 BP. Between the two was a 1m-long fossilised oak baulk, dated to 8910 ± 150 BP. No artefactual evidence was found associated with this structure, but on the basis of the dates and pollen evidence Mitchell (*op. cit.*, 94) concluded that a small Mesolithic population had lived on Valencia and made minor sporadic clearances of the island's forests. The evidence for forest clearances seems to indicate that Mesolithic groups were living on Valencia, but the nature of such settlement is unclear.

The best evidence for the Mesolithic use of islands is to be found on the east coast. Dalkey Island, Co. Dublin, lies approximately 400m offshore and is about 7ha in area. Between 1956 and 1959 Liversage (1968) excavated five 'sites' (or areas) which revealed multi-period occupation, exhibiting extensive disturbance and a complex stratigraphy. Site II, the 'southern basal midden', was some 10m across. Site V, the 'northern basal midden', was just under 5m in length and produced a date of 5290 ± 170 BP. Both middens are associated with Late Mesolithic artefacts, including flints (of which only a few are finished tool types), elongated pebbles, bevel-ended pebbles and polished stone axes. At least three stake-holes were found sealed under the northern midden and possibly one under the southern midden, but no major structural features were found associated with either midden. Liversage (*op. cit.*, 162–3) concluded that the two middens, with their varying quantities of wild and domesticated animal bones, indicated the survival of Mesolithic groups within an island environment and their gradual assimilation into the Neolithic way of life. The dating of some of the animal remains from the two middens by the Irish Quaternary Fauna Project (Woodman *et al.* 1997), however, suggests that the middens were more contaminated than Liversage had originally thought, and that some of the initial bone identifications were incorrect. It appears that the main phase of Mesolithic activity at Dalkey was between 6800 and 6000 BP, when seal and wild pig were the chief mammals exploited, and the bones of the domesticated animals probably date from the later prehistoric settlement of the site (*ibid.*, 138).

Although today linked to the mainland at Sutton, in the early post-glacial period the headland of Howth was an island, lying approximately 2.5km off the coast and measuring some 700ha in area. Mitchell (1956; 1972b) excavated a midden measuring approximately 30m in length at Sutton on the western side of Howth 'island' in 1949 and 1970. The artefacts recovered included Late Mesolithic flints, 'limpet hammers' and polished stone axes, and charcoal produced a date of 5250 ± 100 BP. The range of finished flaked flint/stone tools at Sutton is much greater than at Dalkey, but still less than that found on some mainland sites. The only structural evidence consisted of four pits and a hearth under the midden, although only a small area of the original midden was excavated. A radiocarbon date on a bone which was initially identified as cattle (6660 ± 80 BP, 6560 ± 75 BP), but was more probably bear or another large mammal, and another on a wild pig bone (7140 ± 100 BP) have indicated that the Sutton midden might be around 1000 years older than previously thought (Woodman *et al.* 1997, 144). Mitchell (1956, 25) believed that the island of Howth in Mesolithic times would have been 'an attractive place to settle', but it is not clear whether this was short- or long-term settlement. Approximately 11km north of Howth is the island of Lambay, where, despite recent extensive research, no Mesolithic material has been recovered (Cooney 1993, 26).

Much further north is Rough Island, one of the many small islands within the sea lough of Strangford Lough, Co. Down. Rough Island is a low drumlin composed of boulder clay and connected to the mainland today by a causeway accessible at low tide. In 1936 the Harvard Archaeological Expedition, under the direction of Hallam L. Movius, excavated a number of trenches on the island, some of which revealed midden material, largely oysters (Movius 1940). The full extent of the midden was not established, but it was at least 14m long in one trench. One hearth was found within the midden, and a second in the raised beach was considered to date from the same period (*ibid.*, 134). The Late Mesolithic flints were primarily recovered from the surface soil and raised beach, although some were retrieved from within the midden. Very few animal bones were recovered and the majority came from an area of disturbance. Movius (*op. cit.*, 134) concluded that the island had been used by people from the mainland as a base for food-collecting activities. Mesolithic material has also been found on several of the other islands within Strangford Lough, including Island Reagh, Mahee and Sketrick islands, and it is possible that they were exploited in a similar manner.

The evidence indicates, therefore, that a number of offshore islands, particularly along the eastern seaboard of Ireland, were exploited during the Mesolithic. With the exception of a possible obliquely trimmed microlith from Sutton (Mitchell 1956, fig. 9, b), the finds indicate that the islands were exploited during the later part of the Mesolithic. Some islands may only have been suitable for short-term use for specific purposes such as collecting shellfish, but others may have had the potential for longer-term, permanent settlement, given their size, geology, diverse ecology and so forth. While it is clear that coastal resources played a vital role in the subsistence strategy of Mesolithic groups (Cooney and Grogan 1994; Woodman 1986), the role of offshore islands within this strategy is unclear. The main advantage of an offshore island over the mainland is the isolation that can ensure security. Islands, however, have restricted resources, of both raw materials and food, and the over-exploitation of available resources would have had detrimental consequences for the island environment and population. The problem of restricted resources could possibly have been resolved through a system of trade and exchange networks, but the sociological constraints may have been harder to overcome, and the sustainability and long-term survival of an island population would have been dependent on social links with other hunter-gatherer groups. Consequently, the offshore islands may simply have been used for short-term task-specific activities, with more permanent base camps on the mainland coast. The structural evidence from Dalkey, Sutton and Rough Island seems to confirm this view of short-term use rather than major habitation.

RATHLIN ISLAND

Rathlin Island, Co. Antrim (Fig. 2), lies just over 9.5km off the north Antrim coast and 22.5km from the Mull of Kintyre, Scotland. This position between Ireland and Scotland has greatly influenced its archaeology and history. Of particular interest is its relative proximity to Kintyre and some of the western Scottish islands where there is evidence for Mesolithic activity.

Rathlin is 'L'-shaped in outline and is approximately 11km long, though nowhere more than 1.5km across, and roughly 1300ha in area. The island is now almost treeless, with only a few small pockets of weather-beaten trees growing in some of the more sheltered valleys. The coastline is mostly cliff, much of it 60m high, and Church Bay, facing the Antrim coast, is the main harbour. There are a few small lakes on the island, the largest and best known being Lough Ushet in the south-east. The raised beach is visible in some areas, particularly running southwards from Church Bay towards Rue Point.

The *Preliminary survey of the ancient monuments of Northern Ireland* (*PSAMNI* 1940) mentions only five archaeological sites on the island, all of which date from the later prehistoric and historic periods. A new assessment of the island's archaeological sites was undertaken in the late 1980s by the Environment and Heritage Service (DoENI) as part of the archaeological survey of County Antrim. As a result, the Sites and Monuments Record now lists 82 sites on Rathlin, although most of these either date from the historic period or are undated enclosures and hut sites.

The island's archaeology, particularly that of the prehistoric period, has been rather neglected. Rathlin is probably best known for the volcanic plug of porcellanite at Brockley, and as a consequence has featured greatly in Neolithic stone axe studies (Clough and Cummins 1979; 1988; Cooney and Mandal 1998; Jope 1952; Sheridan 1986). Only three excavations have taken place on the island, and these have been of Neolithic and Bronze Age

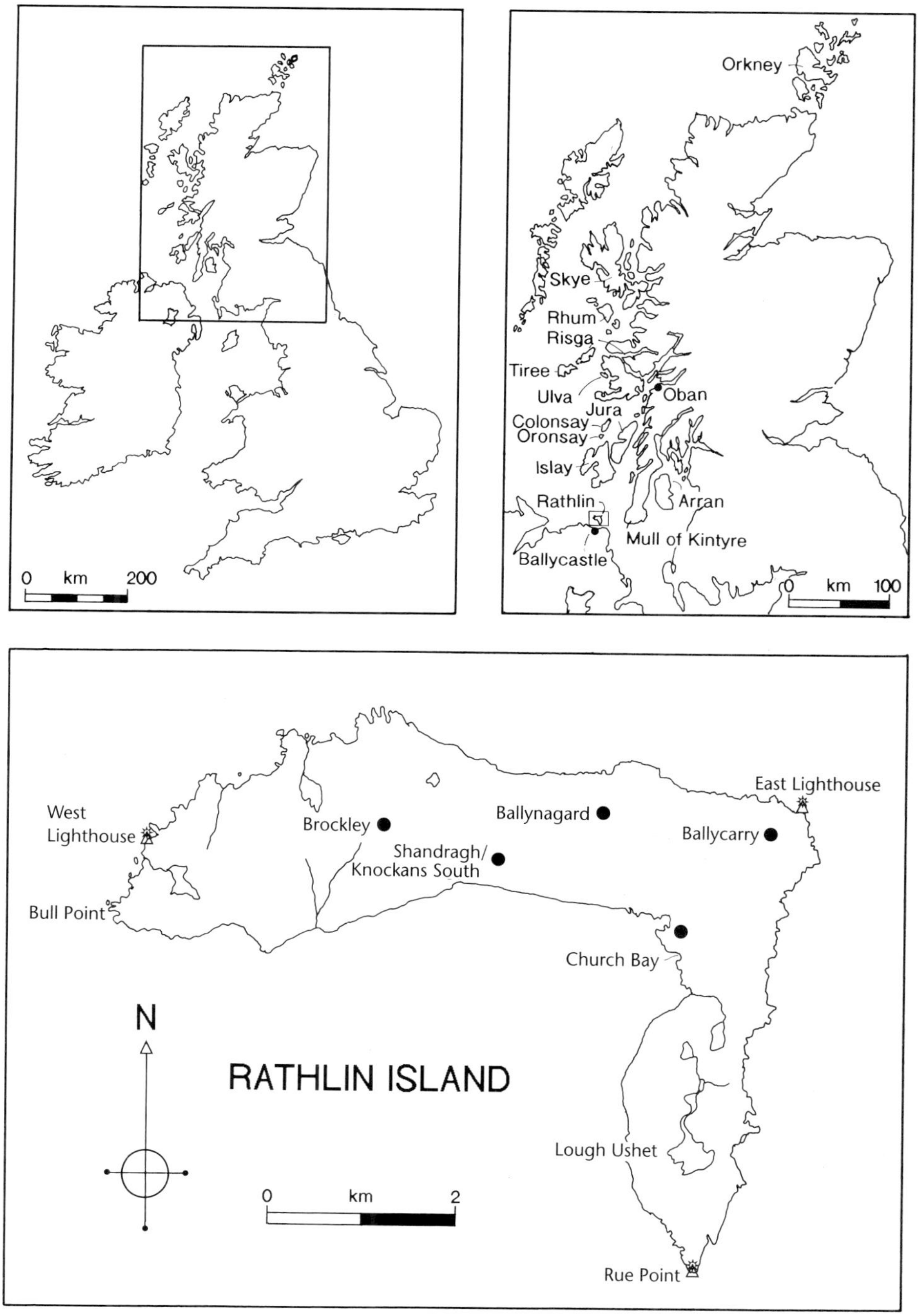

Fig. 2—Map of Rathlin Island.

sites. Whelan (1933–4; 1934–5) explored a Neolithic site at Ballynagard; a Bronze Age cemetery was uncovered in advance of quarrying at Church Bay (Wiggins 1988); and most recently a primarily Late Neolithic site was excavated at Shandragh, Knockans South (Conway 1995). When Woodman (1978) compiled his gazetteer of Mesolithic sites in Ireland, Rathlin did not warrant an entry. The first summary of the island's archaeology was published by Williams (1990), who remarked on the absence of evidence for use in the Mesolithic period, particularly since this contrasted so dramatically with the extensive evidence along the Antrim coast. The scarcity of Mesolithic material also stood in contrast to the evidence of later occupation on Rathlin, particularly that of the Neolithic period, and the absence of megalithic tombs prompted Williams (1990, 48) to suggest that even during the Neolithic, when the island was certainly settled, the occupation was either seasonal or of insufficient status to merit the building of large tombs.

Williams's paper was largely concerned with the monumental evidence. The artefactual evidence, however, tells a slightly different story for the Mesolithic. Within the Ulster Museum collections there are two groups of material which demonstrate a Mesolithic presence on Rathlin. The first is in the collection of the Rev. Canon Grainger and is provenanced only to 'Rathlin Island'. This material shows several different types of patination, suggesting that it might have been collected from a number of different sites (Fig. 3, 1–5). Although there are no diagnostic types, such as microliths or 'Bann Flakes', the laminar blades, some butt-trimmed flakes and a possible roughout for a flint axe (Fig. 3, 5) suggest a Late Mesolithic presence. The second group of material is from the McFadden collection and was recovered from Church Bay. Again, this material has at least three different types of patination and some of it appears to be Late Mesolithic (Fig. 3, 6–8).

The most conclusive evidence for a Mesolithic presence on Rathlin was brought to archaeological attention in 1994, when the late Tommy Cecil of Church Bay, Rathlin, reported his private collection to the Ulster Museum. It includes typical Late Mesolithic artefacts from Ballycarry, near the East Lighthouse, most of which is knapping debris, including the distinctive uniplane core, flakes and blades with distinctive steep platform preparation and some retouched pieces including tanged and butt-trimmed flakes (Fig. 4). No midden material was reported as having been found with these artefacts, suggesting that the nature of the activity at Ballycarry was different to that on Dalkey and Sutton. The latter sites are also right on the coast, unlike Ballycarry, which is slightly inland from a high cliff face.

The Late Mesolithic evidence on Rathlin raises a number of issues that it is hoped will be addressed through fieldwork over the next few years. The first issue is the extent of Late Mesolithic activity or settlement on Rathlin. Field-walking on ploughed land is the chief method by which flint scatter sites are discovered in Ireland, but this is a rare activity on Rathlin today and therefore the discovery of new sites will be difficult. Field-walking ploughed or worked land will, of course, be done when the opportunity arises, but work has also commenced on the detailed recording of the islanders' private collections of archaeological material, which it is hoped will shed further light on artefacts from the island. The second issue relates to the chronology of the Mesolithic use of Rathlin—when the island was first used, whether there is any evidence for Early Mesolithic activity, and whether this

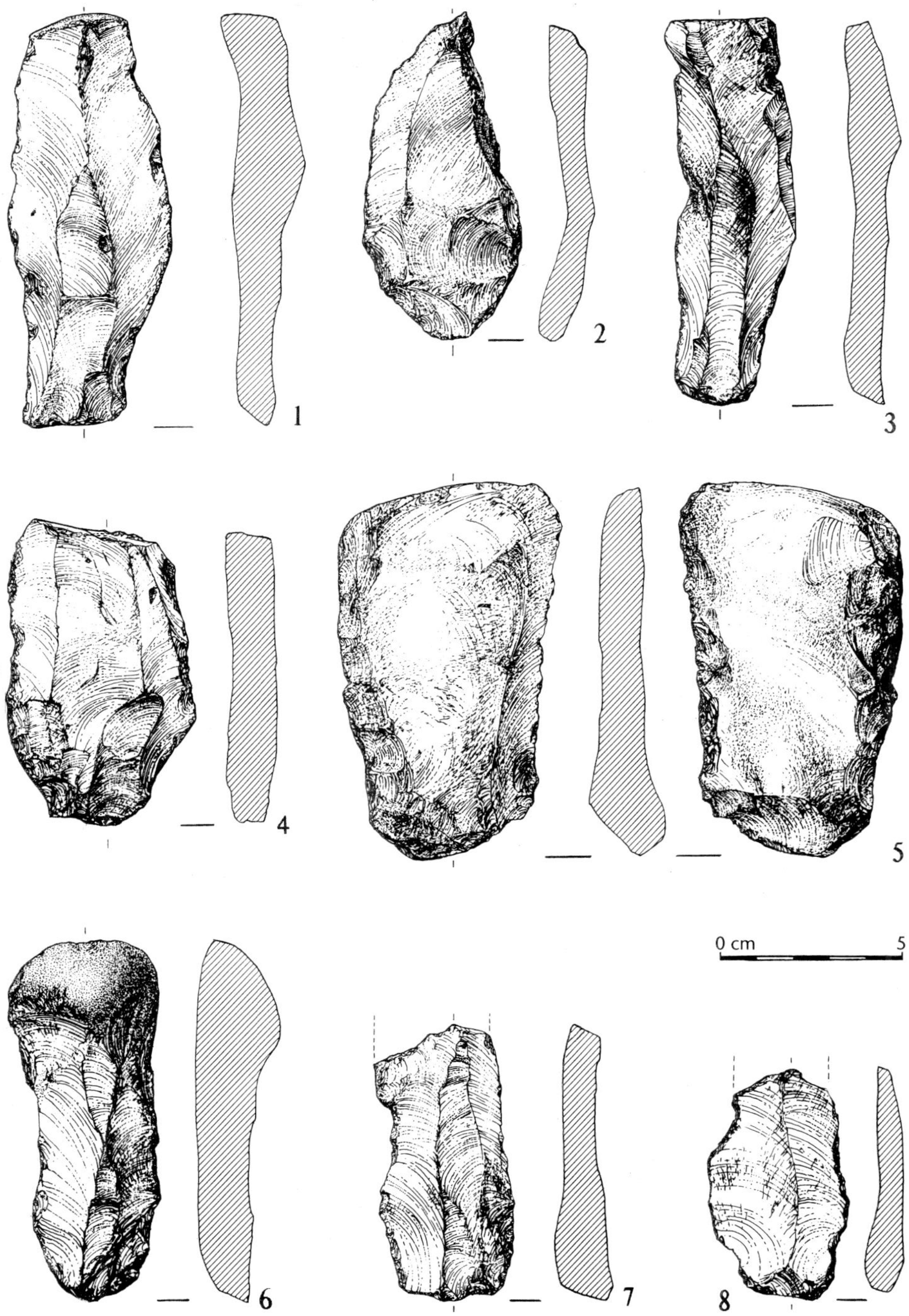

Fig. 3—Grainger Collection of flint artefacts from Rathlin Island, 1–5; McFadden Collection of flint artefacts from Church Bay, Rathlin Island, 6–8.

island might have allowed the vestiges of Mesolithic life to survive longer than on the mainland. The nature of the Late Mesolithic activity on Rathlin also requires investigation—was the island utilised for the exploitation of seasonal resources, or was it permanently settled? Today, part of the island is a bird sanctuary, and seals still frequent its rocky coastline. In the past, the collection of nesting seabirds' eggs and the hunting of birds and seals would have provided seasonally exploitable resources. Of the three main offshore islands under discussion (Dalkey, Howth and Rathlin) which exhibit evidence of Late Mesolithic activity, Rathlin is the largest and therefore probably had the greater potential to sustain long-term settlement. If settlement on Rathlin was permanent, however, the population would have been required to 'manage' their food resources in order to avoid resource depletion. Island groups might well have exchanged local island goods (such as seal meat, birds' eggs, fish and shellfish) with mainland groups for non-island resources. Such a system of exchange or barter would have made long-term, permanent residence on Rathlin much more feasible.

Within a broader context, the nature of the relationship between hunter-gatherer groups on Rathlin and those on the mainland, as well as those on the neighbouring Scottish mainland and islands, needs to be explored. If Rathlin was merely an extension to an Irish mainland group's subsistence pattern, its role is easier to understand. However, if settlement on Rathlin was of a more permanent nature, the issue of how the island groups were organised socially, not only within the island context but also within a broader geographical framework, must be addressed.

Research on the occupation and exploitation of the Scottish islands should help to shed light on the role of Rathlin Island. Mesolithic material has been found both on the larger islands of Orkney (Saville 1996), Skye (Saville and Miket 1994a; 1994b), Islay (Mithen 1995; Mithen and Lake 1996; Mithen *et al.* 1992), Jura (Mercer 1980) and Arran (Affleck *et al.* 1988; Allen and Edwards 1987; Gorman *et al.* 1995), and on the smaller islands of Rhum (Wickham-Jones 1990), Tiree (Livens 1956; MacKie 1963), Risga (Pollard *et al.* 1996), Ulva (Bonsall 1996; 1997; Russell *et al.* 1995), Colonsay (Mithen 1995; Mithen and Finlayson 1991; Mithen and Lake 1996) and Oronsay (Mellars 1987; Mithen and Finlayson 1991). It would appear that these smaller islands, some of which are comparable in size to Rathlin, were primarily used on a temporary basis. Recent work by the Southern Hebrides Mesolithic Project (SHMP) at Staosnaig on Colonsay has indicated that the Mesolithic occupation of the island was of a very 'ephemeral' nature (Mithen 1995, 267–8; Mithen and Finlayson 1991, 7; Mithen and Lake 1996, 138–42). The nature of the occupation of Oronsay has been the subject of debate, with opinions favouring both continuous and intermittent exploitation by Mesolithic groups (Mellars 1987; Mithen and Finlayson 1991, 7). The smaller islands, therefore, may have acted as satellites to base camps on the larger islands or on the mainland. On Islay a short-term seasonal site has been discovered at Newton (McCullagh 1988–9), and work by the SHMP has also shown the existence of both a short-term hunting camp (Gleann Mor) and a large residential camp (Bolsay Farm) on the island (Mithen 1995, 268–70; Mithen and Lake 1996).

It is not clear whether the pattern of island exploitation evident in Scotland existed in Ireland. The Irish evidence to date indicates the short-term use of the islands by Mesolithic hunter-gatherers, and islands such as Rathlin may have been used on a seasonal basis by

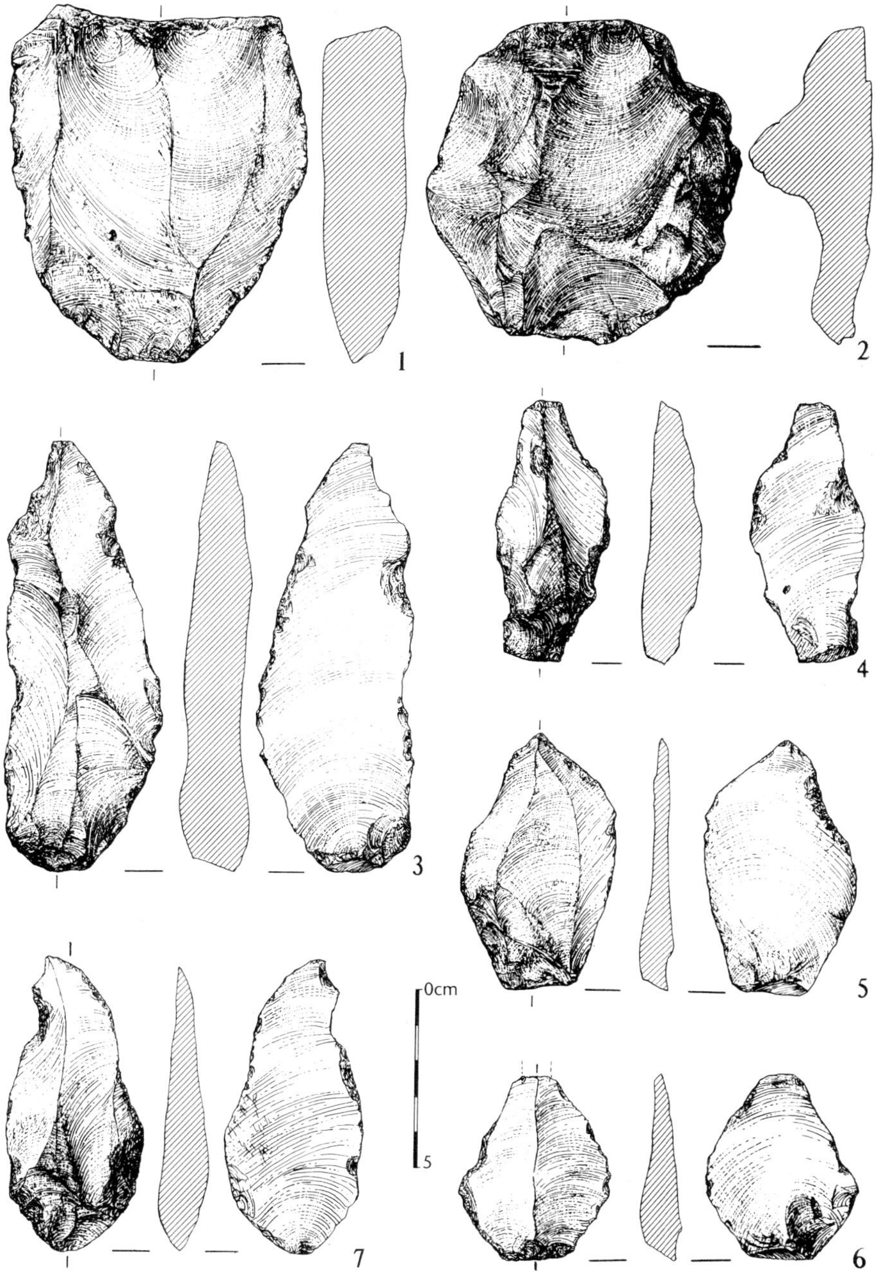

Fig. 4—Cecil Collection.

groups whose base camp was on the Antrim coast. Although there is no evidence for the long-term exploitation of some of the larger Irish islands, it cannot be ruled out.

Of particular interest is the difference between the stone tool assemblages of Rathlin and the Scottish sites. In Ireland, the Late Mesolithic macrolithic stone tool industry dates from between 7000 and 5500 BP (Woodman and Anderson 1990, 377), but the quite different microlithic assemblages from western Scotland date from approximately the same period (Ashmore 1997; Bonsall 1996). Why do two areas so close together have such different contemporaneous stone tool traditions? Do these traditions mark some form of social identity? Despite arguments for an Irish Sea Province in the Mesolithic (Livens 1972), the artefactual evidence does not sustain such claims. The Isle of Man still remains the only area outside of Ireland where a macrolithic Late Mesolithic tradition exists (McCartan 1991–3; Woodman 1978, 206). The Manx–Irish connection, however, serves to highlight the apparent absence of connections with western Scotland.

CONCLUSIONS

Much insight can be gained by the study of islands during the Mesolithic period. Their role in the subsistence and settlement patterns of Mesolithic hunter-gatherers appears to have been to a great extent dependent on the nature of each individual island—size, resources, access to off-island resources, and social connections with hunter-gatherer groups elsewhere. Some Irish islands were certainly suitable only for short-term settlement (the exploitation of seasonal food resources), and others may have been exploited for even shorter periods (for the procurement of raw materials such as chert). The issue of the feasibility of the long-term settlement of the islands remains unresolved. Why, for instance, would people settle on an island where there were fewer, and possibly inferior, resources to those on the mainland? To isolate oneself on an island is not unlike the construction of an 'enclosing' space that occurs in the later prehistoric periods, and may be symptomatic of economic or social stresses. It is hoped that the ongoing research into the Mesolithic settlement of Rathlin Island will throw light on the role of islands within the economic, settlement and social strategies of the Irish Mesolithic hunter-gatherers, as well as addressing the issues raised specifically by the Rathlin evidence.

ACKNOWLEDGEMENTS

I would like to thank the Trustees of the National Museum and Galleries of Northern Ireland for providing facilities. Thanks are also due to Mary Cecil and her family on Rathlin Island for encouraging investigations into the island's past history. I am grateful to Rhoda Cronin for preparing Figs 1 and 2, and to Deirdre Crone for preparing Figs 3 and 4.

REFERENCES

Affleck, T.L., Edwards, K. and Clarke, A. 1988 Archaeological and palynological studies at the Mesolithic pitchstone and flint site of Auchareoch, Isle of Arran. *Proceedings of the Society of Antiquaries of Scotland* **118**, 37–59.

Allen, C. and Edwards, K.J. 1987 The distribution of lithic materials of possible Mesolithic age on the Isle of Arran. *Glasgow Archaeological Journal* **14**, 19–24.

Ashmore, P. 1997 Radiocarbon dates from archaeological sites in Argyll and Arran. In G. Ritchie (ed.), *The archaeology of Argyll*, 236–83. Edinburgh University Press.

Atkinson, G.M. 1872–3 Kitchen-middens in the estuary of Cork Harbour. *Journal of the Royal Historical and Archaeological Association of Ireland* **2** (4th series), 258–61.

Bonsall, C. 1996 The 'Obanian Problem': coastal adaptations in the Mesolithic of Western Scotland. In T. Pollard and A. Morrison (eds), *The early prehistory of Scotland*, 183–97. Edinburgh University Press.

Bonsall, C. 1997 Coastal adaptation in the Mesolithic of Argyll: rethinking the 'Obanian Problem'. In G. Ritchie (ed.), *The archaeology of Argyll*, 24–37. Edinburgh University Press.

Bradley, J. 1999 Excavations at Moynagh Lough, Co. Meath, 1997–98. *Ríocht na Midhe* **10**, 1–17.

Brunicardi, Mrs 1914 The shore-dwellers of ancient Ireland. *Journal of the Royal Society of Antiquaries of Ireland* **44** (3), 185–213.

Clough, T.H.McK. and Cummins, W.A. (eds) 1979 *Stone axe studies*. Research Report No. 23. London. Council for British Archaeology.

Clough, T.H.McK. and Cummins, W.A. (eds) 1988 *Stone axe studies. Volume 2*. Research Report No. 67. London. Council for British Archaeology.

Conway, M. 1995 Shandragh, Knockans South, Rathlin Island. In I. Bennett (ed.), *Excavations 1994*, 6. Bray. Wordwell.

Cooney, G. 1993 Lambay: an island on the horizon. *Archaeology Ireland* 7 (4), 24–8.

Cooney, G. and Grogan, E. 1994 *Irish prehistory: a social perspective*. Bray. Wordwell.

Cooney, G. and Mandal, S. 1998 *The Irish stone axe project. Monograph 1*. Bray. Wordwell.

Cross, R.E. 1953 Lough Gara: a preliminary survey. *Journal of the Royal Society of Antiquaries of Ireland* **83**, 93–6.

Cuppage, J., Bennett, I., Cotter, C. and O'Rahilly, C. 1986 *Archaeological survey of the Dingle Peninsula*. Ballyferriter. Oidhreacht Chorca Dhuibhne.

Evans, J.D. 1973 Islands as laboratories for the study of culture process. In C. Renfrew (ed.), *The explanation of culture change: models in prehistory*, 517–20. London. Duckworth.

Fosberg, F.R. 1963 The island ecosystem. In F.R. Fosberg (ed.), *Man's place in the island ecosystem*, 1–6. Hawaii. Bishop Museum Press.

Fredengren, C. 1998 Lough Gara through time. *Archaeology Ireland* **12** (1), 31–3.

Gorman, F., Murray, B. and Lambie, E. 1995 Kildonan and Machrie, Arran (Kilmory parish): Mesolithic sites. In C.E. Batey (ed.), *Discovery and excavation in Scotland 1995*, 72. Edinburgh. Council for Scottish Archaeology.

Gosling, P. 1993 *Archaeological Inventory of County Galway. Volume 1: West Galway.* Dublin. Stationery Office.

Jope, E.M. 1952 Porcellanite axes from factories in north-east Ireland: Tievebulliagh and Rathlin. Part 1. Archaeological survey. *Ulster Journal of Archaeology* **15**, 31–55.

Kirch, P.V. 1986 Introduction: the archaeology of island societies. In P.V. Kirch (ed.), *Island societies: archaeological approaches to evolution and transformation,* 1–5. Cambridge University Press.

Knowles, W.J. 1889–91a Report on the prehistoric remains from the sand-hills of the coast of Ireland. *Proceedings of the Royal Irish Academy* **1** (3rd series), 173–87.

Knowles, W.J. 1889–91b Second report on the prehistoric remains from the sandhills of the coast of Ireland. *Proceedings of the Royal Irish Academy* **1** (3rd series), 612–25.

Knowles, W.J. 1893–6 The third report on the prehistoric remains from the sandhills of the coast of Ireland. *Proceedings of the Royal Irish Academy* **3** (3rd series), 650–63.

Knowles, W.J. 1900–2 The fourth report on the prehistoric remains from the sandhills of the coast of Ireland. *Proceedings of the Royal Irish Academy* **6** (3rd series), 331–89.

Lacy, B. 1983 *Archaeological Survey of County Donegal.* Lifford. Donegal County Council.

Leonard, H. 1868 Kitchen midden on Omey Island, Co. Galway. *Geological Magazine* **5** (48), 266–8.

Livens, R.G. 1956 Three tanged flint points from Scotland. *Proceedings of the Society of Antiquaries of Scotland* **89**, 438–43.

Livens, R.G. 1972 The Irish Sea element in the Welsh Mesolithic cultures. In F. Lynch and C. Burgess (eds), *Prehistoric man in Wales and the West,* 19–29. Bath. Adams and Dart.

Liversage, G.D. 1968 Excavations at Dalkey Island, Co. Dublin, 1956–1959. *Proceedings of the Royal Irish Academy* **66**C, 53–233.

Lymbery, J. 1864 Correspondence quoted in Proceedings and Papers of the Quarterly General Meeting. *Journal of the Kilkenny and South-east of Ireland Archaeological Society* **5** (new series, part 1, 1864), 121–2.

McCartan, S.B. 1991–3 A Later Mesolithic site at Rhendhoo, Jurby, Isle of Man. *Proceedings of the Isle of Man Natural History and Antiquarian Society* **10** (2), 87–117.

McCullagh, R. 1988–9 Excavations at Newton, Islay. *Glasgow Archaeological Journal* **15**, 23–51.

MacKie, E.W. 1963 A dwelling site of the earlier Iron Age at Balevullin, Tiree, excavated in 1912 by A. Henderson Bishop. *Proceedings of the Society of Antiquaries of Scotland* **96**, 155–83.

Mellars, P. 1987 *Excavations on Oronsay: prehistoric human ecology on a small island.* Edinburgh University Press.

Mercer, J. 1980 Lussa Wood 1: the Late Glacial and early Post-Glacial occupation of Jura. *Proceedings of the Society of Antiquaries of Scotland* **110**, 1–32.

Mitchell, G.F. 1956 An early kitchen-midden at Sutton, Co. Dublin. *Journal of the Royal Society of Antiquaries of Ireland* **86**, 1–26.

Mitchell, G.F. 1970 Some chronological implications of the Irish Mesolithic. *Ulster Journal of Archaeology* **33**, 3–14.

Mitchell, G.F. 1972a Some Ultimate Larnian sites in Lake Derravaragh, Co. Westmeath.

Journal of the Royal Society of Antiquaries of Ireland **102**, 160–73.

Mitchell, G.F. 1972b Further excavation of the early kitchen-midden at Sutton, Co. Dublin. *Journal of the Royal Society of Antiquaries of Ireland* **102**, 151–9.

Mitchell, G.F. 1989 *Man and environment in Valencia Island.* Dublin. Royal Irish Academy.

Mithen, S. 1995 Mesolithic settlement and raw material availability in the southern Hebrides. In A. Fischer (ed.), *Man and sea in the Mesolithic,* 265–72. Oxbow Monograph 53. Oxford.

Mithen, S.J. and Finlayson, B. 1991 Red deer hunters on Colonsay? The implications of Staosnaig for the interpretation of the Oronsay middens. *Proceedings of the Prehistoric Society* **57**, 1–8.

Mithen, S. and Lake, M. 1996 The Southern Hebrides Mesolithic Project: reconstructing Mesolithic settlement in western Scotland. In T. Pollard and A. Morrison (eds), *The early prehistory of Scotland,* 123–51. Edinburgh University Press.

Mithen, S.J., Finlayson, B., Finlay, N. and Lake, M. 1992 Excavations on Bolsay Farm, a Mesolithic settlement on Islay. *Cambridge Archaeological Journal* **2**, 242–53.

Movius, H.L. 1940 Report on a Stone Age excavation at Rough Island, Strangford Lough, County Down. *Journal of the Royal Society of Antiquaries of Ireland* **70**, 111–42.

O'Kelly, M.J. and Shee, E. 1976 *Cork Harbour archaeology.* Cork. Department of Archaeology.

O'Sullivan, A. 1998 *The archaeology of lake settlement in Ireland.* Discovery Programme Monographs 4. Dublin. Royal Irish Academy.

O'Sullivan, A. and Sheehan, J. 1996 *The Iveragh Peninsula. An archaeological survey of south Kerry.* Cork University Press.

Pollard, T., Atkinson, J. and Banks, I. 1996 It is the technical side of the work which is my stumbling block: a shell midden site on Risga reconsidered. In T. Pollard and A. Morrison (eds), *The early prehistory of Scotland,* 165–82. Edinburgh University Press.

Power, D., Byrne, E., Egan, U., Lane, S. and Sleeman, M. 1992 *Archaeological Inventory of County Cork, Volume 1: West Cork.* Dublin. Stationery Office.

Power, D., Byrne, E., Egan, U., Lane, S. and Sleeman, M. 1994 *Archaeological Inventory of County Cork, Volume 2: East and South Cork.* Dublin. Stationery Office.

PSAMNI 1940 *A preliminary survey of the ancient monuments of Northern Ireland.* Belfast. HMSO.

Renfrew, C. and Wagstaff, M. 1982 Introduction: an initial perspective. In C. Renfrew and M. Wagstaff (eds), *An island polity: the archaeology of exploitation in Melos,* 1–8. Cambridge University Press.

Russell, N.J., Bonsall, C. and Sutherland, D.G. 1995 The exploitation of marine molluscs in the Mesolithic of western Scotland: evidence from Ulva Cave, Inner Hebrides. In A. Fischer (ed.), *Man and sea in the Mesolithic,* 273–88. Oxbow Monograph 53. Oxford.

Saville, A. 1996 Lacaille, microliths and the Mesolithic of Orkney. In T. Pollard and A. Morrison (eds), *The early prehistory of Scotland,* 213–24. Edinburgh University Press.

Saville, A. and Miket, R. 1994a An Corran rock-shelter, Skye: a major new Mesolithic site. *Past* **18**, 9–10.

Saville, A. and Miket, R. 1994b An Corran, Staffin, Skye (Kilmuir parish): rock-shelter. In

C.E. Batey and M. King (eds), *Discovery and excavation in Scotland 1994*, 40–1. Edinburgh. Council for Scottish Archaeology.

Sheridan, J.A. 1986 Porcellanite artifacts: a new survey. *Ulster Journal of Archaeology* **49**, 19–32.

Whelan, C.B. 1933–4 Further excavation at Ballynagard, Rathlin Island, County Antrim. *Proceedings and Reports of the Belfast Natural History and Philosophical Society* (1933–4), 107–11.

Whelan, C.B. 1934–5 Studies in the significance of the Irish Stone Age: the Campignian question. *Proceedings of the Royal Irish Academy* **42**C, 121–43.

Wickham-Jones, C.R. 1990 *Rhum, Mesolithic and later sites at Kinloch: excavations 1984–86.* Society of Antiquaries of Scotland, Monograph 7. Edinburgh.

Wiggins, K. 1988 Keeping ahead of the quarrying. Church Bay, Rathlin, Co. Antrim. In A. Hamlin and C. Lynn (eds), *Pieces of the past*, 14–15. Belfast. HMSO.

Williams, B. 1990 The archaeology of Rathlin Island. *Archaeology Ireland* **4** (2), 47–51.

Windle, B. 1911 A note on some kitchen-middens in the north of Ireland. *Journal of the Royal Society of Antiquaries of Ireland* **41**, 1–4.

Woodman, P.C. 1978 *The Mesolithic in Ireland: hunter-gatherers in an insular environment.* British Archaeological Reports, British Series 58. Oxford.

Woodman, P.C. 1986 Problems in the colonisation of Ireland. *Ulster Journal of Archaeology* **49**, 7–17.

Woodman, P.C. and Anderson, E. 1990 The Irish Later Mesolithic: a partial picture. In P.M. Vermeersch and P. van Peer (eds), *Contributions to the Mesolithic in Europe*, 377–87. Leuven University Press.

Woodman, P., McCarthy, M. and Monaghan, N. 1997 The Irish Quaternary Fauna Project. *Quaternary Science Review* **16**, 129–59.

VARIATION AND CONTEXT: ECOLOGY AND SOCIAL EVOLUTION IN IRELAND'S LATER MESOLITHIC

Michael J. Kimball

INTRODUCTION

The Irish Later Mesolithic (*c.* 7500–5500 BP) evolved within an island landscape delineated and perforated by aquatic ecosystems. Of the island's total land area of 84,000km^2, there are 16,000km of primary streams, at least 10,000km of tributaries, and more than 200,000ha of lakes (Whelan 1989, 9). However, compared to Britain and the Continent, Ireland possesses a low diversity of indigenous plant and animal resources (Mitchell 1990).

What should be expected from a mid-Holocene foraging society adapted to this kind of island environment? In this paper two main considerations are explored: (1) global ecological trends and (2) regional-level ecology, both of which conditioned social evolution in prehistoric foraging societies.

The paper focuses on cultures that developed along the Northwest Coast of North America and southern Scandinavia to highlight a trend toward sedentism and social complexity that emerged within many mid-Holocene foraging societies. Regional-level temporal and spatial ecological variables and their relation to society are then discussed, and the role of resource diversity in Ireland's Later Mesolithic adaptation is explored.

While post-depositional processes play a role in forming Ireland's archaeological record, it is possible that a lack of evidence for sedentism, social complexity and intensive resource exploitation in Ireland may accurately represent Later Mesolithic society. In this light, a model that takes into account ecological and biogeographic factors conditioning the evolution of Irish forager societies is proposed. Finally, it is argued that there is a need for studies of the Later Mesolithic that incorporate an evolutionary perspective, which would emphasise variation and appreciate Ireland's island context.

GLOBAL ECOLOGICAL TRENDS

For many prehistoric foraging societies the emergence of sedentism and incipient social complexity roughly coincides with a mid-Holocene appearance of productive and reliable marine ecosystems (Yesner 1998). This is not accidental—the period during which post-glacial eustatic sea-levels were stabilising (approximately 6500–4000 BP) (see Mann *et al.* 1998) created environments that very likely promoted the development of productive migratory fish runs and shellfish beds in many areas (Yesner 1980; Fladmark 1983). As a result, societies with the technological capacity (see Hayden 1981; 1992) and cultural inclination—i.e. historically contingent factors predisposing the behaviour (see Kelly 1995; Cannon 1998)—broadened their subsistence base and intensified their exploitation of

	Sedentism	**Large shell middens**	**Social differentiation**	**Exploitation technology**
Northwest Coast	4000 BP, Namu	5000 BP, Namu	5000 BP, labrets	4000 BP, fish-weirs
Southern Scandinavia	6000 BP, Norsminde	6000 BP, Ertebølle	6000 BP, Danubian axes	6300 BP, fish-weirs

Table 1—Evidence for a global trend toward sedentism and social complexity in mid-Holocene foraging societies.

coastal and migratory fish resources during this period (Price 1985; Hayden 1995).

Archaeological evidence for this phenomenon can be found from both the Northwest Coast of North America and southern Scandinavia (Table 1). For example, in both areas there is the development of semi-sedentary to sedentary occupations, at Namu on the central Northwest Coast by *c.* 4000 BP (Coupland 1998) and at Norsminde in Jutland by *c.* 6000 BP (Andersen 1991). Large shell middens appear at Namu by *c.* 5000 BP (Cannon 1998) and at Ertebølle in Jutland by *c.* 6000 BP (Andersen 1995). Possible evidence for social differentiation includes labret faceting on the teeth of a skeleton at Pender Canal in British Columbia *c.* 5000 BP (Carlson 1998) and trade in Danubian shaft-hole axes in southern Scandinavia by 6000 BP (Fischer 1982; Pedersen *et al.* 1997).

In addition, technologies permitting intensive exploitation of aquatic resources—e.g. fish-weirs at the Glenrose Cannery site in British Columbia dated to *c.* 4000 BP (Coupland 1998) and at Halsskov in Denmark dated to *c.* 6300 BP (Pedersen 1995)—have bolstered the evidence for intensification of resource exploitation during these periods.

Stationary fish-trap evidence, however, can be misleading. Owing to a wealth of ethnographic evidence for riverine fish-weirs among Northwest Coast societies, there has been a tendency to associate the use of fish-weirs with the emergence of cultural complexity (Erlandson *et al.* 1998). Indeed, large fish-weirs do represent a capacity to capture a large number of fish—potentially larger than the number needed to support a family or even a group of families, depending on the abundance of the fish resources. However, fish-weirs alone do not necessarily represent intensified exploitation. For example, prehistoric fish-weirs found along the southern Northwest Coast of North America (specifically coastal Oregon) have led to the following distinction (*ibid.*, 18):

> In general, estuarine weirs (as opposed to riverine salmon weirs) seem to have taken less effort to construct and maintain, to have been used for a greater part of the year (possibly year round), and to have captured a wider range of species. Ethnographic accounts suggest that some coastal groups used weirs communally, but the smaller and simpler estuarine weirs may have been more amenable to individual or family use. On the southern Northwest Coast, the assumption that the mere presence of fishing weirs

implies communal or corporate behavior requiring elite management or control seems to be unfounded.

After 2500 BP, for many societies of the Northwest Coast, trajectories of social change led to the 'Developed Northwest Coast Pattern' (Coupland 1998, 36). This pattern includes archaeological evidence for 'a sedentary village-based cultural system with a seasonal round, storage and preservation of foodstuffs, and elaboration of arts and crafts and social institutions comparable to that achieved by many agricultural societies' (Carlson 1998, 24). Ultimately, these social institutions included competitive feasting, slavery and warfare (Cannon 1992; Ames 1994). This pattern continued up to and beyond contact with Europeans, when competition for European goods among native Northwest Coast peoples was added to competition for salmon resources (Kelly 1995).

In contrast, the emergence of aspects of social complexity within southern Scandinavian forager societies coincides with evidence for contact with Neolithic groups. Late Ertebølle foragers opted for agriculture around 5050 BP (Price *et al.* 1995; Stafford 1999). Thus Neolithic settlement, subsistence and social constructs were gradually integrated into forager society.

In summary, it can be argued that during the mid-Holocene, in disparate regions, a global pattern of sea-level stabilisation created environmental conditions that permitted intensive exploitation of marine (including migratory fish) resources. Forager societies such as those of the Northwest Coast of North America and southern Scandinavia focused on coastal and riverine resources, thereby laying the foundation for an ensuing trend towards sedentism and social complexity.

The Irish case

Aquatic orientation

In 1995 an archaeological survey of a 296km^2 region in eastern County Donegal was conducted (Kimball 1998). The purpose of the Lough Swilly Archaeological Survey (LSAS) was to investigate the transition from the Later Mesolithic to the Neolithic from a regional-scale perspective in a part of Ireland with no history of systematic field collection.

For the purposes of this paper, two findings are presented.

(1) Later Mesolithic settlement in eastern Donegal exhibits an estuarine, coastal, and riverine locational preference; there is no evidence for inland terrestrial settlement. A map (Fig. 1) of the area in which Later Mesolithic artefact types were identified demonstrates this orientation toward aquatic ecozones.

(2) Later Mesolithic artefacts occur both in small lithic concentrations and in dispersed background distributions. This pattern is consistent with an interpretation of small-scale and/or short-term occupations.

These results are consistent with—indeed, representative of—Ireland's overall record of Later

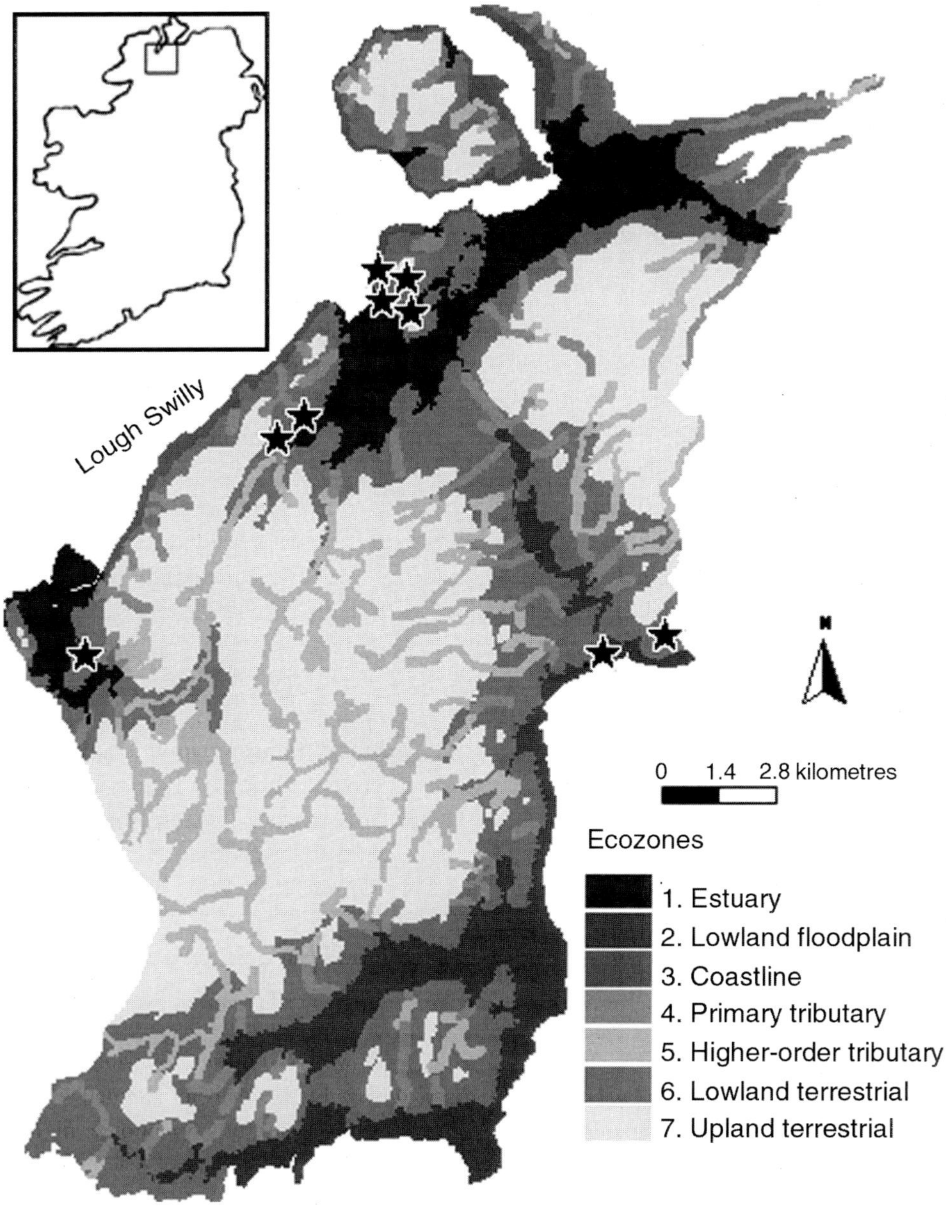

Fig. 1—Distribution of Later Mesolithic artefact types (stars) in Lough Swilly study region. Note orientation towards estuarine and lowland floodplain ecozones.

Ecosystem	% LSAS study region	Subsistence resources
Woodland	65%	*Wild pig; small mammals; hazelnuts; terrestrial plants*
Freshwater (riverine, wetland, forested wetland)	24%	*Wild pig; small mammals; hazelnuts; terrestrial plants*; migratory fish; wetland birds; wetland plants
Estuary and saltwater wetland	9%	*Wild pig; small mammals*; migratory fish; sea fish; shellfish; seabirds; sea mammals; wetland birds; wetland plants
Coastal shoreland	2%	*Wild pig*; shellfish; sea fish; seabirds; sea mammals

Table 2—Estimated distribution of critical subsistence resources within the LSAS study region. Woodland resources are italicised to emphasise their redundancy in other ecosystems.

Mesolithic settlement (Woodman 1978; Anderson 1993).

However, is the Later Mesolithic defined by an aquatic adaptation or might there be an as yet undiscovered inland terrestrial component? Table 2 shows that, although the aquatically oriented ecosystems of the study area represent a minority (35%) of the entire region, an estimate of the distribution of faunal and floral subsistence resources, based on preferred habitat types, suggests that this relatively small area probably possessed a majority of the critical subsistence resources, including those that would also be found in inland terrestrial zones (Kimball 1998).

Given the limited terrestrial biodiversity in Ireland (see below), it is not surprising that Later Mesolithic settlement would be focused on the aquatic margins. Thus it can be argued that the current pattern of Later Mesolithic settlement preference in Ireland is real, rather than an apparent pattern produced by an incomplete archaeological record.

Sea-level stabilisation

Although the dynamics of relative sea-level change are complex for Ireland, overall the mid-Holocene reveals a relatively stable history (Carter *et al.* 1989). For example, although the sea-level in southern Ireland rose continuously between 8000 and 4000 BP, it has remained within 2–3m of the present level since then. In the north-east, sea-level peaked around 6500 BP to about 2m above the present level and fell 2m below the present level by about 4000 BP before attaining its present level. In the north-west (i.e. County Donegal), rapid relative sea-level rise appears to have halted about 5000 BP at between approximately 1m above and 1m below the present level from east to west respectively (Shaw 1985).

These trends are summarised in Table 3 and conform to Fladmark's (1983) criteria for a 'quasi-stable' (vs unstable) sea-level state. Thus Ireland's history of sea-level change would

Quadrant	Sea-level history	Mid-Holocene period
South-east	Increase from 8000 BP	± 2–3m since 4000 BP
South-west	Increase from 8000 BP	± 2–3m since 4000 BP
North-east	Peak at 6500 BP	± 2m since 6500 BP
North-west	Rapid rise stops at 5000 BP	± 1m since 5000 BP

Table 3—General trends for Ireland's sea-level history (derived from Carter et al. *1989).*

appear to agree with a mid-Holocene global pattern of sea-level stabilisation. It may therefore be expected that stable migratory fish and shellfish resources were established during the mid-Holocene in areas with favourable coastal physiographic characteristics.

Sedentism and social complexity

At present, there is no evidence for emerging sedentism and social complexity coincident with sea-level stabilisation. It has been suggested (e.g. Cooney and Grogan 1994) that large Mesolithic settlements may have been obscured or erased by post-depositional processes. Indeed, in many places these are likely to be major reasons for the current state of the archaeological record. Ireland is well known for its blanket and raised bogs (Mitchell 1990); there are many places where high-energy coastal processes could have destroyed prehistoric coastal sites, and rising sea-levels are likely to have inundated many sites.

Ireland's archaeological record is also mute about social differentiation in the Later Mesolithic. This stands in contrast to the archaeological record for the Northwest Coast of North America and southern Scandinavian societies (see above). Of course, it is likely that artefacts marking social differentiation during the Later Mesolithic would have been subjected to the same post-depositional processes that have destroyed or obscured settlement sites.

Significant post-depositional hazards notwithstanding, an important observation must be acknowledged. These factors have also been active for the Northwest Coast of North America (e.g. coastal erosion and acidic soils) and southern Scandinavia (e.g. sea-level rise, coastal erosion, bog development) and yet there is evidence in coastal and riverine environments for the emergence of sedentism and social complexity during the mid-Holocene in both areas. Indeed, given Ireland's record of sea-level change, if there was a trend from mobile, simple societies to relatively sedentary and complex societies, one would expect the latter to be comparatively well represented in the archaeological record, at least in the northern part of the country. This is the case in southern Scandinavia, which has a similar sea-level history (Andersen 1995). Thus some evidence should be visible for sedentism, social differentiation and intensive resource exploitation in Ireland if these actually occurred.

There is a very limited amount of direct evidence for the use of fish-weirs by Later Mesolithic groups. Woodman (1978) has mentioned weirs found in the area of Toome, Co. Antrim, whose disposition may indicate that they were Mesolithic features. Woodman (*op. cit.*) has also suggested that a small arc of stones in the basal layer of Newferry Site 3 (Woodman 1977) may represent the remains of a weir.

Common name	Scientific name
Wrasse	Labridae
Bream	Sparidae
Gurnard	Triglidae
Common eel	*Anguilla anguilla*
Conger eel	*Conger conger*
Shark-type fish	Elasmobranches
Thornback ray	*Raja clavata*
Tope	*Galeorhinus galeus*
Mullet	Muglidae
Scad	*Trachurus trachurus*
Cod-type fish	Gadidae
Whiting	*Merlangius merlangus*
Haddock	*Melanogrammus aeglefinus*

Table 4—Fish species excavated from the Later Mesolithic site of Ferriter's Cove (see Woodman and O'Brien 1993). Faunal analysis conducted by Margaret McCarthy, University College Cork.

If the aquatic component of Later Mesolithic faunal remains is considered, however, then it is possible to suggest a line of indirect evidence for the use of fish-weirs. Extensive analysis of fish bones from Danish Mesolithic sites found that faunal assemblages represent a 'non-selective sample of whatever fish was present in the local coastal waters during the summer half of the year' (Enghoff 1995, 72). According to Enghoff, the pattern of fish remains, varying in size, class and species, strongly suggests the use of stationary capture technologies such as fish-weirs. Indeed, over the last ten years an increasing amount of archaeological evidence for fish-weirs in Denmark has emerged from coastal and underwater archaeological research projects employing predictive models for Mesolithic site location (Pedersen 1995).

Most of the fish remains recovered from Irish Later Mesolithic midden sites are of inshore species, such as mullet, wrasse, sole and tope (Woodman 1978, 166). The fish species list from the Ferriter's Cove excavations (Woodman and O'Brien 1993) provides a good example of this pattern (Table 4). Both large (tope) and small fish are represented, and some (e.g. whiting) were present in large numbers (M. McCarthy, pers. comm.). Although it lacks a fortifying level of detail, this pattern is consistent with that used by Enghoff (1995) to justify the predominant use of stationary fish-weirs in the Danish Mesolithic. Thus it is possible to hypothesise that fish-weirs played a major role in the Irish Later Mesolithic subsistence system as well. Testing of this hypothesis must await further archaeological and zooarchaeological research.

However, as is the case for southern Northwest Coast prehistory (Erlandson *et al.* 1998; see above), evidence for fish-weirs during the Irish Later Mesolithic—should it increase with more archaeological research and analysis—will only demonstrate a technological capacity among foragers for accessing the most available subsistence resources. It will not in itself demonstrate the emergence of social complexity.

In summary, the current archaeological evidence for Later Mesolithic settlement location is consistent with expectations derived from what is known about the modern habitat preferences of critical subsistence resources in Ireland. Moreover, Irish sea-level data are in agreement with a mid-Holocene global pattern of sea-level stabilisation. This phenomenon would probably have created optimal conditions for the development of migratory fish and shellfish resources. There is, however, no archaeological evidence in Ireland that correlates with the emergence of sedentism and social complexity. At this time there is indirect evidence for the use of stationary fish-traps, but it does not necessarily suggest a pattern of intensified exploitation. Although post-depositional processes may have significantly altered the archaeological record, it can be argued that, based on Ireland's sea-level history, the latest Mesolithic societies should be over-represented in the archaeological record. Thus, if sedentism, social differentiation and intensive exploitation actually developed, some evidence for these should be detectable.

REGIONAL-LEVEL ECOLOGY

At an inter-regional level, cultural diversity is the rule for forager societies, in part because of environmental differences that occur at a regional level (Kelly 1995).

Aquatic resource availability and abundance are governed by a host of spatial and temporal factors. Cannon (1996) and Schalk (1977) have identified factors influencing anadromous fish productivity active at different temporal and spatial scales, all of which affect the local environment of foragers. These include global environmental variables such as stabilisation of sea-levels and stream gradients, variable precipitation affecting stream run-off, post-glacial transitions in stream forest cover, and temperature changes affecting the primary productivity of ocean feeding areas. Regional-level factors include marine nutrient upwelling patterns, which affect primary and secondary productivity (Yesner 1983); distance upstream from a river's mouth and variation in stream discharge rate, which affect fish abundance; shifts in the migration routes of major salmon runs; changes in stream water temperature, run-off, stream gradients and sedimentation; and spatially variable features such as lakes (which control run-off extremes), floodplains (which control sediment deposition), and vegetation cover and aspect (which moderate temperature variations).

These factors can also be expected to influence the productivity and distribution of other resources, such as freshwater fish, catadromous fish and shellfish. For example, the size, timing and spatial patterns for the upstream migration of eels are affected by (1) changing patterns or magnitudes of freshwater inflows to bays or estuaries and (2) the availability of soft, undisturbed bottom sediments (Facey and van Den Avyle 1987). Likewise, the interaction between sea-level change and local coastal geomorphology influences factors such as intertidal sedimentation and salinity, which in turn either promote or discourage colonisation and growth of shellfish resources (Yesner 1983).

Variability in the structure of aquatic resources as a function of geography and periodicity requires the development of different adaptations. Meldgaard's (1995) study of Inuit adaptations in west Greenland highlights the impact on technology, hunting strategy and mobility of seasonal and annual trends in the occurrence of marine mammals and seabirds.

Likewise, O'Leary's (1996) ethnographic research has shown that seasonality in the availability and abundance of anadromous fish resources in Canada's south-west Yukon territory leads forager groups to change their settlement pattern on a seasonal basis (*ibid.*, 14):

> When seasonality determines the clumping of salmon, it creates a kind of temporary environment which tends to increase group size and the logistical forays. But once this 'abundant' resource is over, the people at Klukshu village find themselves in an environment which, because of the scattered, dispersed nature of other game . . . tends to decrease group size but increase likelihood and number of moves to a new residence.

The Irish case

Resource variability

Just as in the cases of the Northwest Coast of North America and southern Scandinavia, variability should be anticipated in the adaptations and culture of Ireland's Later Mesolithic societies.

To support this contention, migratory fish (anadromous and catadromous) are taken as a heuristic example for the following reasons: Ireland's zooarchaeological record demonstrates exploitation of these resources (e.g. Woodman 1977, 193; Woodman and O'Brien 1993, 31); they are known to be rich sources of nutrition (e.g. Kew 1992); they are known to run in numbers that, with the appropriate extractive technology, can supply an abundant food source; and it is probable that Irish Later Mesolithic people had the technology (e.g. fish-weirs; see above) to exploit them.

Whelan (1989, 19) has compared Ireland to a 'dog-shaped saucer with a central oval plain of soft carboniferous limestone and outer margins of progressively harder rock'. The waters of the limestone plain are alkaline and thus create favourable environments for brown trout and 'coarse' fish such as cyprinids, eel and stoneloach. The granite coastline waters are acidic and thus favourable for salmonids such as salmon and sea trout, which have adapted to waters with low productivity by migrating to the sea to feed and grow. Thus availability of migratory fish species can be expected roughly to track the pH of the parent material that underlies freshwater systems. This means a high degree of inter-regional spatial variability of this resource in Ireland.

Variability in fish abundance is another critical factor. Although many Irish streams carry migratory fish of one or more species (e.g. salmon, sea trout and eel), their abundance varies according to the nature of stream channel morphology (see above). Furthermore, tributaries carry fewer fish than primary channels (Kew 1992). In addition, following Schalk (1977), the discharge volumes of Ireland's many small rivers may have increased the chances for inter-annual variability in the structure of the migratory fish resource.

The timing of migratory fish runs also plays a major role in conditioning forager settlement and subsistence systems. As discussed above, the 'clumping' of salmon runs along

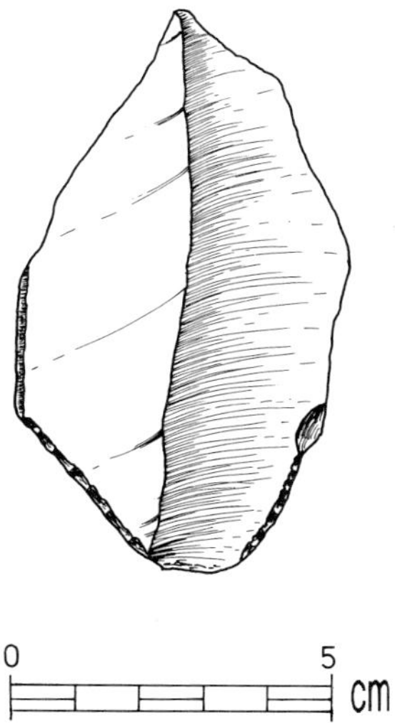

Fig. 2—A Later Mesolithic 'butt-trimmed' artefact, illustrated by Liz Anderson.

rivers in the south-west Yukon, Canada (O'Leary 1996), creates an intra-annual pattern of summer aggregation and off-season dispersal for foragers who depend on this resource. If salmon were important for some Later Mesolithic foraging groups, a similar pattern might have evolved. The response would vary according to the distribution of local secondary resources. Alternatively, if eels were the primary resource—as was the case for some Mesolithic groups in Denmark (Enghoff 1995)—then one might expect autumn aggregations corresponding to eel spawning runs. Regardless of which migratory species is the primary resource, forager adaptations should be expected to vary at an inter-regional scale according to the availability of resources.

Resource diversity

The above discussion begs the following question. If cultural variability should be expected, why is it not apparent in the archaeological record?

Known Later Mesolithic sites consist entirely of ephemeral occupations of aquatically oriented environments, e.g. the margins of coastal areas, estuaries, rivers and lakes. The lithic industry represented across all sites typically includes retouched and unretouched broad blades and flakes (e.g. Fig. 2; see also Woodman and Anderson 1990; Anderson 1994; Anderson and Johnson 1995). With the exception of the Isle of Man (McCartan 1994), there is no counterpart to this artefact type outside Ireland. Within Ireland, no regional variations have been identified—'butt-trimmed' forms look relatively similar anywhere they occur, regardless of the raw material out of which they were made. Thus there is homogeneity in the Later Mesolithic lithic industry that, at first glance, leads one to believe that the culture itself was homogeneous from one end of the island to the other.

The addition of resource diversity as a factor may serve to elucidate this pattern. As indicated above, Ireland's terrestrial biodiversity is comparatively impoverished. Using Mitchell's (1990, 75) summary of native biodiversity in Ireland and Britain, it is possible to construct a histogram that shows Ireland's biota as a proportion of Britain's. Figure 3 reveals that the range of resources available to Ireland's foragers would have been quite restricted even compared to those of another island. This is probably due in part to the 'species–area relationship', i.e. smaller islands support fewer species than larger islands (MacArthur and Wilson 1967; Case and Cody 1983).

Technological homogeneity may thus represent a generalised adaptation to an environment defined by spatial and temporal ecological variability and restricted resource diversity. As Woodman (e.g. 1978; 1992) has suggested, ground stone axes and hafted blades and flakes could represent tools used in the production of an array of more complex procurement technologies, such as stationary fish-traps. As these would be made from organic materials, it is only the stone tools that endure in most contexts. The apparent homogeneity of the production technology may mask actual heterogeneity in procurement technology that is driven by the vicissitudes and extractive requirements of Ireland's aquatic resource base. As a result, actual heterogeneity in subsistence adaptations and society may be occluded by the durable record of a generalised stone toolkit.

DISCUSSION

In summary, there is a global ecological trend to which many mid-Holocene foraging societies responded by intensifying their exploitation of marine resources, thereby establishing a base for the emergence of sedentism and social complexity. In addition, there is an absence of evidence for such a response in the archaeological record for Ireland's Later Mesolithic societies. Switching to the regional level, it is suggested that Ireland's island environment would probably have led to foraging strategies adapted to resource variability and restricted resource diversity.

Aside from explanations that implicate post-depositional processes, what other possibilities exist for the Later Mesolithic pattern, which reflects non-sedentary, simply organised societies? In response to this question, I offer an alternative scenario, which I have termed 'biogeographical constraints'.

Biogeographical constraints

In addition to intensive exploitation of one or more resources, complex foraging societies exploit a wide range of subsistence resources (Hayden 1995). This is reflected in both faunal assemblages and settlement patterns. For example, in ethnographic Fraser River (e.g. Romanoff 1992) and prehistoric Late Ertebølle societies (e.g. Price *et al.* 1995), deer and other secondary terrestrial resources play a significant role in the diet. Moreover, in both cases settlement consists of an array of site types, including short-term and long-term inland and coastal occupations (e.g. Alexander 1992 for Fraser River; Stafford 1999 for Late Ertebølle evidence).

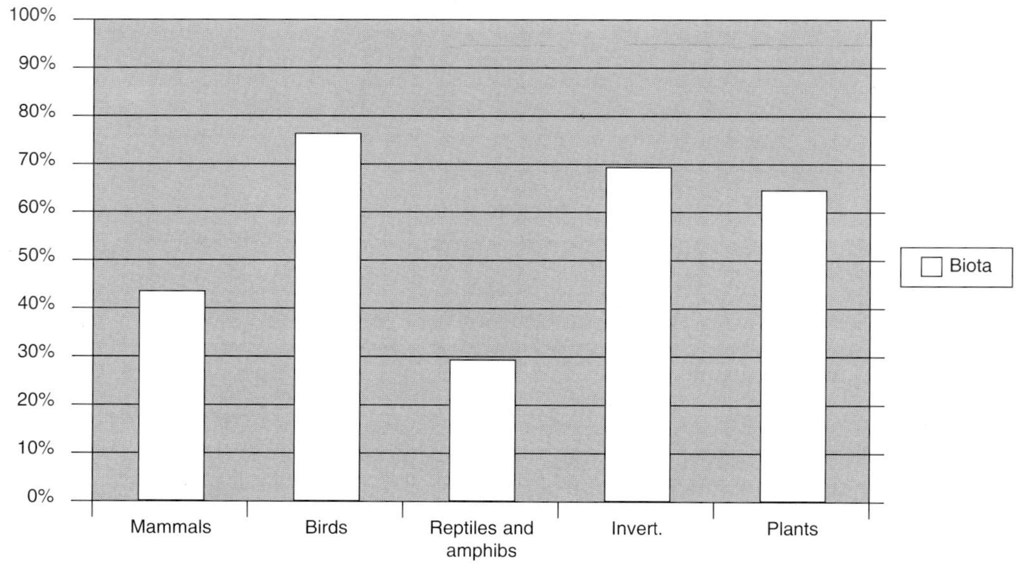

Fig. 3—Ireland's biodiversity as a proportion of Britain's (based on data from Mitchell 1990).

Ireland's relatively impoverished biodiversity may not have permitted a subsistence base that was broad enough to support sedentism and the development of social complexity. It is now reasonably certain that, for whatever reason, large ungulates were not available during the Later Mesolithic. For some years the absence of good evidence for red deer remains in archaeological contexts has been noted (e.g. van Wijngaarden-Bakker 1985). Recent results from the Irish Quaternary Fauna Project (Woodman *et al.* 1997) indicate that the earliest unequivocal occurrence of red deer is from Neolithic contexts. Thus the largest terrestrial mammals available to Irish foragers were likely to have been wild pigs.

There are certainly examples of sedentism among prehistoric foraging societies on islands with impoverished terrestrial biodiversity, e.g. Kodiak Island in the Alutiq Region of Alaska (Haggerty *et al.* 1991; Fitzhugh 1996). However, Kodiak Island foragers were able to intensively exploit cod all year round and to take advantage of concentrated and diverse marine resources, including shellfish, harbour seals, dolphins and whales. This underscores the importance of biogeographic studies that include marine as well as terrestrial biota and measures of the spatial distribution, abundance and periodicity of marine resources. It may be that, for some Northwest Coast island foragers, the availability and diversity of marine fauna sufficiently offset the paucity of terrestrial fauna.

Although it is clear that Ireland's environment offered resources sufficient to permit a successful forager adaptation—if its persistence for *c.* 2000 years is any indication—it is not clear that they were available and diverse enough to form the kind of base that occurred for the Northwest Coast of North America, southern Scandinavian, and other mid-Holocene societies. It may not have been until the appearance of Neolithic domesticates (and red deer) that a critical threshold in resource availability and diversity was crossed, thereby laying the economic foundations for sedentism and social complexity.

Variation and context

Ethnographic and archaeological data demonstrate that sedentism, social complexity and dependence on aquatic resources are positively correlated in foraging societies (Yesner 1980; Pálsson 1988; Kelly 1995). High primary productivity of coastal waters, low relief of coastal plains, and periodic abundance of aquatic resources have been cited as influential factors (Yesner 1980; Perlman 1985; Pálsson 1988). This general pattern encourages an implicit expectation that foraging societies depending on aquatic resources will exhibit sedentism and social complexity.

However, at the regional level such a generalisation becomes suspect. Local environmental factors such as coastal geomorphology, hydrography and biodiversity conspire to create highly variable contexts for social evolution. Yesner (1980, 730) hinted at this when he called for more study of the northern temperate coastal zone, 'where horticulture is only a marginal possibility, wild food plants are not greatly abundant, and high-fat, high-calorie sea mammals are less available than farther north'. Ireland presents a tantalising target for this agenda.

In conclusion, assuming that the interpretation submitted in this paper is correct, should Ireland's Later Mesolithic be seen as a departure from a norm in the evolution of mid-Holocene foraging societies? In a word: no. This would amount to, as McLaughlin (1998, 25) has termed it, an 'essentialist' argument, i.e. one that 'conceptualizes diversity as a "deviation" from a natural state or path of change'. In other words, the expectation that sedentism and complexity *should* arise within maritime foraging societies is based on an assumption that sedentism and complexity are *natural states or trends* for foragers who depend on aquatic resources. Alternatively, it is suggested that cultural change be viewed from an evolutionary perspective, i.e. as 'the product of the continuous interaction between variation and context' (*ibid.*, 28). Ireland's ecology, its 'islandness' and historical contingency converged to create a unique context for social evolution—one that must be appreciated before expectations for Later Mesolithic society are envisioned.

ACKNOWLEDGEMENTS

I obtained funding for my research in County Donegal from a Fulbright Award, the National Science Foundation (SBR-9320499), the Wenner-Gren Foundation for Anthropological Research (5764), and Sigma Xi, and both funding and fieldworkers from the Center for Field Research (Earthwatch). I wish to thank K. Whelan of the Salmon Research Agency in Newport, Co. Mayo, for his advice and assistance concerning Irish migratory fish, and K. Pedersen for his discussions about Denmark's Mesolithic. I also gratefully acknowledge the helpful reviews of M. Partlow, M. Stafford and J. Shokler. I thank the organisers of the New Agendas conference for their invitation to participate.

REFERENCES

Alexander, D. 1992 A reconstruction of prehistoric land use in the mid-Fraser River area based on ethnographic data. In B. Hayden (ed.), *A complex culture of the British Columbia Plateau: traditional Stl'átl'imx resource use*, 99–176. Vancouver. University of British Columbia Press.

Ames, K.M. 1994 The Northwest Coast: complex hunter-gatherers, ecology, and social evolution. *Annual Review of Anthropology* **23**, 209–29.

Andersen, S.H. 1991 Norsminde. A køkkenmødding with Late Mesolithic and Early Neolithic occupation. *Journal of Danish Archaeology* **8**, 13–40.

Andersen, S.H. 1995 Coastal adaptation and marine exploitation in Late Mesolithic Denmark—with special emphasis on the Limfjord region. In A. Fischer (ed.), *Man and sea in the Mesolithic: coastal settlement above and below present sea level*, 41–66. Oxbow Monograph 53. Oxford.

Anderson, E. 1993 The Mesolithic in Munster: fishing for answers. In E. Shee Twohig and M. Ronayne (eds), *Past perceptions: the prehistoric archaeology of south-west Ireland*, 16–24. Cork University Press.

Anderson, E. 1994 Later Mesolithic flint technology. Unpublished MA thesis, University College Cork.

Anderson, E. and Johnson, G. 1995 Irish Later Mesolithic flint technology: further developments. In E. Grogan and C. Mount (eds), *Annus Archaeologiae. Proceedings of the OIA Winter Conference 1993*, 7–22. Organisation of Irish Archaeologists.

Cannon, A. 1992 Conflict and salmon on the Interior Plateau of British Columbia. In B. Hayden (ed.), *A complex culture of the British Columbia Plateau: traditional Stl'átl'imx resource use*, 506–24. Vancouver. University of British Columbia Press.

Cannon, A. 1996 Scales of variability in Northwest salmon fishing. In M. Plew (ed.), *Prehistoric hunter-gatherer fishing strategies*, 25–40. Boise, Idaho. Boise State University.

Cannon, A. 1998 Contingency and agency in the growth of Northwest Coast maritime economies. *Arctic Anthropology* **35** (1), 57–67.

Carlson, R.L. 1998 Coastal British Columbia in the light of North Pacific maritime adaptations. *Arctic Anthropology* **35** (1), 23–35.

Carter, R.W.G., Devoy, R.J.N. and Shaw, J. 1989 Late Holocene sea levels in Ireland. *Journal of Quaternary Science* **4** (1), 7–24.

Case, T. and Cody, M. 1983 Synthesis: pattern and processes in island biogeography. In T. Case and M. Cody (eds), *Island biogeography in the Sea of Cortéz*, 307–41. Berkeley. University of California Press.

Cooney, G. and Grogan, E. 1994 *Irish prehistory: a social perspective.* Bray. Wordwell.

Coupland, G. 1998 Maritime adaptation and evolution of the developed Northwest Coast pattern on the central Northwest Coast. *Arctic Anthropology* **35** (1), 36–56.

Enghoff, I.B. 1995 Fishing in Denmark during the Mesolithic period. In A. Fischer (ed.), *Man and sea in the Mesolithic: coastal settlement above and below present sea level*, 67–74. Oxbow Monograph 53. Oxford.

Erlandson, J.M., Tveskov, M.A. and Byram, R.S. 1998 The development of maritime adaptations on the southern Northwest Coast of North America. *Arctic Anthropology* **35** (1), 6–22.

Facey, D.E. and van Den Avyle, M.J. 1987 Species profiles: life histories and environmental requirements of coastal fishes and invertebrates (North Atlantic)—American eel. *U.S. Fish and Wildlife Service Biological Report* **82**, 11–74.

Fischer, A. 1982 Trade in Danubian shaft-hole axes and the introduction of Neolithic economy in Denmark. *Journal of Danish Archaeology* **1**, 7–12.

Fitzhugh, B. 1996 The evolution of complex hunter-gatherers in the North Pacific: an archaeological case study from Kodiak Island, Alaska. Unpublished Ph.D thesis, Department of Anthropology, University of Michigan, Ann Arbor.

Fladmark, K.R. 1983 A comparison of sea-levels and prehistoric cultural developments on the east and west coasts of Canada. In R.J. Nash (ed.), *The evolution of maritime cultures on the northeast and northwest coasts of America*, 65–75. British Columbia. Department of Anthropology, Simon Fraser University.

Haggerty, J.C., Wooley, C.B., Erlandson, J.M. and Crowell, A. 1991 *The 1990 Exxon Cultural Resource Program: site protection and maritime cultural ecology in Prince William Sound and the Gulf of Alaska.* Anchorage. Exxon Shipping Company and Exxon Company.

Hayden, B. 1981 Research and development in the stone age: technological transitions among hunter-gatherers. *Current Anthropology* **22**, 519–48.

Hayden, B. 1992 Introduction: ecology and culture. In B. Hayden (ed.), *A complex culture of the British Columbia Plateau: traditional Stl'átl'imx resource use*, 3–46. Vancouver. University of British Columbia Press.

Hayden, B. 1995 A new overview of domestication. In T.D. Price and A.B. Gebauer (eds), *Last hunters, first farmers*, 273–99. Santa Fe. School of American Research Press.

Kelly, R. 1995 *The foraging spectrum: diversity in hunter-gatherer lifeways.* Washington, D.C. Smithsonian Institution Press.

Kew, M. 1992 Salmon availability, technology, and cultural adaptation in the Fraser River watershed. In B. Hayden (ed.), *A complex culture of the British Columbia Plateau: traditional Stl'átl'imx resource use*, 177–221. Vancouver. University of British Columbia Press.

Kimball, M.J. 1998 The Lough Swilly archaeological survey: investigations into the Neolithic transition in eastern County Donegal, Ireland. Unpublished Ph.D thesis, University of Wisconsin-Madison.

MacArthur, R.H. and Wilson, E.O. 1967 *The theory of island biogeography.* New Jersey. Princeton University Press.

McCartan, S. 1994 A Later Mesolithic site at Rhendhoo, Jurby. *Proceedings of the Isle of Man Natural History and Antiquarian Society* **10** (2), 87–117.

McLaughlin, P. 1998 Rethinking the agrarian question: the limits of essentialism and the promise of evolutionism. *Human Ecology Review* **5** (2), 25–39.

Mann, D.H., Crowell, A.L., Hamilton, T.D. and Finney, B.P. 1998 Holocene geologic and climatic history around the Gulf of Alaska. *Arctic Anthropology* **35** (1), 112–31.

Meldgaard, M. 1995 Resource pulses in a marine environment: a case study from Disko

Bugt, West Greenland. In A. Fischer (ed.), *Man and sea in the Mesolithic: coastal settlement above and below present sea level*, 361–8. Oxbow Monograph 53. Oxford.

Mitchell, F. 1990 *Reading the Irish landscape*. Dublin. Country House.

O'Leary, B. 1996 The structure of a salmon resource: the southern Tutchone fishery in the Southwest Yukon, Canada. In M. Plew (ed.), *Prehistoric hunter-gatherer fishing strategies*, 6–24. Boise, Idaho. Boise State University.

Pálsson, G. 1988 Hunters and gatherers of the sea. In T. Ingold, D. Riches and J. Woodburn (eds), *Hunters and gatherers*, 189–204. New York. Berg Publishers.

Pedersen, L. 1995 7000 years of fishing: stationary fishing structures in the Mesolithic and afterwards. In A. Fischer (ed.), *Man and sea in the Mesolithic: coastal settlement above and below present sea level*, 75–86. Oxbow Monograph 53. Oxford.

Pedersen, L., Fischer, A. and Hald, N. 1997 Danubian shafthole axes—long distance transport and the introduction of agriculture. In L. Pedersen, A. Fischer and B. Aaby (eds), *The Danish Storebælt since the Ice Age*, 201–5. Copenhagen. A/S Storebælt Fixed Link.

Perlman, S.M. 1985 Group size and mobility costs. In S.W. Green and S.M. Perlman (eds), *The archaeology of frontiers and boundaries*, 33–50. New York. Academic Press.

Price, T.D. 1985 Affluent foragers of Mesolithic southern Scandinavia. In T.D. Price and J.A. Brown (eds), *Prehistoric hunter-gatherers: the emergence of cultural complexity*, 341–63. New York. Academic Press.

Price, T.D., Gebauer, A.B. and Keeley, L.H. 1995 The spread of farming into Europe north of the Alps. In T.D. Price and A.B. Gebauer (eds), *Last hunters, first farmers*, 95–126. Santa Fe. School of American Research Press.

Romanoff, S. 1992 The cultural ecology of hunting and potlatches among the Lillooet Indians. In B. Hayden (ed.), *A complex culture of the British Columbia Plateau: traditional Stl'átl'imx resource use*, 470–505. Vancouver. University of British Columbia Press.

Schalk, R. 1977 The structure of an anadromous fish resource. In L.R. Binford (ed.), *For theory building in archaeology: essays on faunal remains, aquatic resources, spatial analysis, and systemic modeling*, 207–49. New York. Academic Press.

Shaw, J. 1985 Holocene coastal evolution, Co. Donegal, Ireland. Unpublished Ph.D thesis, University of Ulster, Coleraine.

Stafford, M. 1999 *From forager to farmer in flint: a lithic analysis of the prehistoric transition to agriculture in southern Scandinavia*. Aarhus University Press.

van Wijngaarden-Bakker, L. 1985 Quaternary vertebrates. In K.J. Edwards and W.P. Warren (eds), *The Quaternary history of Ireland*, 233–49. New York. Academic Press.

Whelan, K. 1989 *The angler in Ireland: game, coarse, and sea*. Dublin. Country House.

Woodman, P.C. 1977 Recent excavations at Newferry, Co. Antrim. *Proceedings of the Prehistoric Society* **43**, 155–99.

Woodman, P.C. 1978 *The Mesolithic in Ireland: hunter-gatherers in an insular environment.* British Archaeological Reports, British Series 58. Oxford.

Woodman, P.C. 1992 Filling in the spaces in Irish prehistory. *Antiquity* **66**, 295–314.

Woodman, P.C. and Anderson, E. 1990 The Irish Later Mesolithic: a partial picture. In P.M. Vermeersch and P. van Peer (eds), *Contributions to the Mesolithic in Europe*, 377–87.

Leuven University Press.

Woodman, P.C. and O'Brien, M. 1993 Excavations at Ferriter's Cove, Co. Kerry: an interim statement. In E. Shee Twohig and M. Ronayne (eds), *Past perceptions: the prehistoric archaeology of south-west Ireland*, 25–34. Cork University Press.

Woodman, P.C., McCarthy, M. and Monaghan, N. 1997 The Irish Quaternary Fauna Project. *Quaternary Science Review* **16**, 129–59.

Yesner, D.R. 1980 Maritime hunter-gatherers: ecology and prehistory. *Current Anthropology* **21** (6), 727–50.

Yesner, D.R. 1983 On explaining changes in prehistoric coastal economies: the view from Casco Bay. In R.J. Nash (ed.), *The evolution of maritime cultures on the northeast and northwest coasts of America*, 77–89. British Columbia. Department of Anthropology, Simon Fraser University.

Yesner, D.R. 1998 Origins and development of maritime adaptations in the Northwest Pacific region of North America: a zooarchaeological perspective. *Arctic Anthropology* **35** (1), 204–22.

RECOGNISING REGIONALITY IN THE IRISH NEOLITHIC

Gabriel Cooney

CURRENT APPROACHES TO REGIONALITY

Regionality in Ireland is a subject of much current discussion because of both the issue of European Union funding and subsidiarity and the ongoing discourse about the place of Ulster as part of the wider island. In a sense these issues can be placed in a broader context as part of the debate about how we sustain local identities in a world increasingly dominated by global forces, represented in our case most forcefully in the concept of a Euroland with strong internal links (e.g. see discussion in Lee 1999; Tomlinson 1991). The concern about the scale at which social systems operate is also a continuing focus of enquiry in anthropology, with the recognition that the traditional concept of self-sustaining, unchanging small-scale communities fails to take account of the range of ways in which communities can be linked to the larger world (e.g. Eriksen 1995). Archaeologists writing about the past widely agree about the necessity of looking at the evidence from different perspectives and at different scales to understand the character of societies in the past. This is not to say that different scales of analysis can be treated separately, but rather that they should be utilised in combination as a way of altering our focus, to bring into view different aspects of the archaeological record. We can see how people in particular places used material culture on a daily basis and how this articulates with the broader issues of the use and reproduction of material life, traditions and principles of doing things over wider areas and over time (see discussion in Thomas 1996, 95–8). Marquardt and Crumley (1987) introduced the idea of what they referred to as 'effective scale', meaning both the range at which archaeologists can detect cultural patterns and the area over which particular cultural processes may have operated in the past. It has long been recognised that a regional approach is very useful in trying to identify effective scale (e.g. Binford 1964, 440).

Leaving aside for the moment the difficult question of how we actually identify regions from the archaeological record, there has been widespread recognition that regionality is a feature of much of Irish prehistory. This is a theme that can be seen in all the recent general texts (Herity and Eogan 1977; Harbison 1988; O'Kelly 1989; Cooney and Grogan 1994; Waddell 1998). Bearing this in mind, it might seem surprising that we have actually thought and written about Irish prehistory, including the Neolithic period, primarily in the context of an island-wide approach. Alongside the recognition of regionality in the literature, important regional studies have been carried out, but the focus has tended to be on examining particular areas in relation to what have been interpreted as presumed norms of behaviour and material culture across the whole island (see discussions in Mallory and McNeill 1991; Ronayne and Shee Twohig 1993). The dominance of this island-wide approach can be linked in a broad political and ideological sense with the concept of national identity. More pragmatically it reflects the centralised nature of the Republic and the institutions of government concerned with archaeology (see Cooney 1995; 1996; Woodman 1992a; 1995).

This is not a problem unique to Ireland. Harding (1997) has commented in relation to the Neolithic in Britain that an approach which recognises regionality but consigns it to a minor role in narratives, treating the whole island as a unit, has had a dominant place in the recent literature. This is despite the continued calls for the need to acknowledge the central importance of regionality, for example in discussions of the Neolithic period in Scotland (e.g. Kinnes 1985; Sharples 1992; Barclay 1996; 1997). In identifying North Yorkshire as an area that had a particular history during the Neolithic, Harding (1997, 279–81) suggests that a number of factors have caused the recognition of such regionality to be very much underplayed. These include the influence of the interpretation of the evidence from southern Britain in wider interpretative schemes. Concepts and explanations used to understand the Neolithic of southern Britain tend to be uncritically expanded to cover the whole of Britain (and in many cases Ireland). This is a tradition in Neolithic studies that can be traced back to Piggott's (1954) seminal book. Harding also points out that in terms of scale there has recently been a concentration on understanding the archaeological record either in terms of human behaviour in specific contexts and places, or at the very large scale at which the Neolithic can be seen as a social package or a set of structuring principles. What is missing is a focus on the considerable amount of regional contrast within Britain during the Neolithic. Indeed, as Harding points out, the conceptualisation of the Neolithic as a shared set of codes and practices by definition has tended to shift the focus away from a consideration of regional issues or to relegate them to a minor role.

So, regionality has been played down, perhaps for somewhat different reasons, in both Ireland and Britain. There is, however, an important link in the way regionality is treated if we consider the impact of present-day social contexts on the way archaeologists think and write about the past. I suggested above that the focus in Ireland on an island-wide approach to the past might be linked to issues of identity. The implicit and explicit links between archaeology and nationalism in Ireland are being explored (e.g. Cooney 1995; 1996; Woodman 1995; J. O'Sullivan 1998; Tierney 1998). In Britain it could be suggested that the playing down of regionality reflects the dominance of a universalist view of the past (Barclay, forthcoming). Hingley (1996, 140) has commented that, despite the loss of the British Empire, imperial concepts still have an influence in Romano-British studies. However, relatively little attention seems to have been paid to the possibility of a link between the complex interdigitation of ideas of empire, Britain and England, and the writing of prehistory (but see, for example, Champion 1996). Where is the recognition of the possible impact of British nationalism in the writing of British and European prehistory? Could this impact be reflected in a concern with the 'big picture' rather than regional issues? Modes of writing about the Neolithic in Britain are relevant to Ireland because Britain and Ireland are so often lumped together. It is implicitly assumed that the Neolithic was similar across both these islands off the north-west coast of continental Europe (see Cooney 1997). In addressing the question of why regionality has not been to the fore in the discussion and interpretation of the Irish Neolithic, it is relevant therefore to consider the broader issue of how regionality is currently examined in the context of the Neolithic of Britain and north-west Europe, before grappling with the more specific problem of identifying regionality in an Irish context.

Leading on from the points made above, in many recent treatments of the British and European Neolithic there seems to be something akin to a lack of concern or confidence in talking about regionality. The ability to present an interpretative approach based on the detail of individual sites and local sequences has led to a wealth of what could be called local histories, particularly for southern Britain (e.g. Barrett 1994). On the other hand, attention has been focused on understanding the structuring principles of Neolithic life played out over large areas (e.g. Hodder 1990; Thomas 1996). One such principle that has been given prominence in recent years is the concept that Neolithic lifestyles were essentially mobile and that agriculture was adopted only gradually. This idea was intended to break down a supposed older orthodoxy that being Neolithic always meant being sedentary and to provide a basis for a regional perspective (see discussion in Thomas 1993). However, what in effect has happened is that mobility has become the established orthodoxy underlining much recent work (e.g. Thomas 1996; Whittle 1996; Bradley 1998; Edmonds 1999). While this work celebrates the diversity of Neolithic worlds, it depends on mobility as the central explanatory concept. Whittle (1996, 355), for example, writes of the Neolithic way of life in Europe as one in which 'while people moved around, the sense of community continued to be maintained, to be re-affirmed by periodic gatherings, gift exchange, sharings of food and drink, joint participation in ritual and an ever-present web of materiality'. In effect this idea of a mobile lifestyle appears for some archaeologists to represent an overarching principle by which to interpret Neolithic ways of life. Thus Bradley (1997, 6), writing about Atlantic Europe, suggested 'a fundamental distinction in the archaeology of many regions where fixed settlements are first found with any regularity in the latter second and first millennia BC'. In this scenario regional diversity is seen as the local playing out of ways of doing things and struggles for social position reflected through material culture (Thomas 1998, 52). Some authors, such as Sherratt (e.g. 1990; 1995), have seen in this approach the value of a return to the 'big picture' or grand narrative tradition of interpretation. Others, such as Whittle and Thomas, appear to adopt a somewhat contradictory position. From a post-modern stance, they advocate a concern with multiple interpretations and lives and societies created locally. But on the other hand, they argue that all of this diversity is based on a broadly similar mobile lifestyle over very large areas and long periods of time.

Within this style of thought and writing it is not surprising that Ireland would be treated as a unit; indeed, as we have seen, Ireland and Britain often tend to get lumped together as one region. Writing about the Iron Age, James (1999) identified the great diversity of Iron Age communities in Ireland and Britain in contrast to a very strong trend in Iron Age studies which seeks to identify variation from some supposedly typical Celtic Iron Age society. James argues that the idea of a homogeneous insular Celtic Iron Age society is a myth created from the eighteenth century onwards to serve modern needs. I would argue that a similar critique needs to be applied to the way we write about the Neolithic. The image we have created of the Irish (and British) Neolithic may say more about the ideology of the nation state, the legacy of empire, the European project and current theoretical approaches in archaeology than about the realities of life as lived in prehistory.

The central theme of this paper is that the local and the regional were the effective scales of life during the Irish Neolithic. People lived in different ways in different parts of the island. The big question is how we go about identifying such differences. A number of lines of enquiry can be suggested for identifying the effective scale of regions during the Irish Neolithic period.

REGIONALITY OF LANDSCAPE

We might begin by considering variations in the physical and biotic fabric of the land. Discussions about regionality from an archaeological perspective now tend to focus on the idea of the local or regional playing out of more widely employed structures of life (e.g. Thomas 1998). At least in part this seems to be linked to a change in focus from a concern with the physical component of landscapes to their perceptual elements (e.g. Bender 1998; see relevant discussion in Keller 1994). This reflects a wider shift of interest from what Soja (1999) calls 'firstspace', the world of empirically measurable and mappable phenomena, to 'secondspace', i.e. the cognitive, conceptual and symbolic worlds created within cultural contexts, and 'thirdspace', where the first two types of space are brought together. But it seems deeply ironic that, at a time when we are becoming increasingly conscious of the need to understand the close links between people and the land in such a geographical thirdspace, we are paying less attention to how the shape, form, contours and colour of the land would have influenced how people lived their lives.

During the Neolithic the look of the land would certainly have varied across the island of Ireland and over time. In some areas field boundaries were used, suggesting very organised agricultural practices; in other areas there may have been a more flexible pattern of land use. There were areas that would have been used on a seasonal basis, and coastal and wetland areas would have continued to be used for fishing, gathering and hunting (e.g. see discussion in Cooney 1991; 1997; A. O'Sullivan 1997; 1998). All of this activity was going on in a land that was still predominantly wooded. It seems likely that the woods were seen as alive (O'Sullivan 1996). The idea that the woodland was part of a wild, untamed landscape perhaps underplays the range of ways in which it would have been used throughout the Neolithic. If we are right in saying that one of the metaphoric meanings of the large oak posts used in structures in the Late Neolithic was as a recreated wood (see Newman 1996), then this is one indication that concepts of the woodland world must have been important in people's lives.

As Carmichael (1972, 167) observed, human customs, traditions and rituals assume the complexion, colours and composition of their surroundings. The materials that people used emphasised the connection between people and the land (e.g. Lynch 1998; A. Jones 1997). A recent collaborative synthesis (Mitchell *et al.* 1996) has suggested that Ireland can be divided into three broad biogeographical regions (Fig. 1). In the Atlantic fringe there is much upland and mountainous ground, mainly underlain by acid rocks, with restricted areas of good land-use potential. North-east Ireland is characterised by many varied rock types and terrain and fertile lowlands. Central and south-east Ireland has very large areas of lowlands,

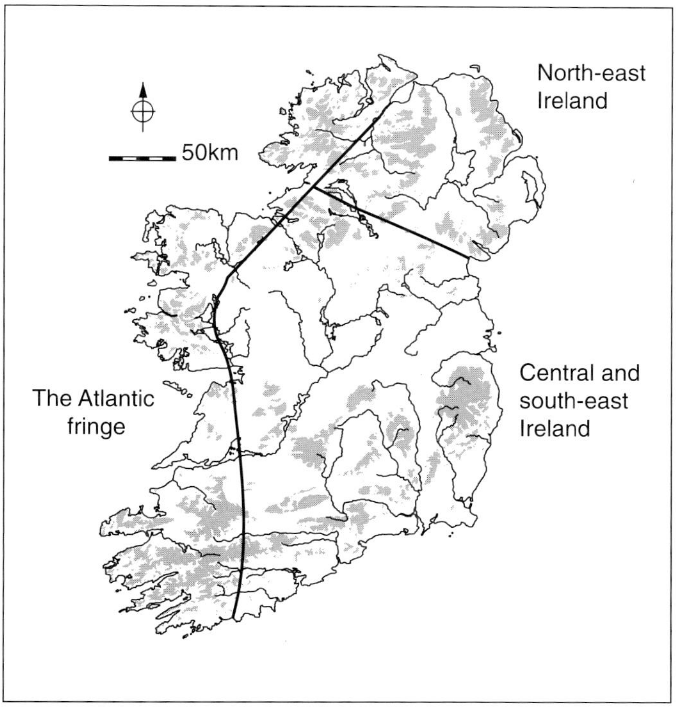

Fig. 1—Biogeographical regions of Ireland (after Mitchell et al. *1996).*

mostly on limestone, with ridges of acid rocks forming uplands. Much of the land in this region is suitable for a variety of uses. This is probably too generalised a regional distinction to fit with more subtle regional variation in human life, but at least it provides a considered basis against which to look at the archaeological evidence. Mitchell and Ryan (1997, 144) point out that in these biogeographical regions there would have been differences in the distribution of plants and animals in the prehistoric period. For example, in Neolithic woodlands elm would have been abundant on the calcareous soils of central Ireland, but pine would have been more prominent on the acid soils of the west. There would have been very considerable diversity in the materials, colours and textures of the landscape. This is not to make an unnecessary divide between natural and cultural landscapes but rather to suggest that the materiality of people's surroundings must have had an influence on how they socialised the landscape. Indeed, during the Neolithic the introduction of new animal and plant species would have greatly added to this diversity (see Kimball, this volume). It now seems likely that red deer may have been brought onto the island during the Neolithic (Woodman, McCarthy *et al.* 1997; McCormick 1999), indicating that it was not only domesticated species that were introduced. In terms of identifying regional landscapes perhaps we should be paying more attention to the catchment areas of the large rivers. In a forested landscape people who moved on foot or by boat would have had a very good knowledge of river systems, and the value of thinking of the landscape in terms of river catchments has been demonstrated both in Ireland (e.g. Smyth 1982) and Britain (e.g. Sherratt 1996).

REGIONALITY AND MATERIAL CULTURE

One of the classic methods of identifying regionality is through variations in observable patterns in material culture. For example, archaeologists frequently use the distribution of monument types to infer a sense of identity. If people were building the same kind of monument, then the argument goes that they must have shared ideas about how social life was to be organised and lived. However, we have come to appreciate that when we look at the evidence of how these monuments were used, each individual site has a different history. When we look at where they were located in the landscape, then we can see patterns where sites belonging to the same monument type are placed in quite different ways in different landscapes. Taking court tombs as an example, in some cases they are located in what appear to be bounded agricultural areas, as in the Céide Fields, Co. Mayo (Caulfield 1983; Caulfield *et al.* 1998); in other cases they are located on what appear to be the margins of the settled landscape, as in the Mourne Mountains, Co. Down, and the Cooley Peninsula, Co. Louth, on either side of Carlingford Lough (e.g. Evans 1978). Court tombs are often placed on the gentler slopes of drumlins; in other terrains they have a dramatic location on a terrace overlooking lower ground (e.g. Cooney 1979; 1983; Mount 1996). Patterns of location are also likely to have changed through time. For instance, Bergh (1995) has detailed how, within the Irish passage tomb tradition, ideas about the role of the monuments in the landscape seem to have altered during the development of this tradition.

A map showing the distribution of different monument traditions current during the Neolithic period (Fig. 2) reflects cumulative activity in monument construction and use spanning hundreds of years. This may help to convey an image of blurred, shifting identities and meanings over time and space during the Neolithic. This is a more realistic picture than any assumption that regional identities were fixed or had defined edges. What is very clear is that we have to move away from the simplistic idea that these traditions represent different ethnic or population groups (see S. Jones 1997). In relation to megalithic tombs, for example, it is clear that court, portal and passage tombs were in use at the same time. There are some areas where monuments belonging to these traditions occur in proximity to each other. In this context it seems more reasonable to think of such structures as having different but related roles (Cooney and Grogan 1994).

Another way of conveying the message that the diversity of life that we see in the landscapes of Neolithic Ireland was actively created by people is to consider the patterns of distribution of objects. Different kinds of objects may have different kinds of life histories and move in different spheres. Pots, in most cases, appear never to have been moved very far from where they were made, but ideas about how to shape and decorate pots were widely shared. On the other hand, the increased regionality of pottery styles through time is also a feature of the ceramic evidence (e.g. Sheridan 1991; 1995). Stone axeheads are the best surviving evidence for the exchange networks that express the web of contacts and exchanges of materials, ideas, and probably people, in the form of marriage and other social alliances, that linked different groups together (see discussion in Cooney and Mandal 1998). We can also look at stone axes in terms of the materials that would have been most widely used in different areas for their production (Fig. 3). In this way we can focus on the axehead as a

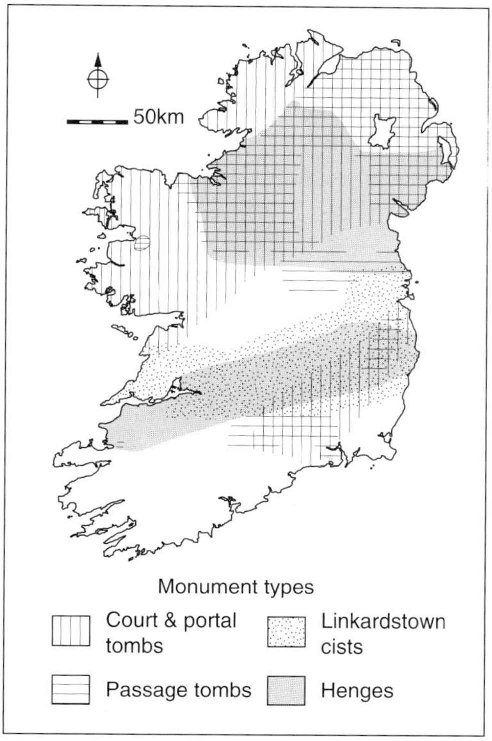

Fig. 2—The distribution of various Neolithic monument traditions in Ireland (various sources).

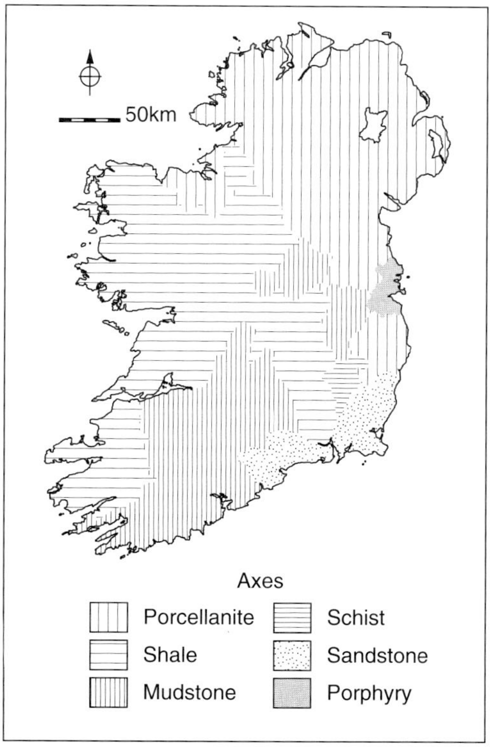

Fig. 3—The dominant sources used to make stone axeheads in different parts of Ireland (after Cooney and Mandal 1998).

symbol of local or regional identity.

Shale and mudstone axeheads are the most common lithologies over much of southern and western Ireland. There are widely occurring sources for these related sedimentary rocks here, so we are seeing in the axeheads a reflection of the land. It may be appropriate to think of these areas as sharing this dominance of shale and mudstone axes as a feature of everyday life, just as for much of the north and north-east (where the two sources are) porcellanite axes were the most common. There would appear to be a more fragmented pattern in the south-east with, for example, porphyry relatively abundant in the Dublin area (probably related to sources such as Lambay; see Cooney 1998). This localised pattern of differentiation in the south-east may not have any real significance in terms of regionality in the Neolithic, particularly given the relatively small number of axes from some of the counties in this area. However, the broader pattern of regional differences may be important. This is not to say that these areas can be seen as unified cultural zones, or that porcellanite, shale and mudstone axes were not used elsewhere, but rather to make the point that items such as axes offer us opportunities to understand that a sense of cultural identity shared by people may have been built on the daily use of similar kinds of objects. It was against this background that non-local axeheads, or indeed any non-local material, would have stood out.

REGIONALITY AND HISTORY

Another approach to identifying different human regions in Ireland during the Neolithic might be to think about the history of settlement in different areas. In relation to the stone axeheads discussed above, it is clear that shale and mudstone axeheads were in use from early in the Mesolithic period onwards (e.g. Woodman 1978; 1987; Woodman and Johnson 1991/2). It would seem that there is a continuity in some areas of life across the Mesolithic/Neolithic transition. For example, in the Ballylough area of County Waterford there is a broad continuity in the areas that seem to have been a focus of settlement in both periods (Green and Zvelebil 1990). Would areas that were foci of activity during the Mesolithic have developed differently to those which appear to have been first used in any extensive way during the Neolithic? One interesting related issue is the way in which the apparently island-wide similarity of the Later Mesolithic is transformed into a picture of increasing regionality during the Neolithic. This theme of the history of settlement has been explored by Whittle (1996) for different parts of Europe and of course brings us to the complex issue of the relationship between foragers and early farmers. Were they one and the same but using new ways of life? Was there an element of new population involved in the beginnings of the Neolithic?

At the moment these are questions to which there are no clear answers, and the evidence which archaeologists use to debate points can be interpreted to support different viewpoints (see O'Sullivan 1997). For example, the suggestion that the tradition of building passage tombs at Carrowmore was begun by Mesolithic foragers (Burenhult 1984; 1995) is difficult to sustain given the absence of any diagnostic Later Mesolithic material. The continuity between the Mesolithic and the Neolithic suggested on the basis of field-walking surveys (e.g.

Green and Zvelebil 1990; Zvelebil *et al.* 1996) has to be seen in the context of the lack of any chronological control on this evidence and the distinction between the lithic technologies of the two periods, which suggests little overlap (Woodman 1994). It is the evidence from sites like Ballydown, Co. Antrim (Crothers 1996), and Ferriter's Cove, Co. Kerry (Woodman, Anderson *et al.* 1999), where there is evidence of Mesolithic and Neolithic activity in the same location, that may offer us the opportunity to resolve some of these issues through rigorous dating and analysis. However, we have to start from the hypothesis that people explored the whole of the island over the long course of the Mesolithic and Neolithic. This exploration would have been by foot and by boat. As pointed out above, the latter perspective in particular is one that as archaeologists we are really only beginning to appreciate as an approach to the Neolithic. Where people settled was a choice based on a range of criteria, but the fundamental need for a secure supply of food and water should never be forgotten. Regardless of the nature and degree of overlap between people in the transition between the Mesolithic and the Neolithic, it is likely that some areas, such as wetlands, would have continued to be exploited because of the range and richness of wild resources. In the search for Neolithic regions that may be distinguished by different earlier histories we are really only beginning to ask the relevant questions.

Some of the points raised above may seem simplistic and very basic, but then perhaps basic points need to be appreciated before we talk about the complex issue of regionality. One other issue that needs to be raised brings us back to the way we tack between archaeological analysis and its interpretation in terms of human patterns of life in the past. At first sight it would appear that we can read the results of different research projects as suggesting that there were very distinctive regional differences in the Neolithic. For example, there are the monumental landscapes of places like Brú na Bóinne (e.g. O'Kelly 1982; O'Kelly *et al.* 1983; Eogan 1986; 1991; Condit and Cooney 1997) and Ballynahatty, Co. Down (Hartwell 1998). There are the landscapes of everyday activities suggested by the results of field-walking projects like that at Ballylough (Green and Zvelebil 1990), the Barrow Valley (Zvelebil *et al.* 1996) and Mount Oriel, Co. Louth (Cooney 1990). The evidence of excavation and survey at Glencloy, Co. Antrim (Woodman 1983; 1992b; Mallory 1991/2; Woodman, Doggart *et al.* 1991/2; Woodman and Johnson 1996), suggests a landscape where activities of different types and duration were carried out in different places. The Céide Fields project indicates a place where various activities were carried out within a structured landscape bounded by stone walls (Caulfield 1983; 1988; Caulfield *et al.* 1998; Molloy and O'Connell 1995). It is worth reiterating the importance of Céide Fields in the wider context of the dominance of the mobility model for the Neolithic (Cooney 1994; 1997). It is clear that in Ireland there are other places apart from Céide Fields where the landscape was organised into fields, suggesting sedentary occupation (e.g. C. Jones and Gilmer 1999). Indeed, Céide Fields forms only the best-known of a wide range of Neolithic field boundaries in north Mayo itself (see discussion in Caulfield *et al.* 1998).

There are physical differences between the landscapes mentioned above, and the pattern of regional differences in the record of human activities would fit with the general thrust of what has been said here. But we also have to bear in mind that the history of many of these landscapes since the Neolithic has been quite different. Some have become marginal for agriculture and therefore have been fossilised to a greater or lesser extent; others form part of what are now, and were in the historic past, intensively farmed landscapes. There is an interplay between the nature and extent of the evidence that survives in these different landscapes and our ability to talk about past settlement from the traces that are left. We also have to be conscious that different archaeological methodologies will lead to a focus on different aspects of the evidence. The lithics and other artefacts that we find in the modern ploughzone bring us directly into contact with the materials that people used in the past and with everyday activities, but they occur in landscapes that have changed out of all recognition over the millennia since people used these tools (see Monk, this volume). This latter comment could also be applied to places like Brú na Bóinne, where the focus of research has been on the monumental complexes. Here the passage tombs, earthen enclosures and other sites are located in a modern agricultural landscape (Stout 1997). In other less intensively utilised landscapes a greater range of evidence may survive. In pastoral landscapes we will not find the lithics that may be all that is left of the Neolithic landscape. In wetlands we may have the survival of trackways and other features, with nothing visible on the surrounding dry ground to tell us where people were moving to and from along the trackways. It follows from all of this that we have to be careful when we talk about regional differences that we are not just talking about differential survival of the archaeological record, or indeed the result of the application of different strategies to recover that record. For example, recent programmes of geophysical survey have altered and enhanced our understanding of the landscape of the complexes of monuments at Tara, Co. Meath (Newman 1997), and Rathcroghan, Co. Roscommon (e.g. Fenwick *et al.* 1999).

CONCLUSION

If we are to see regionality as being important in our approach to the Neolithic then we have to shift our focus away from the comparison of regions to a recognition of the differences between them. At the same time it is clear that there were links between regions, reflected in aspects of material culture such as shared architectural traditions or the occurrence of artefacts originating outside the region. If we think of regions not just in physical terms but as the expression of a shared sense of social identity then we should be able to look at the evidence from new perspectives. For instance, the contacts between north-east Ireland and south-west Scotland (Fig. 4) have tended to be viewed in terms of the broader context of links between Ireland and Britain and the direction of the flow of cultural influences, such as traditions in the construction of megalithic monuments and pottery. Now, while this is the case and we have to see north-east Ireland and south-west Scotland in a wider north Irish Sea cultural zone (e.g. Waddell 1991/2), what we perhaps need to emphasise much more is that this area constitutes a region with shared traditions on either side of the North Channel. In the movement of material culture we can see the cultural web that bound people together in a regional world in which the sea was the vital link between different parts of this region. That there were sustained contacts maintaining these links is indicated by the movement of porcellanite axeheads from Antrim, pitchstone from Arran and flint from Antrim (Saville

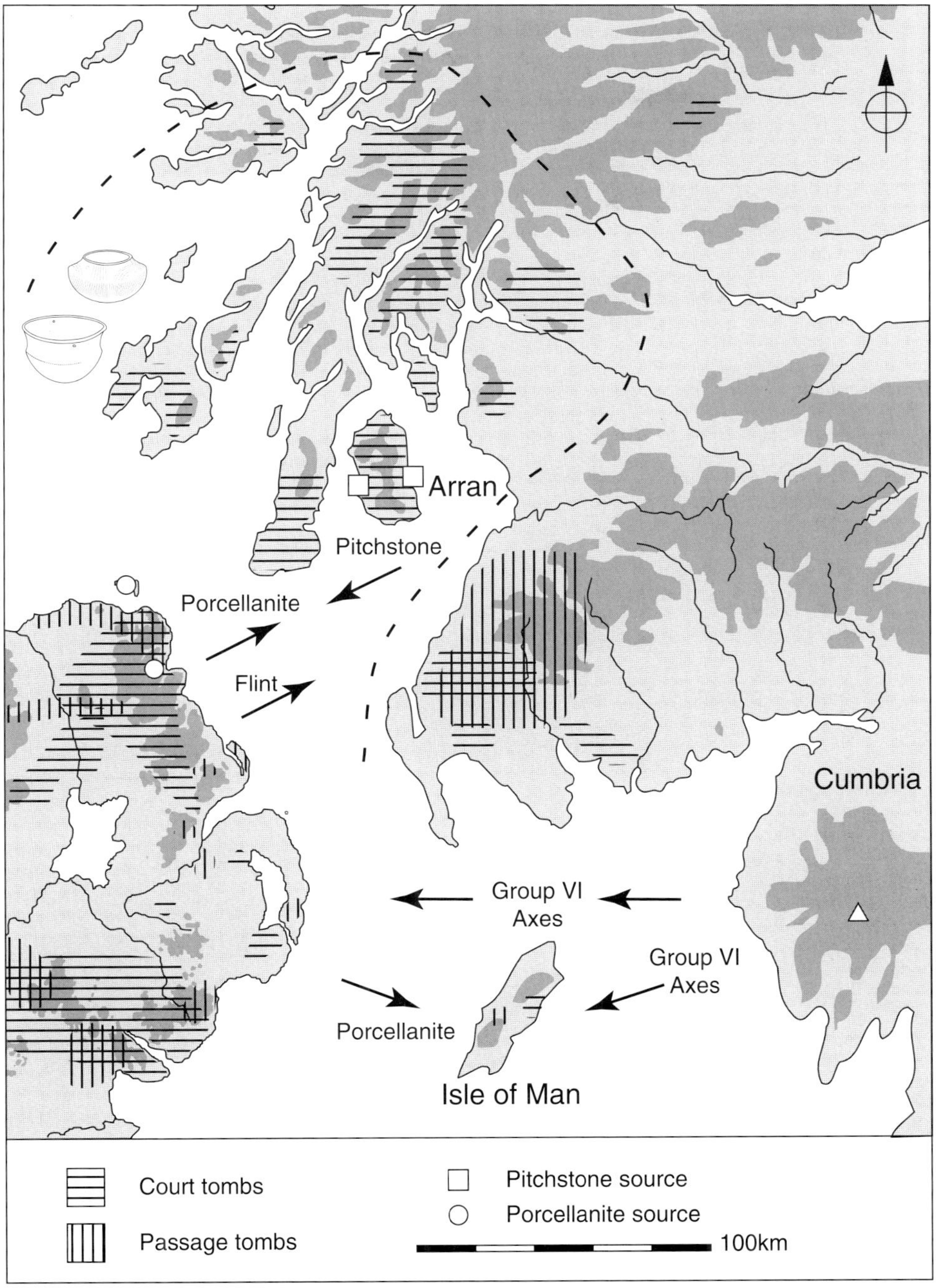

Fig. 4—North-east Ireland and south-west Scotland as a region during the Neolithic (various sources).

1994, 62–3; Sheridan *et al.* 1992, 402, 405; Simpson and Meighan 1999).

The central theme of this paper is that material culture was actively employed at local and regional levels to create different histories of settlement and society in different parts of this island. Physical, geographical or 'firstspace' regions do not determine cultural character, but they form an important part of social identity which we see in 'thirdspace'. There is also a need to get away from the perception that island-wide contacts and use of similar styles of artefacts can be read as implying island-wide uniformity. There may have been shared traditions and practices, for example in domestic architecture, but these were lived out and carried on differently. We also have to recognise the problem that different methodologies of archaeological research and differential survival of archaeological information may create an impression of regional identities and regional differences which has more to do with the present than the past. However, important regional differences were present in the Neolithic. The great challenge now facing archaeologists is to understand the implications of different scales of identity. What we also have to realise is that regional identities would have changed over the long course of the Neolithic as people made their history. It should not be expected that there would be a fixity about people's lives when we take a gaze at a period that lasted around 1500 years. The Late Neolithic world was different in many ways from the way things had been around 4000 BC. It is only by appreciating different regional developments over time and the active use of material suggested by those histories that we are likely to reach a better understanding of social change in the Irish Neolithic. There was no one Irish Neolithic but a number of regionally differentiated Neolithics which changed through time.

REFERENCES

Barclay, G.J. 1996 Neolithic buildings in Scotland. In T. Darvill and J. Thomas (eds), *Neolithic houses in northwest Europe and beyond*, 61–75. Oxbow Monograph 57. Oxford.

Barclay, G.J. 1997 The Neolithic. In K. Edwards and I. Ralston (eds), *Scotland: environment and archaeology, 8000 BC to AD 1000*, 63–82. Chichester. Wiley.

Barclay, G.J. (forthcoming) Living in the shadow of Orkney: the Neolithic of lowland Scotland. In A. Ritchie (ed.), *Neolithic Orkney in its European context.* Edinburgh University Press.

Barrett, J.C. 1994 *Fragments from antiquity: an archaeology of social life in Britain, 2900–1200 BC.* Oxford. Blackwell.

Bender, B. 1998 *Stonehenge: making space.* Oxford. Berg.

Bergh, S. 1995 *Landscape of the monuments.* Stockholm. Riksantikvarieämbet Arkeologiska Undersökningar.

Binford, L. 1964 A consideration of archaeological research design. *American Antiquity* **29**, 425–41.

Bradley, R. 1997 *Rock art and the prehistory of Atlantic Europe: signing the land.* London. Routledge.

Bradley, R. 1998 *The significance of monuments.* London. Routledge.

Burenhult, G. 1984 *The archaeology of Carrowmore: environmental archaeology and the megalithic tradition at Carrowmore, Co. Sligo, Ireland.* Theses and Papers in North-European Archaeology 14. Institute of Archaeology, University of Stockholm.

Burenhult, G. 1995 *The illustrated guide to the megalithic cemetery at Carrowmore, Co. Sligo.* Tjornarp, Sweden. Burenhult.

Carmichael, A. 1972 *Carmina Gadelica, volume 1.* Edinburgh. Scottish Academic Press.

Caulfield, S. 1983 The Neolithic settlement of north Connaught. In T. Reeves-Smyth and F. Hamond (eds), *Landscape archaeology in Ireland,* 195–215. British Archaeological Reports, British Series 116. Oxford.

Caulfield, S. 1988 *Céide Fields and Belderrig guide.* Killala. Morrigan Book Company.

Caulfield, S., O'Donnell, R.G. and Mitchell, P.I. 1998 Radiocarbon dating of a Neolithic field system at Céide Fields, County Mayo, Ireland. *Radiocarbon* **40**, 629–40.

Champion, T. 1996 Three nations or one? Britain and the national use of the past. In M. Díaz-Andreu and T. Champion (eds), *Nationalism and archaeology in Europe,* 119–45. University College London Press.

Condit, T. and Cooney, G. (eds) 1997 *Brú na Bóinne.* Dublin. Archaeology Ireland.

Cooney, G. 1979 Some aspects of the siting of megalithic tombs in County Leitrim. *Journal of the Royal Society of Antiquaries of Ireland* **109**, 74–91.

Cooney, G. 1983 Megalithic tombs in their environmental setting, a settlement perspective. In T. Reeves-Smyth and F. Hamond (eds), *Landscape archaeology in Ireland,* 179–94. British Archaeological Reports, British Series 116. Oxford.

Cooney, G. 1990 The Mount Oriel Project: an introduction. *County Louth Archaeological and Historical Journal* **22** (2), 125–33.

Cooney, G. 1991 Irish Neolithic landscapes and landuse systems: the implications of field systems. *Rural History* **2** (2), 123–39.

Cooney, G. 1994 Sacred and secular Neolithic landscapes in Ireland. In D.L. Carmichael, J. Hubert, B. Reeves and A. Schanche (eds), *Sacred sites, sacred places,* 32–43. London. Routledge.

Cooney, G. 1995 Theory and practice in Irish archaeology. In P. Ucko (ed.), *Theory in archaeology: a world perspective,* 263–77. London. Routledge.

Cooney, G. 1996 Building the future on the past: archaeology and the construction of national identity in Ireland. In M. Díaz-Andreu and T. Champion (eds), *Nationalism and archaeology in Europe,* 146–63. University College London Press.

Cooney, G. 1997 Images of settlement and the landscape in the Neolithic. In P. Topping (ed.), *Neolithic landscapes,* 23–31. Neolithic Studies Group Papers 2 Oxbow Monograph 86. Oxford.

Cooney, G. 1998 Breaking stones, making places: the social landscape of axe production sites. In A. Gibson and D.D.A. Simpson (eds), *Prehistoric ritual and religion,* 108–18. Stroud. Sutton Publishing.

Cooney, G. and Grogan, E. 1994 *Irish prehistory: a social perspective.* Bray. Wordwell.

Cooney, G. and Mandal, S. 1998 *The Irish Stone Axe Project Monograph I.* Bray. Wordwell.

Crothers, N. 1996 Ballyharry's Game. *Archaeology Ireland* **38**, 12–14.

Edmonds, M. 1999 *Ancestral geographies of the Neolithic.* London. Routledge.

Eogan, G. 1986 *Knowth and the passage tombs of Ireland.* London. Thames and Hudson.

Eogan, G. 1991 Prehistoric and Early Historic culture change at Brugh na Bóinne. *Proceedings of the Royal Irish Academy* **91**C, 105–32.
Eriksen, T.H. 1995 *Small places, large issues.* London. Pluto Press.
Evans, E.E. 1978 *Mourne Country: landscape and life in south Down* (3rd edn). Dundalk. Dundalgan Press.
Fenwick, J., Brennan, Y., Barton, K. and Waddell, J. 1999 The magnetic presence of Queen Medb. *Archaeology Ireland* **47**, 8–11.
Green, S.W. and Zvelebil, M. 1990 The Mesolithic colonisation and agricultural transition of south-east Ireland. *Proceedings of the Prehistoric Society* **56**, 57–88.
Harbison, P. 1988 *Pre-Christian Ireland.* London. Thames and Hudson.
Harding, J. 1997 Interpreting the Neolithic: the monuments of North Yorkshire. *Oxford Journal of Archaeology* **16** (3), 279–95.
Hartwell, B. 1998 The Ballynahatty complex. In A. Gibson and D.D.A. Simpson (eds), *Prehistoric ritual and religion*, 32–44. Stroud. Sutton Publishing.
Herity, M. and Eogan, G. 1977 *Ireland in prehistory.* London. Routledge and Kegan Paul.
Hingley, R. 1996 The shared moral purposes of two empires and the origin of Romano-British archaeology. In J.A. Atkinson, I. Banks and J. O'Sullivan (eds), *Nationalism and archaeology*, 135–42. Glasgow. Cruithne Press.
Hodder, I. 1990 *The domestication of Europe.* Oxford. Blackwell.
James, S. 1999 *The Atlantic Celts: ancient people or modern invention?* London. British Museum Press.
Jones, A. 1997 On the earth colours of Neolithic death. *British Archaeology* **22**, 6.
Jones, C. and Gilmer, A. 1999 Roughan Hill, a Final Neolithic/Early Bronze Age landscape revealed. *Archaeology Ireland* **47**, 30–2.
Jones, S. 1997 *The archaeology of ethnicity: constructing identities in the past and present.* London. Routledge.
Keller, C. 1994 The theoretical aspects of landscape study. In T. Collins (ed.), *Decoding the landscape*, 79–97. Centre for Landscape Studies, University College Galway.
Kinnes, I. 1985 Circumstance not context: the Neolithic of Scotland as seen from outside. *Proceedings of the Society of Antiquaries of Scotland* **115**, 15–57.
Lee, J. 1999 A sense of place in the Celtic Tiger? In H. Bohan and G. Kennedy (eds), *Are we forgetting something? Our society in the new millennium*, 71–93. Dublin. Veritas.
Lynch, F. 1998 Colour in prehistoric architecture. In A. Gibson and D.D.A. Simpson (eds), *Prehistoric ritual and religion*, 62–7. Stroud. Sutton Publishing.
McCormick, F. 1999 Early evidence for wild animals in Ireland. In N. Benecke (ed.), *The Holocene history of the European vertebrate fauna: modern aspects of research. Workshop, 6th to 9th April 1998*, 355–71. Berlin. Verlag Marie Leidorf GmbH.Rahden/Westf.
Mallory, J.P. 1991/2 A Neolithic settlement at Bay Farm II, Carnlough, Co. Antrim. *Ulster Journal of Archaeology* **54–5**, 3–12.
Mallory, J.P. and McNeill, T.E. 1991 *The archaeology of Ulster.* Institute of Irish Studies, Queen's University, Belfast.
Marquardt, W.H. and Crumley, C.L. 1987 Theoretical issues in the analysis of spatial patterning. In C.L. Crumley and W.H. Marquardt (eds), *Regional dynamics: Burgundian*

landscapes in historical perspective, 1–18. San Diego. Academic Press.

Mitchell, F.J.G., Bradshaw, R.H.W., Hannon, G.E., O'Connell, M., Pilcher, J.R. and Watts, W.A. 1996 Ireland. In B.E. Berglund, H.J.B. Birks, M. Ralska-Jasiewiczoma and H.E. Wright (eds), *Palaeoecological events during the last 15,000 years. Regional studies of palaeoecological studies of lakes and mires in Europe*, 1–13. Chichester. Wiley.

Mitchell, G. and Ryan, M. 1997 *Reading the Irish landscape* (3rd edn). Dublin. Country House.

Molloy, K. and O'Connell, M. 1995 Palaeoecological investigations towards the reconstruction of environment and land-use changes during prehistory at Céide Fields, western Ireland. *Probleme der Küstenforschung im südlichen Nordseegebiet* **23**, 187–225.

Mount, C. 1996 The environmental siting of Neolithic and Bronze Age monuments in the Bricklieve and Moytirra uplands. *Journal of Irish Archaeology* 7, 1–11.

Newman, C. 1996 Woods, metamorphosis and mazes—the 'otherness' of timber circles. *Archaeology Ireland* **37**, 34–6.

Newman, C. 1997 *Tara: an archaeological survey.* Discovery Programme Monograph 2. Dublin. Royal Irish Academy.

O'Kelly, M.J. 1982 *Newgrange, archaeology, art and legend.* London. Thames and Hudson.

O'Kelly, M.J. 1989 *Early Ireland, an introduction to Irish prehistory.* Cambridge University Press.

O'Kelly, M.J., Cleary, R. and Lehane, D. 1983 *Newgrange, Co. Meath, Ireland: the Late Neolithic/Beaker Period settlement.* British Archaeological Reports, International Series 190. Oxford.

O'Sullivan, A. 1996 Exploring ancient woodlands. *Archaeology Ireland* **36**, 14–15.

O'Sullivan, A. 1997 Last foragers or first farmers? *Archaeology Ireland* **40**, 16–18.

O'Sullivan, A. 1998 *The archaeology of lake settlement in Ireland.* Discovery Programme Monograph 4. Dublin. Royal Irish Academy.

O'Sullivan, J. 1998 Nationalists, archaeologists and the myth of the Golden Age. In M. Monk and J. Sheehan (eds), *Early medieval Munster: archaeology, history and society*, 178–89. Cork University Press.

Piggott, S. 1954 *The Neolithic cultures of the British Isles.* Cambridge University Press.

Ronayne, M. and Shee Twohig, E. 1993 A new agenda: the south-west and beyond. In E. Shee Twohig and M. Ronayne (eds), *Past perceptions: the prehistoric archaeology of south-west Ireland*, 155–64. Cork University Press.

Saville, A. 1994 Exploitation of lithic resources for stone tools in earlier prehistoric Scotland. In N. Ashton and A. David (eds), *Stories in stone*, 57–70. Lithic Studies Society Occasional Paper 4. London.

Sharples, N. 1992 Aspects of regionalisation in the Scottish Neolithic. In N.M. Sharples and A. Sheridan (eds), *Vessels for the ancestors*, 322–31. Edinburgh University Press.

Sheridan, A. 1991 Pottery production in Neolithic and Early Bronze Age Ireland: a petrological and chemical study. In A. Middleton and I. Freestone (eds), *Recent developments in ceramic petrology*, 305–35. British Museum Occasional Paper 81. London.

Sheridan, A. 1995 Irish Neolithic pottery: the story in 1995. In I.A. Kinnes and G. Varndell (eds), *Unbaked urns of rudely shape*, 3–22. Oxbow Monograph 55. Oxford.

Sheridan, A., Cooney, G. and Grogan, E. 1992 Stone axe studies in Ireland. *Proceedings of the Prehistoric Society* **58**, 389–416.

Sherratt, A.G. 1990 The genesis of megaliths; monumentality, ethnicity and social complexity in Neolithic north-west Europe. *World Archaeology* **22**, 147–67.

Sherratt, A.G. 1995 Reviving the grand narrative: archaeology and long-term change. *Journal of European Archaeology* **3**, 1–32.

Sherratt, A.G. 1996 Why Wessex? The Avon route and river transport in later prehistoric Britain. *Oxford Journal of Archaeology* **15**, 211–34.

Simpson, D.D.A. and Meighan, I. 1999 Pitchstone—a new trading material in Neolithic Ireland. *Archaeology Ireland* **48**, 26–30.

Smyth, A.P. 1982 *Celtic Leinster: Towards an historical geography of early Irish civilization A.D. 500–1600.* Dublin. Irish Academic Press.

Soja, E. 1999 Thirdspace: expanding the scope of the geographical imagination. In D. Massey, J. Allen and P. Sarre (eds), *Human geography today*, 260–78. Cambridge. Polity Press.

Stout, G. 1997 The bend of the Boyne, County Meath. In F.H.A. Aalen, K. Whelan and M. Stout (eds), *The atlas of the Irish rural landscape*, 299–315. Cork University Press.

Thomas, J. 1993 Discourse, totalisation and 'the Neolithic'. In C. Tilley (ed.), *Interpretative archaeology*, 357–94. Oxford. Berg.

Thomas, J. 1996 *Time, culture and identity*. London. Routledge.

Thomas, J. 1998 Towards a regional geography of the Neolithic. In M. Edmonds and C. Richards (eds), *Understanding the Neolithic of north-western Europe*, 37–60. Glasgow. Cruithne Press.

Tierney, M. 1998 Theory and politics in early medieval archaeology. In M. Monk and J. Sheehan (eds), *Early medieval Munster: archaeology, history and society*, 190–9. Cork University Press.

Tomlinson, J. 1991 *Cultural imperialism*. London. Pinter.

Waddell, J. 1991/2 The Irish Sea in prehistory. *Journal of Irish Archaeology* **6**, 29–40.

Waddell, J. 1998 *The prehistoric archaeology of Ireland*. Galway University Press.

Whittle, A. 1996 *Europe in the Neolithic, the creation of new worlds*. Cambridge University Press.

Woodman, P.C. 1978 *The Mesolithic in Ireland: hunter-gatherers in an insular environment*. British Archaeological Reports, British Series 58. Oxford.

Woodman, P.C. 1983 The Glencloy Project in perspective. In T. Reeves-Smyth and F. Hamond (eds), *Landscape archaeology in Ireland*, 25–34. British Archaeological Reports, British Series 116. Oxford.

Woodman, P.C. 1987 The impact of resource availability on lithic industrial traditions in prehistoric Ireland. In P. Rowley-Conwy, M. Zvelebil and H.P. Blankholm (eds), *Mesolithic northwest Europe: recent trends*, 138–46. Department of Archaeology and Prehistory, University of Sheffield.

Woodman, P.C. 1992a Filling in the spaces in Irish prehistory. *Antiquity* **66**, 295–314.

Woodman, P.C. 1992b Excavations at Mad Man's Window, Glenarm, Co. Antrim: problems of flint exploitation in east Antrim. *Proceedings of the Prehistoric Society* **58**, 77–106.

Woodman, P.C. 1994 Towards a definition of Irish Early Neolithic lithic assemblages. In N. Ashton and A. David (eds), *Stories in stone*, 213–18. Lithic Studies Society Occasional Paper 4. London.

Woodman, P.C. 1995 Who possesses Tara? Politics in archaeology in Ireland. In P.J. Ucko (ed.), *Theory in archaeology: a world perspective*, 278–97. London. Routledge.

Woodman, P.C. and Johnson, G. 1996 Excavations at Bay Farm 1, Carnlough, Co. Antrim, and the study of the 'Larnian' technology. *Proceedings of the Royal Irish Academy* **96**C, 137–235.

Woodman, P.C. and Johnson, I. 1991/2 A petrological examination of some Mesolithic stone artifacts. *Ulster Journal of Archaeology* **54–5**, 134–7.

Woodman, P.C., Anderson, E. and Finlay, N. 1999 *Excavations at Ferriter's Cove 1983–1995. Last foragers/first farmers in the Dingle Peninsula.* Bray. Wordwell.

Woodman, P.C., Doggart, R. and Mallory, J.P. 1991/2 Excavations at Windy Ridge, Co. Antrim, 1981–82. *Ulster Journal of Archaeology* **54–5**, 13–35.

Woodman, P.C., McCarthy, M. and Monaghan, N. 1997 The Irish Quaternary Fauna Project. *Quaternary Science Reviews* **16**, 120–59.

Zvelebil, M., Macklin, M.G., Passmore, D.G. and Ramsden, P. 1996 Alluvial archaeology in the Barrow valley, southeast Ireland: the 'Riverford' culture revisited. *Journal of Irish Archaeology* 7, 13–40.

SEEDS AND SOILS OF DISCONTENT: AN ENVIRONMENTAL ARCHAEOLOGICAL CONTRIBUTION TO THE NATURE OF THE EARLY NEOLITHIC

Michael Monk

INTRODUCTION

In recent years there has been considerable debate about the nature of the Neolithic, prompted largely by a review of the evidence for the Neolithic in southern Britain in the light of changes in archaeological theory. The idea of a less sedentary, mobile Neolithic, based to a greater extent on animal husbandry, has not been accepted by all, but it is only recently that some prehistorians have taken exception to the generalisations to which this has given rise (see, for example, Cooney and Grogan 1994; Cooney 1997; 1999b).

There are several reasons for entering this debate, not least because, as an environmental archaeologist and in common with a number of colleagues (especially Tony Legge, who has been critical for some time, and more recently Glynis Jones (forthcoming a)), I have not been happy with the way that palaeoeconomic evidence (remains of plants and animals) has been used uncritically to make this case. In addition, I have worked on and published some key Irish evidence that could be used to offer an alternative view. While the following thoughts have been gestating for over seven years, six years ago I did publish a preliminary critique (Monk 1993, 45). At that time I remember discussing my thoughts about the beginnings of the Neolithic with Liz Anderson in one of those post-5pm chats we had from time to time, when I would wander into her office, with its always-open door, and we would just talk about whatever was on our minds at the time. I know that I am not the only one who misses those occasional casual chats. I offer this paper in memory of Liz, by way of remembrance of and thanks for those conversations.

BACKGROUND

It has been the case that a number of prehistorians with post-processual agendas (e.g. Thomas 1991; 1996; Barrett 1994; Edmonds 1997; Bradley 1997) have extrapolated from the results of various environmental archaeological studies to support their case for a mobile Neolithic. In particular they have referenced the paper by Moffett *et al.* (1989).

The conditional interpretation made by the authors of this paper, and another, less cautious, work on Neolithic animal husbandry as against plants in the same volume (Entwhistle and Grant 1989, 203–4), was questioned at the time by Tony Legge (1989). Also, the data they were all drawing on are now well over a decade old.[1] Since that time some extremely relevant palaeoeconomic evidence has come to light in occupation deposits from

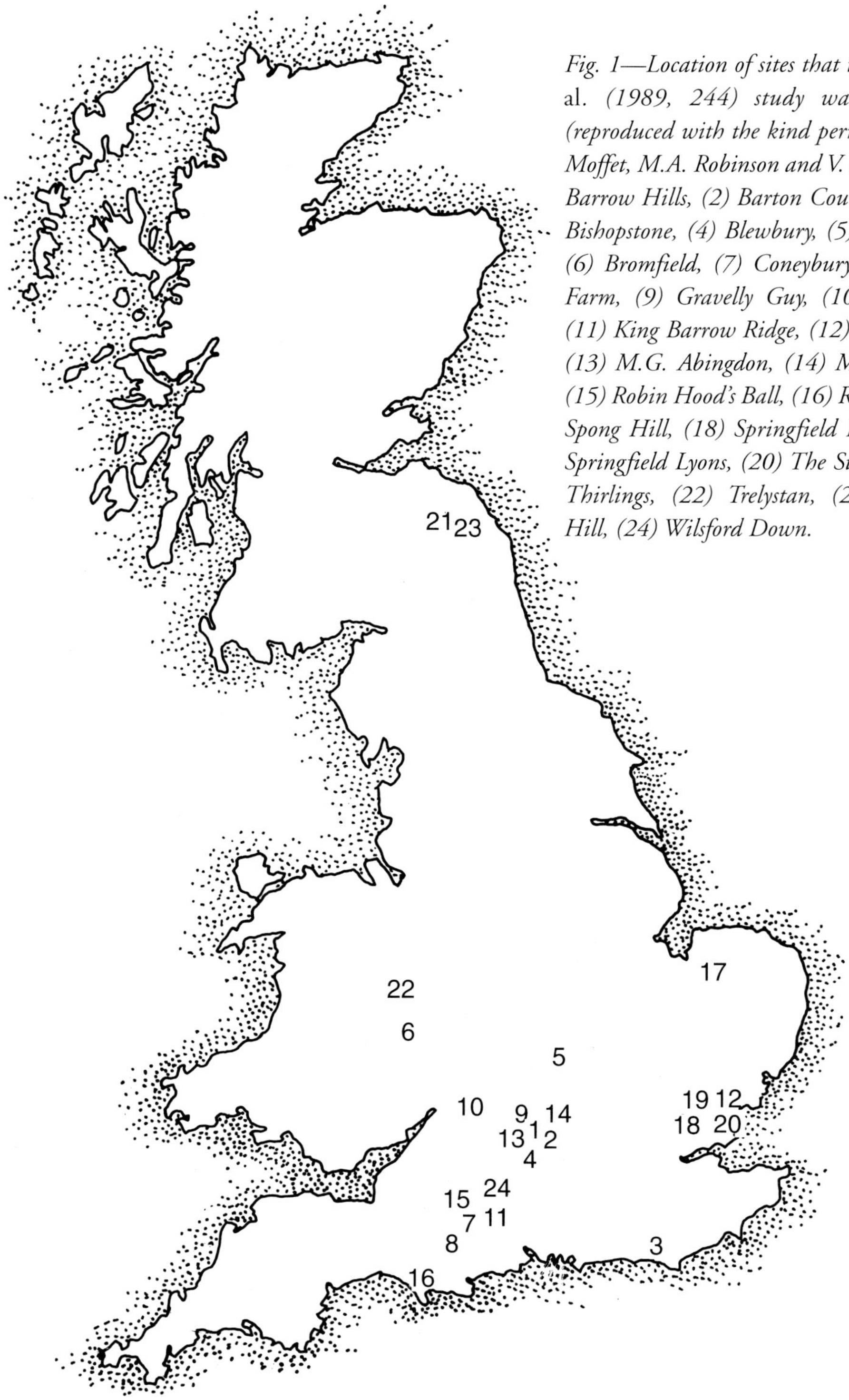

Fig. 1—Location of sites that the Moffet et al. *(1989, 244) study was based on (reproduced with the kind permission of L. Moffet, M.A. Robinson and V. Straker). (1) Barrow Hills, (2) Barton Court Farm, (3) Bishopstone, (4) Blewbury, (5) Briar Hill, (6) Bromfield, (7) Coneybury, (8) Down Farm, (9) Gravelly Guy, (10) Hazleton, (11) King Barrow Ridge, (12) Lofts Farm, (13) M.G. Abingdon, (14) Mount Farm, (15) Robin Hood's Ball, (16) Rowden, (17) Spong Hill, (18) Springfield Barnes, (19) Springfield Lyons, (20) The Stumble, (21) Thirlings, (22) Trelystan, (23) Whitton Hill, (24) Wilsford Down.*

several areas in Britain and Ireland. This evidence has not, apparently, been assimilated by the aforementioned proponents of a mobile Neolithic.

Also ignored, it seems, has been the large body of geoarchaeological sedimentary evidence for considerable landscape change through erosion and depositional processes in southern Britain since the Neolithic. It is therefore perhaps no surprise that the most telling body of evidence for a sedentary Neolithic comes from outside southern Britain, particularly in Ireland. Not only is there evidence for substantial Neolithic field systems in the west of Ireland (in counties Mayo and Kerry)—as also pointed out in Cooney's critique (1997, 28—referencing Caulfield 1983)—but over the last ten years there has been an explosion in the number of substantially built Neolithic houses discovered in Ireland (nine sites, several with more than one building) and in the midlands and north of Britain, a number of them producing evidence for cereal husbandry. The evidence and its implications from one of these, Tankardstown, Co. Limerick (Gowen 1988; Monk 1988; forthcoming b), will be discussed below.

CRITIQUE OF MOFFETT *ET AL.* 1989

In this pivotal paper the author s brought together the evidence for carbonised Neolithic plant remains from 26 contexts and over 24 sites. Eleven of these contexts were dated to the Earlier Neolithic and the remaining fifteen to contexts grouped under the general heading 'Later Neolithic' (including Grooved Ware sites and Beaker sites). Only four of the sites were outside southern and eastern Britain (Fig. 1; Tables 1 and 2).

In the majority of cases the contexts from which the remains came were pit fills, many of these isolated features with little other Neolithic cultural context (ibid., 256–7).

The Earlier Neolithic

Within those sites grouped as Earlier Neolithic, two contexts were described as occupation deposits/debris (Hazleton and The Stumble). Ten of the eleven sites dated to this period produced remains of cereals, and in five of these (including the occupation debris contexts) cereals were the most frequent remains. Of the remaining six samples, in five instances the most frequent remains were hazelnut fragments. The sixth had an equal representation of cereals and hazelnuts. Several of the samples also produced isolated incidences of sloe stones, hawthorn pips, bramble/blackberry pips and crab-apple remains. It is worth noting that many of the samples also produced an occasional-to-frequent incidence of seeds of plants that could be described as weeds of cultivation.

The Later Neolithic

Thirteen of the Later Neolithic samples came from pits, one from a cursus and another from a henge ditch fill, but no further specific details of context were given (i.e. from where exactly in these fills the remains came).

While cereals were present in fourteen of the contexts, their incidence was low. By comparison a variable incidence of hazelnut fragments was recovered from thirteen of the

		Hazleton	Rowden	Bromfi
		2970bc	**2910bc**	**2730b**
Triticum cf. *monococcum* (einkorn)	glume base	1	0	0
T. dicoccum and *T.* cf. *dicoccum* (emmer)	grain	49	2	0
T. dicoccum and *T.* cf. *dicoccum* (emmer)	glume base	1	0	0
T. dicoccum or *spelta* (emmer/spelt)	grain	0	6	0
T. aestivum s.l. and *T.* cf. *aestivum* s.l. (bread-type wheat)	grain	33	0	0
Triticum sp. (wheat)	grain	186	0	1
Triticum sp. (wheat)	glume base	5	0	0
Hordeum sativum (hulled six-row barley)	grain	0	0	0
H. sativum var. *nudum* (naked six-row barley)	grain	0	0	0
H. sativum and *H.* cf. *sativum* (barley)	grain	3	2	3
Indeterminate cereals	grain	11	31	0
Total cereal grain		**282**	**41**	**4**
Rubus spp (raspberry and blackberry)	stone	0	0	0
Prunus spinosa L. (sloe)	stone	0	0	0
Crataegus sp. (hawthorn)	stone	0	1	0
Malus sylvestris Mill. (crab-apple)	seed	0	0	0
M. sylvestris Mill. (crab-apple)	endocarp frags	0	0	0
Malus or *Pyrus* sp. (crab-apple or pear)	seed frags	0	0	1
Malus or *Pyrus* sp. (crab-apple or pear)	calyx	0	0	1
Malus or *Pyrus* sp. (crab-apple or pear)	epidermal frags	0	0	0
Corylus avellana L. (hazel)	nut shell frags	1000+	0	*
Weed seeds		42	0	3
Unidentified seeds (mostly weeds)		10	0	0
Number of samples		61	23	2
Total volume of samples (litres)		550	66	7

* = present

Table 1—Carbonised cereal, fruit and nut remains from Earlier Neolithic samples (after Moffet et al. *1989, 248).*

riar Hill 635bc	Bishop -stone 2510bc	The Stumble	Coneybury	Wilsford Down	Robin Hood's Ball	Lofts Farm	Spong Hill
0	0	0	0	0	0	0	0
0	6	30	0	0	0	0	0
0	*	9	1	0	0	0	0
0	0	0	10	0	0	0	0
0	0	0	0	0	0	0	0
0	9	0	0	0	0	0	2
0	0	0	0	0	0	0	0
0	0	0	0	0	0	0	0
1	0	0	0	0	0	0	0
0	10	0	0	0	0	0	0
2	0	25	40	0	1	2	2
3	**25**	**55**	**50**	**0**	**1**	**2**	**4**
0	0	0	0	0	0	0	0
1	0	0	0	0	0	cf1	0
0	0	0	0	0	0	0	0
0	0	0	0	0	0	0	0
0	0	0	0	0	0	0	0
0	0	0	0	0	0	0	0
0	0	0	0	0	0	0	0
0	0	0	0	0	0	0	0
5	0	*	0	2	26	*	2
13	14	1	0	0	0	1	0
7	0	2	0	0	0	0	0
3	1	6	6	1	8	17	4
6			61	10	102	292	15

		Trelystan 2180bc	Barton Court 2020bc	Down Farm 2160bc	Barrow Hills	Blewbur
Triticum cf. *monococcum* (einkorn)	glume base	0	0	0	0	0
T. dicoccum and *T.* cf. *dicoccum* (emmer)	grain	0	2	0	0	0
T. dicoccum and *T.* cf. *dicoccum* (emmer)	glume base	0	1	0	0	0
T. dicoccum or *spelta* (emmer/spelt)	grain	0	0	0	0	0
T. aestivum s.l. and *T.* cf. *aestivum* s.l. (bread-type wheat)	grain	0	3	0	0	6
Triticum sp. (wheat)	grain	0	9	1	2	3
Triticum sp. (wheat)	glume base	0	0	0	0	0
Hordeum sativum (hulled six-row barley)	grain	0	0	0	0	0
H. sativum var. *nudum* (naked six-row barley)	grain	0	0	0	0	0
H. sativum and *H.* cf. *sativum* (barley)	grain	0	3	11	0	2
Indeterminate cereals	grain	0	4	13	8	8
Total cereal grain		**0**	**22**	**25**	**10**	**19**
Rubus spp (raspberry and blackberry)	stone	1	0	0	0	0
Prunus spinosa L. (sloe)	stone	0	0	0	0	0
Crataegus sp. (hawthorn)	stone	0	0	0	0	0
Malus sylvestris Mill. (crab-apple)	seed	cf.1	23	1	1	0
M. sylvestris Mill. (crab-apple)	endocarp frags	0	0	0	106	0
Malus or *Pyrus* sp. (crab-apple or pear)	seed frags	0	0	0	39	0
Malus or *Pyrus* sp. (crab-apple or pear)	calyx	0	0	0	6	0
Malus or *Pyrus* sp. (crab-apple or pear)	epid-ermal frags	0	0	0	171	0
Corylus avellana L. (hazel)	nut shell frags	*	84	2	340	76
Weed seeds		1	8	1	6	15
Unidentified seeds (mostly weeds)		2	3	5	7	1
Number of samples		5	4	14	22	2
Total volume of samples (litres)		114	115		260	25

Table 2—Carbonised cereal, fruit and nut remains from Later Neolithic samples (after Moffet et al. *1989, 250).*

G. …gdon	Thirlings	Whitton Hill	Coney-bury	Mount Farm	King Barrow Ridge	Springfield Barnes	Springfield Lyons	Gravelly Guy	Spong Hill
	0	0	0	0	0	0	0	0	0
	0	1	0	1	0	2	0	0	0
	0	0	0	0	0	0	0	0	0
	0	0	0	0	1	0	0	0	0
	0	0	0	1	0	4	0	0	0
	0	0	0	1	0	1	3	0	0
	0	0	0	0	0	0	0	0	0
	0	0	102	0	0	0	0	0	0
	1	1	159	0	0	0	0	0	0
	0	2	43	8	0	0	0	2	0
	1	1	27	0	0	6	2	6	1
	2	**5**	**331**	**11**	**1**	**13**	**5**	**8**	**1**
	1	0	0	0	0	0	0	0	0
	0	0	0	0	1	1	0	0	0
	1	0	1	0	0	2	0	0	0
	0	0	0	0	0	0	0	0	0
	0	0	0	0	0	0	0	0	0
	0	0	0	0	0	0	0	0	0
	0	0	0	0	0	0	0	0	0
	0	0	0	0	0	0	0	0	0
6	1587	9	0	425	160	*	0	156	1
	18	5	5	4	1	8	2	14	0
	4	1	0	7	0	1	0	4	0
	4	3	3	2	14	18	4	16	1
8	168	21	26		125	440	32	170	

contexts, but these were dominant over cereals in only four contexts. In all cases there was a presence of seeds of weed plants.[2]

Some general observations

(i) Cereals were present in most samples, with a higher incidence in the Earlier Neolithic samples than in the later ones.

(ii) While not abundant, there was a consistent presence of seeds from those plants usually described as weeds of cultivation.

(iii) Of the plants described as gathered foods, hazelnut shells were the most common, with a very high incidence of fragments in some contexts.

It is mainly from the high incidence of hazelnut fragments that Moffett *et al.* conclude that gathering was as important as cereal-growing on a number of British Neolithic sites.

Taphonomic and contextual problems

Concluding that gathering was as important as cereal-growing on the basis of such an overall low incidence of remains could be seen as problematic, especially from what is in effect one or, at best, two juxtaposed regions within Britain and Ireland (see Fig. 1). Perhaps an even greater problem is the relatively undiscussed acceptance of the contexts of these remains. While it could be argued that Moffett *et al.*'s review was carried out at a time when archaeobotanists were only beginning to become aware of the taphonomic processes and contextual/preservation biases which could affect the representation of plant remains studied, Legge (1989, 218–20) in the same volume indicates his awareness of some of these issues.

All but two contexts were fills of pits. The problem with pit fills in non-anaerobic situations is that, unless there is clear evidence to the contrary from the primary deposits, most of the content will have been derived (often at two or three stages removed from the activity that produced it), and there is every likelihood that the material content would have been altered and moved by soil-forming processes within the pit after deposition.

Because of slumping and infilling, consequent on biological decay and physical movement (the degree of both depending on individual situations), the complete infilling of a pit could span a long period. In the case of large pits and ditches, for example, the tertiary fills could have accumulated several hundred years after the original digging of these features—an example might be the Iron Age grain-storage pits at Micheldever Wood (Monk 1991, 106–8; forthcoming a). In effect, the larger the dug feature, the greater the problem in terms of tertiary infill occurring many years after primary use.

Considering the lack of primary occupation debris and the formation history of pit fills, it is likely that at least some of the carbonised plant remains surveyed by Moffett *et al.* had been subjected to considerable movement and probable attrition.

Plant remains taphonomy and hazelnut shells

As Legge pointed out in his paper (1989, 218), in the movement of deposits and attrition of remains in them, carbonised hazelnut shell fragments, being generally larger and having a denser cellular structure, are more robust and fare better in terms of preservation in identifiable form than carbonised cereal remains. Hazelnuts are usually stored in the shell, the shell often removed only at the point of consumption. Hazelnut shells are primary waste; eating hazelnuts therefore leads to a high wastage rate per unit volume of the complete nut. While it is possible that hazelnuts could have become charred accidentally during roasting before storage, the main reason for the preservation in carbonised form of their shells on sites is that they were thrown into domestic fires after kernel extraction. By comparison, cereal grains are primary food items and generally, while they may go through a series of crop-cleaning processes, they would be destined for consumption, only becoming carbonised secondarily, by accident or because they became part of crop-processing waste, one use for which is as tinder for lighting fires. There is hence a strong tendency to curate cereal grains until consumption or use as seed corn. This tendency may have been even more likely in earlier prehistoric subsistence-based societies than in later times after the establishment of redistributive networks and more specialised market-based economies.

In an important discussion of this issue, Jones (forthcoming a) has noted from her own work several points relevant to this discussion (see also Boardman and Jones 1990). In the first instance, while the dense waste from hazelnut consumption, the shells, cannot be used for anything else but fuel, the waste from cereal use, the chaff element, could be used as animal fodder and therefore is less likely to become carbonised. She has also noted that the denser the cellular structure of the plant material, the greater the possibility for intact preservation both in charring fires and after deposition; consequently, hazelnut shells will be preserved over cereal grains and cereal grains over chaff waste (rachis fragments, straw fragments and spikelet forks of the glumed wheats) from crop-processing.

Sampling and recovery biases

Obviously the level of sampling can greatly affect the incidence and frequency of potentially recoverable plant remains. It should go without saying that the lower the number of samples and the smaller the size (in volumetric terms) of the soil sample taken (conditioned by context size), the lower the overall incidence and frequency of remains, whether cereals or gathered plants. This point is relevant in terms of the comparability of different sites sampled differently, as well as the relative frequency of the different types of remains. The problem of possible sample size bias for those sites in the Moffett *et al.* survey has recently been raised by Legge *et al.* (1999, 91). However, simply on the basis of grain size alone, all other things being equal, one might expect a higher incidence of cereal grains relative to hazelnut shells in smaller volumes of deposit sampled (but see the arguments above).

There are likely to be biases in the recovery of hazelnut shells and cereals. While hazelnut shells, with a dense internal structure, will often sink in the flotation recovery process, they are still very likely to be easily found and identified, not only in sieving residues but also during excavation because of their distinctive curved shape (even with fragments). This is especially so by comparison with the smaller, fragile cereal remains whose surfaces are more likely to be obscured by earth encrustation than are the smoother-surfaced hazelnut shells.

It is the case that charred cereal remains are more easily separated by flotation recovery than hazelnuts because of their occluded structure (containing pockets of air). However, such a less-dense porous structure (accentuated by carbonisation) does create a certain fragility and can lead to grains being broken down into small unidentifiable pieces during redeposition,

Tankardstown, Co. Limerick	
on emmer grain	OxA-1476: 4890 ± 80 BP
	OxA-1477: 4840 ± 80 BP
on charcoal	Gr-14713 : 5105 ± 45 BP
	Gr-15386: 5005 ± 25 BP
	Gr-15387: 4880 ± 110 BP
Ballygalley, Co. Antrim	
on charcoal	UB-3491: 4830 ± 117 BP (3639 BC)
	UB-3471: 5219 ± 104 BP (3998 BC)
on charcoal associated with barley grain (after Simpson *et al.* 1990, 44)	4995 (3992–3788 BC)
Newtown, Co. Meath	
on charcoal from wall line	UB-3521: 5033 ± 42 BP (3948–3760 or 3744 –3712 BC)
	UB-3522: 4978 ± 32 BP (3906–3878 or 3804 –3696 BC)
on charcoal from pit	UB-3568: 4996 ± 39 BP (3940–3862 or 3816 –3698 BC)
	UB-3569: 5059 ± 31 BP (3948–3790 BC) (dates courtesy of Anna Brindley)
Balbridie (Grampian region), Scotland	
on wheat grain	GU-1421: 4745 ± 160 BP
on oat grain type	OxA-1767: 4820 ± 80 BP
on flax seed	OxA-1768: 4940 ± 70 BP
on crab-apple	OxA-1769: 5010 ± 90 BP

Table 3—Radiocarbon dates for plant remains and associated contexts in Neolithic houses.

and even during flotation recovery.

It is therefore inevitable that hazelnut fragments are likely to survive better in identifiable form in secondary and tertiary contexts than cereal remains. However, for the Later Neolithic, even given the biases favouring the preservation in identifiable form of hazelnut shells, their higher incidence does need to be addressed.

The problem of context bias caused by landscape formation history

The lack of identifiable domestic and structural-type contexts (i.e. post-holes, house wall-trenches, hearth surrounds and floor layers) amongst those considered by Moffett *et al.* is significant. This may, however, have more to do with post-Neolithic landscape formation processes than the total absence of these contexts at the time of the Neolithic.

A good number of geoarchaeological studies, particularly in the chalkland and limestone areas of southern Britain (e.g. Bell 1982; 1983; Allen 1988; 1992; Bell and Boardman 1992) have indicated that there has been considerable landscape change since the Bronze Age, resulting from slope degradation activated by clearance and well over 3000 years of tillage. This change has been particularly marked over the last 100 years. These processes have given rise to considerable colluvial accumulation at the base of slopes and then alluvial deposition in the streams and river systems and their valleys in southern Britain since the Iron Age (Robinson 1992).

The relevance here is that while early foot-slope and river valley sites have become buried and sealed by these processes, sites on upper slopes and former slope terraces have been at best truncated and at worst eroded completely, with shallow structural remains obliterated and occupation debris dispersed, mixed and destroyed (Allen 1991).

In this context it is worth making reference to the comments of Frank Green on the discovery of Mesolithic and Neolithic structural remains at Bowman's Farm, near Romsey, Hampshire. He states that the fills of these structural remains included modern, partially decayed material as well as the ancient remains (Green 1996, 116):

> the shallow nature of the surviving structural evidence clearly demonstrates the vulnerability of such evidence within intensively farmed landscapes in lowland Britain. It is clear that if intensive cereal cultivation had occurred, as on adjacent fields, in the period after the Second World War, then it is doubtful if the site at Bowman's Farm would have yielded anything other than a thin lithic scatter associated with high concentrations of comminuted charcoal.

Discussion of these crucial factors of landscape formation factors and taphonomic biases affecting the remains did not feature in the Moffett *et al.* (1989) paper. Awareness of these factors has increased since then but has not been reflected in the recent theory-based interpretations of the British Neolithic.

THE LESSONS OF THE IRISH AND NORTHERN BRITISH EVIDENCE

A major change in recent years is that the much-altered, distorted and fragmented southern British evidence can now be set beside the less-altered, less-piecemeal evidence that has been coming to light from Ireland and northern Britain.

These regions have, overall, suffered less from prolonged intensive agricultural practice over time (and particularly twentieth-century deep ploughing) but are now being subjected to modern infrastructural development and in some areas large-scale topsoil removal (for pipelines, roads, and industrial and housing estates). While this is threatening the archaeological heritage in these areas, it is also revealing extensive subsurface evidence. Large areas of occupational deposits of non-monumental prehistoric sites, some dated to the Neolithic, have been revealed. These construction and occupation surfaces have remained largely intact and in several cases have revealed sizeable quantities of plant remains.

In Ireland the recently discovered Neolithic sites containing this evidence include

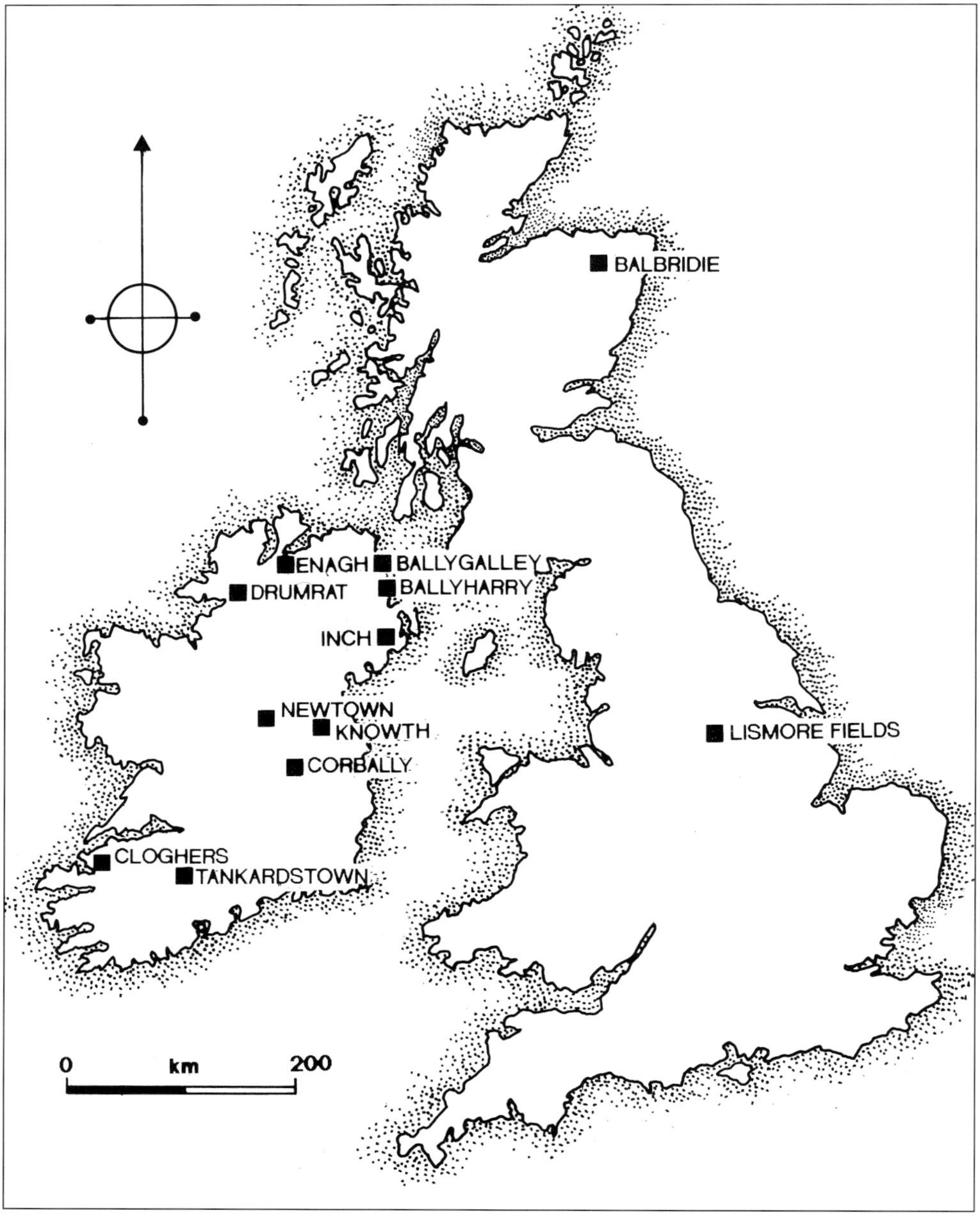

Fig. 2—Location map of recently discovered Neolithic house sites.

Tankardstown, Co. Limerick (Gowen 1988; Monk, forthcoming b); Ballygalley (Simpson *et al.* 1990; Simpson 1993; 1995) and Ballyharry, Co. Antrim; Enagh, Co. Derry; Inch, Co. Down; Cloghers, Co. Kerry; Corbally (near Kilcullen), Co. Kildare; Newtown (Gowen and Halpin 1992) and Knowth, Co. Meath (Eogan and Roche 1997; Cooney 1999a); and a site at Drumrat found during excavations in advance of the Donegal town bypass. Examples in

Scotland include Balbridie (the Grampian area), and in England Lismore Fields, Buxton, Derbyshire (see Fig. 2).[3] The ^{14}C dates obtained from some of these sites (Table 3) indicate that they are all early in the Neolithic, centring on 4800–5000 BP—for example, Tankardstown (Gowen and Tarbett 1988; M. Gowen, pers. comm.), Newtown (A. Brindley, pers. comm.), Ballygalley and Balbridie (Fairweather and Ralston 1993, 314).

The Tankardstown evidence in a broader context

In the case of Tankardstown, the plant remains came from the fills of post-holes and foundation trenches of two houses. A particularly high incidence of charred emmer wheat, *Triticum dicoccum*, grains was recovered from the structural features of House 1 (Gowen 1988, 30, figs 3 and 4; Cooney and Grogan 1994, 38, fig. 4:1). At least one of the wall-trenches and two post positions showed distinct signs of burning.

The presence of emmer was confirmed by the occasional incidence of spikelet forks and glume bases. However, the indications are that this was a cleaned product of crop-processing with a relatively low incidence of the chaff element and a low incidence of weed seeds, such as *Rumex* sp., *Atriplex* sp. and unidentifiable grasses (Monk 1988; forthcoming b).

Carbonised remains of gathered plants were also present, including a few fragments of hazelnuts, *Corylus avellana*, but also charred pips and endocarps of wild (crab) apples, *Malus sylvestris*, found especially along the wall line of House 1. Their presence in this form would suggest that they were being dried prior to being caught up in the fire that destroyed the wall of this building (Monk, forthcoming b). A similar spectrum of remains has been recovered from the northern Irish sites of Ballygalley and Ballyharry, according to preliminary information, but the grain is mainly emmer wheat (plus possible einkorn, *Triticum monococcum*, from Ballygalley), with some barley, *Hordeum* sp., from both sites (Simpson 1995, 38; D. Weir, pers. comm.; B. Collins, pers. comm.). In addition, preliminary information from the Cloghers site in County Kerry (L. Dunne, J. Kiely and M. Hannon, pers. comm.) and from Corbally in County Kildare (P. Johnston and A. Purcell, pers. comm.) also indicates the presence of cereals, in the latter case mainly emmer type or emmer/einkorn wheat (with also a possible presence of a free-threshing wheat). In this case the incidence of grains is low but consistently present. However, hazelnut shells have also been noted, with a couple of concentrations.

At Balbridie, Scotland, in addition to emmer, the free-threshing wheat *Triticum aestivo-compactum* was also represented, as well as a higher incidence of barley, *Hordeum* sp., flax, *Linum usitatissimum*, and a Neolithic-dated oat, *Avena* sp.[4]

The highest frequency of remains at all sites seems to be wheat. In her work on the Lismore Fields site at Buxton, Glynis Jones (forthcoming b) has noted a similar spectrum of cereal remains and gathered plants to those so far identified from the Irish sites and from Balbridie. A ^{14}C date on the grain (of 4930 ± 70 BP) is also within the same date range as the sites listed in Table 3.

It is worth noting that where there is evidence for a catastrophic fire destroying part or all of these buildings, there is a high incidence of cereal remains (as in the case of Tankardstown 1 by comparison with Tankardstown 2). In such situations the quality of the evidence is also better (as noted by Jones (forthcoming a)), particularly where storage areas have also been affected. Where cereal remains are present on sites with little or no evidence for burning, other than disturbed domestic hearth debris, their incidence is much lower, particularly relative to hazelnut shells.

The incidence, and in some cases quantity, of cereal remains from these sites contrasts sharply with those included in the Moffett *et al.* paper. One suspects that if they had had more occupation/structural-type contexts to draw on, their conclusions might have been different.

The structural evidence for sedentism

Apart from the plant remains of cereal cultivation, the archaeological evidence itself, not least the substantial timbers used in the buildings on the sites mentioned, indicates a considerable degree of sedentism.[5] While building structures *per se* do not indicate sedentism, the size of these buildings and the building timbers used, mainly oak,[6] suggest a level of investment in energy unlikely to be expended by a nomadic or mobile society (see note 5). In addition, there is evidence at some of these sites for rebuilding of the structures on the same spot, for example Tankardstown 2 and Ballyharry, which would itself suggest a degree of longevity of use (M. Gowen, pers. comm.; Crothers 1996). As mentioned earlier, and also discussed by Cooney (1997, 28), the construction of field systems in areas like the west of Ireland is hardly the practice of a mobile society.

It is perhaps important to note from preliminary general information that a majority of these sites in Ireland are located on, or close to, some of the better soils available for sedentary agricultural practices, either grey-brown podzolic or brown earth soils which have developed on drift geology consisting of limestone and shales. In the case of two of the northern sites—Ballygalley and Ballyharry—the general soil associations are gleys, but there is also local occurrence of brown soils (Gardiner and Radford 1980).

The faunal evidence

While this is not the place to go into this important area of discussion in detail (see van Wijngaarden-Bakker 1986; McCormick 1987; and for the later prehistoric animal remains McCarthy, this volume), it is necessary to point out that while there are not that many quantitatively large collections of animal bones from Neolithic sites in Britain and Ireland (such collections are particularly lacking in the latter case), few bones of wild, hunted animals have been identified in these collections (McCormick 1999, 360). This is not to say that the exploitation of wild fauna was not continued into the Neolithic, but its importance in the contribution of protein to the diet had diminished relative to the preceding Mesolithic.

The quantity of cattle bones from Neolithic sites, particularly from the ditches of causewayed enclosures in southern Britain, has been used to support the argument for structured deposition of animal remains by a society operating a mobile economy (Edmonds 1993). There is likely to be site context bias as well as recovery bias affecting this evidence (depending on whether sieving was selective or extensive at these sites), but this is not the place to tease out the detail of arguments involving taphonomy, context and recovery. Suffice it to say that the quantities of securely dated Neolithic animal bone are at present too small to form a strong basis for argument. It would seem, then, that the evidence is not sufficient to justify an interpretation of a society more mobile than one exploiting seasonal variability (transhumance) within a territory with topographic and ecological variability.

Gathering in the Neolithic

It is the case that even from sites with plant remains from Ireland and northern Britain a high incidence of remains of gathered food plants has been found, which, while it cannot be taken as an indicator of a nomadic society, does nevertheless suggest that gathered plant foods were readily available in the vicinity and were significant in the diet.

It can be argued that there was an increased availability of such resources and the reason for this lies in the ecological response of plants to the effects of clearance in the Early Neolithic, resulting in a vegetation succession back to regenerated woodland in the Later Neolithic.

Discussing the beginnings of the Irish Neolithic from the pollen evidence, Groenman-van Waateringe (1983) suggested that with increased clearance of the forest those species that thrive on the outer fringes of wooded areas, or 'mantle vegetation' (consisting of hawthorn, wild rose, bramble, blackthorn/sloe, crab-apple and hazel), would have expanded (relative to other species) to match the increase in potential habitat, i.e. increases in new clearings leading to increased areas of woodland fringe around them (see also Groenman-van Waateringe 1968; O'Kelly 1989, 37; Moffett *et al.* 1989, 246).

What would now be described as a 'hedgerow' or outskirt field-edge type of vegetation, with its fruit- and nut-bearing plants, would not have been left to idle even by farming groups. The increase in such vegetation may have been the incidental ecological consequence of Neolithic clearance, but it was 'one which Neolithic man could profit from' (Groenman-van Waateringe 1983, 227). It would also have been a convenient resource to exploit close to Neolithic farms. If anything, such a readily available resource would have helped to reinforce their sedentism.

Food values

One area of discussion concerning pre- and post-Neolithic subsistence that is seldom considered is the food value of exploited resources. In terms of subsistence, we often think of plant foods before and after the Neolithic in opposite terms simply because the resources involved are acquired in different ways—gathering on the one hand and cultivation on the other. Moffett *et al.* (1989) have perhaps inadvertently fallen into this way of thinking in the presentation of their discussion. We seldom think in terms of the complementarity of different plant foods in a dietary/nutritional sense. This point is very relevant in the case of hazelnuts on the one hand and cereals on the other.

Hazelnuts are, for example, high in fats (63.57g per 100g) and at the same time rich in certain vitamins, particularly Vitamin E (29.98 per 100g) (S. Gannon, pers. comm.). By contrast, and in a complementary sense, cereals are high in carbohydrates, an area of food value that hazelnuts do not score highly in. Therefore, while the two food sources have a different energy base, it could be argued that they complement one another, providing a sound nutritional dietary package for Neolithic people who continued to an extent to be supported by the proceeds of gathering. In this context it is important to appreciate that a whole range of essential vitamins and minerals were not available in the narrow range of livestock and crops domesticated. This, however, is unlikely to have been perceived as a problem while the wild fruits and green foods were as readily available as the bulk storable carbohydrates or meats provided by domesticated sources.

CONCLUSION

The archaeobotanical basis for interpreting Neolithic societies as essentially mobile has been discussed and has been found wanting, especially in the light of more recent evidence from sites in Ireland and northern Britain, two areas that, by comparison with southern Britain, have been less subjected to landscape changes and consequent selective destruction of the plant remains evidence. However, while Neolithic societies were not mobile, their activities gave rise to an expansion in plants with gathering potential around the woodland and field margins created by the farmers, plants for which there was no substitute in the range of domesticated species. The archaeobotanical evidence clearly indicates that these food plants were exploited by the early farmers, but this activity meant neither that these groups were nomadic nor that gathering was more important than cultivation. This activity did mean, however, that, at least during the first part of the Neolithic, farming communities had a broad and diverse food base (see Kimball, this volume), and indeed a nutritionally complementary diet. In the course of time, however, and probably consequent on the expansion in population and environmental change, this dietary advantage was reduced. In the Later Neolithic there may have been a contraction in human activity, and the ecological effect of this could have been an expansion of secondary woodland, including those plants producing edible fruit and nuts. The higher incidence of the remains of these plants on later-dated Neolithic sites could indeed be a reflection of an expansion of gathering activities against a contraction in cereal husbandry. Such an interpretation, like that for many areas of the Neolithic as a whole, is based on relatively meagre evidence which has been subjected to many taphonomic processes. There is a need for more detailed studies in every region within Britain and Ireland to be able to account for the biases and tease out the regional similarities and variations through time. The exciting new evidence from Ireland and northern Britain must serve as a lesson against generalisations within a period that is at least 2000 years long.

ACKNOWLEDGEMENTS

I am in debt to a number of archaeobotanical and archaeological colleagues for reference to their unpublished work, for their comments and their inspiration: to Brenda Collins, David Weir, Penny Johnston, Martha Hannon, Meriel McClatchie and Sandra McKeown for reference to their ongoing archaeobotanical work. In addition, I would like to acknowledge Lisa Moffett, Vanessa Straker and Mark Robinson, whose paper helped to kick-start and inspire this study and for kindly allowing me to use their table and map. Thanks are also due to Gordon Hillman for discussion of this issue at an early stage and to Glynis Jones for a more recent discussion and reference to her unpublished work. Gabriel Cooney has provided an important complementary perspective on this subject and I wish to thank him for reference to his (then) unpublished book. Simon Gannon provided engaging discussion on the use of hazelnuts and nutrition. I am also very grateful to the excavators whose sites have produced the remains that allow us to see the economy of the Irish Neolithic in a better light—Margaret Gowen and Christine Tarbett, Avril Purcell, George Eogan and Helen Roche, Lar Dunne and Jacinta Kiely, John Channing, Sylvia Desmond and Paula King. Thanks are also due to Anna Brindley and Jan Lanting for reference to the Newtown dates. Finally, thanks are due to those people who were crucial in the final draft of the paper, not least Rhoda Cronin for expertly drawing the maps, Margaret McCarthy and Mark Brisbane for making pertinent comments and editorial suggestions, and Judith Monk, Gina Johnson and Angela Desmond for their final editorial work.

REFERENCES

Allen, M. 1988 Archaeological and environmental aspects of colluviation in south-east England. In W. Groenman-van Waateringe and M. Robinson (eds), *Man-made soils*, 67–92. British Archaeological Reports, International Series 410. Oxford.

Allen, M.J. 1991 Analysing the landscape: a geographical approach to archaeological problems. In A.J. Schofield (ed.), *Interpreting artefact scatters: contributions to ploughzone archaeology*, 39–57. Oxford. Oxbow.

Allen, M. 1992 Products of erosion and the prehistoric land-use of the Wessex Chalk. In M. Bell and J. Boardman (eds), *Past and present soil erosion*, 37–52. Oxford. Oxbow.

Barrett, J.C. 1994 *Fragments from antiquity: an archaeology of social life in Britain, 2900–1200 BC.* Oxford. Blackwell.

Bell, M. 1982 The effects of land-use and climate on valley sedimentation. In A.F. Harding (ed.), *Climate change in later prehistory*, 127–42. Edinburgh University Press.

Bell, M. 1983 Valley sediments as evidence for prehistoric land-use on the South Downs. *Proceedings of the Prehistoric Society* **49**, 119–50.

Bell, M. and Boardman, J. (eds) 1992 *Past and present soil erosion.* Oxbow Monograph 22. Oxford.

Boardman, S. and Jones, G. 1990 Experiments on the effects of charring on cereal plant components. *Journal of Archaeological Science* **17**, 1–11.

Bradley, R. 1997 *Rock art and the prehistory of Atlantic Europe: signing the land.* London. Routledge.

Caulfield, S. 1983 The Neolithic settlement of north Connaught. In T. Reeves-Smyth and F. Hamond (eds), *Landscape archaeology in Ireland*, 195–215. British Archaeological Reports, British Series 116. Oxford.

Clutton-Brock, J. 1989 Introduction to pastoralism. In J. Clutton-Brock (ed.), *The walking larder: patterns of domestication, pastoralism and predation*, 115–18. One World Archaeology Series. London. Unwin and Hyman.

Coles, J. and Hall, D. 1998 *Changing landscapes: the ancient fenland.* Cambridge County Council.

Collins, B. 1997 Appendix 3: plant remains. In G. Eogan and H. Roche, *Excavations at Knowth 2—settlement and ritual sites of the fourth and third millennia BC*, 295–300. Dublin. Royal Irish Academy.

Cooney, G. 1997 Images of settlement and the landscape in the Neolithic. In P. Topping (ed.), *Neolithic landscapes*, 23–31. Neolithic Studies Group Papers 2. Oxbow Monograph 86. Oxford.

Cooney, G. 1999a A boom in Neolithic houses. *Archaeology Ireland* **13** (1), 13–16.

Cooney, G. 1999b *Landscapes of Neolithic Ireland*. London. Routledge.

Cooney, G. and Grogan, E. 1994 *Irish prehistory: a social perspective*. Bray. Wordwell.

Crothers, N. 1996 Ballyharry's game. *Archaeology Ireland* **10** (4), 12–14.

Edmonds, M. 1993 Interpreting causewayed enclosures in the past and present. In C. Tilley (ed.), *Interpreting archaeology*, 99–142. Oxford. Berg.

Edmonds, M. 1997 Taskscape, technology and tradition. *Analecta Praehistorica Leidensia* **29**, 99–110.

Entwhistle, R. and Grant, A. 1989 The evidence for cereal cultivation and animal husbandry in the southern British Neolithic and Bronze Age. In A. Milles, D. Williams and N. Gardiner (eds), *The beginnings of agriculture*, 203–15. British Archaeological Reports, International Series 496. Oxford.

Eogan, G. and Roche, H. 1997 Pre-tomb Neolithic house discovered at Knowth, Co. Meath. *Archaeology Ireland* **11** (2), 31.

Fairweather, A.D. and Ralston, I.B.M. 1993 The Neolithic timber hall at Balbridie, Grampian Region, Scotland: the building, the date, the plant macrofossils. *Antiquity* **67**, 313–23.

Gardiner, M.J. and Radford, T. 1980 *Soil associations of Ireland and their land use potential* (Explanatory Bulletin to Soil Map of Ireland 1980). Soil Survey Bulletin No. 36. National Soil Survey of Ireland. Dublin. An Foras Taluntais.

Gowen, M. 1988 *Three Irish gas pipelines: new archaeological evidence in Munster*. Dublin. Wordwell.

Gowen, M. and Halpin, E. 1992 A Neolithic house at Newtown. *Archaeology Ireland* **6** (2), 25–7.

Gowen, M. and Tarbett, C. 1988 A third season at Tankardstown. *Archaeology Ireland* **2** (4), 156.

Green, F.J. 1996 Mesolithic or later houses at Bowman's Farm, Romsey Extra, Hampshire, England. In T. Darvill and J. Thomas (eds), *Neolithic houses in northwest Europe and beyond*, 113–22. Neolithic Studies Group Seminar Papers 1. Oxbow Monograph 57. Oxford.

Groenman-van Waateringe, W. 1968 The elm decline and the first appearance of *Plantago major*. *Vegetatio* **15**, 292–6.

Groenman-van Waateringe, W. 1983 The early agricultural utilisation of the Irish landscape: the last word on the elm decline. In T. Reeves-Smyth and F. Hamond (eds), *Landscape archaeology in Ireland*, 217–32. British Archaeological Reports, British Series 116. Oxford.

Ingold, T. 1980 *Hunters, pastoralists and ranchers*. Cambridge University Press.

Jones, G. (forthcoming a) Evaluating the importance of cultivation and collecting in Neolithic Britain.

Jones, G. (forthcoming b) Evidence for the importance of cereals in the Neolithic: charred plant remains from the Neolithic settlement at Lismore Fields, Buxton. In D. Garton, *The excavation of a Mesolithic and Neolithic settlement area at Lismore Fields, Buxton, Derbyshire.*

Khazanov, A.M. 1984 *Nomads and the outside world* (translated by J. Crookenden). Cambridge University Press.

Legge, A.J. 1989 Milking the evidence: a reply to Entwhistle and Grant. In A. Milles, D. Williams and N. Gardiner (eds), *The beginnings of agriculture*, 217–42. British Archaeological Reports, International Series 496. Oxford.

Legge, T., Payne, S. and Rowley-Conwy, P. 1999 The study of food remains in prehistoric Britain. In J. Bayley (ed.), *Science in archaeology*, 89–94. London. English Heritage.

Lennon, A.-M. 1988 Examination of charred wood in macrofossil flots submitted to Mick Monk. In M. Gowen, *Three Irish gas pipelines: new archaeological evidence in Munster*, 198. Dublin. Wordwell.

McCormick, F. 1987 Faunal remains from prehistoric burials. *Journal of Irish Archaeology* **3** (1985/6), 37–48.

McCormick, F. 1999 Early evidence for wild animals in Ireland. In N. Benecke (ed.), *The Holocene history of the European vertebrate fauna: modern aspects of research. Workshop, 6th to 9th April 1998*, 355–71. Berlin. Verlag Marie Leidorf GmbH.Rahden/Westf.

Moffett, L., Robinson, M.A. and Straker, V. 1989 Cereals, fruit and nuts: charred plant remains from Neolithic sites in England and Wales and the Neolithic economy. In A. Milles, D. Williams and N. Gardiner (eds), *The beginnings of agriculture*, 243–61. British Archaeological Reports, International Series 496. Oxford.

Monk, M.A. 1986 Evidence from macroscopic plant remains for husbandry in prehistoric and early historic Ireland. *Journal of Irish Archaeology* **3**, 31–6.

Monk, M.A. 1988 Appendix 3: archaeobotanical study of samples from gas pipeline sites. In M. Gowen (ed.), *Three Irish gas pipelines: new archaeological evidence in Munster*, 185–91. Dublin. Wordwell.

Monk, M.A. 1991 The archaeobotanical work carried out for the M3 Project—a retrospective view. In P.J. Fasham and R.J.B. Whinney (eds), *Archaeology and the M3*, 105–10. Monograph 7. Stroud. Alan Sutton for the Hampshire Field Club and the Trust for Wessex Archaeology.

Monk, M.A. 1993 People and environment: in search of the farmers. In E. Shee Twohig and M. Ronayne (eds), *Past perceptions: the prehistoric archaeology of south-west Ireland*, 35–52. Cork University Press.

Monk, M.A. (forthcoming a) Formation processes and plant remains studies [provisional title].

Monk, M.A. (forthcoming b) Tankardstown: plant remains report on the samples from the 1987–89 seasons. (To be published in M. Gowen, *Excavations at Tankardstown.*)

O'Kelly, M.J. 1989 *Early Ireland: an introduction to Irish prehistory.* Cambridge University Press.

Robinson, D. and Rasmussen, P. 1989 Botanical investigations at the Neolithic lake village at Weier, N.E. Switzerland: leaf hay and cereals as animal fodder. In A. Milles, D. Williams and N. Gardiner (eds), *The beginnings of agriculture*, 149–63. British Archaeological Reports, International Series 496. Oxford.

Robinson, M. 1992 Environment, archaeology and alluvium on the river gravels of the South Midlands. In S. Needham and M.G. Macklin (eds), *Alluvial archaeology in Britain*, 197–208. Oxbow Monograph 27. Oxford.

Scannell, M. 1988 Appendix 6 (i). Identification of wood species from charcoal and wood samples. In M. Gowen, *Three Irish gas pipelines: new archaeological evidence in Munster*, 196. Dublin. Wordwell.

Simpson, D. 1993 Ballygalley. *Current Archaeology* **134**, 60–2.

Simpson, D.D.A. 1995 The Neolithic settlement site at Ballygalley, Co. Antrim. In E. Grogan and C. Mount (eds), *Annus Archaeologiae: Proceedings of the OIA Winter Conference 1993*, 37–44. Dublin. Office of Public Works.

Simpson, D.D.A., Conway, M.G. and Moore, D.G. 1990 The Neolithic settlement at Ballygalley, Co. Antrim. Excavations 1984 interim report. *Ulster Journal of Archaeology* **53**, 40–9.

Thomas, J. 1991 *Rethinking the Neolithic.* Cambridge University Press.

Thomas, J. 1996 Neolithic houses in mainland Britain and Ireland—a sceptical view. In T. Darvill and J. Thomas (eds), *Neolithic houses in northwest Europe and beyond*, 1–12. Oxford. Oxbow.

van Wijngaarden-Bakker, L.H. 1986 The animal remains from the Beaker settlement at Newgrange, Co. Meath: final report. *Proceedings of the Royal Irish Academy* **86**C, 2–111.

Endnotes

1 Moffett, Robinson and Straker (pers. comm.) fully appreciate the fact that their paper (Moffett *et al.* 1989) has dated in terms of both plant remains evidence for the Neolithic and archaeobotanical methodology, but additionally feel that their work and results have been taken up more definitively than intended in subsequent discussions on the nature of the British Neolithic. The conditional points they made have not been noted.

2 This discussion centres on those plant remains preserved by direct or indirect exposure to fire and which have consequently become carbonised. There is an inevitable bias towards a narrow spectrum of plants, including cereals and other plant foods, that are exposed to fire during their processing. A few Neolithic sites have been found with a broader range of preserved plant remains, particularly sites with anaerobic conditions. Although Moffett *et al.* (1989, 246) refer to the site at Etton in Cambridgeshire which, in common with other fenland sites, has waterlogged deposits present, the evidence had not been fully studied at that time. The range of remains that can be produced from waterlogged sites is demonstrated by the study of the Neolithic lake village at Weier, Switzerland (Robinson and Rasmussen 1989, 153–5). This site, in common with those with a similar range of preservation, continues to highlight the importance of domesticated plant remains, but it also produced a consistent presence of gathered plants.

In addition there is an inevitable bias towards plants of damp ground, reflecting its particular wetland location and suggesting, as may have been the case at Etton, its seasonal use for herded animals (Coles and Hall 1998, 18).

3 Of those Neolithic house sites identified and excavated before the mid-1980s, few were sampled or produced carbonised plant remains. Some samples were taken from Ballynagilly, Co. Tyrone, but a study by this author produced only carbonised bracts of pine cones, which may have been used as tinder for fires. An important collection of samples taken from Ballyglass has recently been examined and a low incidence of charred grain, unfortunately indeterminate to species, has been identified (M. McClatchie, pers. comm.). Occupation surfaces under other megalithic tombs have also produced some remains, e.g. Townley Hall and Knowth, Co. Meath, and Baltinglass, Co. Wicklow (Monk 1986, 31).

4 A possible oat was also discovered in a Neolithic context from Knowth (Collins 1997, 296).

5 There has been a lack of clarity in some discussions in the use of the terms 'sedentism', 'mobility' and 'nomadism'. Clutton-Brock (1989, 117–18), drawing on the discussions of Ingold (1980) and Khazanov (1984), has clarified some of the terms related to pastoral societies. The author would argue that sedentism should not be seen in absolute terms, i.e. it should not be seen to negate the budding-off of 'daughter' settlements into new territories or, more importantly (in the light of this critique), to negate transhumance or seasonal movement back and forth to one or more base locations in order to exploit different ecological zones in a particular locale.

6 Where there is clear evidence from carbonised remains, the timber used in these house structures was mainly oak—e.g. Tankardstown (Scannell 1988), with a few hazel twigs (Lennon 1988). At the Ballyglass site a mixture of wood species was identified from a recent charcoal study, but it did include oak from the wall-trenches of the house, some of which may have been part of the structure (S. McKeown, pers. comm.).

FRAMEWORKS FOR THE MEGALITHIC ART OF THE BOYNE VALLEY

Elizabeth Shee Twohig

'There are some stories which have to be retold by each generation
—Virginia Woolf

INTRODUCTION

It is now axiomatic that any interpretation of the past is inevitably situated in the present. I think this may be even more true for megalithic art than for other areas of investigation that might be regarded as more tractable, because tensions will inevitably arise between the recording/classifying of art and its interpretation. In this paper I propose briefly to look back over the changing contexts of the study of the megalithic art at Newgrange during the past hundred years. I will then re-view the art in a manner that I believe to be informed by current ways of thinking about material culture and show how the motifs relate to the architecture of the monument. To do this I will obviously be drawing largely on Brian and Claire O'Kelly's work at both the main tomb and the immediately adjacent sites. Finally, I will show that three main phases of carvings can be identified at Newgrange and Knowth and that these provide us with a framework for understanding the use of the art in the Boyne Valley.

From early this century the study of megalithic art followed the diffusionist approach, as did the study of megalithic tombs generally. For megalithic art two threads seem to have been followed, both suggesting an exotic and even glamorous source for specific aspects of the art. In the 1890s George Coffey published a series of papers on prehistoric ornament in Ireland and in 1912 revised them under the title *New Grange (Brugh na Bóinne) and other incised tumuli in Ireland: the influence of Crete and the Aegean in the extreme west of Europe in early times.* Like many others before and since he was fascinated by the spirals, and in the 1912 book he proposed an eastern Mediterranean origin for the art, seeing spirals as being brought from Bronze Age Mycenae/Crete via Scandinavia to Ireland. The point was fully argued, and there seems no justification for Ian Kinnes's (1995, 51) hint of a nationalist agenda in Coffey's circuitous route for the spiral around Britain to Ireland. Immediately afterwards the French archaeologist Déchelette brought the spiral further south, from Ireland to Gavrinis in Brittany. Within the decade, however, Macalister argued that 'it is a fundamental error to consider Crete as a parent of European Civilisation . . . the spiral may appear independently of Crete' (Macalister 1921, 219). Meanwhile other French prehistorians had been pursuing a female divinity across Europe, from Egypt through the Aegean up to the collective tombs of the Paris Basin (Cartailhac 1889; Déchelette 1908). Déchelette then used Coffey's (1912) illustrations to suggest that the carvings showed human representations (Déchelette 1912, 37) or tattooed women (*ibid.*, 42). As discussed elsewhere (Hutton 1997; Shee Twohig

1998), this theme was very prevalent until the 1960s when Andrew Fleming (1969) called into question the whole concept of a Mother Goddess in western European passage tombs, as Peter Ucko (1968) had just done for eastern Mediterranean idols. These papers represent moves to challenge the diffusionist approach as, for example, in Renfrew 1967. However, an anthropomorphic interpretation is still occasionally invoked for some of the Irish material (e.g. in O'Sullivan 1997), though the Mother Goddess interpretations—as promoted by Gimbutas (1989) and others seeking a sort of prehistory for matriarchy and feminism—are generally rejected (Shee Twohig 1998).

Interpretations outside the diffusionist genre include astronomical, especially solar, symbolism. This goes back to the late eighteenth-century ideas of Charles Vallencey and has many followers in this century (e.g. Brennan 1983). These were particularly common following the discovery that the Newgrange tomb is orientated on the midwinter sunrise, but space does not allow for these or the many other interpretations to be discussed here.

In the 1960s several new examples of megalithic art were discovered during the course of excavations at Newgrange and Knowth (published mainly in M.J. O'Kelly 1982 and Eogan 1986a respectively). As discussed by O'Sullivan (1986) and Shee Twohig (1997), most of those studying the art retreated from the minefield of interpretation to the safer territories of classification and the identification of styles of ornament.

In the past decade new approaches to megalithic art have been suggested as a result of Lewis-Williams and Dowson's work on the rock art of southern Africa, and the proposals, based on ethnography, that much of the San/Bushman art is related to shamanism, with images derived from designs neurologically generated in trance or altered states of consciousness (ASC). This idea has not been universally accepted by those researching the San art because of the problems of applying the ethnography of the Kalahari San to those of the south. It was suggested that European Upper Palaeolithic art was also shamanistic (Lewis-Williams and Dowson 1988), and this idea was then applied to megalithic tomb art by Bradley (1989) and developed further for Ireland by Lewis-Williams and Dowson (1993) and in a number of papers by Dronfield (1995a; 1995b; 1996a; 1996b). Many, though not all (see discussion in Dronfield 1996a), are now prepared to accept the possibility that some of the motifs in Irish passage tombs are derived from images seen in Stage 1 of ASC and that they have been culturally processed. These are known as entoptic motifs (Lewis-Williams and Dowson 1988) or endogenous visual phenomena (Dronfield 1995a). What Dronfield terms 'endogenous diagnostic shapes' occur relatively rarely in comparison with 'general undiagnostic shapes'. The latter are those shapes that occur frequently but not exclusively as endogenous images (*ibid.*, fig. 4). One of the possibilities which follows from the derivation of motifs from Stage 1 of ASC is that wherever the designs occur in passage tombs of a particular region they may have developed independently in those areas and not have been copied from one area to another (Shee Twohig 1997). I am not convinced, however, that it is possible to identify the precise methods of achieving ASC on the basis of the varying motifs at individual sites, *pace* Dronfield (1995b, 272–3). Nor do I find at all persuasive Dronfield's (1996a) attempts to identify circular motifs and the tunnel or vortex of trance, or to correlate the occurrence of lattice motifs with mortuary deposits. The latter argument was made even less convincing by Dronfield's selective replication of carved panels at Newgrange, e.g.

Dronfield 1996a, fig. 9, is credited 'after C. O'Kelly' but has many motifs deleted from the O'Kelly illustration.

There are several problems with the application of the shamanism hypothesis to megalithic art—firstly the acceptance that any of these arts is ASC-derived, secondly the fact that so-called ASC-derived arts are generally associated with hunter-gatherers rather than farming societies, and finally the validity of cross-cultural transfers of explanations for behaviour.

Few other new approaches have been presented for the study of megalithic art. One recurrent feature in recent years, however, is the replacement of terms such as 'religion', in relation to both megalithic tombs and megalithic art, by, for example, 'ritual', and figures formerly interpreted as goddesses are now being referred to as women, sometimes in opposition to what are seen as male emblems, such as axes (e.g. Hodder 1990, 232; see also Thomas and Tilley 1993). Is this, to steal a phrase out of context, a 'sign of the times', reflecting an increasing secularisation of society, or is it just the adoption of more circumspect language?

One of the more constructive approaches to megalithic art studies in the post-processual mode is that which considers how the art might be encountered inside megalithic tombs, e.g. Thomas 1990. An exercise of this kind has already been carried out for Loughcrew (Shee Twohig 1997), and here the carvings at the main tomb at Newgrange and those adjacent to it are examined in the context of the tomb architecture. There is a demonstrable sequence for the Newgrange art that can be correlated with the phasing of the art at Knowth, the biggest 'megalithic art gallery', which has been studied by both the excavator, George Eogan, and by Muiris O'Sullivan. The latter's distinction between 'depictive' and 'plastic' art, based mainly on a case study of Knowth (O'Sullivan 1986), has been very helpful in understanding megalithic art in the Boyne Valley. The depictive art is two-dimensional, while the plastic approaches the three-dimensional and is related to the form of the stone. The plastic was superimposed on the depictive, and in the tombs it tends towards large-scale ribbon-like designs, lacking in specific motifs. On the kerbstones of the main tomb at Knowth (Knowth 1) a variant of plastic art (mainly circles and serpentiforms) was superimposed on smaller depictive motifs.

George Eogan has recently discussed the phasing of the art at Knowth in two papers, arising partly from a detailed examination of some of the stones and partly from the discovery of carvings on several hitherto buried surfaces in the passage of the western tomb in Knowth 1. Eogan (1998) suggested a sequence of building on the site starting with Sites 16 and 13, which have incised art, followed by another monument which is now destroyed. From this a number of stones that were decorated with picked curvilinear and angular designs were reused in the building of both the tombs in Knowth 1). Orthostats with almost identical ornament were also incorporated into the passage (and possibly elsewhere) at Newgrange. The Knowth 1 art proper follows this, as outlined in Eogan 1997, which shows a sequence beginning with incised designs in the inner section of the tombs, which may be overlain by angular picked motifs, and these in turn may be overlain by loose picking. These were followed by ribbon art (basically O'Sullivan's plastic art) and close area picking. The chronological relationship between incised designs and the curvilinear/angular art reused in the outer parts of the passages at Knowth 1 is, however, not yet determined.

Pl. 1—Orthostat 81 from the passage of Knowth 1 western tomb. The pointed end was found set in the socket. (Photo: author.)

NEWGRANGE

Four passage tombs have been excavated at Newgrange . O'Kelly excavated the main tomb (M.J. O'Kelly 1982) as well as Sites K and Z, while Lynch excavated Site L (O'Kelly *et al.* 1978).

Main tomb

Of primary concern here are the carvings, which are well preserved and have been thoroughly documented by Claire O'Kelly (1982).

The main cairn, which covers *c.* 0.5ha, is sited midway along a low ridge to the north of the River Boyne. It is visible from much of the surrounding countryside, but the approach to it was probably from the south, towards the glistening white and grey wall of quartz and granite that topped a band of green kerbstones. Traces of ceremonial activities survived at the entrance in the form of an oval setting of stones in which a phalloid stone was deposited

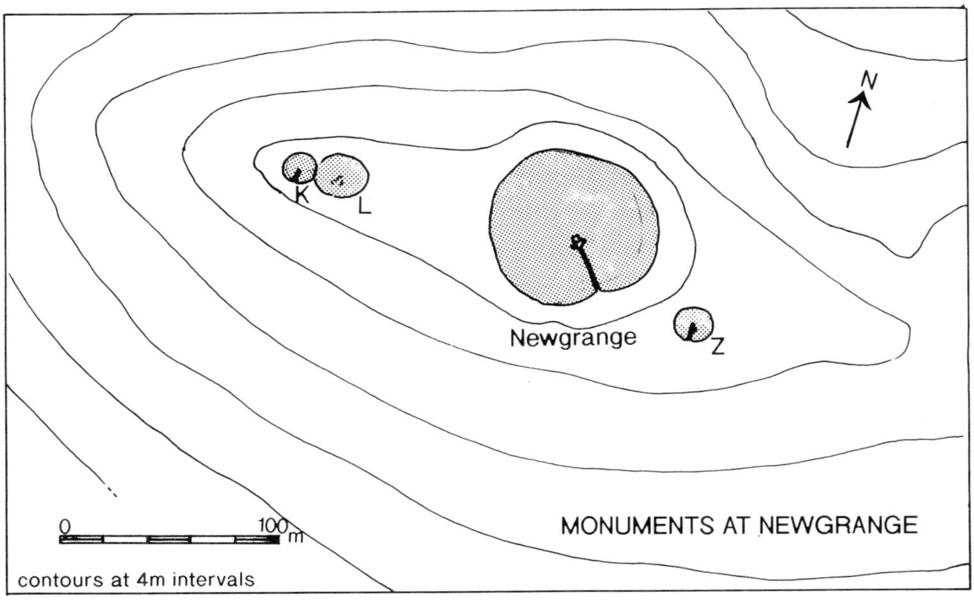

Fig. 1—Relative positions of passage tombs at Newgrange (after O'Kelly et al. *1978).*

amongst a collection of quartz, granite and water-rolled pebbles.

The focal point of the cairn was the tomb entrance, with the most spectacular carved kerbstone (K1) signalling something special (Pl. 2). Above it projected the horizontal edge of the roofbox lintel, which was decorated with lattice/lozenges in relief.

The passage

There must always have been a problem in providing access to the passage without damaging the stones once K2 and K97 were put in place on each side of K1. The only way to enter would have been by clambering over the kerbstones, thus crossing *over* a threshold and then entering into the passage opening, going *under* another special carving, the roofbox lintel. The height of the passage roof allows one to walk along almost without bending, the lowest points being under the first roofslab and under the lintel RS12. The passage is in two sections, with the inner element starting where the lowest lintel (RS12) rests on R12 and L13. Beyond this the roof rises like steps to its corbelled vault. There is also a slight change in direction in the plan at this point, which is almost exactly halfway between the entrance and the backstone of the chamber. This threshold between outer and inner passage is also distinguished through the carvings which are to be found in both the passage and the roof at this point.

The carvings in the passage were executed in at least three phases. Three stones, R3, L19 and L20, must have been carved before the stones were put in place, because the carvings were concealed in the ground when the stones were set upright. All the carvings are on the passage-facing surface and comprise mainly spirals or circles with a few angular motifs near them. These hidden designs are all very similar to those found in similar positions at Knowth

Pl. 2—Newgrange K1, at tomb entrance. (Photo: author.)

1 (see above). Eogan's suggestion that they all came from a pre-existing monument at Knowth seems reasonable at first glance in view of the number (15) found there. Alternatively they may have been specially carved for incorporation in these major tombs. In the Newgrange chamber several of the orthostats have similar spiral carvings, particularly one stone with spirals and a lozenge which was noted by George Coffey in the wall behind a chamber orthostat (see below).

Apart from the stones with hidden motifs, the carvings in the passage are generally small-scale, comprising lozenge/triangle panels (L15, R8, R12, R21) and zigzag panels (L22, R18) or small-scale outline circles and lozenges (Fig. 2). The structural change at the beginning of the inner section of the passage is marked by some random carvings on the south (outer) edge of L13 and a panel of triangles on the outer edge of R12. In each case these must have been carved before the adjacent stone to the south was put in place. The passage face of R12 has a small panel of triangles low down, which is respected by the pick dressing that occupies most of the main surface.

The third stage of carvings visible in the passage comprises what is generally termed 'pick dressing'. This must have been done when the stones were *in situ* as it never occurs on inaccessible parts of the stones and it generally stops along a line parallel with the ground surface and about 20cm above it (e.g. on L19). On two stones (R12 and R21) the pick dressing was done quite deeply in bands to produce a corrugated effect. These are located at two particular structural points: on R12 at the junction between the inner and outer passage, and on R21 at the junction between passage and chamber. Eogan (Eogan and Aboud 1990, fig. 3) has shown that in the cruciform tomb at Knowth 1 the boundary between the inner

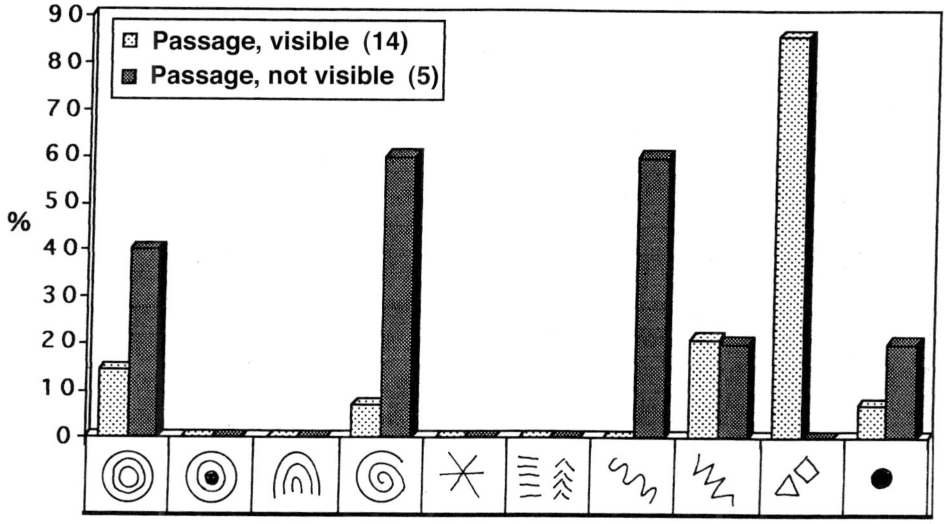

Fig. 2—Relative occurrence of motifs on nineteen surfaces in the passage at Newgrange. Percentages are based on total number of decorated stones in each area.

and outer parts of the passage is also marked by special carvings on the roofslab and by the beginning of rectilinear designs on the orthostats. Most of the corbels in the chambers were also pick-dressed. Whatever the explanation for this form of embellishment, it was obviously very important at Newgrange and it was done on some stones at the smaller tombs nearby (see below).

The chamber

In the chamber, designs can be seen on ten of the seventeen orthostats, on the underside of a large roofslab, and on the leading edges of ten corbels or roofslabs. The chamber plan is irregular, cell 1 (to the left on entering) being only one orthostat deep, while cells 2 and 3 are both two orthostats deep. The right side cell is distinguished not only through its architecture but by a magnificently carved roofslab and two basin stones. Each cell contains spiral designs, and it has been suggested that looking at these may have helped to induce a state of trance, or that they might signify the passage through which the dead could enter the spirit world (Dronfield 1996a, fig. 9). It would, however, be necessary to assume different positions to look at the spirals in each cell—looking into cell 1, out from cell 2 or up to the roof of cell 3.

Cell 1, to the left on entering, is the shallowest cell and this adds to the immediate impact of the spirals on its backstone (C3); the central spiral is comprised of a dizzying 13–14 closely set turns, with arcs above making it seem even larger. Overall, spirals dominate here, with a range of other designs having a somewhat peripheral role. Apart from a small spiral on the edge of C10 (in cell 2), all the spirals on the chamber orthostats turn anticlockwise from the centre outwards.

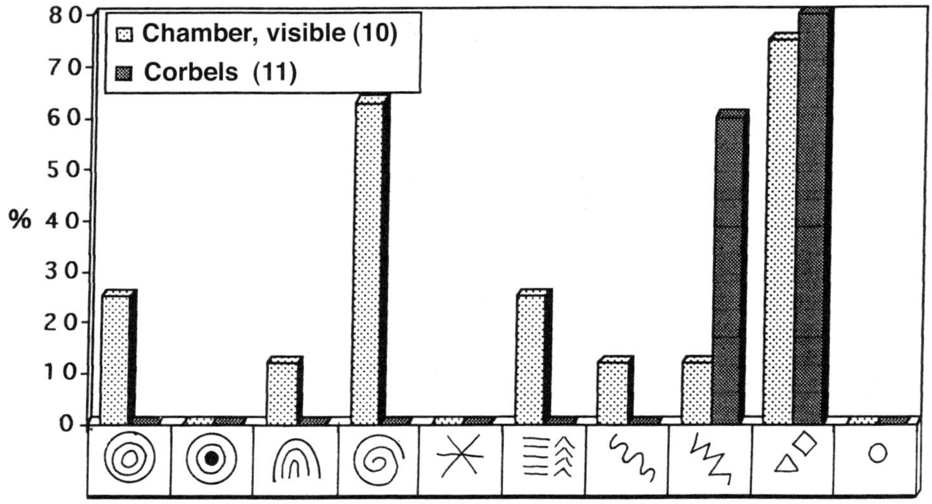

Fig. 3—Relative occurrence of motifs on 21 surfaces in the chamber at Newgrange. Percentages are based on total number of decorated stones in each area.

Cell 2, the end cell, faces the passage. At first glance one gets the impression that it is almost devoid of carvings. However, a small spiral on the edge of the right-hand orthostat (C10) looking inwards signals a special spiral design, which can only be seen by approaching the threshold of the cell. This is the distinctive 'three-spiral figure', composed of three conjoined double spirals. Much of the stone was pick-dressed, but the spiral was left untouched. The spirals can best be seen by looking out from the cell towards the passage, from which point one views the lozenges on the leading edge of RS17 marking the line of the passage. At the midwinter solstice, the three-spiral figure is illuminated by reflection from the beam of light that enters through the roofbox and reaches the end cell. In the nineteenth century this was recorded as having fallen forward and carvings were described on the back of 'some of the neighbouring stones' by Fergusson (1872, 203). Coffey's (1912, fig. 10) illustration of the underside of 'a stone in the walling' shows spirals and a lozenge that are very like those on the reused slabs in the passage (R3, L19, L20).

Cell 3 contains two basin stones, and above them is a very elaborately carved roofstone on which is a wide range of motifs, including spirals, zigzags and lozenges. The designs run beyond the supporting orthostats into the roof structure and so must have been carved before the slab was placed in position. The other orthostats in this cell have virtually no carvings. A panel of lozenges/triangles is carved at the top of the west-facing edge of both C15 and C16. These angular designs at or above eye-level continue round the cell, a feature noted by Eogan, who termed it a frieze (Eogan and Aboud 1990, 135).

Generally, in the chamber the corbels show exclusively angular designs of zigzag or lozenge/triangle panels, while the orthostats have mainly lozenge/triangle, spirals and some circles (Fig. 3).

Passage roof

The conservation project with which the 1962–75 excavations were associated necessitated the dismantling of much of the passage, in the course of which designs were found on six stones in the outer part of the roof. In the roof three styles of art can be identified. All use a wider range of designs than is found in any other part of the monument.

(a) On the outer passage there is a wide variety of picked motifs, which are associated with the grooves that were cut to allow water to run off the top of the roofstones and seem to have been cut at the same time.

(b) On the inner passage, where the roof starts to rise, stones X and Y (C. O'Kelly 1982, fig. 13) have both incised and deeply picked designs, as has a loose stone Z, found nearby; there are also carvings in the passage beneath this point.

(c) A corbel in cell 2 has motifs that are more like the kerbstone hidden art.

The kerbstones

All 97 of the kerbstones that surrounded the cairn have been revealed in recent excavations, except for the lower parts of a section of the western zone (numbers 21 to 47, Fig. 4). Also included here are a number of carvings recorded by staff of National Parks and Monuments Service, Office of Public Works, during conservation work on the north side of the cairn in the 1980s, when K55 through to K80 were set upright. These carvings are on the following kerbstones: 56 (back), 58 (back), 65, 66 (back), 72, 73, 76, 78. In all, carvings have been recorded on the outer face of 33 of the kerbstones and on the back, base or side of nine more.

The kerbstone designs can be divided as follows (Fig. 5).

(a) Visible faces of kerbstones (total 30): these have mainly concentric circles or zigzags. Radials and cupmarks are less common, but the full range of designs is represented.

(b) Hidden surfaces of kerbstones (total 9): despite the small number of stones, the full range of designs is found. K13 and K18 each have a surface area of *c.* 4m^2 completely covered with a wide range of designs. Concentric circles and circles with central dot are common, the latter particularly so in comparison with the overall total of this design in the tomb. Four stones have angular incised designs, which are so well preserved that they cannot have been exposed to weathering agencies for any length of time before being incorporated into the monument. The picked designs are also well preserved.

(c) Plastic-style designs (total 3): three of the kerbstones (K1, K52 and K67) are clearly very special, having designs in plastic style. K1 (Pl. 2) is in front of the tomb entrance and K52 is diametrically opposite it, marking the maximum extent of the cairn 'bulge', which apparently accommodates a pre-tomb turf mound (M.J. O'Kelly 1982, 92). Both of these stones were carved *in situ,* their carving stopping at the old ground level. Their sculptural quality is well captured by O'Sullivan's (1986) term 'plastic style', being adapted to the contour of the stone, particularly on K1 and the right half of K52. The designs are based principally on spirals and lozenges. Depictive ornament appears to underlie the large spirals on K67. The lintel of the roofbox, which features lozenges in relief, may also be regarded as belonging to this group.

Many of the kerbstones were pick-dressed, particularly those in the vicinity of the tomb entrance. Practices at megalithic tombs involved choreography and patterns of procedure.

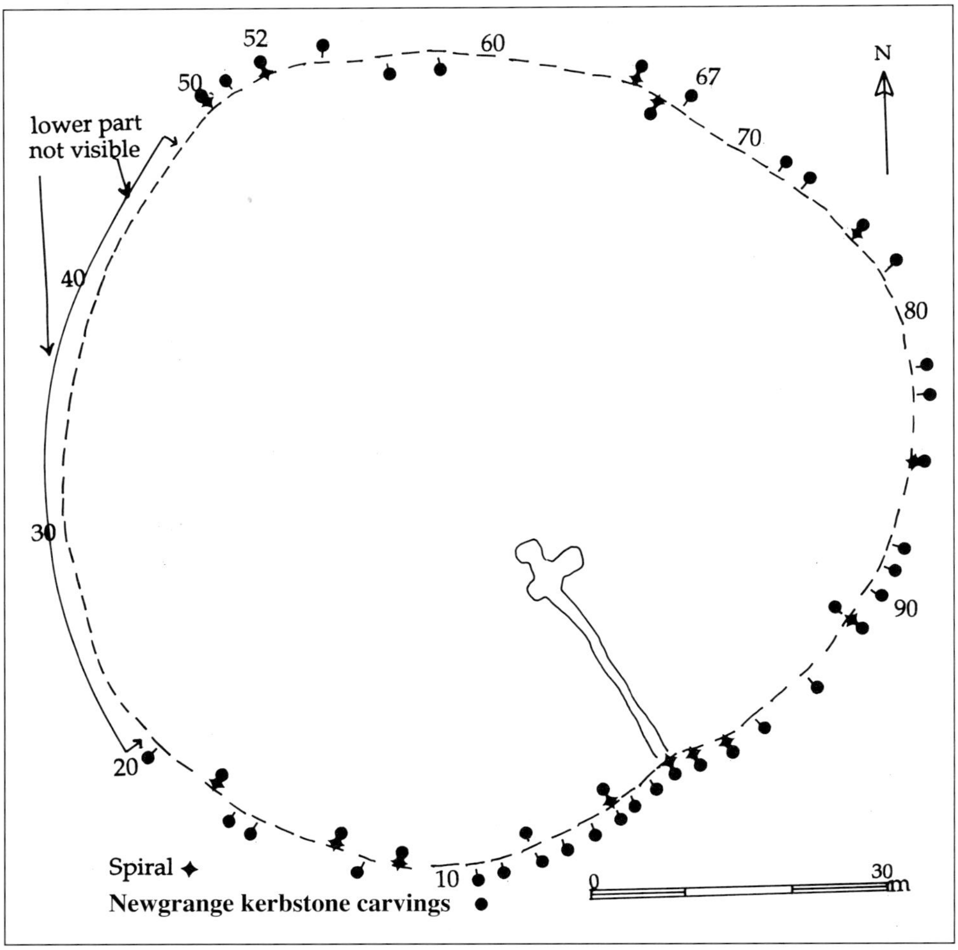

Fig. 4—Location of carvings on the kerbstones at Newgrange (plan after M.J. O'Kelly 1982).

Eogan (1986a) and Thomas (1990) have both envisaged processions around Knowth—Thomas in particular interpreting such processions as having been accessible to large numbers of the population, while entry to the tomb would have been the privilege of certain people in the community only. At Newgrange a circuit of the kerbstones would surely have been punctuated by some ceremony at the highly decorated kerbstones, K1, K52 and K67. Moving clockwise around the site, the imminent appearance of these was marked by the presence of spirals on stones immediately preceding the special kerbstones (Fig. 4). The variety of motifs present, however, does not support the suggestion made by Bradley (1997, 124) that the outer limit of the Boyne Valley monuments was defined by a range of circular motifs and that this was a public art in contrast to the angular art inside the monuments, which could only be seen by special people.

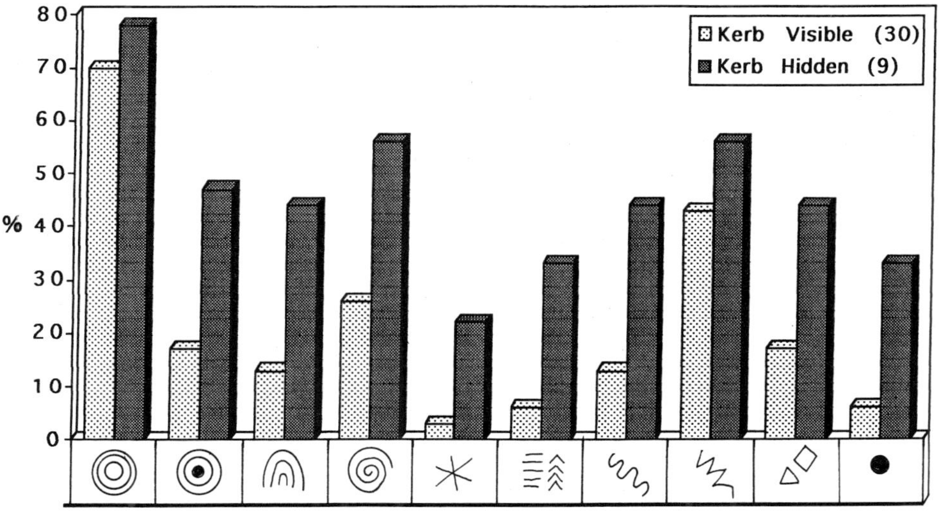

Fig. 5—Relative numbers of depictive-style motifs on 39 surfaces on the kerbstones at Newgrange. Percentages are based on total number of decorated stones in each area.

ADJACENT PASSAGE TOMBS

Site K

Site K was built in two phases. It was initially a 5m-long 'V'-shaped tomb, with a side chamber set to the right (north-east) of the chamber. In Phase II the passage was extended and a mound built over the entire earlier structure. A sillstone divided the passage and a closing stone was placed at the end (O'Kelly *et al.* 1978). I suggest that the enlargement of this monument came with the building of the big tombs at Newgrange and Knowth, and that it reflects practices at both those sites, such as the use of rounded stones in front of the entrance. At first glance the Site K carvings seem undistinguished, with arcs and concentric designs dominating and with designs also on the backs or edges of some orthostats. Closer study shows two stones with later plastic style of carving. One is the inner face of the backstone (No. 5), with concentric circles and arcs picked in broad bands, which Claire O'Kelly (*ibid.*, 321) compared with the Newgrange entrance stone and the basin stone in Site Z. The other plastic-style feature is the use of close pick dressing on the top edge of the sillstone that delimits the chamber (*ibid.*, fig. 33). Thus certain activities at Site K belong to the later stages of passage tomb use in the valley.

Site L

Excavation (O'Kelly *et al.* 1978) revealed that this area had been occupied for some time before the tomb was built. The tomb was cruciform in plan, but much of it was destroyed by the insertion of a lime-kiln. Four of the nine surviving chamber orthostats display carvings. No real patterning of location can be claimed for the carvings in the tomb, but the designs clearly belong to O'Sullivan's (1986) 'depictive' style. Only about twelve of a possible total of 60 kerbstones survived, and one (LB) was found buried on the edge of the mound, adjoining Site K. Face 1 of this stone has circles and natural hollows or cupmarks enclosed with circles, a serpentiform and some dots. Face 2 has a line of cupmarks (partly natural?), solidly picked triangles in a panel, well-executed zigzags, radials and an incised offset motif. I would suggest that Face 2, with its more formal decoration, was the outer one and that its position here signalled the presence of Site K alongside. Its area-picked motifs suggest that it is later than the simpler depictive style on the chamber stones in Site L and that it fits more readily with the extension (Phase II) or alterations (addition of plastic-style art) at Site K.

Site Z

Built just south-east of the main mound at Newgrange, this tomb was 10m long, opened to the south/south-east and was 'V'-shaped in plan. A side cell opened off the right (east) of the passage, just before the sillstone that separated the passage and chamber. The area had been stripped of turves and M.J. O'Kelly interpreted this as having been done in order to provide material for the construction of the main mound, with the tomb being built after the turf had begun to grow again (O'Kelly *et al.* 1978, 294). This reading of the evidence implies that Site Z is later in date than the main mound. Alternatively, these turves could have been used in the construction of the pre-tomb mound (see above). Site Z was severely disturbed and almost all the orthostats had been removed from their sockets and broken up. A decorated basin stone probably came from the centre of the chamber and still contained some cremated bone and two beads. The basin stone carving is pick-dressed and has rubbed out motifs characteristic of the plastic style, while a hollow on the upper surface of the basin recalls the twin hollows on one of the basins in the right side cell of the main tomb at Newgrange. Thus the art style fits with the interpretation of the tomb as being relatively late in the Newgrange tomb group sequence. The only other carving at Site Z was an incised zigzag found on a fragment of stone, presumably broken from an orthostat.

DISCUSSION

This examination of the carvings at Newgrange identifies three main phases of carvings, and these can be correlated with the evidence from Knowth (Table 1), and possibly with that from Dowth.

Newgrange

Earliest phase

This is seen on orthostats in the passage with distinctive spiral/zigzag designs, which appear to be reused from another monument.

Main phase

The main phase has a variety of depictive motifs, both picked and incised, used during the building and in the main phase of carving. Subgroups that can be identified within this phase include:

(a) the carvings associated with the water grooves in the passage roof;
(b) the carvings in the roof where the corbelled vault starts to rise;
(c) spirals in the cells of the chamber, including the elaborate roofstone of cell 3;
(d) the appearance of picked and plain panels in the chamber and passage;
(e) the frieze of angular motifs carved on the face of *in situ* corbels in the chamber;
(f) the marking of the junction between the inner and outer parts of the passage by carvings both within the passage and in the roof above it;
(g) the depictive motifs on kerbstones, on both inner and outer faces; also most of the carvings at Sites K and L.

Phase	Newgrange	Knowth
Mature	Pick dressing of orthostats, plastic style on 3 kerbs + roofbox. Some at sites K, X and ?L.	Close picking. Plastic/ribbon art K1 kerb and chambers. + Site 4.
Main	Depictive, picked + incised, plain and picked panels. + Sites K and L.	Loose picking. Depictive, incl. picked and plain panels.
Early	Spiral/zigzag on inverted passage orthostats.	Spiral/zigzag on inverted passage orthostats, and roof stones. +? Incised motifs

Table 1—Outline of phases suggested for megalithic art at Newgrange and Knowth.

Mature phase

The mature phase is characterised by the following:
(a) pick dressing on a number of stones within the tomb, particularly in the passage;
(b) completion of the whole design with plastic-style carving of K1, K52 and K67, where it overlies depictive motifs, and also on the roofbox lintel; some pick dressing and plastic style at Site K and the basin stone at Site Z.

Knowth

Early phase

At Knowth this consists of incised designs on the inner sections of both the western and eastern tombs in Knowth 1 and in certain smaller tombs, notably Sites 13 and 16, both of which are stratigraphically earlier than the final phase of the Knowth 1 mound. The postulated monument with spiral/zigzag designs, whose stones were incorporated into the outer part of the passages of Knowth 1, must also be early. As noted, the similarly situated and decorated stones at Newgrange must also belong with this group. At Newgrange incised art may be quite early also, occurring on stones incorporated into the construction.

Main phase

The main phase has the depictive style, using a range of motifs and picked and plain panels. This is also found most commonly on the surrounding tombs.

Mature phase

The mature phase consists mainly of the ribbon/plastic style and all-over picking. Stones with these designs are always in the inner section of the passages of Knowth 1, with the exception of the kerbstone in front of each tomb. The occurrence of such carvings on the outer face of both orthostats marking the start of the inner section of the passage of Knowth 1 east shows that the ribbon design style must have been developed before the construction of the outer part of the passage at Knowth 1 east. Ribbon/plastic style is found on only a few of the stones in the surrounding tombs, such as Stone A from Site 4, a sillstone which also has incised designs overlain by depictive (Eogan 1986b, fig. 62).

Dowth

The tomb at Dowth is much more difficult to understand, because we know very little about its sequence of construction. For the most part the art is depictive, with some incised designs (O'Kelly and O'Kelly 1983). Picked and plain panels are almost absent, except for orthostat C6 in the southern tomb, which is very different from the rest and has much in common with some of the main phase art at Knowth. Pick dressing in the same chamber belongs as usual to the mature phase.

CONCLUSION

In conclusion, I suggest that the approach adopted here, bringing together aspects of both content and context of the art, can lead us further towards understanding the way it was used at these sites. We see that the motifs were not randomly placed but form an integral part of the tomb design at various stages of construction and that a variety of internal styles can be related to the sequence of construction. This is now possible because of the amount of excavation carried out at Newgrange and Knowth, and understanding the sequence at these sites allows us to extrapolate tentatively for other sites in the area.

To return to Virginia Woolf, with whose reflections on biography I began this paper, I suggest that part of the agenda of Irish archaeologists in the new millennium should be a concern with 'detecting falsity, unreality, and the presence of obsolete conventions'.[1]

ACKNOWLEDGEMENTS

I would like to thank Ann Lynch of *Dúchas* The Heritage Service for allowing me to examine drawings of kerbstone carvings revealed during conservation work at Newgrange. Thanks also to George Eogan for permission to refer to a forthcoming paper and for useful discussion of the Knowth art.

A particular poignancy in presenting this paper in honour of Liz Anderson derives from the fact that she had produced the graphs for an earlier version.

REFERENCES

Bradley, R. 1989 Deaths and entrances: a contextual analysis of megalithic art. *Current Anthropology* **30**, 68–75.

Bradley, R. 1997 *Rock art and the prehistory of Atlantic Europe: signing the land.* London and New York. Routledge.

Brennan, M. 1983 *The stars and the stones.* London. Thames and Hudson.

Cartailhac, E. 1889 *La France préhistorique d'après des sépultures et les monuments.* Paris. Alcan.

Coffey, G. 1912 *Newgrange (Brugh na Bóinne) and other incised tumuli in Ireland: the influence of Crete and the Aegean in the extreme west of Europe in early times.* Dublin. Hodges Figgis.

Déchelette, J. 1908 *Manuel d'archéologie préhistorique*, Vol. I. Paris. Picard.

Déchelette, J. 1912 Une nouvelle interprétation des gravures de New-Grange et de Gavr'inis. *L'Anthropologie* **23**, 29–52.

Dronfield, J. 1995a Subjective vision and the source of Irish megalithic art. *Antiquity* **69**, 539–49.

Dronfield, J. 1995b Migraine, light and hallucinogens: the neurocognitive basis of Irish megalithic art. *Oxford Journal of Archaeology* **14**, 261–75.

Dronfield, J. 1996a Cognition, art and architecture in Irish passage tombs. *Cambridge Journal of Archaeology* **6**, 37–55 and Comments.

Dronfield, J. 1996b The vision thing: diagnosis of endogenous derivation in 'abstract' arts. *Current Anthropology* **37**, 373–93.

Eogan, G. 1986a *Knowth and the passage tombs of Ireland.* London. Thames and Hudson.

Eogan, G. 1986b *Excavations at Knowth, vol. 1: smaller passage tombs, Neolithic occupation and Beaker activity.* Dublin. Royal Irish Academy.

Eogan, G. 1997 Overlays and underlays: aspects of megalithic art succession at Brugh na Bóinne, Ireland. *Brigantium* **10**, III Coloquio Internacional de Arte Megalítico, 217–34.

Eogan, G. 1998 Knowth before Knowth. *Antiquity* **72**, 162–72.

Eogan, G. and Aboud, J. 1990 Diffuse picking in megalithic art. *Revue Archéologique de l'Ouest. Supplément no. 2*, 121–40.

Fergusson, J. 1872 *Rude stone monuments in all countries.* London. Murray.

Fleming, A. 1969 The myth of the Mother Goddess. *World Archaeology* **1**, 247–61.

Gimbutas, M. 1989 *The language of the goddess.* London. Thames and Hudson.

Hodder, I. 1990 *The domestication of Europe.* Oxford. Blackwell.

Hutton, R. 1997 The Neolithic great goddess. *Antiquity* **71**, 91–9.

Kinnes, I. 1995 An innovation backed by great prestige: the instance of the spiral and twenty centuries of stony sleep. In I. Kinnes and G. Varndell (eds), *Unbaked urns of rudely shape,* 49–53. Oxford. Oxbow.

Lewis-Williams, J.D. and Dowson, T.A. 1988 The signs of all times: entoptic phenomena in Upper Palaeolithic art. *Current Anthropology* **29**, 201–45.

Lewis-Williams, J.D. and Dowson, T.A. 1993 On vision and power in the Neolithic: evidence from the decorated monuments. *Current Anthropology* **34**, 55–65.

Macalister, R.A.S. 1921 *Ireland in pre-Celtic times.* Dublin. Maunsel and Roberts.

O'Kelly, C. 1982 Corpus of Newgrange art. In M.J. O'Kelly, *Newgrange: archaeology, art and legend,* 146–85. London. Thames and Hudson.

O'Kelly, M.J. 1982 *Newgrange: archaeology, art and legend.* London. Thames and Hudson.

O'Kelly, M.J. and O'Kelly, C. 1983 The tumulus of Dowth, Co. Meath. *Proceedings of the Royal Irish Academy* **83**C, 135–90.

O'Kelly, M.J., Lynch, F. and O'Kelly, C. 1978 Three passage-graves at Newgrange, Co. Meath. *Proceedings of the Royal Irish Academy* **78**C, 249–352.

O'Sullivan, M. 1986 Approaches to passage tomb art. *Journal of the Royal Society of Antiquaries of Ireland* **116**, 68–83.

O'Sullivan, M. 1997 Megalithic art in Ireland and Brittany: divergence or convergence. In J. L'Helgouac'h *et al.* (eds), *Art et symboles du mégalithisme Européen. Actes du 2e Colloquium International sur l'art mégalithique, Nantes, juin 1995. Revue Archaéologique de l'Ouest. Supplément no. 8,* 81–96. Nantes.

Renfrew, C. 1967 Colonialism and megalithismus. *Antiquity* **41**, 276–88.

Shee Twohig, E. 1997 Context and content of Irish passage tomb art. In J. L'Helgouac'h *et al.* (eds), *Art et symboles du mégalithisme Européen. Actes du 2e Colloquium International sur l'art mégalithique, Nantes, juin 1995. Revue Archaéologique de l'Ouest. Supplément no. 8,* 67–80. Nantes.

Shee Twohig, E. 1998 A 'Mother Goddess' in north-west Europe *c.* 4200–2500 BC? In L. Goodison and C. Morris (eds), *Ancient goddesses: the myths and the evidence,* 164–79. London. British Museum Press.

Thomas, J. 1990 Monuments from the inside: the case of the Irish megalithic tombs. *World Archaeology* **22**, 168–78.

Thomas, J. and Tilley, C. 1993 The axe and the torso: symbolic structures in the Neolithic of Brittany. In C. Tilley (ed.), *Interpretative archaeology,* 225–324. Providence and Oxford. Berg.

Ucko, P.J. 1968 *Anthropomorphic figurines of Predynastic Egypt and Neolithic Crete.* London. Andrew Szmidla.

Endnote

1 Woolf was describing the role of the biographer, who has to be a pioneer going 'ahead of the rest of us, like the miner's canary, testing the atmosphere, detecting falsity, unreality and the presence of obsolete conventions'. From V. Woolf, 'The art of biography', in *Collected Essays* IV, edited by L. Woolf, p. 226, quoted in H. Lee, *Virginia Woolf* (London, 1996), 11.

HUNTING, FISHING AND FOWLING IN LATE PREHISTORIC IRELAND: THE SCARCITY OF THE BONE RECORD

Margaret McCarthy

INTRODUCTION

Although Liz earned her professional recognition as a lithics analyst, she was keenly interested in the role of wild fauna, particularly marine resources, in prehistoric diet. While she admitted to not having the patience to identify small fragments of bone, she was always eager to see the results, and contributed invaluable information on the behaviour and habitat preferences of the species present. (This interest in archaeofauna rarely extended to domesticated animals, and her only real interest in cattle and sheep was when their remains occurred in an early context!) One of Liz's main research ambitions was to locate a Late Mesolithic site in the Blackwater Valley with preservation conditions that would lead to the survival of the full range of organic material. I offer this paper to Liz, in memory of a good friend and an enthusiastic and dedicated colleague.

With the introduction of agriculture in the Neolithic period and the adoption of a settled way of life, it is generally accepted that the range of communities relying upon hunting, fishing and fowling decreased in number. This paper reviews the archaeozoological evidence for the exploitation of non-domestic faunal resources during the late prehistoric period. It details the major wild faunal groups and the significance of their exploitation. The main purpose of the paper is to evaluate the scarcity of non-domestic fauna at excavated sites and to show that many factors conspire to make a sound interpretation of the contribution of wild resources to the diet difficult to achieve. The paper concludes by discussing the limitations of the current faunal database and outlines some priorities for future research.

One of the main obstacles to the reconstruction of past diet is acquiring reliable information on what human populations actually ate. This is not always accurately reflected by the faunal remains recovered from archaeological excavations. Over the last 60 years almost 30 occupation sites dating from the Bronze and Iron Ages have been investigated, but despite all this effort the archaeozoological database remains unsatisfactory. The excavated assemblages differ considerably in terms of the number of surviving bones. Any interpretation of the data should be undertaken mindful of the fact that many of the collections have derived from early excavations, which were often subject to a limited research design at best. Some assemblages, such as those from Clonfinlough, Co. Offaly (Moloney *et al.* 1993), and Curraghatoor, Co. Tipperary (Doody 1997), are too small to represent any more than a partial species list. Others, such as Ballinderry 2, Co. Westmeath (Hencken 1942), and the earlier assemblages from Lough Gur, Co. Limerick (Ó Ríordáin 1949), are very large, but lack the detail of archaeological context that would allow them to be used with confidence. There is now, however, a growing number of relatively large, well-stratified collections, including those from Chancellorsland, Co. Tipperary (Doody 1995), Lough Gur (Cleary 1995), Ross Island, Co. Kerry (O'Brien 1995), Dún Aonghasa, Co. Galway (Cotter 1996), and Mooghaun, Co. Clare (Grogan 1996). Since much of the bone material from these sites is still being analysed, this paper should be seen as a working statement which has been written mindful of the fact that results from these analyses may expand and perhaps modify many of the observations made here.

Another major problem in the investigation of late prehistoric animal-based diet is the fact that the vast majority of the bone collections belong to the middle and later phases of the Bronze Age, with few samples from before or after those periods. The assemblage from Newgrange, Co. Meath (van Wijngaarden-Bakker 1974), is currently the only published report on Early Bronze Age fauna. Likewise, the only Iron Age sites to have produced viable samples of animal bones are the royal centres at Dún Ailinne, Co. Kildare (Crabtree 1985), and Navan, Co. Armagh (Mallory 1995).

Archaeological investigation into settlement patterns for this period indicates that many factors influenced communities in their choice of where to live. For farming groups, such as the inhabitants of Haughey's Fort, Co. Armagh (Mallory 1995), or Chancellorsland and Ballyveelish, Co. Tipperary (Doody 1997), land quality must have been a primary concern. Coastal settlement sites are also represented in the archaeological record. Examples have been excavated at Carrigillihy, Co. Cork (O'Kelly 1951), Aughinish Island in the Shannon Estuary (Kelly 1974) and Dún Aonghasa (Cotter 1996), while recent discoveries in the vicinity of False Bay, Co. Galway (McCormick 1995), include shell middens, hut sites and enclosures, with the earliest midden dated to 2022–1894 BC. Further evidence for the exploitation of coastal resources in the late prehistoric period is indicated by shell middens excavated in Culleenamore, Co. Sligo (Burenhult 1980), Beginish Island, Co. Kerry (O'Sullivan and Sheehan 1996), and Poul Gorm, Co. Cork (A. McCarthy, unpublished). The geographical positioning of a number of lacustrine and estuarine sites, such as Cullyhanna Lough, Co. Armagh (Hodges 1958), Knocknalappa, Co. Clare (Raftery 1942), and Carrigdirty Rock, Co. Limerick (O'Sullivan 1995; 1996), is ideal for the exploitation of migratory fish and various species of wild fowl. O'Sullivan's (1998) study of wetland settlement in Ireland, as well as recent work by the Discovery Programme on the intertidal zones in the Shannon and Fergus estuaries (O'Sullivan and Condit 1995), have provided important new information on the subject of late prehistoric adaptation to marshland and estuarine environments.

In examining the evidence for non-domestic resources in late prehistoric diet, it is necessary to look first at the proportions of the various faunal groups represented by the numbers of bones found on the different sites (Table 1). The data show that over 86% of the bones collected from late prehistoric sites are derived from domesticated animals. The evidence for hunting and fowling activities is scarce and, with the exception of Dún Aonghasa, is almost non-existent for fishing. Bird bones make up a small proportion of the otherwise large assemblage from Newgrange, while the only site other than Dún Aonghasa to produce evidence for fishing is Chancellorsland (McCarthy, forthcoming a). It would seem, therefore, that the demand for meat in the late prehistoric period was almost entirely satisfied by farming. Hunting and collecting wild food resources were apparently minority activities.

Site	Domestic mammals	Wild mammals	Wild bird	Fish
Newgrange	12064	133	7	—
Ballyveelish	820	10	—	—
Chancellorsland	11342	20	120	1
Curraghatoor	264	—	—	—
Lough Gur	1165	3	23	1
Clonfinlough	169	—	—	—
Haughey's Fort	1075	8	—	—
Dún Aonghasa	7688	14	1093	>5000
Navan Fort B	2610	51	—	—
Dún Ailinne	4431	—	—	—

Table 1—Frequency of wild/domestic species.

THE EVIDENCE FOR HUNTING

There is, as yet, no evidence for intensive and specialised hunting of wild mammals during the late prehistoric period in Ireland. Table 2 lists the range of animals that would have been available for exploitation at this time. The flesh of some of these animals is considered palatable and could have supplemented the domestic-based meat supply. Red deer has been recorded on most of the sites listed in Table 1, but not in quantities that would suggest its intensive exploitation. The individual records for deer remains from the various sites are more widely spread than those of other wild mammals and this, presumably, is because of the exploitation of their antlers as a source of raw material for bone-working, as was noted at Navan Fort (McCormick 1994, 184). The debate about the status of red deer in Irish prehistory is well known, with current evidence indicating that the species existed in very small numbers throughout the period (Woodman *et al.* 1997). Deer remains have not been convincingly recorded in any Mesolithic faunal assemblage, and post-cranial elements from the Bronze Age, Iron Age and subsequent periods are also extremely scarce.

The only other large, wild land mammals that may have been considered edible and which were still present during the Bronze Age were wild boar and bear. It is often difficult to distinguish the remains of wild boar from those of domestic pigs, and the possibility of cross-breeding must always be considered. For this reason the extent of the contribution of wild boar to late prehistoric diet cannot yet be fully determined. Individual finds of brown bear have been recovered from just two locations: Sites C and K, Lough Gur (van Wijngaarden-Bakker 1974, 370–5), and there is a debatable occurrence in an Early Bronze Age context at Newgrange (van Wijngaarden-Bakker 1986, 91; McCormick 1999, 359). It can be assumed that this species was either only present in very small numbers during the late prehistoric period or that it was simply not exploited as a food resource.

Common name	Proper name
Red deer	*Cervus elaphus*
Brown bear	*Ursus arctos*
Wild pig	*Sus scrofa*
Wolf	*Canis lupus*
Fox	*Vulpes vulpes*
Badger	*Meles meles*
Pine marten	*Martes martes*
Otter	*Lutra lutra*
Stoat	*Mustela mustela*
Wild cat	*Felis sylvestris*
Irish hare	*Lepus timidus hibernicus*
Red squirrel	*Sciurius vulgaris*
Woodmouse	*Apodemus sylvaticus*
Pygmy shrew	*Sorex minutus*

Table 2—List of wild mammal species present during the late prehistoric period.

During winter months the trapping of small furred animals would have provided soft and warm materials for clothing, but the archaeological evidence for these species in late prehistoric contexts is extremely scarce. Some wild animals, such as badgers, otters, hares, pine martens and foxes, have occasionally been found at different sites while others, such as red squirrel and stoat, have yet to be documented. A ninth-century Irish law-tract (Kelly 1997) lists badgers, as well as deer and wild pigs, among the three game animals. It is also known that badgers were hunted for food in the early medieval period as written sources contain a reference to salted badger meat (McCormick 1999). Two late prehistoric sites have produced badger bones: the wedge tomb at Lough Gur (Ó Ríordáin and Ó hIceadha 1955) and Ballinderry 2 (Stelfox 1942). The remains from both sites, however, seem to have derived from contaminated contexts (McCormick 1999). Otter bones have been recovered from both Ballinderry 2 (*ibid.*) and False Bay, Co. Galway (McCormick 1995). Pine martens are not recorded from any late prehistoric site, but their presence during this period is attested by radiocarbon dates from Foley Cave, Co. Cork, and Kilgreany Cave, Co. Waterford (Woodman *et al.* 1997).

While it is highly unlikely that rodents would have been consumed, the recovery of pygmy shrew and woodmouse from Ballycarty, Co. Kerry (McCarthy 1999a, 78–9), and Chancellorsland (McCarthy, forthcoming a) represents the earliest occurrence of these species on Irish archaeological sites. The question that needs to be posed, then, is whether small species of wild mammal were of only minor economic importance or whether the scarcity of their remains is the result of biased samples. Amongst the factors that could be responsible for an under-representation of such fauna in the assemblages are inadequate sample sizes, poor retrieval strategies and a bias in the type of site excavated. The operation of an extensive on-site sieving programme at Chancellorsland, however, demonstrated that sieving had only a minor influence on the overall proportion of small mammals recovered in the assemblage. It should be emphasised that the occurrence of hare, wild cat and woodmouse at this site, albeit in small quantities, would not have been documented without the on-site bulk sieving.

It is also important to be aware that hunting expeditions organised specifically to capture animals for their pelts may leave little or no trace in the archaeological record. The flesh of otters, pine martens, wild cats and foxes is considered unpalatable and consequently the carcasses of these animals may have been left at the kill site following the removal of their skins. In terms of the large wild mammals, their low occurrence or virtual absence at many of the sites has to be interpreted as representing a gradual decline in the practice of hunting. This, in turn, may be linked with forest depletion and, perhaps, increased farming efficiency.

THE ROLE OF FISHING

The extent to which marine resources contributed to the overall food quest in the late prehistoric period is not yet fully understood. There is plentiful evidence to indicate that Mesolithic populations subsisted almost exclusively on aquatic resources (van Wijngaarden-Bakker 1989; McCarthy 1999b), and the Irish law-tracts emphasise the importance of fish in the early medieval diet (Kelly 1997). It is generally accepted that the onset of the Neolithic saw a decline in the overall importance of fish in the meat diet. Studies on fish remains from late prehistoric Irish sites are almost non-existent, as most of the faunal assemblages come from inland settlements where only freshwater species could be expected to occur (Wheeler 1969). Many of the estuarine and inland wetland sites are thought to have functioned as the temporary camps of sedentary farming groups exploiting summer grasslands (O'Sullivan 1995, 10–11; O'Sullivan and Condit 1995, 8). Despite the current lack of evidence, it seems inconceivable that the occupants of these sites did not take advantage of the migratory runs of fish. The two main species present in Irish rivers and lakes at this time were salmon, *Salmo salar,* and eel, *Anguilla anguilla,* both of which are migratory fish that enter and leave rivers at different times of the year. A number of other fish taxa could also have been caught in estuarine waters, including shad, *Alosa alosa,* trout, *Salmo trutta,* and smelt, *Osmerus eperlanus.* Although herring, *Clupea harengus,* and flounder, *Platichthys flesus,* are essentially marine fish, they shoal in estuarine waters during the summer months when many of the adjoining sites are thought to have been occupied.

The inhabitants of coastal settlement sites, such as Carrigillihy, Co. Cork (O'Kelly 1951), Meadowlands, Co. Down (Pollock and Waterman 1964), and Carrigdirty Rock, Co. Limerick (O'Sullivan 1998), would have had access to a variety of marine fish species, shell fish and seaweed. Remains of marine molluscs have been recovered from Bronze Age and Iron Age midden sites at Culleenamore, Co. Sligo (Burenhult 1980), False Bay, Co. Galway (McCormick 1995), and Beginish Island, Co. Kerry (O'Sullivan and Sheehan 1996). The contents of two shell-filled pits at Aughinish Island (Kelly 1974) indicate that Bronze Age communities living in the Shannon Estuary also exploited local aquatic resources. Sea mammals must also have been an important resource, not only in terms of food and skin but also for blubber and oil. Seals were, it seems, occasionally caught by the occupants of Dún Aonghasa (McCormick 1994).

Most of the excavated coastal sites, however, have failed to produce evidence for fishing. In the case of Carrigillihy, though, it is doubtful whether fish bones would have survived in the acidic soil conditions which prevailed. One important development in recent years has been the recovery through sieving of well over 5000 fish bones from Dún Aonghasa (McCarthy, forthcoming b). The sheer quantities involved clearly demonstrate the bias that must occur in fish data from non-sieved sites. The identification of this material is currently being undertaken by the writer, and the most obvious result to date is the dominance of wrasses, specifically ballan wrasse, *Labrus bergylta*, in the samples. Conger eel, *Conger conger*, scad, *Trachurus trachurus*, cod, *Gadus morhua*, and ling, *Molva molva*, are also present in the assemblage though in smaller quantities. It is likely that as work proceeds on this material the range and size of fish species exploited by the occupants of Dún Aonghasa will increase. The preliminary results are presented here in order to demonstrate the continued significance throughout later prehistory of aquatic resources for groups living in coastal locations.

Various taphonomic agents, both cultural and natural, can influence the quantity and kinds of fish remains found on archaeological sites. These factors can, in turn, affect our ability to establish the true role of fish in ancient diet. Post-depositional processes, such as trampling and scavenging, usually result in the total destruction of fish bones or render them unidentifiable. Some coastal sites, in particular, tend to have fish remains added to them by large seabirds depositing the remains of their own meals. Fish filleted at sea, with just the meat being brought back to the settlement, will only yield a few spines and ribs to the archaeozoologist, although it has to be said that this method of processing is unlikely to have occurred in the prehistoric period. The remains of fish are often rare on archaeological sites because their bones are more vulnerable to the effects of differential preservation than the more substantial bones of mammals (Wheeler and Jones 1989). Fish bones rarely survive in acidic soil and this may be one of the explanations for the absence of fishes from most of the excavated estuarine and lakeshore settlement sites in Ireland. In addition, the small size of fish bones results in failure to recover them unless specialised recovery techniques are employed. It is, however, important to be aware that fish do have hard parts such as scales, teeth and otoliths that might survive and be recovered by intensive sieving methods. These elements were found in large quantities at Ferriter's Cove (McCarthy 1999b), where the sandy soil conditions were conducive, in particular, to the survival of otoliths. It is important to emphasise, however, that these elements will rarely be retrieved unless a programme of intensive sieving is initiated on the site.

Quantifying the contribution of members of the shark family to the diet poses a special problem, since their skeletons do not contain bone and mineralised cartilage does not preserve well. Some soil chemical conditions, such as those experienced at Ferriter's Cove, will favour the survival of the denser vertebrae of sharks. It is also important to point out that coastal areas potentially provide a variety of edible seaweed and other marine resources, such as squids and octopuses, whose remains are highly unlikely to survive.

The absence of fish bones is not always simply related to preservation and recovery. At the recent excavations at Chancellorsland (Doody 1995) and Lough Gur (Cleary 1995), despite extensive fine-mesh sieving, few fish bones were preserved. A single salmonid bone was recovered from the sorted residues at both sites. It is not surprising that fish constitute only a tiny fraction of the assemblages from Chancellorsland, as the nearest fish-producing river is five miles from the site. Lough Gur itself, being a solution feature, could never have received migratory runs of fish. It is telling, however, that these sites have produced more fish bone than the entire group of excavated wetland settlements in Ireland.

THE ROLE OF FOWLING

The practice of identifying, analysing and interpreting bird remains from late prehistoric sites has been much neglected compared with that developed for the domestic ungulates, yet many of the recorded lake-edge camps could have been primarily established to take advantage of migrating waterfowl in spring and autumn. Finds of birds can reflect hunting specialisation, and the presence of migratory species is often used as an indicator of seasonality. Some bird species are available all year round but the most likely season for large-scale exploitation would have been the winter, when major concentrations of wildfowl would have been available. Fewer than ten late prehistoric sites have yielded evidence for the exploitation of birds, and at most of these the total number of remains is less than one hundred. The indications are that wild birds were only occasionally caught and, like wild mammals, were not a significant component of the diet except in so far as they contributed to its variety. The recovery of a small quantity of wildfowl from Knockadoon, Lough Gur, has recently been published by van Wijngaarden-Bakker (1995, 86–8), and the assemblage represents a wide range of species favouring marshland and wooded environments. The species present include white-fronted goose, *Anser albifrons,* teal, *Anas crecca,* the now extinct crane, *Grus grus,* and great crested grebe, *Podiceps cristatus.* By far the largest collection of late Bronze Age bird bones is from Dún Aonghasa, where on-site retrieval methods ensured the recovery of over 1000 specimens (O'Sullivan, forthcoming). Ten different species were identified and seabirds, not surprisingly, made up the greatest part of the assemblage. The guillemot, *Uria aalgae,* was the most commonly represented bird, with lower incidences of razorbill, *Alca torda,* puffin, *Fratercula arctica,* shag, *Phalacrocorax aristotelis,* cormorant, *Phalacrocorax carbo,* kittiwake, *Rissa tridactyla,* and herring gull, *Larus argentatus.* McCormick (1994, 181–3) has interpreted the faunal assemblage from this site as the product of environmental determinism, where poor agricultural land and the lack of tree cover led to an emphasis on the rearing of sheep. The most important natural resources on the Aran Islands during the Bronze Age would have been fish and seabirds and, in an environment that must have presented numerous challenges for agriculturists, wild food resources would have supplemented nutritional requirements.

Despite an intensive programme of sieving at Chancellorsland the meat component of the diet remains dominated by beef, with apparently little use of wildfowl to provide variety (McCarthy, forthcoming a). Wild birds were probably only exploited as an occasional addition to the diet and, together with wild mammals, are best interpreted as an additional source of food rather than as a main one. The local environmental picture presented by the identification of the small sample of bird remains is a mixture of marshland and wooded country. The edible species include white-fronted goose and crane, both of which were also present at Site C at Lough Gur (van Wijngaarden-Bakker 1995). The recovery of crane bones from a number of early cave sites and lakeshore settlements has provided ample proof of the former existence of this species in Ireland. The white-fronted goose is a winter visitor, indicating perhaps that wildfowling was a seasonal pursuit engaged in when a lull in agricultural activity allowed time for hunting. The presence of crane, white-fronted goose and water rail, *Rallus aquaticus,* all birds that favour wet conditions, indicates that during the Bronze Age marshy areas existed in the vicinity of the settlement.

DISCUSSION AND CONCLUSIONS

One of the most important issues in archaeozoological analysis, and presently the single most insurmountable barrier to effective interpretation of the remains, is the scale of the biases introduced by taphonomic and retrieval processes. The constraints of partial excavation, differential preservation and recovery efficiency will result in highly selective assemblages (McCarthy 1998, 61). As stated at the beginning of this paper, many of the late prehistoric assemblages derive from early excavations, which were often subject to only limited research designs. The importance of adequate sampling and sieving for a proper understanding of the role of fish cannot be overstated, and the recent results from Dún Aonghasa confirm this. The implementation of sieving techniques will also inform those bone specialists who previously may have been content to receive samples for analysis without question. It should be acknowledged that in recent years the use of improved sampling strategies in Ireland has led to more representative and varied assemblages. There is still a need, however, for joint participation between bone analysts and archaeologists so that specialists can advise on the retrieval, welfare and correct storage of faunal material prior to the commencement of archaeological projects. The achievement of a more multidisciplinary approach in reconstructing past diet is also essential, and faunal analysts should incorporate the information obtained from plant remains and human bones in their analyses. Significant work has been undertaken elsewhere on the chemical analyses of archaeological human remains (Price and Kavanagh 1982; Subirà and Malgosa 1992). Carbon isotope analysis of a number of early prehistoric human bones was undertaken as part of the Irish Quaternary Fauna Project (Woodman *et al.* 1997), but further examination of large samples of Irish material would undoubtedly prove very useful for future analysis of prehistoric diet.

Bronze Age and Iron Age groups were essentially sedentary pastoralists, but given the lack of an extensive database we should not close our minds to alternative ways of viewing issues relating to late prehistoric diet. It can be argued, for instance, that for many of the Irish sites depositional and preservation factors have to some extent biased the bone record in favour of larger mammals. The question of whether the inhabitants of settlements located in riverine and coastal environments may have continued to exploit non-domestic resources has yet to be resolved. Increased interest has been shown in the remains of birds and fish in recent times and some interesting results are beginning to emerge that will eventually lead to a better appreciation of the role of non-domestic resources in late prehistoric diet. The excavated bone assemblages are still somewhat limited—obvious gaps remain to be filled. With the exception of Dún Aonghasa, where the evidence interestingly suggests a continued emphasis upon collected and hunted resources to supplement land-based farming, there is a lack of substantial bone samples from coastal sites. The examination of the fish bones from Dún Aonghasa will offer a unique insight into late prehistoric fishing activities.

The search for larger bodies of archaeozoological data from coastal, estuarine and lacustrine sites, where wild faunal resources are found in great abundance, should become a priority. Improved recovery methods will hopefully provide more information and, while there will never be complete agreement on what constitutes an adequate sample, the present database for our late prehistoric sites requires close scrutiny. Further excavation in geographically diverse locations, combined with adequate on-site retrieval, should provide a more complete picture of the subsistence customs of late prehistoric Irish society.

ACKNOWLEDGEMENTS

I am grateful to Clare Cotter and Martin Doody for permission to refer to unpublished data from Dún Aonghasa and Chancellorsland respectively. Many thanks are also due to Mick Monk, John Sheehan and Gina Johnson, who read and made helpful comments on the finished text.

REFERENCES

Burenhult, G. 1980 *The Carrowmore excavations: excavation season 1980.* Stockholm Archaeological Reports 7. Stockholm.

Cleary, R.M. 1995 Later Bronze Age settlement and prehistoric burials, Lough Gur, Co. Limerick. *Proceedings of the Royal Irish Academy* **95**C, 109–18.

Cotter, C. 1996 Western Stone Forts Project. *Discovery Programme Reports* **4,** 1–14. Dublin. Royal Irish Academy.

Crabtree, P. 1985 The mammalian fauna from Dún Ailinne, Co. Kildare, Ireland. *MASCA Journal* **3** (6), 179–81.

Doody, M. 1995 The Ballyhoura Hills Project. *Discovery Programme Reports* **2**, 12–44. Dublin. Royal Irish Academy.

Doody, M. 1997 Bronze Age settlements in Co. Tipperary: fifteen years of research. *Tipperary Historical Journal* (1997), 94–106.

Grogan, E. 1996 Excavations at Mooghaun South, 1994. Interim report. *Discovery Programme Reports* **4,** 47–57. Dublin. Royal Irish Academy.

Hencken, H. 1942 Ballinderry crannog no. 2. *Proceedings of the Royal Irish Academy* **47**C, 1–76.

Hodges, H.W.M. 1958 A hunting camp at Cullyhanna Lough near Newtown Hamilton, Co. Armagh. *Ulster Journal of Archaeology* **21**, 7–13.

Kelly, E.P. 1975 Aughinish Island, sites 1 and 2. In T. G. Delaney (ed.), *Excavations 1974. Summary accounts of archaeological work in Ireland*, 20–1. Belfast. Association of Young Irish Archaeologists.

Kelly, F. 1997 *Early Irish farming*. Dublin. Institute of Advanced Studies.

McCarthy, M. 1998 Archaeozoological studies and early medieval Munster. In M.A. Monk and J. Sheehan (eds), *Early medieval Munster: archaeology, history and society*, 60–4. Cork University Press.

McCarthy, M. 1999a Appendix 3: The animal bones. In M. Connolly, *Discovering the Neolithic in County Kerry: a passage tomb at Ballycarty*, 77–83. Bray. Wordwell.

McCarthy, M. 1999b Faunal remains. In P.C. Woodman, E. Anderson and N. Finlay, *Excavations at Ferriter's Cove 1983–95: last foragers, first farmers in the Dingle Peninsula*, 85–92. Bray. Wordwell.

McCarthy, M. (forthcoming a) Faunal material from Chancellorsland, Co. Tipperary.

McCarthy, M. (forthcoming b) The fish bones from Dún Aonghasa, Co. Galway.

McCormick, F. 1994 Faunal remains from Navan and other late prehistoric sites in Ireland. In J.P. Mallory and G. Stockman (eds), *Ulidia. Proceedings of the first international conference on the Ulster Cycle of Tales, Belfast and Emain Macha 8–12 April 1994*, 181–6. Belfast. December Publications.

McCormick, F. 1995 False Bay, Co. Galway, in the Bronze Age. *Archaeology Ireland* **31**, 12–13.

McCormick, F. 1999 Early evidence for wild animals in Ireland. In N. Benecke (ed.), *The Holocene history of the European vertebrate fauna: modern aspects of research. Workshop, 6th to 9th April 1998*, 355–71. Berlin. Verlag Marie Leidorf GmbH.Rahden/Westf.

Mallory, J.P. 1995 Haughey's Fort and the Navan complex in the Late Bronze Age. In J. Waddell and E. Shee Twohig (eds), *Ireland in the Bronze Age*, 73–86. Dublin. Stationery Office.

Moloney, A., Jennings, D.M. and MacDermott, C. 1993 *Excavations at Clonfinlough, Co. Offaly*. Irish Archaeological Wetland Unit Transactions 2. Dublin. Crannóg.

O'Brien, W. 1995 Ross Island and the origins of Irish–British metallurgy. In J. Waddell and E. Shee Twohig (eds), *Ireland in the Bronze Age*, 38–48. Dublin. Stationery Office.

O'Kelly, M.J. 1951 An Early Bronze Age ringfort at Carrigillihy, Co. Cork. *Journal of the Cork Historical and Archaeological Society* **56**, 69–86.

Ó Ríordáin, S.P. 1949 Lough Gur excavations: Neolithic and Bronze Age houses on Knockadoon. *Proceedings of the Royal Irish Academy* **56**C, 297–459.

Ó Ríordáin, S.P. and Ó hIceadha, G. 1955 Lough Gur excavations: the megalithic tomb. *Journal of the Royal Society of Antiquaries of Ireland* **85**, 34–50.

O'Sullivan, A. 1995 Marshlanders. *Archaeology Ireland* **31**, 8–11.

O'Sullivan, A. 1996 Later Bronze Age discoveries on north Munster estuaries. *Discovery Programme Reports* **4**, 63–72. Dublin. Royal Irish Academy.

O'Sullivan, A. 1998 *The archaeology of lake settlement in Ireland*. Discovery Programme Monograph 4. Dublin. Royal Irish Academy.

O'Sullivan, A. and Condit, T. 1995 Late Bronze Age settlement and economy by the marshlands of the upper Fergus estuary. *The Other Clare* **19,** 5–9.

O'Sullivan, A. and Sheehan, J. 1996 *The Iveragh Peninsula. An archaeological survey of south Kerry.* Cork University Press.

O'Sullivan, T. (forthcoming) Report on the bird bones from Dún Aonghasa.

Pollock, A.J. and Waterman, D.M. 1964 A Bronze Age habitation site at Downpatrick. *Ulster Journal of Archaeology* **27**, 31–58.

Price, T.D. and Kavanagh, M. 1982 Bone composition and the reconstruction of diet: examples from the midwestern United States. *Midcontinental Journal of Archaeology* **7** (1), 61–79.

Raftery, J. 1942 Knocknalappa crannog, Co. Clare. *North Munster Antiquarian Journal* **3**, 53–72.

Stelfox, A.W. 1942 Report on the animal bones. In H. Hencken, 'Ballinderry Crannog No. 2'. *Proceedings of the Royal Irish Academy* **47**C, 67–74.

Subirà, M.E. and Malgosa, A. 1992 Multi-element analysis for dietary reconstruction at a Balearic Iron Age site. *International Journal of Osteoarchaeology* **2**, 199–204.

van Wijngaarden-Bakker, L.H. 1974 The animal remains from the Beaker settlement at Newgrange, Co. Meath: first report. *Proceedings of the Royal Irish Academy* **74**C, 313–83.

van Wijngaarden-Bakker, L.H. 1986 The animal remains from the Beaker settlement at Newgrange, Co. Meath: final report. *Proceedings of the Royal Irish Academy* **86**C, 17–111.

van Wijngaarden-Bakker, L.H. 1989 Faunal remains and the Irish Mesolithic. In C. Bonsall (ed.), *The Mesolithic in Europe*, 125–33. Edinburgh. John Donald.

van Wijngaarden-Bakker, L.H. 1995 Appendix VII: Subsistence in the Late Bronze Age at Lough Gur. In R.M. Cleary, 'Later Bronze Age settlement and prehistoric burials, Lough Gur, Co. Limerick'. *Proceedings of the Royal Irish Academy* **95**C, 79–92.

Wheeler, A. 1969 *The fishes of the British Isles and northwest Europe.* London. Macmillan.

Wheeler, A. and Jones, A. 1989 *Fishes.* Cambridge Manuals in Archaeology. Cambridge University Press.

Woodman, P.C., McCarthy, M. and Monaghan, N. 1997 The Irish Quaternary Fauna Project. *Quaternary Science Reviews* **16** (2), 129–59.

THE POTTER'S CRAFT IN PREHISTORIC IRELAND WITH SPECIFIC REFERENCE TO LOUGH GUR, CO. LIMERICK

Rose M. Cleary

INTRODUCTION

The minimal resources required to make pottery are clay, water and fuel for firing. Temper or non-plastic inclusions can be added if required, although raw clays usually contain non-plastic material which itself can facilitate the production of pottery. These naturally occurring impurities include quartz and other forms of silica, organic matter, calcium carbonate and iron (Shephard 1968, 18–19). Temper is added to improve workability and shaping of clay, to prevent excessive shrinkage during the drying stage and to facilitate firing. Temper types were likely to be chosen because of availability, to suit the type of vessel being produced or perhaps to counteract some inherent flaw in the local clay resource. Changes in the exploitation of both clay and temper sources, production techniques and technology and vessel morphology can be indicative of wider cultural changes. The most apparent changes in pottery production are those of shape and decoration.

This paper will examine some of the changes in the ceramic record from the Lough Gur area of County Limerick. The prehistoric settlement and ritual sites in Lough Gur are located in a region with a wide range of natural resources (Fig. 1). In terms of pottery production, the sites around the lake are in areas where the underlying geology is Waulsortian Reef limestone of Carboniferous age and the overlying residual clay is calcareous. Further out from the lake are the 'Limerick Volcanics', where a series of extinct volcanic plugs form a ring-dyke complex almost surrounding Lough Gur. Here the geology is primarily basalt, basaltic tuffs and tuff braccias. The clays in these regions are reflective of the underlying geology, are non-calcareous and include minerals associated with igneous and metamorphic rock formations. Transported clays along the Camoge river valley and its tributaries to the north of Lough Gur and along the Morningstar River to the south may also include volcanically derived clays reflective in mineral composition of the source geology. Prehistoric potters had therefore a variety of clay and crushed rock temper types to choose from. This variety is reflected in the ceramic assemblages from the Lough Gur sites.

THE SITES

The sites used as the base material for this study range in date from the Neolithic to the Later Bronze Age. Two of the sites, Site B on Knockadoon Hill and Grange stone circle, were excavated during the campaign of excavation in Lough Gur by S.P. Ó Ríordáin in the late 1930s and the 1940s (Ó Ríordáin 1951; 1954). The sites were excavated without the benefit of radiocarbon determinations, and the chronology for many of the sites, based on the

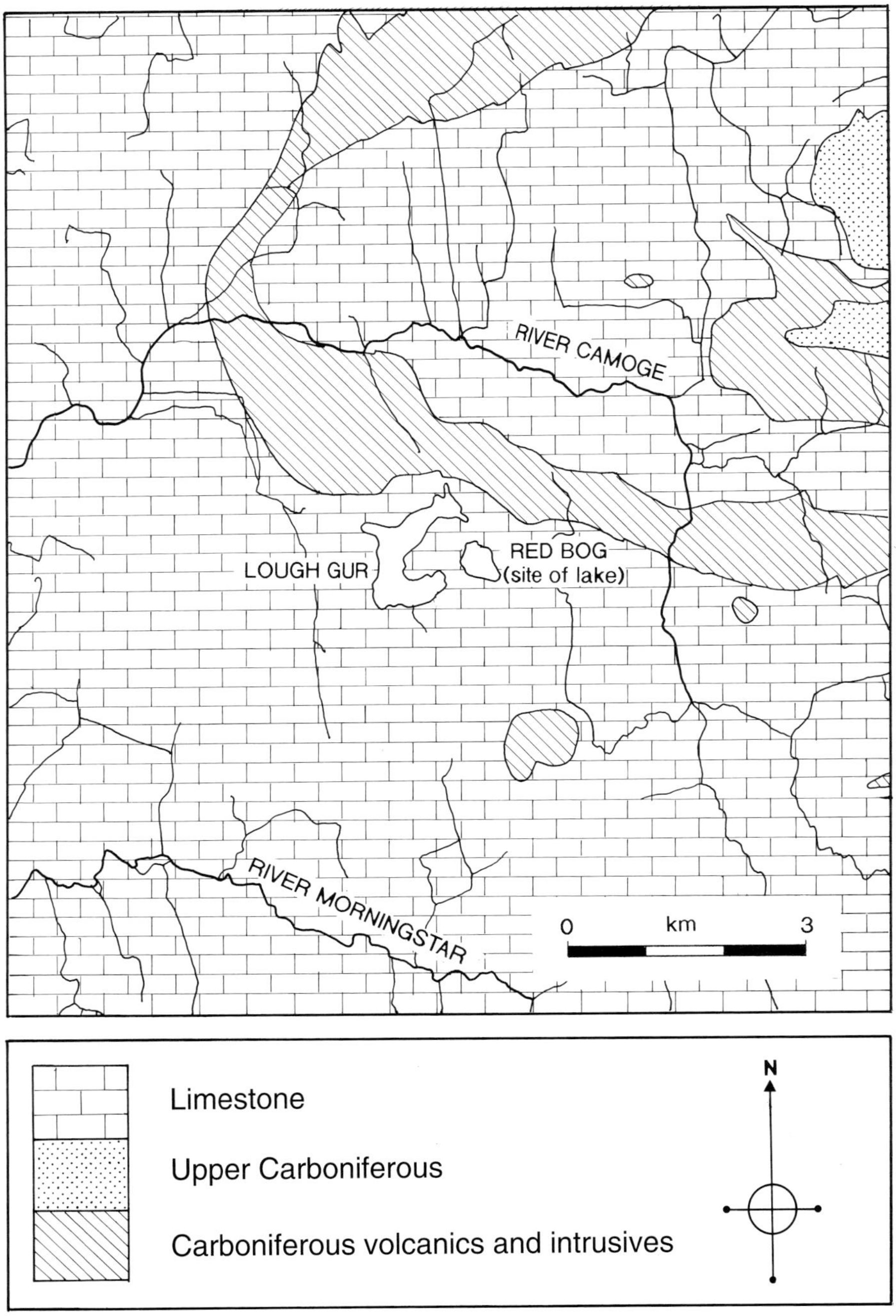

Fig. 1—Geological map of Lough Gur hinterland (Discovery Programme).

ceramic sequence, remained floating until the dating of the sequence was more firmly established by cross-reference to more recent excavations. The ceramic assemblage from the Later Bronze Age site was excavated between 1985 and 1988 (Cleary 1995b). In this paper the ceramic sequences at the sites will be discussed first and then the manufacturing details will be examined with particular reference to choice raw materials.

Site B

The dating of Site B has been discussed elsewhere (Cleary 1993) and the ceramic types found on the site date almost exclusively from the Neolithic period. Ó Ríordáin recognised two phases of building on the site although the structural features could not be clearly assigned to either phase. The pottery was identified as both Class I and Ia of the Limerick style of Western Neolithic Wares[1] (Case 1961). The relative sequence of pottery has been summed up by the excavator as follows: 'In the matter of stratification both classes were clearly contemporary, but Class Ia predominated at the earliest level' (Ó Ríordáin 1954, 317). This level was a burnt layer over the natural boulder clay and was recorded at a depth of 0.75m, while the upper level was a black stratum over the burnt clay and was recorded 0.45m below ground level.[2] The assemblage consists of 650 sherds (2491g). Featureless body sherds can belong to either classification, and in all 18% (444g) with decorated rims can be definitely ascribed to the Class Ia type. Some of the Class I wares from Site B have out-turned simple rims and defined carinated profiles (Fig. 2). These are not dissimilar to pottery dated at the Tankardstown site to 4030–3786 cal. BC[3] (Gowen 1988, fig. 8, 37). Class Ia sherds from Site B have more pronounced rims and sharp angled shoulders (Fig. 3).

Sheridan (1995, 18) has suggested that the Limerick style of Western Neolithic pottery belongs to a tradition of modified carinated bowls with 'a distinctive local variant emerging in Co. Limerick', dating from the Middle Neolithic (*c.* 2900–2500 uncal. BC/*c.* 3650–3100 cal. BC). Decorated and 'modified' carinated bowls are included in this category (*ibid.*, fig. 2.5, no. 3), with the 'classic' carinated vessel continuing into the Middle Neolithic period (*ibid.*, fig. 2.3, no. 2). As regards the dating of the Site B material, some sherds are morphologically similar to the Tankardstown assemblage while others belong to a local Lough Gur variant (Class Ia). In terms of relative dating of the ceramic sequence at Site B, there are parallels in vessel form between the Tankardstown assemblage and the Class I pottery from Site B, and it may be that both date from the early phase of the Middle Neolithic as defined by Sheridan (*ibid.*, 18). The Class Ia pottery appears on stratigraphic grounds to be earlier, but the time interval between the production of both types may not have been great. The occurrence of the heavy-rimmed Class Ia ware could also be a local preference, or indeed may represent a specific functional purpose, and may be unrelated to any modern perception of a typological development.

Grange stone circle

Ó Ríordáin (1951, 45–6) considered that Grange stone circle was constructed as a single-period monument. The basis of this interpretation was that some of the stones were set on or above the original ground level, and could only have been kept in place if externally supported by the bank. Two discrete turf-lines were recorded within the bank in an area

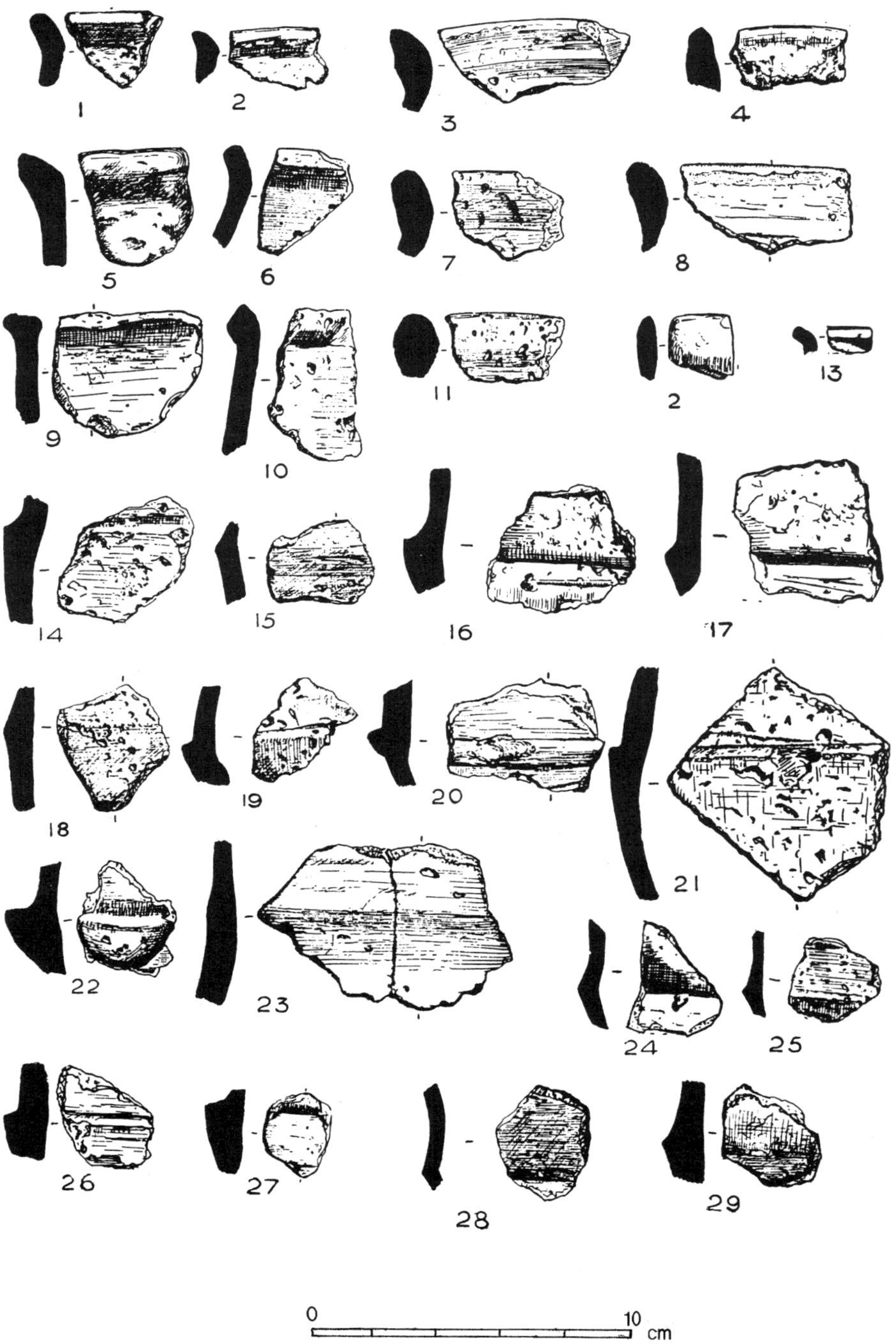

Fig. 2—Site B: Class I pottery (after Ó Ríordáin 1954, fig. 7).

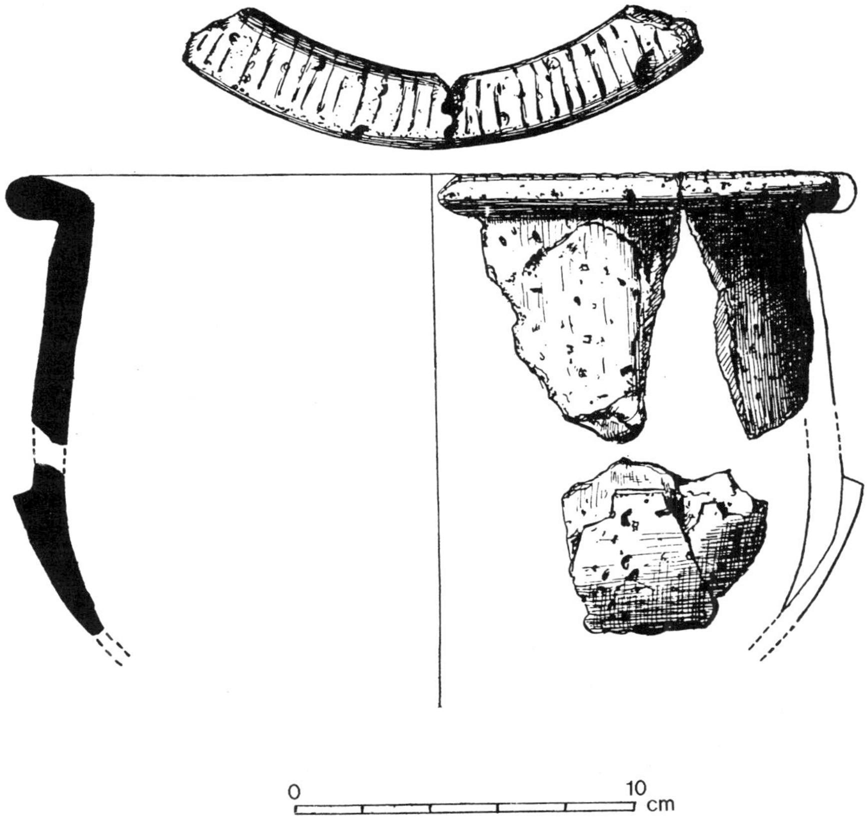

Fig. 3—Site B: reconstructed drawing of Class Ia pot (after Ó Ríordáin 1954, fig. 8).

excavated in the western section of the monument (west of stones 67 and 68). A further western bank cutting also had an intermediary turf-line within the bank (west of stones 73–84). These were interpreted as an accumulation of organic material due to the location of workers' camps on this side of the monument. The turf or buried sod horizon could also have been deliberately laid as part of the bank construction, as Ó Ríordáin (*op. cit.*, 47) suggested that the lowest layer of bank material on the west side was more humic in composition than elsewhere. The explanation for the difference in composition may be that the bank material on the west side was drawn from the upper (humic) levels of the source location rather than the lower boulder (yellow) clay used elsewhere for bank construction.

The ceramic assemblage consisted of 4311 sherds (16,645g) and included a variety of recognisable types, including Class I of the Limerick Style of Western Neolithic pottery, Class II, Grooved Ware, Beaker and Food Vessel. The Class I wares were generally without shoulders or defined carinations on the vessel profiles. Class I pottery at Grange has relatively simple profiles, in contrast to the pronounced angles (carinations) of the Class Ia style. The Class I wares were found in the western quadrant of the interior and under the western bank of the stone circle. Similarly, the Class II wares were 'well represented in the material under the bank on the west' (Ó Ríordáin 1951, 55), mainly from the original ground surface under

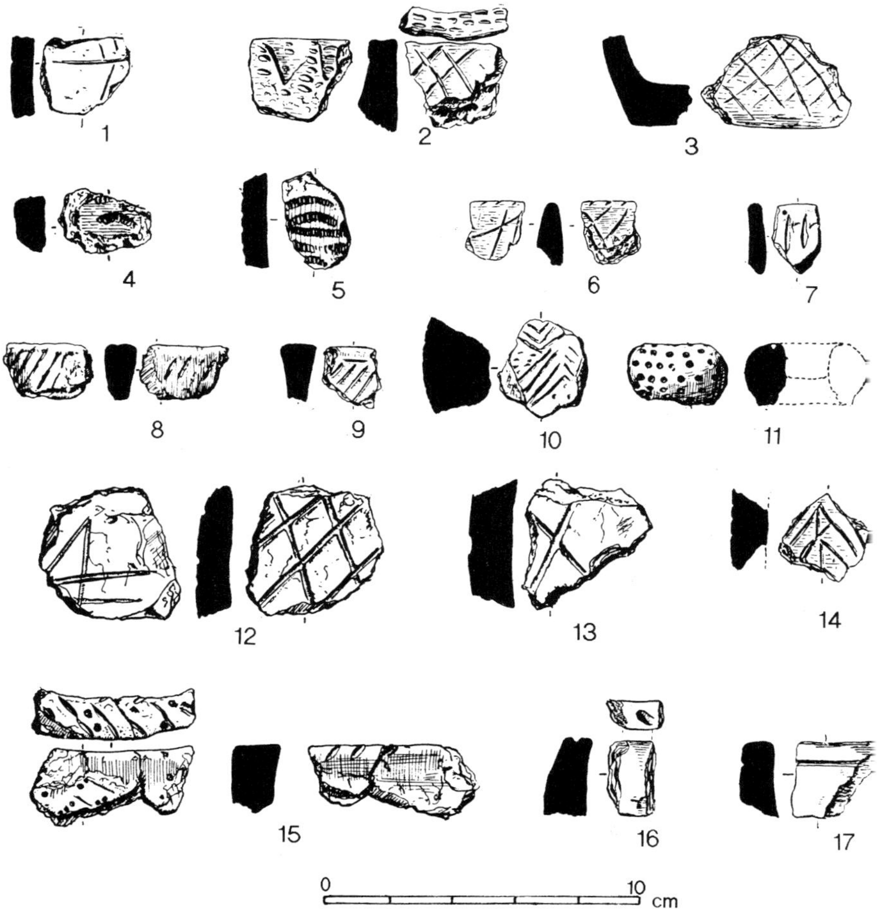

Fig. 4—1–11: Sherds from the interior of the circle. 12–17: Sherds from under the bank (after Ó Ríordáin 1951, figs 8 and 9).

the bank. This level represents the pre-construction phase, but the interval between the deposition of the pottery and the construction of the bank may have not been great. Some sherds of Grooved Ware (*ibid.*, 65, fig. 8, 1–8) were also recovered from the circle interior. The amount of Grooved Ware is difficult to quantify as Grooved Ware and Class II pottery are similar in fabric and in decoration. Incised cross-hatched decoration occurs on pottery both from inside the circle and from under the bank (Fig. 4) and the pottery cannot be easily assigned to either classification.[4] Indeed, it may be that pottery ascribed to the Lough Gur Class II style belongs to the Grooved Ware classification. The Beaker and Food Vessel pottery came exclusively from the stone circle interior. Beaker pottery was recovered both from the sockets and fills of the upright stones and from the enclosed area of the circle. The general date range for the site is within the Later Neolithic period, and the appearance of Grooved Ware in the ceramic sequence may suggest an initial construction phase as early as 2250 uncal. BC/2900–2700 cal. BC.[5]

Late Bronze Age habitation site

The final site chosen for ceramic analysis is a recently excavated site on Knockadoon Hill, where a Later Bronze Age habitation site produced an assemblage of 1307 sherds (2454g) of flat-based coarse wares (Cleary 1995b). This site had the remains of three post-built houses with radiocarbon dates centring on *c.* 1000 uncal. BC/*c.* 1200 cal. BC.

RAW MATERIALS

Clay

The sourcing of raw materials for pottery production in the Lough Gur area from the Neolithic to the Late Bronze Age has been investigated mainly through petrological examination of paste and temper inclusions. Most clays used in the assemblages are sandy or silty in composition and derive from a number of fluvially derived sources. The quartz inclusions are undiagnostic in relation to the source. Some preliminary work on re-firing clays in the locale suggests that the river valleys to the north and south of the lake were potential clay sources. The Neolithic and Beaker period pottery was made from clays with feldsparithic minerals in the matrix and indicates a source of clays derived from the igneous and metamorphic bedrock of the volcanic ring-dyke complex on the perimeter of the lake. Calcium carbonate minerals in the clays also indicate the use of clays derived from the lower Carboniferous Waulsortian Reef limestone in the immediate environs of the lake. There is a marked preference for non-calcareous clays in the Neolithic and Beaker period ceramics, while the Later Bronze Age assemblages appear to be made from at least some limestone-derived clays. It can therefore be suggested that the Neolithic potters chose to travel outside the immediate environs of the lake when sourcing clay and used clay ultimately derived from the volcanic regions on the periphery of the lake. Bronze Age potters exploited both clay sources closer to the settlement sites and to a limited extent sources further afield. A similar scenario can be seen in the Bronze Age site at Ballyveelish, Co. Tipperary (Cleary 1987), where almost 95% of the pottery could have been manufactured from clays in the immediate environs of the site.

Temper

The choice of tempers also varied through time. Most of the assemblage from Site B (Fig. 5; Table 1) had no observable temper (65%) and a pitted or porous surface. This 'corky' texture was interpreted as the result of burnt grass temper or grits dropping out during firing (Ó Ríordáin 1951, 54; 1954, 327). If grass had been used as temper the pores would have presented as narrower linear voids of a fairly uniform width, whereas the pores are discrete and of varying sizes. Grits dropping out during firing is also unlikely as some voids are internal in the vessel wall and grits could not drop out of the middle of a vessel wall. The Class I wares at Site B, however, have obvious rectangular and needle-shaped pores on the surfaces and through the vessel wall sections from external to internal surfaces. These pores are the result of the use of bone temper which has dissolved through time. The pores register optical inactivity under polarised light and if the pores were caused by the dissolution of

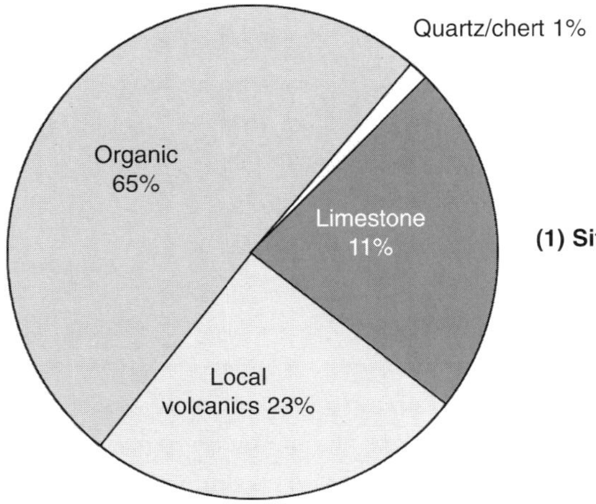

(1) Site B

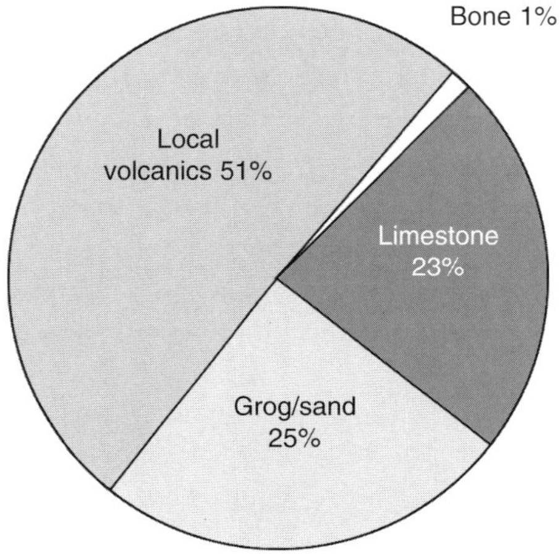

(2) Grange stone circle

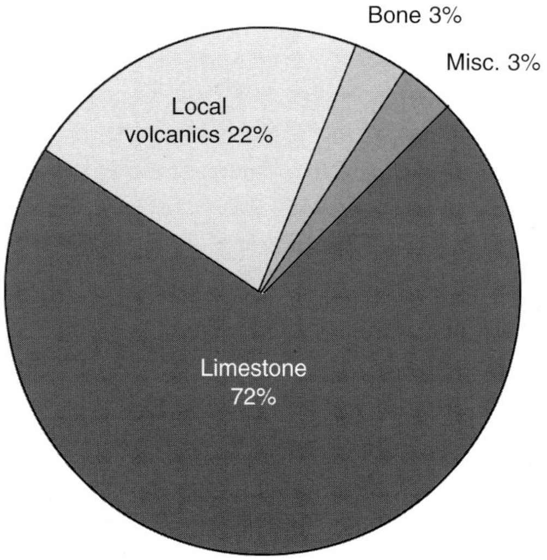

Fig. 5—Temper preferences from Site B (1), Grange stone circle (2) and the Later Bronze Age (3).

(3) Later Bronze Age sites

Site B	Grange stone circle	Late Bronze Age
Bone (organic) (65%)	Local volcanics (51%)	Limestone (72%)
Local volcanics (23%)	Grog/sand (25%)	Local volcanics (22%)
Limestone (11%)	Limestone (23%)	Bone (3%)
Quartz (sand)/chert (1%)	Bone (1%)	Chert/quartz/greywacke (3%)

Table 1—Temper types (in descending order of frequency of occurrence).

calcium carbonate it would be expected that some residual crystals would remain in the voids. The presence of crushed bone in some of the Site B sherds has been confirmed by scanning electron microscopy—the distinct cellular structure of bone is visible under high magnification (x500) along the edges of the pores where residual bone survives. Elemental analysis also confirms the presence of phosphate (apetite), one of the main components of bone. Bone temper produces a light, strong vessel, and the organic content can strengthen the vessel fabric (Grim 1962, 85). The use of bone temper has been recorded in Neolithic pottery from tomb 27 at Carrowmore passage tomb cemetery (Hulthèn 1981) and possibly in a Western Neolithic vessel from Tankardstown (Gowen 1988, 48–9). Bone temper is also known from a classic Beaker vessel at Grange stone circle (Cleary 1984) and in that case the vessel surface was not particularly porous. Some of the Later Bronze Age assemblages at Lough Gur may also have had bone temper as the pore structure in some sherds is similar to the voids in the Neolithic wares (Cleary 1995b, 84–5).

The other temper types in the Site B assemblage are crushed rocks (24%), from the volcanic ring-dyke complex, and limestone (11%). The rock types are mainly local basalts, tuffs and sandstones, and the limestone is from the Waulsortian Reef type in the Lough Gur area.

Limestone temper, though occurring in a small percentage (11%) of the Western Neolithic material from Site B, is not particularly suitable for pottery production. If temperatures between 650°C and 900°C are reached in the original firing, the limestone[6] will begin to decompose and cause the vessel to crack or crumble (Shephard 1968, 30). Subsequent reheating of successfully fired limestone-tempered cooking vessels will also reactivate the process of decomposition and ultimately cause the vessel to crack. It is possible that these vessels were designated as dry goods containers and that the choice of temper was determined by the vessel function.

Grange stone circle pottery (Fig. 5, no. 2; Table 1) is mainly tempered with crushed rock (51%), grog and/or sand (25%) and limestone (23%). Crushed rock, limestone and sand are found in all the types of pottery from Grange, whereas grog or crushed pottery sherds is exclusively found in the Beaker pottery. The rock types are similar to the Site B material and of similar origin. In the case of sand, this is an intrinsic part of the clay and was not added as a temper. Grog is only detectable in thin sections examined under the petrological microscope. It is only possible to say from macroscopic examination where an obvious temper is not visible that either grog or naturally occurring sand acted as the temper. The use of grog temper represents a technological change in pottery production and is generally considered to be a Beaker period innovation (Peacock 1970).[7] Grog is also known in the Beaker assemblage at Newgrange (Cleary 1983) and at Knowth (Brindley 1984; 1997). Grog was not recorded in the Bronze Age material from Lough Gur, but occurs in Bronze Age pottery from Ballyveelish (Cleary 1987) and Dún Aonghusa (Cleary 1995a, 86). The reasons for the use or lack of use of grog as tempering material have been discussed by Cleal (1995, 192), who suggests that one reason for not using grog may have been that pottery was a valuable item and care was taken to prevent breakage. There is, of course, no reason to discard a vessel when chipped or cracked if it functioned as a container for dry goods. Even when pots were broken there may have been a taboo against 'recycling' old pots in new vessels.

The use of limestone temper in the Grange stone circle assemblage occurred in both Class I and II wares and Beakers, although the preference for this temper type was relatively limited (23%). Dolomite, also essentially a calcium carbonate and similar to limestone, was used in All Over Ornamented Beakers and Beaker-influenced pottery at Newgrange (Cleary 1983, 114).

Domestic Bronze Age ceramics at Lough Gur are in the main flat-based bucket-shaped vessels. Two Later Bronze Age sites have been securely dated by a series of ^{14}C determinations to *c.* 1000 uncal. BC/*c.* 1200 cal. BC (Cleary 1995a; 1995b). The pottery from one of these sites (Cleary 1995b) had been tempered with mainly local Waulsortian Reef limestone (72%) and fired mainly in the range 500–600°C. The extensive use of limestone (Fig. 5, no. 3; Table 1) may be related to vessel function in that these vessels were not produced as cooking wares. There was no evidence of cereal production from this site and the faunal assemblage was primarily pig. Vessels may not have been required for storage or cooking as pig may have been roasted and cereals were not in evidence. The remaining types of temper used included crushed local basalt (20%), possibly crushed bone (3%), sandstone, chert and greywacke. The presence of non-local greywacke as temper suggests that some of the pottery was imported onto the site. The greywacke-tempered pottery has an atypical sandy clay also indicating a different origin to the main assemblage. Trade in what can be perceived as low-grade, domestic pottery is also indicated at Ballyveelish, Co. Tipperary, where *c.* 5% of the pottery was made from a non-local clay and tempered with grog. Late Bronze Age pottery from Chancellorsland (Doody 1993; this volume) has basaltic temper inclusions similar to the Later Bronze Age assemblages, and the source of at least some of the Chancellorsland material may be non-local.

Pottery form

The most obvious change in the ceramic record within the Lough Gur area is in the shape of the vessels. The Neolithic Class I wares are round-bottomed, shouldered (carinated) pots with decoration occurring on the upper neck and rim of the Class Ia type. The shape of this type of pottery remained unchanged for perhaps up to 1500 years. It is almost impossible to ascribe undiagnostic body and base sherds to either the Class I or Ia types. Changes in shape may reflect, in part, a change in function for a vessel. The shape of round-bottomed Western

Neolithic pots must have been a predetermined choice on the part of the potters and related to the use of the vessels, probably as cooking vessels over a fire where heat was evenly distributed across the bottom. The pot design is similar to the pot oven or bastible of more recent times where, once the food was cooked, the round-based vessel was left to sit in a 'pot hole' when it was lifted off the fire (Evans 1945, 67). Given the difficulty of transporting these vessels, their use must be related to sedentary societies. There is little direct evidence from the Lough Gur sites of agriculture as opposed to pastoralism, but it is likely that the economy was mixed. Some evidence of transhumance is indicated by Late Neolithic/Beaker period hearths excavated in the Rockbarton area, a mile or so west of the lake (Mitchell and Ó Ríordáin 1942). The more recently excavated Neolithic site at Tankardstown has produced evidence for cereal production (Monk 1988; 1993) and it is likely that this was also the case at Lough Gur. Mitchell (1954) has identified a rise in herbaceous and grass pollen, probably associated with cereal-growing at the beginning of the Neolithic.[8]

Grooved Ware may be a manifestation of a new belief or practice and may be related to a cult involving the construction of the embanked stone circle at Grange. Few stratigraphic details survive from the excavation record of Grange and it is not possible to determine how structured the deposition of Grooved Ware was in relation to the monument. The similarity of decorated Class II ware to what is now recognised as Grooved Ware compounds the difficulty in interpreting the relationship of pottery deposition to the construction of the site. The site was considered to have been constructed as a unit (Ó Ríordáin 1951, 45) and Beaker pottery was recovered from sockets of the internal orthostats, suggesting that Beakers were in use at least at some stage during the monument construction. The Late Neolithic/Beaker period saw the introduction of fine, small, flat-based vessels with innovative decorative motifs, including the use of comb-stamped patterns. The use of comb-stamped motifs is unknown in the ceramic record in pre-Beaker times. The introduction of highly decorated, relatively small Beaker vessels is undoubtedly related to a new cult or change in ritual practice. The use of flat-based wares such as Class II wares, Grooved Ware, and Coarse or Domestic Beaker in the Late Neolithic/Beaker period may indicate a functional change. Pottery vessels may have become primarily containers, as in the eighteenth- and nineteenth-century earthenwares ('crocks') used for storage, or table vessels as we understand the function of cups and mugs today.

The presence of flat-based coarse ware or Lough Gur Class II pots under the bank at Grange stone circle and in association with Class I wares on other sites on Knockadoon suggests that they originate in the Later Neolithic. The undecorated Class II pottery may be a local product of the Lough Gur area. Some of the decorated pottery previously identified as Lough Gur Class II may in fact be Grooved Ware and may represent a discrete settlement phase at Lough Gur. Flat-based bucket-shaped vessels continued to be produced into the Later Bronze Age, being securely dated on recent excavations (Cleary 1995b; forthcoming). The shape is functional for cooking and container vessels, and this may account for the longevity of form.

Bronze Age domestic pottery is invariably flat-based and with a large range of rim diameters and vessel heights. The Lough Gur Bronze Age pottery has average rim diameters of 14–16cm. Pottery of the same period from Chancellorsland is slightly larger, with rim diameters up to 25cm, but some are as small as 12cm. Some of the larger vessels were undoubtedly cooking pots,[9] whereas small vessels may have served as 'table' utensils. Internally bevelled rims may have been lid seatings, suggesting that at least some of the pots were covered containers.

Pottery manufacture

Manufacturing techniques are not, in general, related chronologically to specific periods of pottery production, but are linked to vessel size and ultimately to function. The two main methods of manufacture in the prehistoric period were pinching a clay ball into shape or making a coil pot. Pinched pots are of necessity small, whereas coil-made pottery can be relatively large. The coil manufacturing technique was used in Class I and Ia and Class II wares, the domestic Beaker or associated cooking wares and in the Later Bronze Age assemblages. The method as described by Ó Ríordáin (1951) suggests that the vessels broke at the joint line between two coils. 'In several instances the "false rim" is not rounded but has an angular profile—the lower pointed portion fitting into a corresponding groove in the ring above it' (*ibid.*, 64). This method of manufacture gives a characteristic 'N' profile to the fracture, whereby the clay from one coil is pushed up to adhere to the next coil on one side and down on the other side to adhere to the coil below. This is common in the Lough Gur assemblages, though the 'coils' may have been fairly short and the vessels themselves appear to have been built with small slabs of clay. The result is that the fractures occur along the edges of the slabs rather than uniformly along the upper or lower surfaces of a coil. Ó Ríordáin also suggested that a slip was used over the vessel surfaces to mask the ridges between coils. A slip is a coating of fine clay washed over a vessel surface. The clay may be deliberately levigated to remove large particles. Slip coatings are apparent in thin section as a layer of fine clay and to date this has not been observed in the Lough Gur pottery. It is more likely that the appearance of fine clay was actually the product of smoothing out the coils rather than a deliberate slip coating.

Classic Beakers are by design relatively small and may have been pinched and/or turned on a base. The use of a base would allow the potter to turn the vessel around to facilitate working of the clay to form the wall. The 'classic' Beaker pottery from Lough Gur appears to have been pinched into shape. This is also the case in the Newgrange Beaker pottery assemblage (Cleary 1983, 110). Small vessels are also known from Later Bronze Age assemblages and were described as 'cups' by Ó Ríordáin (see also Cleary 1993; 1995b). Small pinched pots are best made rapidly in order to prevent cracking and splitting of the drying clay (Leach 1973, 63).

Decoration on pottery may have been executed for many reasons, perhaps varying from some type of eschatological belief, a secret code, or some more mundane reason such as a maker's mark identifying the potter, or simply decoration for decoration's sake. The decoration on vessels may have been structured to suit demand or a social requirement. It is invariably abstract and appears mainly to be placed in areas where it would be most visible, i.e. around the mouth or upper sections of vessels. Most prehistoric pottery is decorated with incised, impressed or plastic motifs. The incised motifs may be simple lines or the more complicated herringbone motifs that occur on the Class Ia wares at Site B. Class II wares invariably have incised lines or cross-hatching. Impressed motifs occur on Class II wares and vary from (bird?) bone impressions that look like small pits to fingernail impressions. Plastic decoration includes the use of additional clay strips. These are rare enough in prehistoric pottery, the exceptions being Encrusted Urns and some Food Vessels. Beaker period pottery has a large repertoire of motifs, including comb impressions, which are exclusive to that pottery and to Food Vessels. Lugs and cordons may have been entirely functional and served as handles. Later Bronze Age pottery at Lough Gur is almost entirely undecorated. This is in contrast to the Later Bronze Age assemblage from Chancellorsland (Doody 1993, fig. 11), where a variety of motifs, including twisted cord and incised line motifs, occur.

Prehistoric pottery was undoubtedly produced as a response to demand. The production of pottery is not as essential as other economic activities, such as agriculture, and the presence of pottery on prehistoric sites suggests a certain surplus of wealth and a stable and ordered social structure. Sheridan (1991, 329) has suggested that pottery production was a small-scale, localised effort, and the likely scenario is that craft potters produced for the needs of local communities. The position of craft potters within prehistoric societies is difficult to establish. The pottery from the Lough Gur region is generally well made and this in itself suggests a degree of skill. The Western Neolithic wares are thin-walled, large vessels which would be difficult to manufacture without slumping of the walls. Their production suggests that the potters, be they female or male specialist potters, in a group or tribe had learned to exploit the local natural resources and to manipulate the clays and firing schedule to create useful and durable vessels. In the Late Neolithic/Beaker period, the production of ornate ceremonial 'classic' Beaker pottery types may have elevated the social standing of craft potters if the goods they produced were an intrinsic part of some ritual. The deposition of the Beaker pottery in the sockets of the orthostats at Grange stone circle appears to suggest some rite connected with the construction of the monument. Pottery in the Later Bronze Age is perceived as being a low-grade bulk item, yet there is some evidence of trade.

As archaeologists we have probably removed the human element from the study of pottery in the ways we dissect, analyse and categorise the product of a human hand. The motivation for pottery production and the use of the pottery is reflective of the need, be it profane or ritual or a combination of both, for ceramic vessels in prehistoric communities. Information which may aid our understanding of people's lives in the past can be extrapolated from the sherds. The conference title which led to this publication suggests that we should be looking towards a 'new agenda' in Irish archaeology, and a new agenda for pottery studies must be a more interdisciplinary approach, using whatever techniques and resources are available in other branches of science. It is no longer sufficient to slot excavated pottery into convenient, published typologies and to divorce the ceramic assemblage from its original environment. Archaeologists studying prehistoric people have a limited database on which to draw. Analysis of pottery shows the history of ceramic development, exploitation of resources and the influences that led to the origin and use of specific types of vessels.

REFERENCES

Brindley, J.C. 1984 Petrological examination of Beaker pottery from the Boyne Valley sites. In G. Eogan, *Excavations at Knowth*, 331–42. Dublin. Royal Irish Academy.

Brindley, J.C. 1997 Petrological examination of Earlier 'Western' Neolithic, decorated pottery and Grooved Ware pottery. In G. Eogan and H. Roche, *Excavations at Knowth 2*, 271–82. Dublin. Royal Irish Academy.

Case, H.J. 1961 Irish Neolithic pottery: distribution and sequence. *Proceedings of the Prehistoric Society* **27**, 174–233.

Cleal, R.M.J. 1995 Pottery fabrics in Wessex in the fourth to second millennia. In I. Kinnes and G. Varndell (eds), *Unbaked urns of rudely shape: essays on British and Irish pottery for Ian Longworth*, 185–94. Oxford. Oxbow Books.

Cleary, R.M. 1983 The ceramic assemblage. In M.J. O'Kelly, R.M. Cleary and D. Lehane, *Newgrange, Co. Meath, Ireland: the Late Neolithic/Beaker period settlement*, 58–117. British Archaeological Reports, British Series 190. Oxford.

Cleary, R.M. 1984 Bone tempered Beaker potsherd. *Journal of Irish Archaeology* **2**, 73–5.

Cleary R.M. 1987 The ceramic assemblage. In M.G. Doody, 'Late Bronze Age settlement, Ballyveelish 2, Co. Tipperary'. In R.M. Cleary, M.F. Hurley and E.A. Twohig (eds), *Archaeological excavations on the Cork–Dublin natural gas pipeline, 1981–2*, 31–5. Department of Archaeology, University College Cork.

Cleary, R.M. 1993 The Later Bronze Age at Lough Gur: filling in the blanks. In E. Shee Twohig and M. Ronayne (eds), *Past perceptions: the prehistoric archaeology of south-west Ireland*, 114–20. Cork University Press.

Cleary, R.M. 1995a Irish Later Bronze Age pottery: a preliminary technological assessment. *Kungl. Vitterhets Historie och Antikvitets Akademien Konferenser* **34**, 77–90. Stockholm.

Cleary, R.M. 1995b Later Bronze Age settlement and prehistoric burials, Lough Gur, Co. Limerick. *Proceedings of the Royal Irish Academy* **95**C, 1–92.

Cleary, R.M. (forthcoming) An enclosed Later Bronze Age habitation site and field fence at Lough Gur, Co. Limerick.

Doody, M. 1993 Ballyhoura Hills Project. *Discovery Programme Reports* **2**, 17–18. Dublin. Royal Irish Academy.

Eogan, G. and Roche, H. 1997 *Excavations at Knowth 2: settlement and ritual sites of the fourth and third millennia BC*. Dublin. Royal Irish Academy.

Evans, E.E. 1945 *Irish heritage: the landscape, the people and their work*. Dundalk. Dundalgan Press.

Gowen, M. 1988 *Three Irish gas pipelines: new archaeological evidence in Munster*. Dublin. Wordwell.

Grogan, E. 1988 The pipeline sites and the prehistory of the Limerick area. In M. Gowen, *Three Irish gas pipelines: new archaeological evidence in Munster*, 148–57. Dublin. Wordwell.

Grim, R.E. 1962 *Applied clay mineralogy*. New York. McGraw Hill.

Herity, M. 1982 Irish decorated Neolithic pottery. *Proceedings of the Royal Irish Academy* **82**C, 247–404.

Hulthèn, B. 1981 A pottery study. An investigation of some sherds from north-western Ireland. In G. Burenhult (ed.), *The Carrowmore excavations*, 174–9. Stockholm Archaeological Reports. Institute of Archaeology. University of Stockholm.

Leach, B. 1973 *A potter's book*. London. Faber and Faber.

Mitchell, G.F. 1954 A pollen diagram from Lough Gur, Co. Limerick (Studies in Irish Quaternary Deposits, No. 9). *Proceedings of the Royal Irish Academy* **56**C, 481–8.

Mitchell, G.F. and Ó Ríordáin, S.P. 1942 Early Bronze Age pottery from Rockbarton Bog, Co. Limerick. *Proceedings of the Royal Irish Academy* **48**C, 255–72.

Monk, M. 1988 Archaeobotanical study of samples from pipeline sites. In M. Gowen, *Three Irish gas pipelines: new archaeological evidence in Munster*, 185–91. Dublin. Wordwell.

Monk, M. 1993 People and environment: in search of the farmers. In E. Shee Twohig and M. Ronayne (eds), *Past perceptions: the prehistoric archaeology of south-west Ireland*, 35–52. Cork University Press.

Ó Ríordáin, S.P. 1951 Lough Gur excavations: the great stone circle (B) in Grange townland. *Proceedings of the Royal Irish Academy* **54**C, 37–74.

Ó Ríordáin, S.P. 1954 Lough Gur excavations: Neolithic and Bronze Age houses on Knockadoon. *Proceedings of the Royal Irish Academy* **56**C, 297–459.

Peacock, D.P.S. 1970 Scientific analysis of ancient ceramics: a review. *World Archaeology* **1** (3), 375–89.

Shephard, A. 1968 *Ceramics for the archaeologist*. Washington. Carnegie Institution of Washington.

Sheridan, A. 1991 Pottery production in Neolithic and Early Bronze Age Ireland: a petrological and chemical study. In A. Middleton and I. Freestone (eds), *Recent developments in ceramic petrology*, 305–35. British Museum Occasional Paper No. 81. London.

Sheridan, A. 1995 Irish Neolithic pottery: the story in 1995. In I. Kinnes and G. Varndell (eds), *Unbaked urns of rudely shape: essays on British and Irish pottery for Ian Longworth*, 3–20. Oxford. Oxbow Books.

Endnotes

1 Sheridan (1995, 17) suggests that the term 'Western Neolithic' be replaced by the term 'traditional carinated bowl' or 'Classic carinated bowl' (cf. *ibid.*, fig. 2.5, no. 1) as the original terminology of Case may be outdated. The term 'Western Neolithic' is retained here as it is an intrinsic part of Irish archaeological literature and the introduction of new terminology is considered unnecessary for the purposes of this paper. Lough Gur Class Ia pottery has also been categorised by Herity (1982) under his Style 2 classification of decorated Neolithic pottery. These vessels have a broad rim and incised decoration on the upper sections of the pots.

2 The depth was presumably from the existing ground level or sod layer.

3 A ^{14}C determination of 5105 ± 45 BP for Tankardstown (House 1) is referred to in

Grogan 1988.

4 Some sherds from Grange stone circle are remarkably similar in decorative motifs to Grooved Ware from Knowth (see Eogan and Roche 1997, vessel 51, fig. 44; Ó Ríordáin 1951, fig. 8, nos 29–31). Ó Ríordáin (*op. cit.*, 62) identified some 'miscellaneous' sherds from the circle interior as being similar to British Grooved Ware sites and this identification appears to be valid.

5 This date is based on Sheridan's (1995) reappraisal of Irish Neolithic pottery. Radiocarbon determinations for layers with Grooved Ware at Knowth (Eogan and Roche 1997, 219) are within the range *c.* 2880–2460 cal. BC.

6 Or any material including calcium carbonate, such as shell and calcite.

7 One sherd of Earlier Western Neolithic pottery from Knowth had grog temper, which may have been a casual rather than intentional inclusion in the clay (Brindley 1997, 275).

8 This core was taken from the lake and is dated to the transition between the climatic phases of the Atlantic period (Zone VIIa) and the Sub-Boreal Period (Zone VIIb), or the interface between Mesolithic and Neolithic periods in archaeological terms.

9 Ongoing gas chromatography analyses of the residues on some vessels from Chancellorsland indicate that at least some contain the burnt remains of cereal-based gruel.

BRONZE AGE HOUSES IN IRELAND

Martin Doody

INTRODUCTION

The study of Irish Bronze Age houses and settlements has advanced greatly in recent years. This is due in no small part to an accelerated rate of site discovery resulting from excavations prior to large-scale industrial and infrastructural developments. There has been a steady increase in the frequency of site discovery since the 1930s, with a slight decline in the 1940s and 1950s, and a notable increase in the numbers of sites discovered in the 1990s. The study of Bronze Age settlement had slow beginnings in the history of Irish archaeology. The first recorded instance of a Bronze Age house was at Ballinderry 2, Co. Offaly (Hencken 1942), excavated by the Harvard archaeological expedition to Ireland in 1933; however, this structure is far from typical of Irish Bronze Age houses. It was not until Ó Ríordáin's excavations at Lough Gur, Co. Limerick (Ó Ríordáin 1954), in the 1940s and O'Kelly's work at sites such as Carrigillihy and Ballyvourney, Co. Cork (O'Kelly 1951; 1954), in the early 1950s that more typical examples of Bronze Age houses emerged. In 1964, Eogan, in his article on the Later Bronze Age in Ireland, could list only four examples of domestic sites (Eogan 1964, 314–16). The distribution map of settlement sites (Fig. 1) is gradually being filled in, but it is still a long way from that of the Bronze Age burials or of chance finds of Bronze Age artefacts, which clearly indicate a widespread occupation of the country during this period.

The contribution of rescue excavations to the discovery of Bronze Age sites is undoubtedly great; however, a large part of the work has been done over the years by archaeologists such as M.J. O'Kelly and E.M. Fahy in the south and S.P. Ó Ríordáin and R.M. Cleary in the Lough Gur area. In recent years much has been achieved by the Archaeological Wetlands Unit and the Discovery Programme, which were established in 1990 and 1991 respectively.

The purpose of this paper is to present a list of Irish Bronze Age settlements that have produced house remains dating from the immediate post-Beaker period. The form of the houses is examined and an assessment of possible morphological change as the Bronze Age progressed is presented. The dates for the Early, Middle and Late Bronze Age are based on the radiocarbon chronology for the period published by Brindley (1995).

Thirty-eight Irish Bronze Age sites have produced structural remains that may be considered as houses—a total of 78 individual structures. The term 'house' is used loosely, as obviously not all need necessarily have served as domestic dwellings. Some may have been animal shelters or pens or may have been used for storage. The function of a building is not always apparent from the evidence available at the time of excavation, and even such basic structural details as whether or not a building was roofed may not be clear. All 78 structures are included in the following discussion.

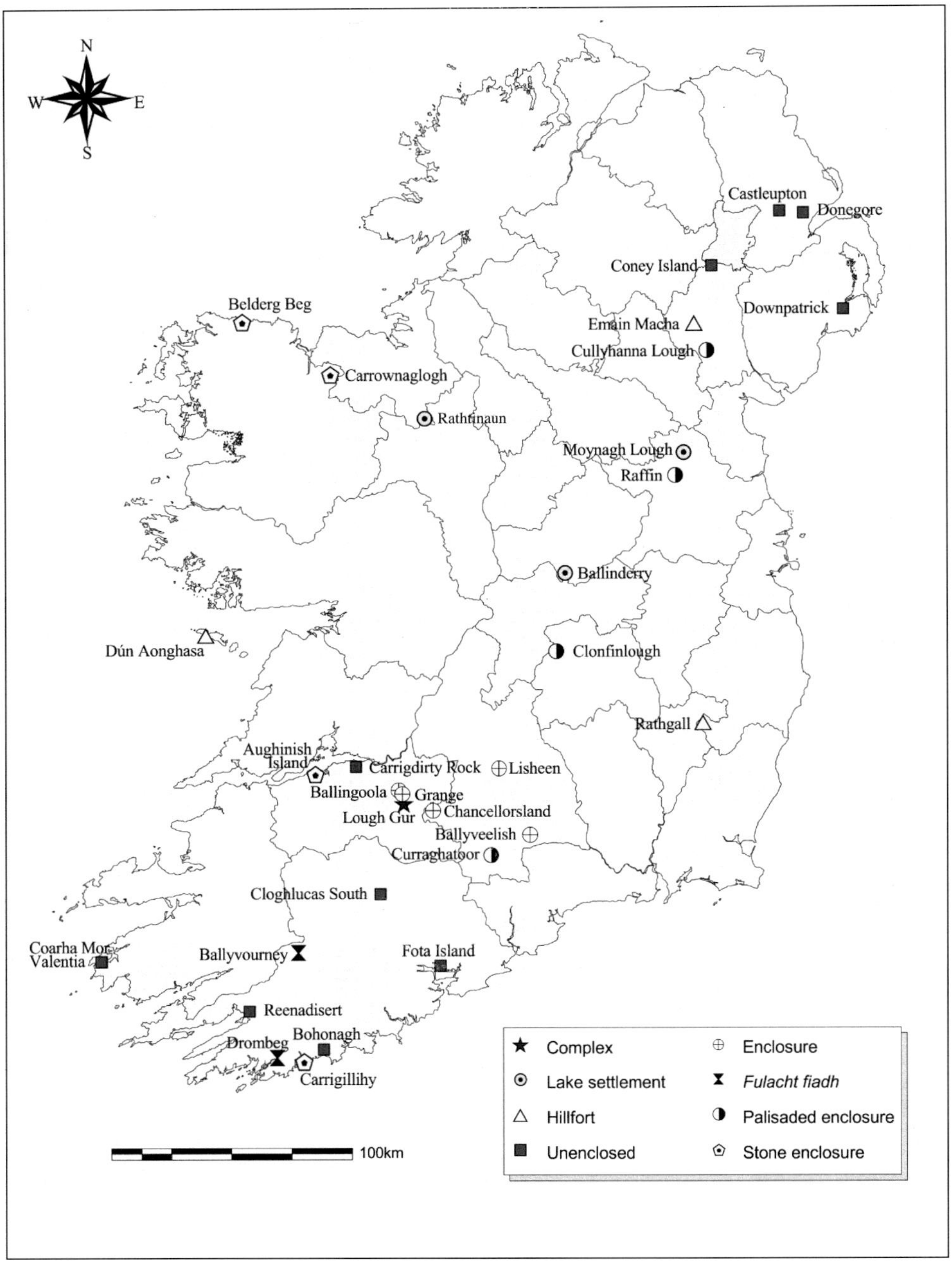

Fig. 1—Distribution map of Bronze Age settlement sites.

HOUSE TYPES

A morphological change, from a largely rectangular house design, began in the Middle Neolithic when some circular houses were being built, and a gradual trend towards circularity becomes apparent as the Neolithic progressed (Grogan 1996, 59). This continued in the Bronze Age, when house design was predominantly circular, although rectilinear examples continued to be built. Both stone and timber were used in construction depending on the local availability of building materials.

Three basic ground-plans were in use (Table 1): round or almost circular, 'U'-shaped/oval, and rectilinear. The houses may be grouped further depending on the number of rings in the perimeter wall, the use of footing trenches and/or an internal arrangement of roof supports. Within these broad types there is considerable diversity in size.

Ground-plan	Perimeter wall	Internal supports	Quantity
Timber round	Single ring		10
	Double ring		2
	Footing trench		7
	Double footing trench		1
	Footing trench	Inner supports	8
Timber 'U'-shaped/oval	Single row/ring		9
	Footing trench		1
Timber rectilinear	Single row/ring		1
	Double row/ring		1
	Single row/ring	Inner supports	1
	Footing trench		8
Stone round			1
		Inner supports	1
Stone rectilinear			3
Stone 'U'-shaped/oval			5
Miscellaneous			8
Combination			4
No details			8
Total			78

Table 1—Summary of Bronze Age house plans and features.

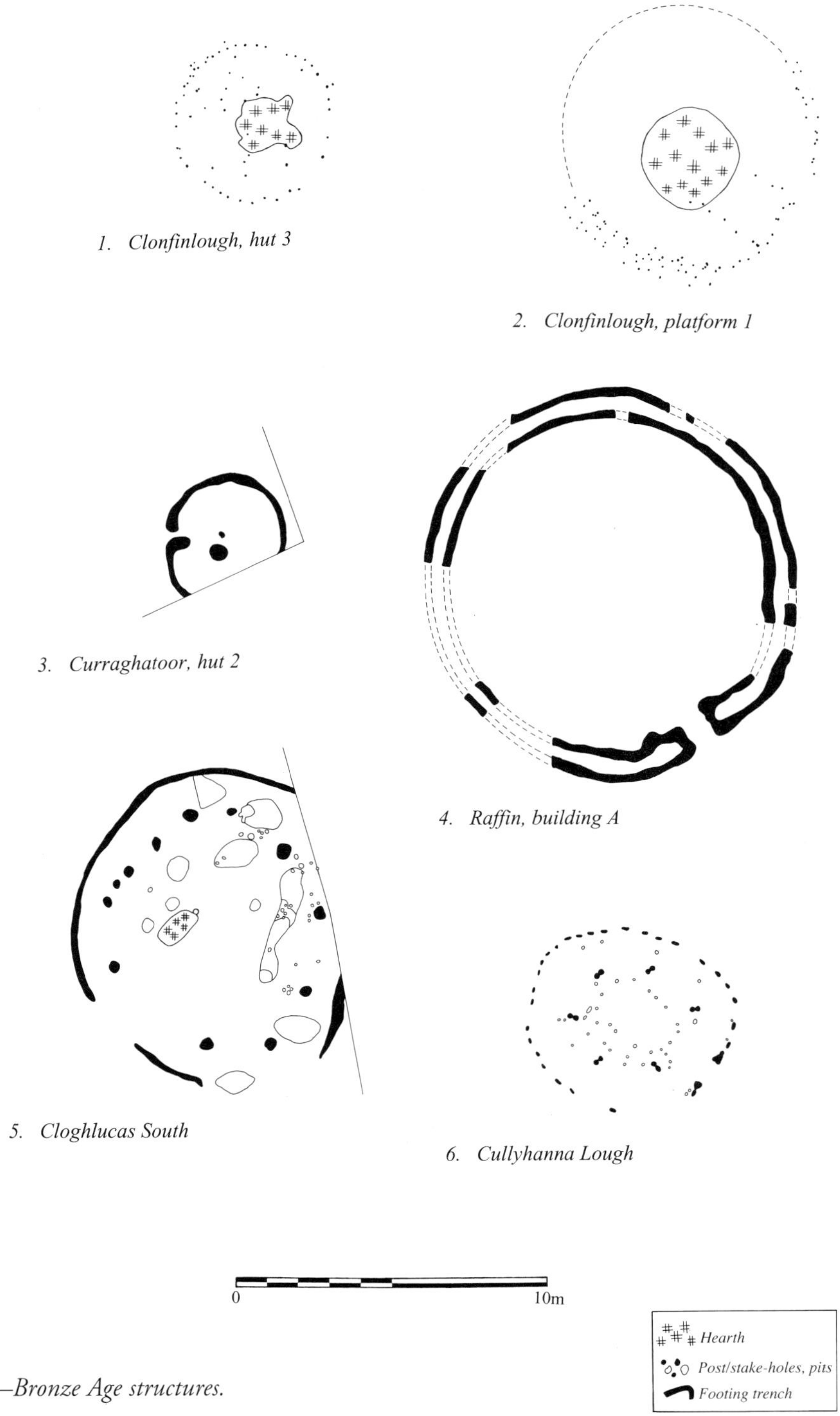

Fig. 2—Bronze Age structures.

Round houses

Round houses in one form or another account for over 87% of excavated Bronze Age house types. The most common type is circular or almost circular in plan; there are 29 examples of these or over 37% of the total. These are further subdivided into five groups based on the form of the perimeter wall, which may consist of a single or double ring of posts or a single or double footing trench, sometimes accompanied by an inner setting of roof supports. The majority of the round houses were constructed of a single ring of posts which formed the wall, and examples are known from Curraghatoor, Co. Tipperary, hut 1 (Fig. 4); Donegore, Co. Antrim; and Clonfinlough, Co. Offaly, hut 3 (Fig. 2, no. 1). Only two examples of round houses with a double ring of posts are known, and both are from the Later Bronze Age site at Clonfinlough (Fig. 2, no. 2).

There are seventeen examples of houses that incorporate one or more footing trenches in the construction. These are equally divided between those with an internal ring of roof supports, e.g. Castleupton (Co. Antrim), Lisheen (Co. Tipperary) and Cloghlucas South (Co. Cork) (Fig. 2, no. 5), and those without an internal ring, as at Curraghatoor hut 2 (Fig. 2, no. 3), Raffin (Co. Meath) and Rathgall (Co. Wicklow). A single example of a house with a double footing trench was also found at Raffin (Fig. 2, no. 4). Prior to the recent excavations at Castleupton and Lisheen there were only two known examples of houses with a footing trench with a true inner ring of roof supports.

The round houses vary considerably in size, ranging in diameter from 3m at Curraghatoor to 13m at Castleupton and 15m at the Later Bronze Age example from Rathgall hillfort. However, in the 28 examples for which accurate measurements are available, the majority (over 60%) are between 5m and 9m in diameter, while eight examples are less than 5m and three are over 10m.

Subcircular, 'U'-shaped or oval houses

Ten examples of houses which are subcircular, oval or 'U'-shaped in plan are known, and all save one are constructed of a single setting of posts without a footing trench. Examples are known from Cullyhanna Lough, Co. Armagh (Fig. 2, no. 6), and Fota Island, Co. Cork. Considerable variation in size is again apparent, the smallest being an example 2.4m in maximum length associated with the *fulacht fiadh* at Ballyvourney 1, while the example at Fota Island was 8m in maximum length. As with the round houses, however, most examples measure between 5m and 9m in maximum length, with only two measuring less than 5m and none exceeding 10m.

There is a single example of an oval or 'U'-shaped house with the wall set in a footing trench at Chancellorsland, Co. Tipperary, structure 15 (Fig. 3, no. 1), where the house was made up of a double setting of closely set stakes.

Rectangular houses

There are eleven recorded examples of rectangular timber houses. These have little in common with their Neolithic predecessors. Few are truly rectangular in plan and many have rounded corners, tending towards a curvilinear plan. The most common type incorporates a footing trench in which the wall is set. Seven of the known examples come from

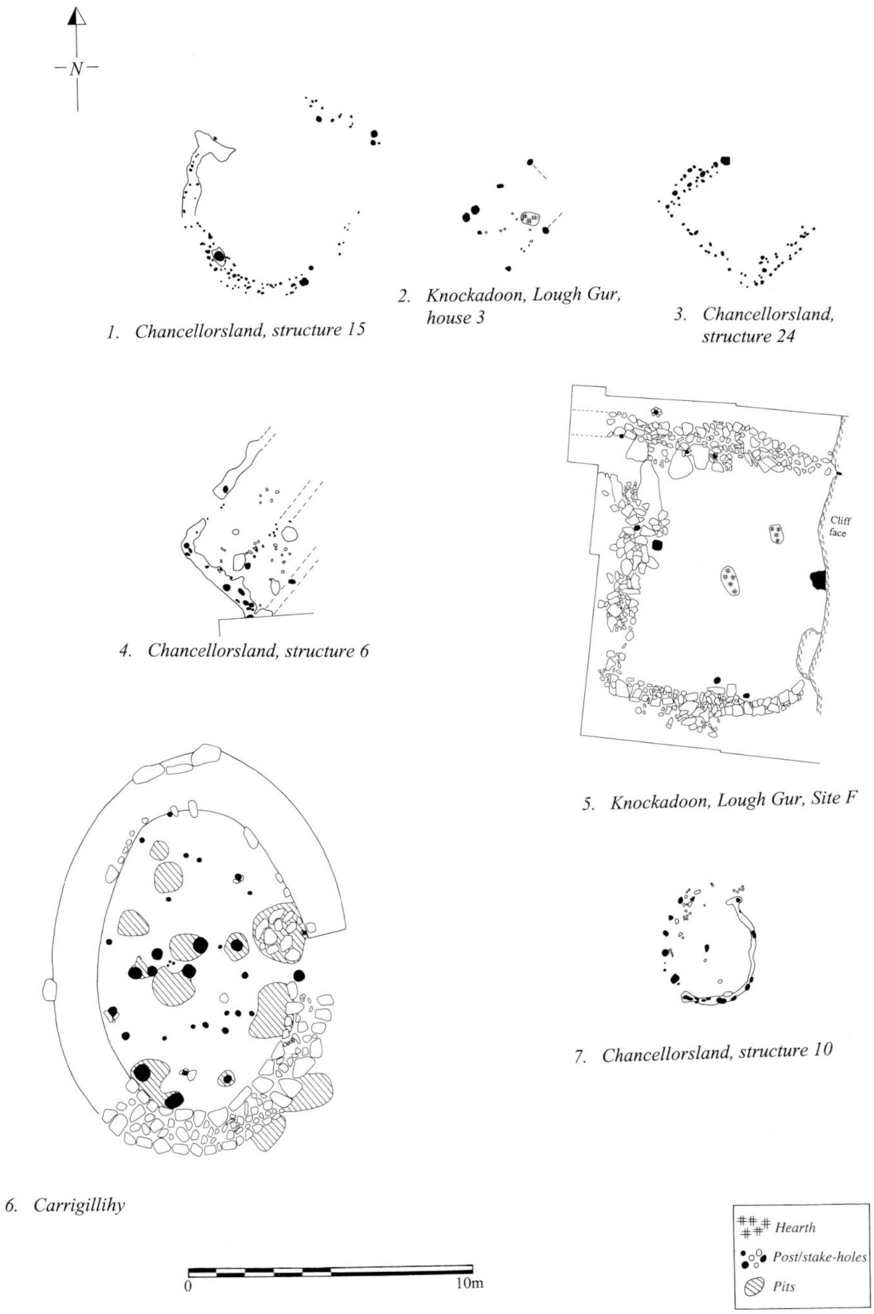

Fig. 3—Bronze Age structures.

Chancellorsland, Co. Tipperary (Doody 1996; forthcoming), and Coney Island, Lough Neagh (Addyman 1965). A house comprised of a row of free-standing uprights was found outside the recently excavated Knockadoon Cave site in Lough Gur (Fig. 3, no. 2; Cleary 1995), while a single example of a house made up of a double row of perimeter posts was recorded at Chancellorsland, structure 24 (Fig. 3, no. 3). A subrectangular house, with an inner row of roof supports, was excavated by Rose Cleary at the Knockadoon Later Bronze Age enclosure, where the cliff face was incorporated into the house construction (Cleary, forthcoming).

The dimensions of the rectangular houses vary considerably, and an example measuring 11m x 4m was excavated at Ballyveelish 3, Co. Tipperary (Doody 1987), while a partly excavated house at Chancellorsland, structure 1, was as little as 2.4m in width. Again the majority have maximum dimensions between 5m and 9m, and only the examples at Ballyveelish 3 and the Knockadoon enclosure exceed these measurements.

Stone houses

Stone houses account for only 12.8% of the excavated Irish examples. Houses that were completely stone-built are as yet unknown in the Irish excavation record. In most cases where the foundation courses of stone remain it is likely that the upper portions of the walls were of a more perishable material, such as wood or sod.

Five of the ten recorded houses are oval or 'U'-shaped in plan and include the impressive Later Bronze Age example from Carrigillihy, which was surrounded by a yard and stone wall (Fig. 3, no. 6). The house measured 10m x 6m and was oval in plan, made up of a double row of orthostats with a rubble core.

Three rectilinear stone houses are known, all from Knockadoon, Lough Gur. These were built up against a cliff face and the largest, site F, measured 8m x 3m (Fig. 3, no. 5). Only two stone round houses are on record. A small example, 3m in diameter, is known from Dún Aonghasa, Inis Mór, and a more elaborate example with an inner ring of roof supports from Belderg Beg, Co. Mayo.

Miscellaneous house types

A number of houses in the archaeological record utilise a combination of techniques in their construction. Examples are known from Chancellorsland, structure 10 (Fig. 3, no. 7), and Downpatrick, Co. Down, where a footing trench is used only in part of the perimeter while the remainder of the posts are free-standing. This was also the case at the Early Bronze Age example from Ballyveelish 3 (Doody 1987) and the rectangular building at Bohonagh, Co. Cork (Fahy 1961).

Other unusual houses are the rectilinear examples from Ballinderry 2, Co. Offaly, which appear to have been constructed on pile foundations, and the huts from Ballingoola 3 and 4 and Grange, Co. Limerick, where the outline of the circular structures was clear; however, there was no detectable evidence of timber uprights.

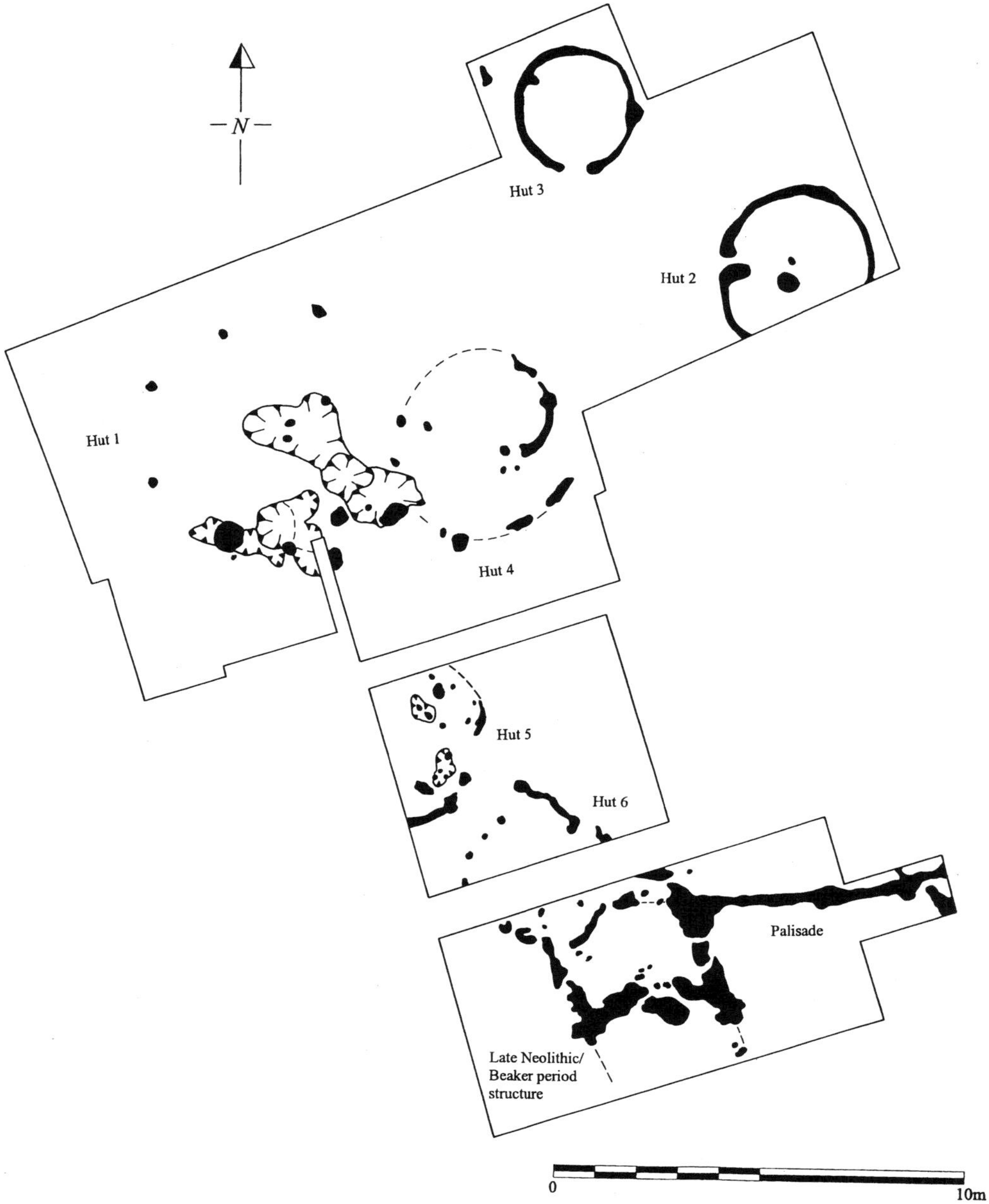

Fig. 4—Curraghatoor, Co. Tipperary: Later Bronze Age settlement.

CHANGE IN STRUCTURAL MORPHOLOGY AS THE BRONZE AGE PROGRESSED

Early post-Beaker Bronze Age (*c.* 1900–1600 BC)

Only eight houses are known from the Early Bronze Age. No particular preference in structural design is apparent, and circular, rectangular and oval examples are known.

Middle Bronze Age (*c.* 1600–1200 BC)

Structural details are available for eighteen houses. Five examples are rectilinear with a footing trench; there are three examples of circular houses with a footing trench and inner ring of roof supports, and a further three of subcircular plan. A greater range of structural dimensions is apparent than was the case with the Early Bronze Age examples, and three houses exceeded 8m in diameter.

Late Bronze Age (*c.* 1200–500 BC)

By far the greatest number of Irish Bronze Age houses date from the later part of the period. Thirty-five examples have been reliably dated to the Later Bronze Age. As one might expect, a wide range of types is present, but circular houses with or without footing trenches account for 48% (17) of the houses present. Of these, the most common types are those with a single ring of free-standing stakes and those with a footing trench. The Later Bronze Age houses are generally slightly larger than the Early/Middle Bronze Age examples. Four considerably larger structures with diameters in excess of 10m are known. The largest Late Bronze Age house is 15m in diameter and was recorded at Rathgall hillfort.

If comparison is made between a combination of Early/Middle Bronze Age houses and the Later Bronze Age examples, of which there is reliable dating evidence for 26 and 35 houses respectively, some differences in ground-plan emerge. Circular houses with or without a footing trench become more common in the later part of the period, from around 19% in the Early/Middle Bronze Age to 48% in the Later Bronze Age. Other types, such as oval, stone-built and circular houses with a footing trench, appear in the archaeological record towards the end of the period.

The question of whether there is a significant change in house design towards the end of the Bronze Age is rather difficult to deal with. There is an obvious imbalance between the numbers of known Early, Middle and Late houses in the archaeological record. There appears to have been a trend towards circular houses, with some larger examples occurring in the Later Bronze Age. A note of caution is advisable, however, as the statistical sample of houses is quite small and the discovery of even a single major site could radically alter our perception of house change throughout the period—in many ways such a discussion is premature. It should also be pointed out that on stylistic grounds there is very little difference between the earlier Bronze Age houses at, for example, Downpatrick and the Later Bronze Age example at Curraghatoor hut 1.

Evidence for superstructure

Except in conditions of exceptional preservation, notably at sites such as Cullyhanna Lough and Clonfinlough, little is preserved of the superstructures of the dwellings. Furthermore, the scarcity of specialist environmental studies, especially from the earlier excavations, has resulted in little indication of the type of wood used in the construction and little interpretation of the finished appearance of the structures. Now, however, with the development of environmental aspects of archaeology, a more complete picture of Bronze Age buildings is emerging.

Types of wood used

Many factors influenced the choice of material used in house construction. Local availability apart, the size and nature of the building will dictate the dimensions and species of wood to be used. For example, some of the lighter turnover-type huts, such as Curraghatoor huts 2, 3 and 4 and Chancellorsland structure 10, would require light flexible timbers that could be drawn towards the centre and tied; young ash, hazel and willow/poplar were suitable. On the other hand, more substantial structures capable of supporting a heavy thatched roof would require much more sturdy posts, perhaps up to 30cm in diameter, such as Chancellorsland structure 12, where oak and elm were used. Wattle screens are sometimes indicated by the presence of suitably sized willow and hazel rods.

The evidence from excavated sites is for the use of a wide variety of wood species in house construction. The results from the Chancellorsland excavations were especially useful in this regard owing to the preservation of charred wood remains from the structural features themselves and waterlogged wood from the surrounding ditches. Structure 6 (Fig. 3, no. 4) appears to have been a substantial rectangular building and was constructed of oak, hazel and ash. Oak, hazel and willow/poplar were used in structure 10 (Fig. 3, no. 7). Alder was used in structure 15, hazel and oak occurred in structure 24, while oak and elm were among the species used in structure 12.

Superstructure

The spacing of the uprights varied considerably in different structures, from virtually contiguous at Chancellorsland structure 15, to 1.5m at Moynagh Lough, Co. Meath, and 2m at Downpatrick, Co. Down, and Curraghatoor hut 1. O'Kelly (1954) addressed this aspect of house design in his reconstruction of the wigwam-type structure at Ballyvourney 1. He found that the widely spaced uprights provided insufficient support for the roof, resulting in roof sag. He wove light timbers between the uprights only as far as ground level, where they would leave no detectable archaeological trace, and found that it greatly strengthened the structure and eliminated the sag.

Evidence for wall coverings is less forthcoming. Wattling of willow and hazel is known from a number of sites, including Ballyveelish 3, Clonfinlough and the structures outside the recently excavated Knockadoon Cave site at Lough Gur; however, evidence for how this may have been weatherproofed, if at all, is not as obvious. Mud daub, animal skins and sod have all been proposed, but except in exceptional circumstances these are not evident at the time of excavation. Examples of daub are known from Grange and Ballingoola, Co. Limerick, and Lisheen and Curraghatoor, Co. Tipperary. Ó Ríordáin proposed a plastered 'bird cage' reconstruction for the Grange example, while O'Kelly suggested a covering of animal skins for the Ballyvourney 1 hut. There was evidence for sod walls at the Early Bronze Age house on Coney Island, while Hodges suggested that the gaps between the uprights at Cullyhanna Lough could have been filled with peat blocks. Finally, the evidence from Navan Fort, slot E3, suggests the presence of upright planking positioned between pairs of stakes. It is likely that most roofs were thatched, although the use of skins and sods is also a possibility.

Internal divisions, furnishings, and internal and external hearths

Many of the excavated houses are practically devoid of internal features. Unlike some of the Neolithic examples, there are only a few houses with obvious internal subdivisions. In many ways this reflects the size of the structures, which are often too small to accommodate more than a single compartment. Two rooms were noted at the Fota Island house and this was also the case at the Early Bronze Age house at Ballyveelish 3, where there was a clearly marked doorway between the two compartments. Chancellorsland structures 1 and 6 also appear to have had internal subdivisions, and what may have been a 'hallway' ran from the entrance of the large house at Rathgall hillfort towards the centre of the structure.

Evidence for internal furnishings is not immediately so obvious. This is not surprising as benches, beds, etc. need not necessarily leave any detectable remains at the time of excavation. O'Kelly, however, interpreted some of the features at the Ballyvourney 1 hut as a possible bed or table.

Internal hearths were recorded in only 24 of the 78 known structures. This may mean that those structures without hearths had a function other than a domestic one, or it may simply indicate that the houses were used mainly as sleeping quarters while most of the domestic or industrial activity took place in daylight outside the huts. External hearths close to huts have been recorded at Castleupton, Chancellorsland, Rathgall and Moynagh Lough.

Reconstruction

The house reconstructions presented here (Figs 5 and 6) were executed on AutoCAD 14 and involved firstly digitising the excavated ground-plan and then inserting appropriately sized uprights into the post-holes and stake-holes. The skeletal structure was then draped to create the impression of the walls and roof. The reconstructed image is ultimately three-dimensional and can be rotated and viewed from any angle, including internally.

The reconstructed houses are based on the evidence from two different structural types excavated at Chancellorsland. The smaller of the two is based on the evidence from structure 10, which is almost circular in plan and measured 3.6m north–south x 3.25m east–west (Fig. 5). It was made up of light stakes, some of which were set in a slight footing trench, and there was a central roof support. The reconstruction is in the form of a turnover-type hut, where the uprights are bent inwards towards the centre to form a framework similar to an upturned basket. There was no evidence from the excavation to suggest how the framework of the hut was covered. In this case a covering of thatch is used, although sods or hides may have been viable alternatives.

The reconstruction of the larger house is based on Chancellorsland structure 12 (Fig. 6). It measured 6.6m north–south x 5.4m east–west and was constructed of closely set substantial uprights, the majority of which appear to have been driven into the ground. A

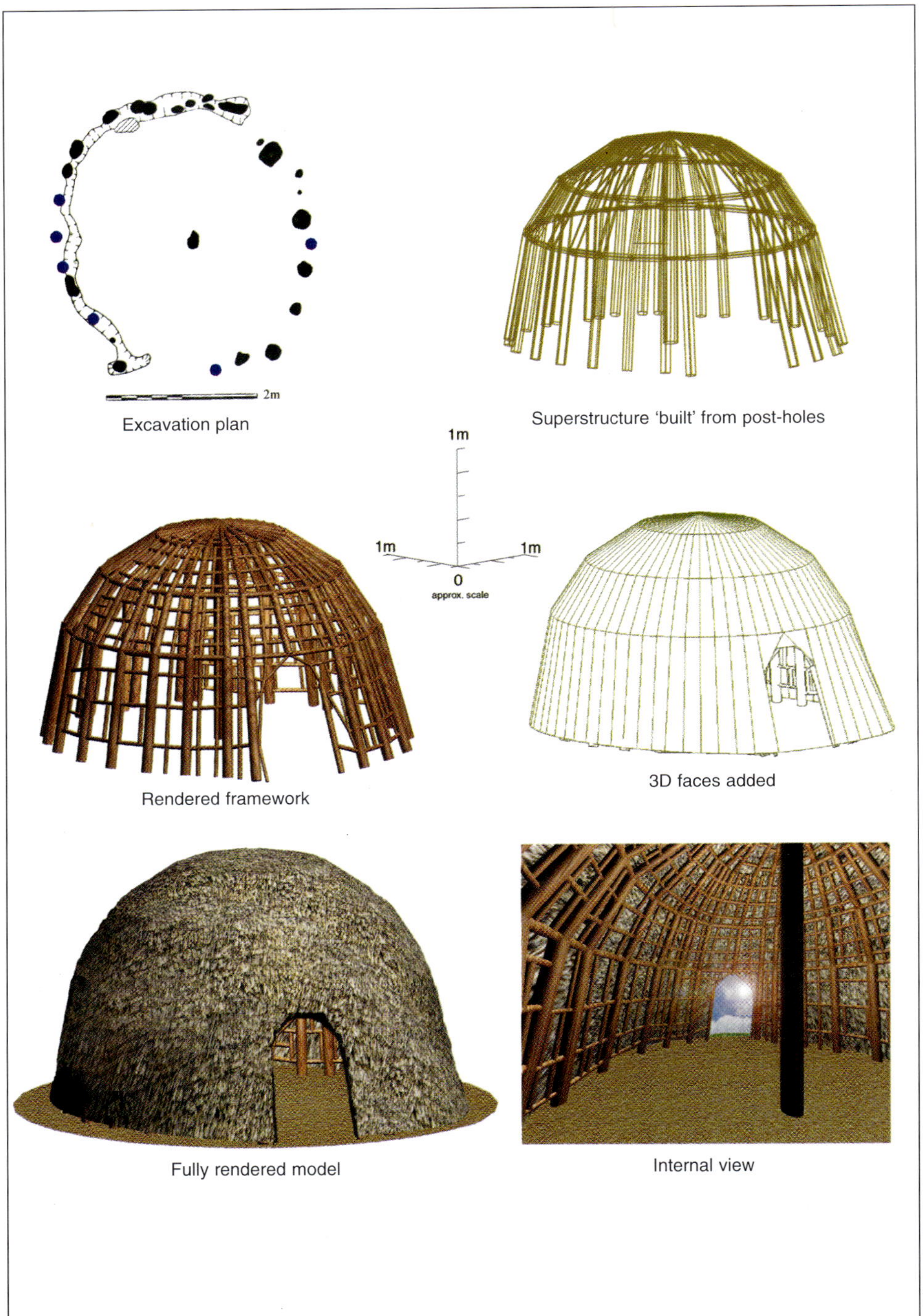

Fig. 5—Reconstruction of structure no. 10 at Chancellorsland, Co. Tipperary.

number of assumptions are made in the reconstruction of structure 12. Firstly, there is no direct evidence that the building was roofed or, if so, that it was in the manner proposed. Secondly, there is no evidence from the excavation for the daub rendering of possible wattle walls. Nevertheless, the reconstruction is presented as representing how a substantial Bronze Age house may have appeared.

Successive building phases and house clusters: is there any evidence for village communities in the excavation record?

There is ample evidence for the construction of two or more houses on many excavated sites. This was the case in fifteen out of the 38 sites that have produced house remains. A number of sites are known where a particular ground-plan is repeated two or more times. At Chancellorsland there are at least three examples that follow a roughly similar ground-plan, which is rectilinear and relatively small, with little evidence for uprights. Similarly, at Curraghatoor four of the huts are strikingly similar to each other, with a circular plan and a slight footing trench (Fig. 4). At Lisheen and Castleupton several examples of houses with footing trenches and an inner ring of roof supports are known. This type of construction was almost unknown in Ireland prior to the excavation of these houses.

In many sites the multiple occurrence of houses clearly represents the successive construction of buildings, owing to structural deterioration, on the same location. Such was the case at Downpatrick and the Early Bronze Age Moynagh Lough, where the two round houses were not contemporary—nor indeed were all ten structures at Chancellorsland. Similarly, Curraghatoor hut 1 clearly post-dates hut 4 and appears to be the latest of the buildings on the site.

Less frequent is the evidence for clusters of houses that may have been in use contemporaneously. This appears to have been the case at Clonfinlough, where the dating evidence indicates a relatively short duration of use of the settlement, perhaps by an extended family group. At Curraghatoor, the smaller huts (2–6), with the exception of hut 6, were similar to each other morphologically. They may all have been in use at the same time and were perhaps enclosed by a palisade. The hut entrances appear to face each other towards a common central area (Fig. 4). One could imagine these huts, which would have been cramped as domestic quarters, functioning mainly as sleeping quarters, while most of the domestic activity could have taken place in the area outside.

There is no evidence from the excavated sites for village communities, i.e. groups of several extended families together. Rather, the evidence supports a system of single farmsteads or at best clusters of huts of an extended family living together.

EVIDENCE FOR ENCLOSURES

Perhaps as many as seventeen of the 38 excavated sites appear to have been enclosed in one form or another at some stage during their use. A number of different forms of enclosure existed, ranging from very elaborate hillfort defences, such as at Rathgall and Mooghaun, to ditched enclosures like Chancellorsland and palisaded examples like Curraghatoor and

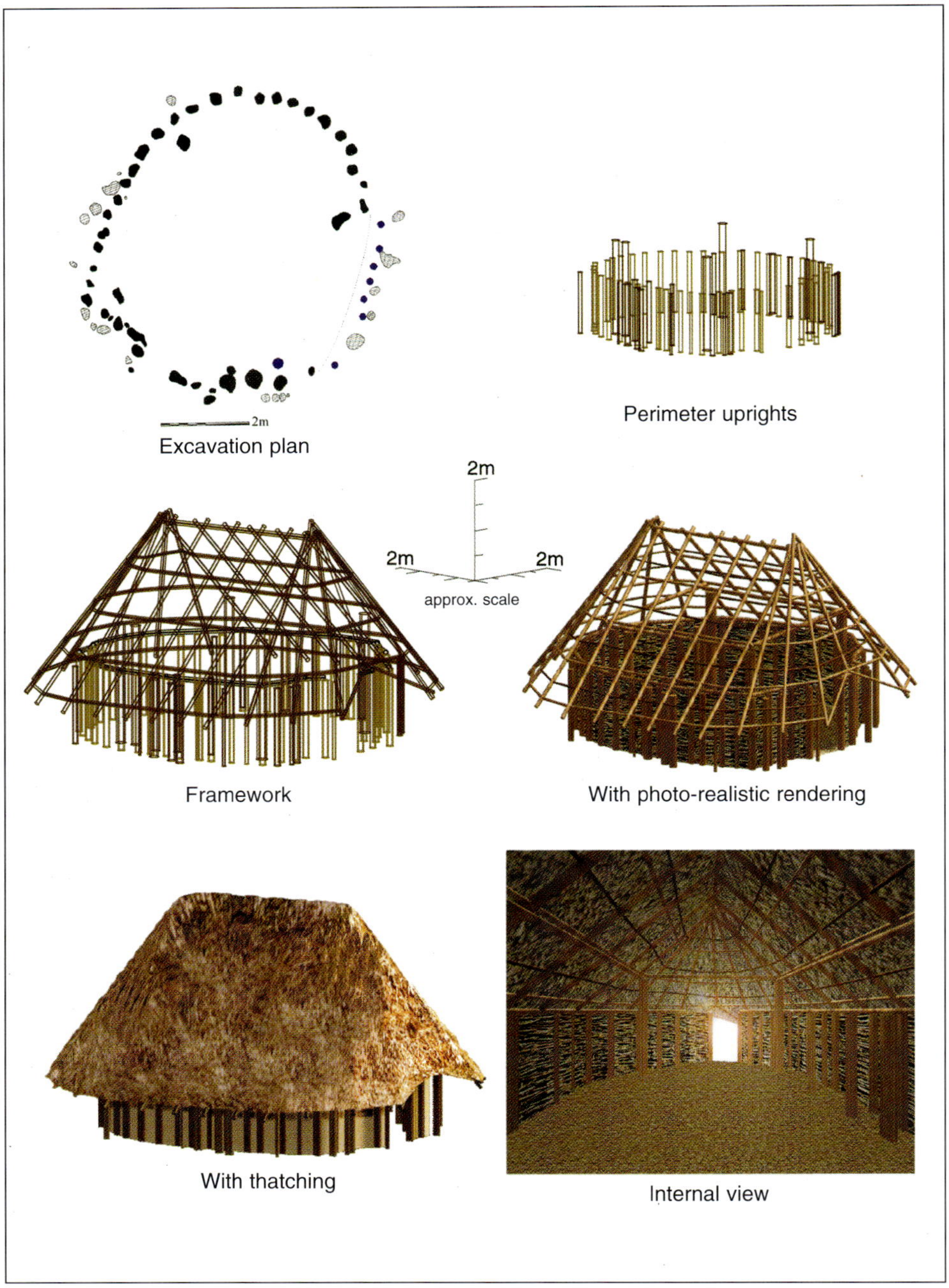

Fig. 6—Reconstruction of structure no. 12 at Chancellorsland, Co. Tipperary.

perhaps Raffin and Donegore. Simple stone and earthen enclosures surrounding a single dwelling are also known, such as at Carrigillihy, Co. Cork, and Aughinish and Ballingoola 3 and 4, Co. Limerick.

Many of the unenclosed settlements were excavated in rescue conditions where often it was not possible to examine a sufficiently large area around the houses. A case in point is Curraghatoor which, when originally excavated as part of the Cork–Dublin pipeline in 1982, was thought to be unenclosed. It was only after further large-scale excavation from 1987 to 1991 that the evidence for an enclosing palisade was recognised. It is possible that enclosed sites may have been far more common than the evidence as yet suggests. The reconstruction of the Chancellorsland house and enclosure (Fig. 7) is based largely on the excavated structural features and environmental and economic information inferred from specialist studies of the organic remains.

DISCUSSION

Analysis of the corpus of Irish Bronze Age houses has focused attention on a number of issues relating to the distribution and nature of Bronze Age settlement, the factors that influenced house design throughout the period and the general social context to which they belong.

The distribution map of Bronze Age settlements is in marked contrast to those of the burials (Waddell 1990, 36, fig. 7) and metalwork of the period (Eogan 1983, 217–18, figs 1 and 2), both of which point to a widespread occupation of the country. The occurrence of settlement sites is by comparison patchy, despite the increased rate of site discovery in recent years. The reasons for the under-representation of domestic sites are many, but principal among these are the difficulties of recognising Bronze Age settlement sites in the absence of excavation. Bronze Age structures were predominantly built of wood and, as such, leave few above-ground detectable remains. Apart from sites such as hillforts and crannogs, for example, it has been difficult to identify a distinctive Bronze Age site type that might increase the visibility of settlement sites on the ground. Recent aerial reconnaissance in an area around Bruff, Co. Limerick, has been instructive in this regard (Doody 1993). The survey has highlighted the existence of a number of subcircular and subrectangular enclosures of types that are not readily accommodated by existing archaeological classifications. The juxtaposition of some of these enclosures with barrow cemeteries, e.g. Lattin and Chancellorsland, Co. Tipperary, has raised the possibility of a Bronze Age date for the enclosures. This was confirmed by excavation in the Chancellorsland example, with obvious consequences for the recognition of part of the Bronze Age landscape in the survey area.

Analysis of changing trends in house design throughout the Irish Bronze Age is fraught with difficulties. As was the case in Britain, round or at least curvilinear house design became predominant in the Bronze Age. Once this basic round house design was adopted it remained remarkably constant throughout the period, albeit with many variations and an apparent increase in the occurrence of larger houses towards the end of the Bronze Age. It has been suggested that the general similarities that exist in house plans are due to the comparable nature of domestic life and social organisation in an area, while the variations that exist may

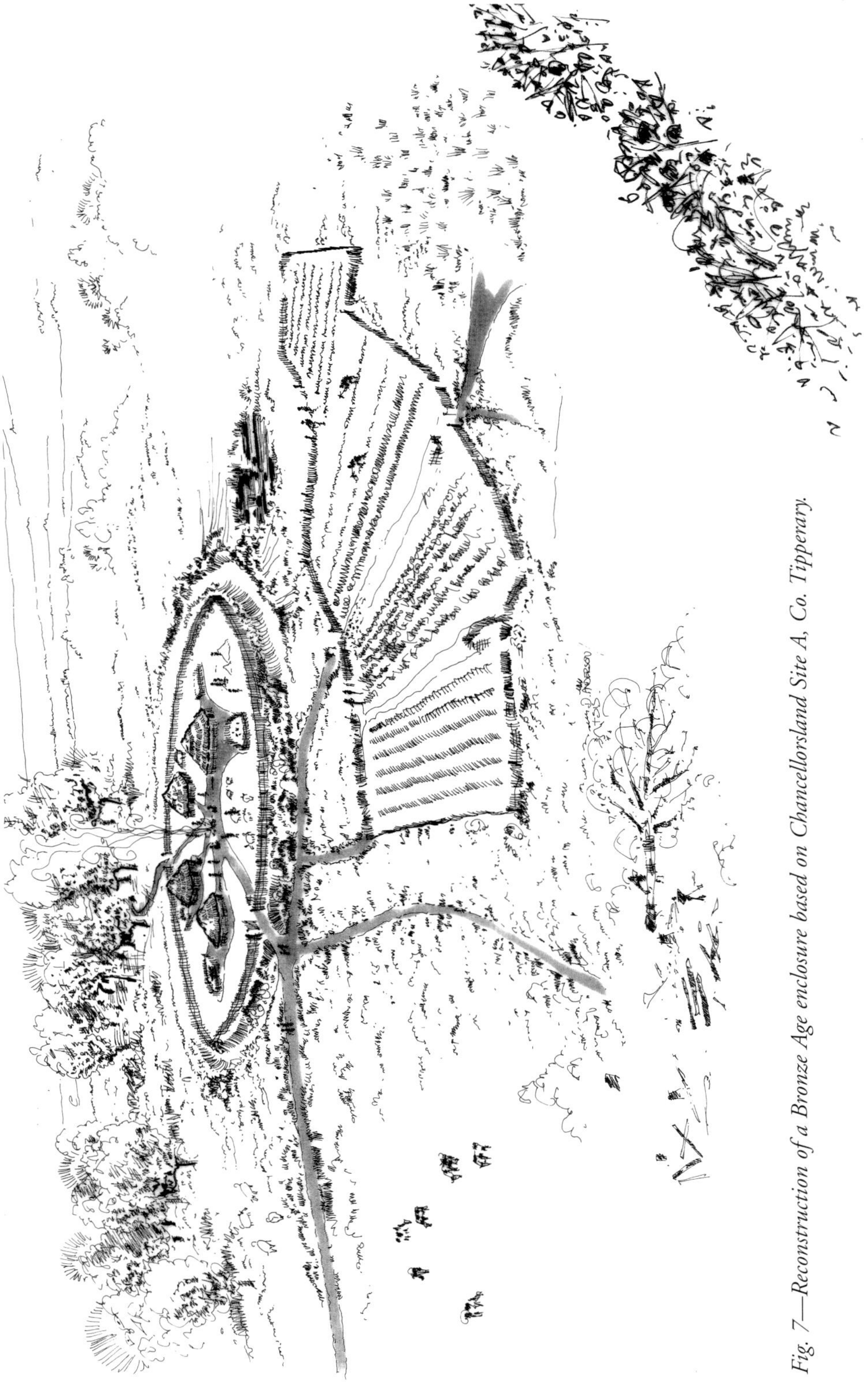

Fig. 7—Reconstruction of a Bronze Age enclosure based on Chancellorsland Site A, Co. Tipperary.

be due to diversity caused by different tribal or ethnic groups (Reid 1993, 5). This appears to hold true for Britain, where a number of regionally distinctive house styles had developed by the Bronze Age. There is no evidence, as yet, to suggest that this was the case in Ireland, where no regional preferences are apparent. It is difficult to chronologically assess changing house styles from earlier and later periods of the Bronze Age as the majority of the recorded houses date from the Later Bronze Age, with only a few belonging to the earlier part of the period. As a result any analysis of house styles will be biased in favour of the Late Bronze Age. This also appears to be the case in Britain, where Early Bronze Age houses are especially rare (Barclay 1998, 58).

The reconstruction of two very different house types from Chancellorsland illustrates the potential diversity of roughly contemporary houses from a single site. Structure 12, at least, indicates that Bronze Age houses had achieved a considerable degree of sophistication. Evidence from Ireland and Britain points to the use of advanced woodworking techniques, with mortise and tenon joints and wooden pegs being employed to secure timbers in place (Reid 1993, 16).

The social context of the Bronze Age houses appears to have been complex. Grogan (1996, 38) and Eogan (1998, 324) propose a speculative model for social organisation in the Bronze Age in which the elaborate hillforts, having a communal function, represented the highest-status sites. The next tier in the proposed hierarchy comprised medium-sized enclosures, essentially family farmsteads, such as those at Chancellorsland and Curraghatoor, which was surrounded by a palisade. Single enclosed house sites, for example Aughinish and Ballingoola, and presumably unenclosed sites formed the lowest stratum of society. The extent to which this hierarchy in settlement types may have been reflected in a similar hierarchy of house types is not yet fully understood; this will only become possible with the excavation of a representative cross-section of sites from the various stages of the Bronze Age.

SUMMARY OF EXCAVATED SITES WITH HOUSE REMAINS

Aughinish, Co. Limerick

Two stone enclosures were excavated at this Later Bronze Age site in 1974. The remains of a circular wooden structure were found in one, while a platform for another was recorded in the second enclosure. Associated artefacts included pottery, bronze, possible mould fragments, saddle querns and part of an iron bridle-bit.
(Kelly 1975)

Ballinderry 2, Co. Offaly

This lakeside settlement was excavated as part of the Harvard archaeological expedition to Ireland in 1933. The Later Bronze Age component contained at least two unusual rectangular houses that appear to have been constructed on a pile foundation. A wealth of associated Dowris Phase artefacts was found, which included pottery, bronze, amber, lignite, stone, flint and worked bone.
(Hencken 1942)

Ballingoola 3 and 4, Co. Limerick

These enclosures are described by the excavator as marshland habitation sites. They may date from the Bronze Age and consist of small banked and ditched subcircular enclosures, each containing a house. The few recorded finds included fragments of stone axes and crudely chipped flint.
(Ó Ríordáin 1949)

Ballyvourney 1 and 2, Co. Cork

Two *fulachta fiadh* were excavated by M.J. O'Kelly in the early 1950s as part of his experiments into ancient Irish cooking places. In addition to the cooking troughs, both sites produced evidence of hut structures, one at Ballyvourney 1 and two successive buildings at the second site. The only artefact was a stone pounder from the trough at site 1.
(O'Kelly 1954)

Ballyveelish, Co. Tipperary

Excavated in 1981–2 as part of the Cork–Dublin natural gas pipeline, the site produced evidence for Earlier (site 3) and Later (sites 2 and 3) Bronze Age activity. An oval-shaped Earlier Bronze Age house was associated with an encrusted urn burial, while a subrectangular structure was constructed in the same location during the Later Bronze Age. No house remains survived on site 2 owing to later disturbance of the enclosure. Artefacts included an encrusted urn, two pygmy cups, worked flint and two saddle querns.
(Doody 1987)

Belderg Beg, Co. Mayo

A circular stone house was associated with a stone field system that is part of the Céide Fields. The only domestic artefacts were saddle querns and rubbing stones. An Early/Middle Bronze Age date is suggested.
(Caulfield 1988)

Bohonagh, Co. Cork

A rectangular timber house in close proximity to a recumbent stone circle was excavated in 1959 and the only finds recorded were several undiagnostic pieces of flint.
(Fahy 1961)

Carrigdirty Rock, Co. Limerick

This site, situated in the Shannon Estuary, was excavated as part of the Discovery Programme's North Munster Project. A light, oval timber structure was associated with animal bone. The radiocarbon evidence suggests a Middle Bronze Age date.
(O'Sullivan 1996)

Carrigillihy, Co. Cork

This site produced evidence from the Bronze Age and Early Christian periods. The Later Bronze Age horizon produced evidence for an oval stone-built house within an oval stone

enclosure. Associated artefacts included pottery, a bronze awl, a stone disc and a hone stone.
(O'Kelly 1951)

Carrownaglogh, Co. Mayo
This circular house was marked by a bank inside a stone-walled enclosure. There were no associated finds. It was dated to the Middle Bronze Age.
(Herity 1981)

Castleupton, Co. Antrim
Rescue excavations in 1996 uncovered an apparently unenclosed site with three circular houses. Finds included pottery, stone and flint.
(A. Gahan, pers. comm.)

Chancellorsland, Co. Tipperary
A ditched enclosure, oval in plan, was discovered through aerial photography in 1986 and later excavated as part of the Discovery Programme's Ballyhoura Hills Project in 1992–6. The site included the remains of at least ten houses, a large quantity of organic remains, pottery, chert and flint, stone, amber, worked bone and a small amount of bronze. The radiocarbon evidence suggests use of the enclosure during the Middle Bronze Age.
(Doody 1996; forthcoming)

Cloghlucas South, Co. Cork
An unenclosed circular house was uncovered during the construction of the Limerick gas pipeline. There were no associated finds. A Bronze Age date is suggested by the proximity of a *fulacht fiadh* and close parallels with other excavated Bronze Age houses.
(Gowen 1988)

Clonfinlough, Co. Offaly
This palisaded enclosure, located on the shore of Finlough, was excavated by the Irish Archaeological Wetlands Unit in 1991. Excellent preservation conditions led to the survival of the remains of two substantial hut platforms and two smaller huts. Associated finds included pottery, amber and worked wood. The site has been dated by dendrochronology to the Later Bronze Age.
(Moloney 1993)

Coarha More, Valentia Island
This unenclosed stone house was associated with a *fulacht fiadh*. Finds included pottery, flint flakes and a worked wooden object. The site has been radiocarbon-dated to the Late Bronze Age.
(Hayden 1994)

Coney Island, Lough Neagh
Limited excavations at this apparently unenclosed site produced remains dating from the

Early and Late Bronze Age. Two rectangular huts were associated with food-vessel bowls, a plano-convex knife and small scrapers, and dated from the earlier period. Later Bronze Age coarseware and a possible house trench were found in the same area.
(Addyman 1965)

Cullyhanna Lough, Co. Armagh
This temporary hunting camp was enclosed by a wooden palisade and contained a single house. The few associated finds consisted of pottery and flint. It was dated dendrochronologically to the Early Bronze Age.
(Hodges 1958)

Curraghatoor, Co. Tipperary
The site was first excavated in 1982 as part of the Cork–Dublin gas pipeline and later from 1987 to 1991. It was enclosed by a wooden palisade during at least one phase of occupation and consisted of at least five circular houses and one rectangular example. The few associated finds included pottery, flint and stone.
(Doody 1997)

Donegore, Co. Antrim
A single round house dating from the Late Bronze Age was found on Donegore Hill during the excavation of the causewayed enclosure in 1983; it may have been enclosed by a wooden palisade. There were no associated artefacts.
(Mallory and McNeill 1991; J.P. Mallory, pers. comm.)

Downpatrick (Meadowlands), Co. Down
Limited excavations during the construction of the Meadowlands housing estate uncovered the remains of two apparently unenclosed circular houses. Associated finds were a globular lump of bronze, stone, flint and cordoned urn pottery. The site has been dated to the Early/Middle Bronze Age.
(Pollock and Waterman 1964)

Drombeg, Co. Cork
Three successive structures, the earliest of which was timber-built and the other two of stone, were found in association with a *fulacht fiadh*. The only finds were a perforated stone and a saddle quern.
(Fahy 1960)

Dún Aonghasa, Inis Mór
The hillfort was excavated as part of the Discovery Programme's Western Stone Forts Project, 1992–6. The remains of several stone house sites were uncovered, at least one of which appears to be of Bronze Age date. The artefact assemblage was rich and varied and included pottery, bronze, moulds and crucibles, amber, stone and flint.
(Cotter 1996; forthcoming)

Fota Island, Co. Cork

This unenclosed site contained one oval wooden house. The only associated artefact was a chert blade. The site has been dated by radiocarbon to the Early/Middle Bronze Age.
(Rutter 1992)

Grange, Co. Limerick

This was a marshland habitation site, subcircular in plan and enclosed by a bank and ditch, located close to Ballingoola 3 and 4 (see above). A circular house within the enclosure had apparently burnt down. Associated finds were stone, flint, chert and worked bone.
(Ó Ríordáin 1949)

Knockadoon Cave, Lough Gur, Co. Limerick

The excavation at the mouth of a cave on Knockadoon Hill produced evidence for successive periods of occupation during the Later Bronze Age. The remains were unenclosed (as with all the Knockadoon sites, this was effectively enclosed by the lake) and comprised three or possibly four timber huts on a platform outside the cave. Finds included pottery, a small amount of bronze, stone, flint and worked bone.
(Cleary 1995)

Lough Gur, Co. Limerick

This stone enclosure was located on a plateau close to Circle K on the western side of Knockadoon Hill. The site produced evidence for two houses, both of which incorporated the natural cliff face in their construction. The finds included pottery, a small amount of gold and bronze, stone, flint and worked bone.
(Cleary, forthcoming)

Lough Gur, Co. Limerick, Site D

An unenclosed rectangular stone house was located on the southern side of Knockadoon Hill. The structure may have been a metal workshop and the finds included pottery, bronze, moulds, crucibles, stone, flint and worked bone.
(Ó Ríordáin 1954)

Lough Gur, Co. Limerick, Site E

This rectangular unenclosed stone house was located on the southern side of Knockadoon Hill. Finds included pottery and stone.
(Ó Ríordáin 1954)

Lough Gur, Co. Limerick, Site F

A rectangular unenclosed stone house was located at the western end of Knockadoon Hill. Finds included stone axe fragments, Class I and II pottery, and mould fragments of looped spearheads and rapiers.
(Ó Ríordáin 1954)

Lough Gur, Co. Limerick, Site G

An unenclosed semicircular stone house was located on the southern side of Knockadoon Hill. Finds included pottery, flint, a bone point and two small pieces of bronze.
(Ó Ríordáin 1954)

Lough Gur, Co. Limerick, Site H

An irregularly shaped stone and post structure was associated with a small quantity of Class I pottery and a few Beaker sherds. Most of the pottery was of Class II.
(Ó Ríordáin 1954)

Lisheen, Co. Tipperary

Five structures were uncovered during a rescue excavation as part of the Lisheen mining project. The structures were located quite close to a *fulacht fiadh* and a wooden trackway. Finds included pottery, flint, stone and a spearshaft. The site has been radiocarbon-dated to the Middle Bronze Age.
(J. O'Neill, pers. comm.)

Moynagh Lough, Co. Meath

This complex lakeside habitation site produced evidence for multi-period occupation from Mesolithic times. The Bronze Age occupation dates from the Early and Later Bronze Age. There was evidence for two timber structures from the earlier part of the period and one from the later phase. A wealth of associated artefacts included pottery, flint, stone, bone and beads from the earlier Bronze Age deposits, and pottery, bronze, amber, lignite, stone, bone and antler from the later deposits.
(Bradley 1997)

Raffin, Co. Meath

The main phase of activity at this complex ritual and settlement site was in the Iron Age, from the second to the fifth century AD, but the dates ranged from the Neolithic through to the sixth and seventh centuries AD. The site produced two Bronze Age houses, both of which date from the Later Bronze Age. The earlier of the two appears to have been enclosed by a palisade.
(Newman 1995; pers. comm.)

Rathtinaun, Co. Sligo

The remains of a possible circular timber house at this lakeside settlement were associated with a small but varied assemblage of artefacts, including pottery, bronze and gold, mould fragments, amber, lignite and worked wood.
(Raftery 1994)

Rathgall, Co. Wicklow

The hillfort excavations at Rathgall produced evidence for extensive metal production during the Later Bronze Age, and artefacts included pottery, bronze, gold, mould fragments, amber,

lignite and stone. A large circular house was recorded in the innermost enclosure, and other smaller buildings were excavated outside the enclosure.
(Raftery 1994)

Reenadisert, Bantry, Co. Cork
A rescue excavation has produced the remains of a circular structure associated with pottery.
(J. Tierney, pers. comm.)

ACKNOWLEDGEMENTS

The author wishes to thank the following, who allowed access to material in advance of publication: Rose Cleary, Mags Gowen, John O'Neill, John Bradley, Jim Mallory, Aidan O'Sullivan, Audrey Gahan, John Tierney and Conor Newman. Thanks are also due to Nigel McGuirk for the computer-aided reconstructions, Donal Anderson for the site reconstruction, and Niamh O'Callaghan for the line drawings and helpful discussion on the text.

REFERENCES

Addyman, P.V. 1965 Coney Island, Lough Neagh: prehistoric settlement, Anglo-Norman castle and Elizabethan fortress. *Ulster Journal of Archaeology* **28**, 78–101.

Barclay, G. 1998 *Farmers, temples and tombs: Scotland in the Neolithic and Early Bronze Age.* Edinburgh. Canongate Books with Historic Scotland.

Bradley, J. 1997 Archaeological excavations at Moynagh Lough, Co. Meath, 1995–1996. *Ríocht na Midhe* **9** (3), 50–61.

Brindley, A.L. 1995 Radiocarbon, chronology and the Bronze Age. In J. Waddell and E. Shee Twohig (eds), *Ireland in the Bronze Age,* 4–13. Dublin. Stationery Office.

Caulfield, S. 1988 *Céide Fields and Belderrig guide.* Killala. Morrigan Book Company.

Cleary, R.M. 1995 Later Bronze Age settlement and prehistoric burials, Lough Gur, Co. Limerick. *Proceedings of the Royal Irish Academy* **95**C, 1–92.

Cleary, R.M. (forthcoming) An enclosed Later Bronze Age habitation site and field fence at Lough Gur, Co. Limerick.

Cotter, C. 1996 Western Stone Forts Project, interim report. *Discovery Programme Reports* **4**, 1–14. Dublin. Royal Irish Academy.

Doody, M. 1987 Ballyveelish, Co. Tipperary. In R.M. Cleary, M.F. Hurley and E.A. Twohig (eds), *Archaeological excavations on the Cork–Dublin natural gas pipeline 1981–82,* 8–35. Department of Archaeology, University College Cork.

Doody, M. 1993 The Bruff Aerial Photographic Survey. *Tipperary Historical Journal* (1993), 173–80.

Doody, M. 1996 Ballyhoura Hills Project, interim report. *Discovery Programme Reports* **4**,

15–25. Dublin. Royal Irish Academy.

Doody, M. 1997 Bronze Age settlement in Co. Tipperary: fifteen years of research. *Tipperary Historical Journal* (1997), 94–106.

Eogan, G. 1964 The Later Bronze Age in Ireland in the light of recent research. *Proceedings of the Prehistoric Society* **30**, 268–351.

Eogan, G. 1983 *Hoards of the Irish Later Bronze Age.* University College Dublin.

Eogan, G. 1998 Homes and homesteads in Bronze Age Ireland. In H. Bernhard (ed.), *Mensch und Umwelt in der Bronzezeit Europas*, 307–26. Kiel. Oetker-Voges Verlag.

Fahy, E.M. 1960 A recumbent stone circle at Drombeg, Co. Cork. *Journal of the Cork Historical and Archaeological Society* **64**, 1–27.

Fahy, E. 1961 A stone circle, hut and dolmen at Bohonagh, Co. Cork. *Journal of the Cork Historical and Archaeological Society* **50**, 42–9.

Gowen, M. 1988 *Three Irish gas pipelines: new archaeological evidence in Munster.* Dublin. Wordwell.

Grogan, E. 1996 Neolithic houses in Ireland. In T. Darvill and J. Thomas (eds), *Neolithic houses in northwest Europe and beyond*, 41–62. Oxford. Short Run Press.

Hayden, A. 1994 Coarha More, Valentia Island, Bronze Age settlement. In I. Bennett (ed.), *Excavations 1993*, 42–3. Bray. Wordwell.

Hencken, H. O'Neill 1942 Ballinderry crannog no. 2. *Proceedings of the Royal Irish Academy* **47**C, 1–76.

Herity, M. 1981 A Bronze Age farmstead at Glenree, Co. Mayo. *Popular Archaeology* **2**, 258–65.

Hodges, H.W.M. 1958 A hunting camp at Cullyhanna Lough near Newtown Hamilton, Co. Armagh. *Ulster Journal of Archaeology* **21**, 7–13.

Kelly, E. 1975 Aughinish Island, sites 1 and 2. In T.G. Delaney (ed.), *Excavations 1974. Summary accounts of archaeological work in Ireland*, 20–1. Belfast. Association of Young Irish Archaeologists.

Mallory, J.P. and McNeill, T.E. 1991 *The archaeology of Ulster from colonization to plantation.* Institute of Irish Studies, Queen's University, Belfast.

Moloney, A. 1993 *Excavations at Clonfinlough, Co. Offaly.* Irish Archaeological Wetland Unit Transactions 2. Dublin. Irish Archaeological Wetland Unit.

Newman, C. 1995 Raffin Fort, Co. Meath: Neolithic and Bronze Age activity. In E. Grogan and C. Mount (eds), *Annus Archaeologiae*, 55–66. Dublin. Organisation of Irish Archaeologists.

O'Kelly, M.J. 1951 An Early Bronze Age ringfort at Carrigillihy, Co. Cork. *Journal of the Cork Historical and Archaeological Society* **56**, 69–86.

O'Kelly, M.J. 1954 Excavations and experiments in Irish cooking places. *Journal of the Royal Society of Antiquaries of Ireland* **84**, 105–55.

Ó Ríordáin, S.P. 1949 Lough Gur excavations; three marshland habitation sites. *Journal of the Royal Society of Antiquaries of Ireland* **79**, 126–39.

Ó Ríordáin, S.P. 1954 Lough Gur excavations: Neolithic and Bronze Age houses on Knockadoon. *Proceedings of the Royal Irish Academy* **56**C, 297–459.

O'Sullivan, A. 1996 Later Bronze Age intertidal discoveries on north Munster estuaries.

Discovery Programme Reports **4**, 63–71. Dublin. Royal Irish Academy.
Pollock, A.J. and Waterman, D.M. 1964 A Bronze Age habitation site at Downpatrick. *Ulster Journal of Archaeology* **27**, 31–58.
Raftery, B. 1994 *Pagan Celtic Ireland: the enigma of the Irish Iron Age.* London. Thames and Hudson.
Reid, M.L. 1993 *Prehistoric houses in Britain.* Princes Risborough. Shire.
Rutter, A.E. 1992 *Digging up Cork, archaeological excavations in Cork 1992.* Cork Public Museum.
Waddell, J. 1990 *The Bronze Age burials of Ireland.* Galway University Press.

MEGALITHIC TOMBS, METAL RESOURCES AND TERRITORY IN PREHISTORIC SOUTH-WEST IRELAND

William O'Brien

> 'The cause of the distribution of the megalithic culture beyond the area of the Eastern Mediterranean was the search for certain forms of material wealth. Gold, tin, copper, pearls, precious stones, and so forth were eagerly sought after, and where they were discovered, there the megalithic influence soon made itself felt. The search for wealth is the underlying factor in the distribution, and it seems to provide the motive for the widespread travellings of these people' (Perry 1915, 25).

The circumstances surrounding the building of megalithic tombs in western Europe during the Neolithic continue to engender much debate. While modern studies emphasise regional variability and multi-causal explanation, the earlier tendency was to seek unitary interpretations within a migrationist or diffusionist framework. Though widely attributed to religious fervour, more pragmatic theories were also advanced to explain the spread of the 'megalithic idea'. A strong economic incentive, be it the promise of new agricultural land, metal or other commodities, has frequently been raised in this regard. Doubtless this was encouraged by the many historical parallels, from Roman legions to Spanish conquistadors, for the spread of a religious movement in the wake of military conquest in which the search for precious metal was an important objective.

This rationale is evident in the writings of W.J. Perry, a student of Professor Elliot Smith and the Manchester school of hyperdiffusionism. For these scholars, the origins of the megalithic tomb lay in small groups of merchant venturers ('Children of the Sun') setting out from Egypt to civilise the world (see Daniel and Renfrew 1988, 84–96). In his 1915 paper, Perry argued that a search for metal and other precious substances lay behind these wanderings. This notion of a link between megalithic tombs and trade is also apparent in the modified diffusionism of Childe, whose 'apostles of the megalithic faith' moved along routeways and contacts established for the exchange of metals and other commodities. Examples here include the lure of Wicklow gold for the Boyne Valley tomb-builders (Macalister 1935; Childe 1940), or the arrival of metal-seeking 'colonists' of eastern Mediterranean origin in southern Iberia (Siret and Siret 1887; Blance 1961).

Since the 1960s, radiocarbon dating has made a connection between early metal use and the building of megalithic tombs untenable for many parts of western Europe (cf. Renfrew 1967). While this remains possible for the Iberian Peninsula, where metal use extends back to 3000 BC or earlier, megalithic tombs had largely ceased to be built elsewhere by the mid-third millennium BC, when metallurgy was being widely adopted. This is true for Britain and Ireland, where construction and active use of chambered tombs had effectively ceased by *c.* 2800–2500 BC. An important exception here is the wedge tomb, a gallery tomb variant which was built in large numbers in parts of Ireland in the centuries following the introduction of metallurgy around 2500–2300 BC.

With the 'radiocarbon revolution' came the realisation that culture-historical frameworks for this period were seriously flawed (Renfrew 1973a, 84–108). As a result, new approaches for extracting social meaning from archaeological data have emerged in recent decades. The response generally has been to examine how material evidence reflects the internal dynamics of past human societies, or actively constitutes their social relations through symbolic meaning. These new perspectives have gradually made an impact on the study of megalithic tombs in Ireland, where culture-historical thinking has prevailed until recent times. This is especially true in the case of wedge tombs, for which issues of chronology and origins have long dominated the interpretative agenda.

SOUTH-WEST IRELAND

With few monuments of Early–Middle Neolithic date, the first widespread occurrence of megaliths in the Cork–Kerry region is the appearance of wedge tombs in the final Neolithic/Early Bronze Age, *c.* 2500–1500 BC. These are small, single-chambered monuments with a south-westerly orientation (Pl. 1), marked by a consistent size and architecture (see de Valera and Ó Nualláin 1982; O'Brien 1999 for details). Some 139 examples have been identified in this region, with 104 of these in Cork alone (Fig. 1). These fall into two geographical groupings, namely a distribution in the Cork–Kerry peninsulas and a concentration of some 50 tombs in the upper Lee basin and surrounding landscape of mid-Cork. The building of these megalithic tombs appears to have been followed, with some possible overlap, by a broadly complementary distribution of stone circles, rows and related monuments in Middle–Late Bronze Age times (Ó Nualláin 1978; 1984; 1988; O'Brien 1993).

Ó Nualláin linked the appearance of these wedge tombs and stone circle monuments to the arrival of two metal-seeking groups who colonised this region at the beginning of the Bronze Age (de Valera and Ó Nualláin 1982). His culture-migrationist model attributed the appearance of wedge tombs to the arrival of Beaker-using people from north-western France, where *allées couvertes* gallery tombs provided suitable prototypes. In this ethnic interpretation, the peninsular and inland distributions of wedge tombs in the Cork–Kerry region were respectively interpreted in terms of landfall and inland penetration (*ibid.*, 118). A comparison may be drawn with a survey of early copper-mining in Huelva province, Spain (Rothenberg and Blanco-Freijeiro 1981), which also used the proximity of megalithic tombs to provide a cultural context for this activity.

This paper will consider the social context of megalithic tomb-building in south-west Ireland during the final Neolithic and Early Bronze Age. The emphasis will be on understanding the territorial significance of wedge tomb distributions and the implications of resource control for social relations within these small-scale segmentary societies. This analysis will focus on the role of wedge tomb communities in early copper-mining and metal production.

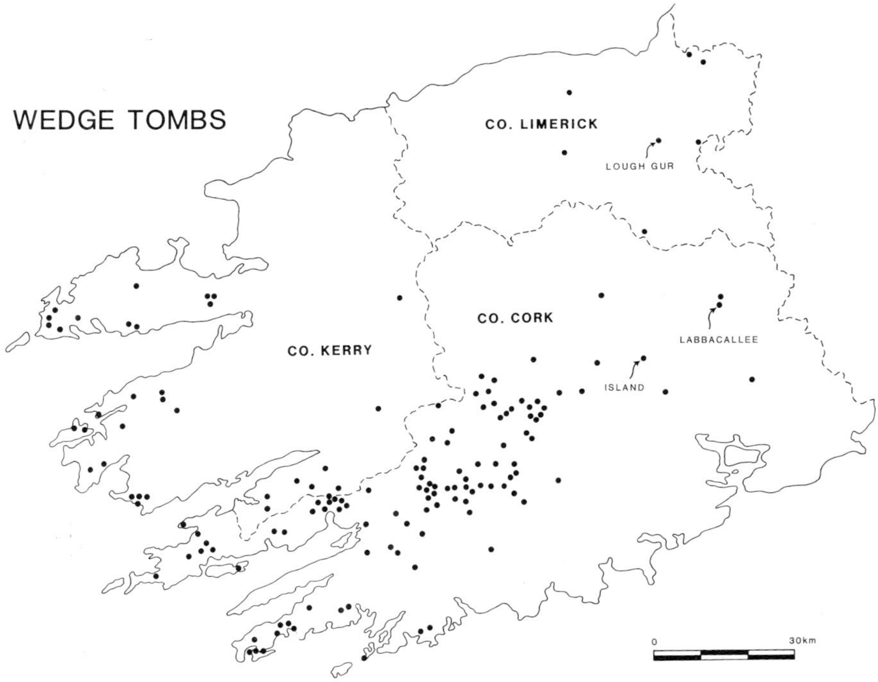

Fig. 1—Wedge tombs in south-west Ireland.

Pl. 1—Rathooragh wedge tomb, Mizen Peninsula, Co. Cork (scale: 2m). Mount Gabriel in background.

THE 'ECONOMY' OF THE TOMB-BUILDERS

Examining the economic concerns of megalithic tomb-builders is central to understanding the process of Neolithicisation in many parts of western Europe. Unfortunately, this analysis is often hampered by the dearth of contemporary settlement information. The general assumption is that most megalithic tombs were an integral part of a lived-in landscape, and were probably sited within their immediate settlement context. In the absence of residential sites, researchers have used the siting and distribution of megalithic tombs to infer settlement economy, where a proximity to fertile soils, fishing grounds and other natural resources is seen to reflect the subsistence concerns of these Neolithic communities. Generally included in this resource catchment analysis is some consideration of raw materials, such as lithic sources and, in a few instances, metals.

The question of whether we can infer subsistence economy from tomb location is highly contentious. Many studies have identified a broad correlation between the distribution of megalithic tombs and good agricultural land (e.g. Renfrew 1979; Cooney 1983; O'Brien 1999). This may be used to support a close relationship with agricultural activity, whereby the monuments served as territorial markers and symbols of resource ownership. The siting of tombs directly on or overlooking farmland may also have been motivated by magico-religious belief and a desire to place agricultural activity under the protection of the tomb spirits. However, by comparing megalithic tomb distributions with land quality, we make certain assumptions about the economic base of these prehistoric communities. That their tombs were located on or near good soils does not mean that the builders were agriculturists, just as a proximity to ore sources does not imply an interest in metal production. Excavation of the tombs themselves is also problematic, as their contents, like their siting, often represent highly symbolic acts which need not reflect the economic concerns of that particular society.

The siting and distribution of wedge tombs in south-west Ireland suggest three different areas which may have been of economic importance to the tomb-builders—agriculture, the exploitation of coastal resources, and an involvement in copper-mining and metal production. From pollen evidence it appears that many wedge tomb communities were involved in agriculture. Others were also able to exploit marine resources to varying levels of intensity, and some groups discovered copper ore deposits within their resource catchment areas (Figs 2 and 3). While there were opportunities for specialisation, most communities probably had a broadly based subsistence economy with much local and seasonal variability. The main factors here were the resource opportunities offered by their respective settlement territories, and the different population requirements and cultural outlook of each community. Also relevant was the willingness of different groups to engage in local and regional exchange, and to exploit resource imbalances for collective or individual gain. The ability to make metal and to control its circulation is particularly significant here. The latter may have introduced an element of instability into small-scale societies which had otherwise achieved a certain equilibrium in their natural and cultural environments.

Metal resources

While many Bronze Age communities in south-west Ireland obtained supplies of metal

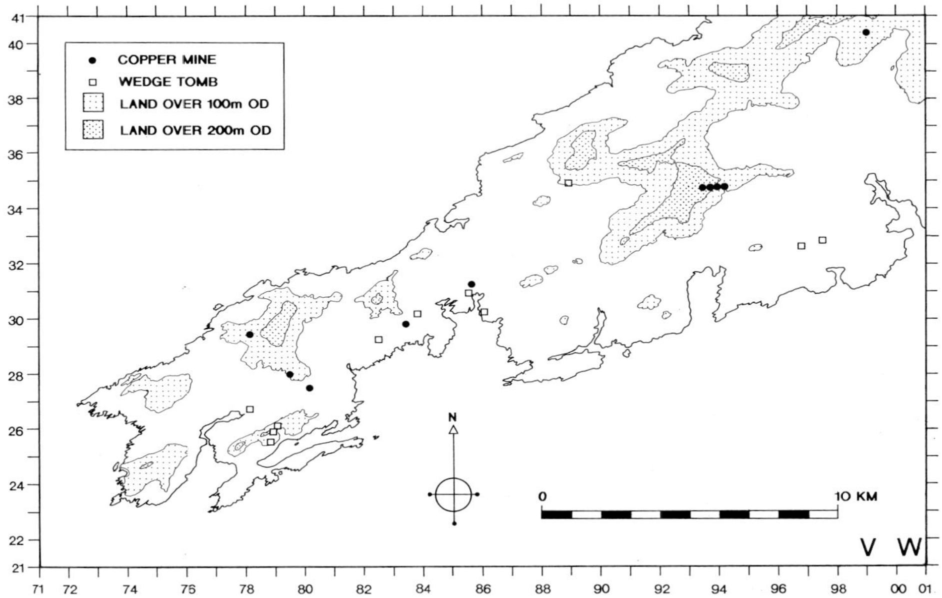

Fig. 2—Wedge tombs and Bronze Age copper mines in the Mizen Peninsula, Co. Cork.

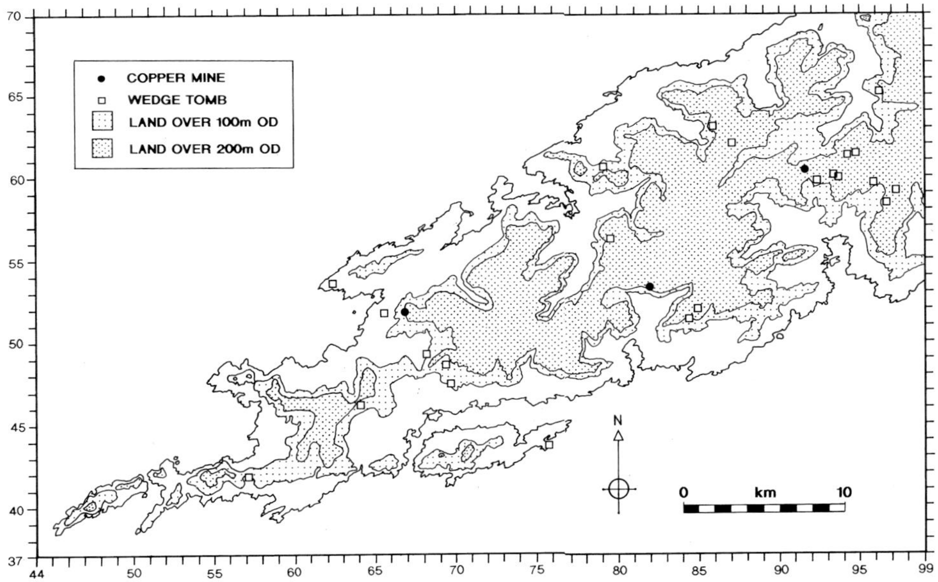

Fig. 3—Wedge tombs and Bronze Age copper mines in the Beara Peninsula, Co. Cork.

through regional exchange networks, an involvement in mining and primary production of metal was limited by natural resource distribution across this region. To identify the resource base of these early metallurgists, we need to consider the availability of different ore resources in both technological and social terms and then demonstrate their *de facto* use by specific tomb-building communities. This requires a consideration and secure dating of mines and metallurgical sites, metal-working artefacts and residues, with scientific provenancing of the metal concerned to local ore deposits.

The Cork–Kerry region offers an ideal environment in which to address some of these questions. This area has a proven record of Bronze Age mining, most notably the distribution of Mount Gabriel-type copper-bed workings in the Mizen and Beara peninsulas of Cork (Figs 2 and 3; O'Brien 1994) and the recent discovery of a Beaker copper mine at Ross Island, Killarney, Co. Kerry (O'Brien 1995). The dense concentration of wedge tombs and stone circle monuments in this region has long been linked to the exploitation of these copper deposits (de Valera and Ó Nualláin 1982). It does appear that copper metallurgy was a significant component in the economy of *some* megalith-building communities in south-west Ireland. Instead of viewing these metal sources as the stimulus for an external colonisation, we should examine the contribution which metal production made to the socio-economic development of indigenous population groups from the end of the Neolithic.

WEDGE TOMBS AND THE TERRITORIAL MODEL

With the processual archaeology of the 1970s came the development of new approaches to understanding the social context of megalithic tombs in western Europe. The most influential research was that carried out by Colin Renfrew, who argued that we can use spatial patterning within the archaeological record to examine how past societies were organised (Renfrew 1973b; 1976; 1977). Observing that human behaviour is territorially organised, he suggested that all past societies had a spatial structure which in some way reflected their social organisation. This can be investigated through archaeological survey and the analysis of settlement patterns, as revealed through the distribution of habitation sites, ritual monuments and artefacts.

In his important 1976 paper, Renfrew proposed that the appearance of megalithic tombs in western Europe was an expression of territorial behaviour in small-scale segmentary societies. He argued that this emerged in response to population pressure experienced by Early Neolithic farming groups in the Atlantic and North Sea coastal zone, where they came into contact with successful forager communities. He recognised that the anthropological definition of a segmentary tribal society could be usefully applied to the social context of megalithic tomb-building. Through various case-studies, he proposed that territorial division of land and resources is given symbolic expression in many segmentary societies. Membership of the social group and the land they occupied was defined by kinship and local residence, expressed in rituals which were often focused upon a specific location. For Renfrew, megalithic tombs functioned as territorial markers in segmentary societies and played a key role in maintaining the structure of contemporary social organisation.

Renfrew's basic theory was subsequently developed by Chapman (1981), using anthropological arguments to examine the link between megalithic tombs and territoriality. While criticised in recent years for its functionalist approach and ecological determinism (see Chapman 1995 for discussion), the territorial model offers several important insights into the structuring of past societies. These may now be applied to an analysis of wedge tombs and final Neolithic/Early Bronze Age society in south-west Ireland.

Wedge tomb society

Following Renfrew's approach, we may consider how the location and distribution of these tombs relate to the Early Bronze Age settlement landscape, and specifically to the concept of wedge tomb 'territories'. The underlying assumption is that the distribution of these monuments reflects kin-based residence patterns, where each wedge tomb or tomb cluster represents a unilineal descent group, bound to neighbouring groups by common descent or marriage relationships. Each wedge tomb can be taken to represent a 'primary tribal segment', for whom the monument may have served many different functions and acquired many different meanings (O'Brien 1999).

The question arises as to whether these small multi-family groupings were integrated into a wider tribal structure, sharing a common ancestry and ethnicity, language and religion. The fissioning or segmentation of tribal societies means that groups separated by considerable distances may be related by kinship, which ensures an ongoing interacting relationship. However, tribes are segmental organisations, marked by basic residential units which enjoy a high degree of economic and political autonomy (Sahlins 1961; Service 1962). This structure can tend towards disunity and constant feuding unless certain mechanisms promote integration through pan-tribal sodality. The wedge tomb is an obvious mechanism to promote kinship and group solidarity, through its articulation of the principle of descent from a common ancestor or its expression of a widely held religious belief.

It appears likely that the social 'territories' suggested by the distribution of wedge tombs do indeed correspond to the home areas of living groups of people. This assumption is supported by the spacing of these monuments in the peninsulas and mid-Cork region, and their occurrence in, or close to, resource-rich areas. Within these locales, there is a spacing of similarly sized tombs or tomb clusters, with no indication of hierarchical ordering of monuments on the basis of size, architecture or location. This tendency to dispersal and uniformity reflects a territorial constraint on the growth of this society, in a cellular pattern broadly repeated across the south-west region.

Essentially, the distribution of wedge tombs in Cork and Kerry represents the geographical spread of unilocal descent groups as part of an expanding tribal/lineage network. While we may conceptualise a mosaic of wedge tomb communities, it is less easy to visually map their respective territories across south-west Ireland. The difficulty here relates to our limited understanding of wedge tomb chronology and the changing configuration of these home areas over time. To identify Early Bronze Age settlement zones in this landscape, we clearly cannot think of equal-distance territories with arbitrary boundaries. The overall settlement pattern was heavily influenced by both terrain and natural resource distribution, which combined to create certain areas that were optimal for human settlement (Fig. 4).

RESOURCES AND SOCIETY

Central to the territorial model is the idea that megalithic tombs were part of a system of socially recognised claims to valuable resources. For Renfrew, these tombs served as a deed of usership of the land, and the bones of the ancestors were physical reminders of the continuity of settlement and the lasting bonds between land and people. He equated the use and location of a megalithic tomb with membership of a corporate group defined by ancestry and place of residence. This idea was further developed by Chapman, who proposed that megalithic tombs were examples of 'formal disposal areas' by which corporate groups utilised lineal ties to the ancestors to control access to crucial but restricted resources. He argued that these monuments began to be used when critical resources came under pressure and communities needed to symbolically control them in a more visible way. The emergence of territorially based descent groups is a response to this process, expressed in the building of megalithic tombs which stake a permanent claim to critical resources through the enduring presence of the ancestors (Chapman 1981; 1995).

In regard to south-west Ireland, such theories prompt the question of whether any imbalance in the distribution of natural resources led to competition between different groups, resulting in social tension which required the building of a megalithic tomb as a territorial/resource marker. While accepting that this may have happened elsewhere, I consider it less likely among the wedge tomb communities of the West Cork peninsulas, where strong lineal ties and marriage relationships probably limited competition in what was after all a resource-rich environment. Each wedge tomb was a territorial marker in the sense that it symbolically denoted a unilocal community; however, these monuments are unlikely to have developed in an environment of demographic pressure and competition for critical resources.

Human resources

It is widely assumed that the building of megalithic tombs implies a considerable input of labour which was only possible in societies that had reached a certain level of economic development. Many large megalithic tombs display an obvious 'command of labour' in the scale of their construction, which allows certain interpretations to be made about the nature of that society. In Late Neolithic Ireland the building of large passage tombs like Newgrange and the other Boyne Valley monuments is generally taken to represent a high degree of centralised organisation and economic surplus. In contrast, the building of smaller megalithic tombs is usually seen as being well within the resources of small local groups, aided on occasions by kinsmen and neighbours.

The wedge tombs of south-west Ireland fall into the latter category, marked by a limited investment of labour that was feasible within the small multi-family groups which constituted the 'primary segments' of this tribal society. The fact that these communities did

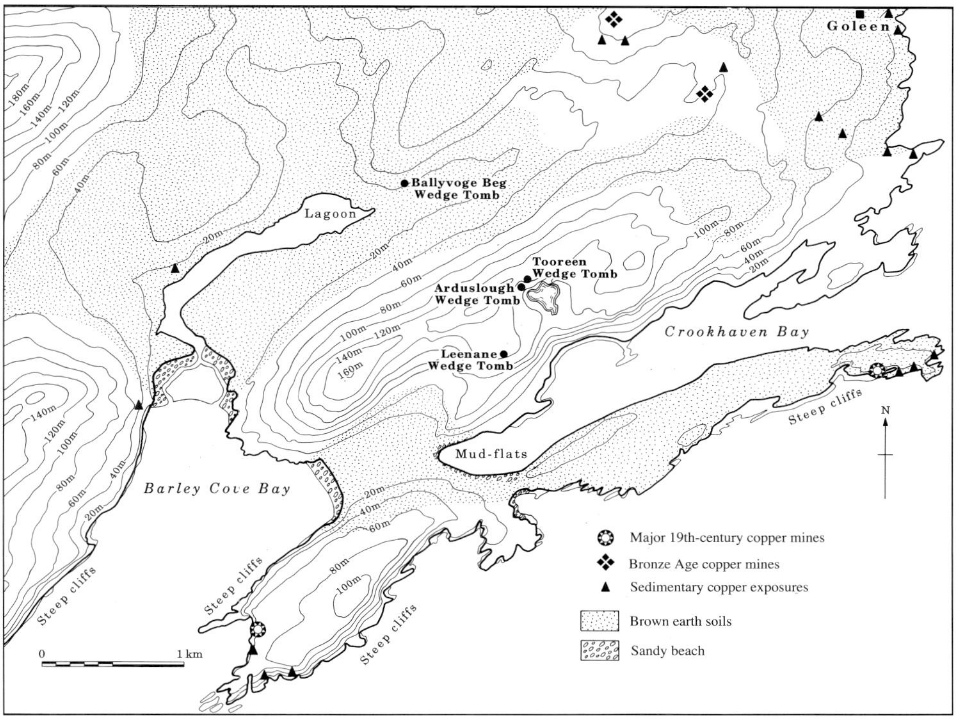

Fig. 4—A wedge tomb 'territory': the Crookhaven–Barley Cove district of the Mizen Peninsula, Co. Cork, containing one low-lying wedge tomb (Ballyvoge Beg) and three upland examples (Arduslough, Leenane and Tooreen). Resources within a 3km radius include fishing and marine food collection in deep-water and inshore areas (rocky shorelines, sandy beach and lagoon environments); lowland soils (brown earths) suitable for cultivation and pasture; hillside grazing; hunting in adjacent mountain terrain; numerous copper deposits, including vein-style and sedimentary mineralisation; Bronze Age copper mines in adjacent hills.

not collaborate in the building of larger monuments is probably indicative of the way their social relations were structured. Low-investment monuments do not have to be indicative of small-scale societies; however, it is likely that the scale of construction seen in the Mizen Peninsula tombs does reflect the segmentary character of this tribal society. This is supported by the spacing of these monuments across the landscape and the consistency of size and architectural detail. Renfrew (1979) argued that the absence of ranking between megalithic tombs is the most important indicator of a 'segmentary society', which is precisely what we see in these wedge tomb distributions.

The structure of this Early Bronze Age society had a direct bearing on how activities such as copper-mining and metal production were organised. The only Bronze Age copper mines which have been identified to date within the main areas of wedge tomb distribution in Cork are of the Mount Gabriel type. In addition to Mount Gabriel itself, similar workings have been identified at up to six other locations in the Mizen Peninsula and at three sites in the

Beara Peninsula (Figs 2 and 3). These small copper-bed mines represent a particular approach to the sourcing of metal in the earlier Bronze Age, possibly indicative of the social context in which this was undertaken. We see a proliferation of small surface workings, each representing a limited investment of time and material resources by groups of between ten and twenty individuals, possibly working on a seasonal or sporadic basis. These short-term commitments to mining across a landscape were adapted to the disseminated occurrence of sedimentary copper mineralisation, which has numerous exposures along the coastline and hilly interior of the West Cork peninsulas. This approach contrasts with most other Bronze Age copper mines in Britain and Ireland, which are generally sited on localised deposits of concentrated mineralisation. Centres like Ross Island in County Kerry, the Great Orme, Pary's Mountain and Cwmystwyth in Wales, and Alderly Edge in England saw a considerable time–energy commitment to copper-mining over long periods (O'Brien 1996).

The question now arises as to why Bronze Age miners in the Mizen Peninsula targeted low-grade sedimentary copper-beds rather than the richer vein-style mineralisation also found in the area. This was partly a question of physical accessibility; however, the Mount Gabriel approach may also represent an ability to mobilise sufficient human and material resources to mine copper-bed exposures but not to engage in deep-mining of vein-style mineralisation. While the latter may have been worked in some instances, it appears that copper-mining in the wedge tomb territories was characterised by the efforts of small local communities, consisting of multi-family groups ('primary tribal segments'), with minimal inter-group collaboration. The Mount Gabriel-type approach to copper-mining is thus partly a consequence of the small-scale segmentary organisation of Bronze Age society in this area. The overall level of production from these mines is low, probably reflecting the perceived need for metal in these small-scale societies.

Following Renfrew and Chapman (above), we may conclude that each wedge tomb community was a corporate group in the sense that it had proprietary rights to land and other resources within its own territory. These rights were primarily established by residence and lineal descent from ancestors whose remains may have been enshrined in the community tomb. The siting of these monuments on or near good agricultural land, or a metal offering like that at Toormore wedge tomb (see below), may have symbolically affirmed these rights. However, it is likely that any overt statement of resource ownership was of secondary significance to the magico-religious context within which these acts took place.

WEDGE TOMBS AND METAL MAGIC

Early metal artefacts are largely absent from wedge tombs across Ireland (O'Brien *et al.* 1989/90). This is surprising in view of the supposed connections between this monument tradition and early metallurgy in south-west Ireland. Indeed, the recent discovery of a decorated bronze axehead and two pieces of raw copper at Toormore, Co. Cork, is the only early metal find from eight wedge tombs excavated in the Cork–Kerry region (O'Brien 1999). The Toormore find provides important evidence for the involvement of wedge tomb communities in metal production during the Early Bronze Age. The axehead and raw copper here constitute a direct link with local metal-working activity *c.* 1900–1600 BC, to which a stone axe-mould from Doonour townland (O'Kelly 1969) in this area can also be linked. Having established this association, the wider significance of the metal deposit at Toormore must be considered. Typological analysis confirms that this axehead is a product of indigenous production during the developed Early Bronze Age, dating possibly from three to five centuries after metal was first introduced to Ireland. This lends no support to the theory that this and other peninsular wedge tombs are 'landfall' sites linked to an external colonisation which introduced metallurgy to this region.

The context at Toormore strongly suggests that this deposit was a ritual act, placed either as a static offering or else used in ritual ceremonies on different occasions. This metal find cannot be linked to funerary ritual; indeed, no human remains were found at Toormore. This is consistent with the wider Bronze Age record in Ireland, where metal axeheads were rarely used as grave-offerings. The placing of this deposit outside the entrance to a megalithic tomb suggests that it represents a votive offering whose function was either one of expiation, thanksgiving or supplication. The value is clearly apparent when one considers the limited scale of Early Bronze Age metal production, as modelled by Flanagan (1979) and indicated locally by the Mount Gabriel output (O'Brien 1994, 195–8).

The presence of decoration on the Toormore axehead suggests that it may represent a special-purpose or prestige object. It has been suggested that unhafted decorated axes were used in a 'role concerned with display [which] was often connected with sacred sites of both funerary and ritual function' (Needham 1988, 245). It is likely that metal axes had a dual role in the Early Bronze Age, being used for utilitarian work practices and occasionally invested with a symbolism connected to their use in prestige transaction and social display. The use of axeheads in this way dates back to the Neolithic period, when the stone axe was a potent symbol for agricultural communities (Bradley 1990, 91). Several researchers have identified a close link between axe exchange and megalithic ritual throughout the Neolithic. For the Armorican Neolithic, Patton (1993) sees stone axeheads playing an important role in socially significant transactions. He argues that only axes from certain sources were considered appropriate for these transactions, where the origin, individual history and mythico-religious associations of the object are more important than functional considerations. In addition, Patton believes that the production of these special axeheads took place at only a few centres, including sites of ritual–ceremonial importance.

We could similarly argue that the production of certain bronze axeheads in Early Bronze Age Ireland occurred at centres of magico-religious significance. This might conveniently explain both the Toormore and Newgrange (O'Kelly and Shell 1979) finds, with the former linked to copper ingots and the latter to metal-working tools. The symbolism and status of these axeheads may partly derive from their association with these sacred places. For the protagonists, the Toormore offering may have been at the centre of rituals performed to invoke metal-making magic or to give thanks to the bountiful Earth. We could also see this as a fertility offering in a broader sense, where the axe as a male symbol expresses an ideological link between production and reproduction (cf. Patton 1993, 31). Finally, a comparison may also be made with the discovery of metal-casting moulds of Middle Bronze Age date at three other wedge tombs elsewhere in Ireland (O'Brien 1999). This suggests that votive deposition of metal-working artefacts continued to be an occasional feature of wedge tomb ritual in later centuries.

METAL AND SOCIETY

The use of wedge tombs is likely to reflect a sense of territoriality and resource ownership among Early Bronze Age populations in south-west Ireland. As a consequence, population groups in the West Cork peninsulas probably controlled access to local copper deposits, using this resource to produce metal for their own needs and for exchange purposes. Certain population groups found themselves in a position to exploit a new raw material that was much in demand across Ireland. Any imbalance in natural resource distribution may have had destabilising effects on the wider society, leading to increased social differentiation, where individuals or groups rose to prominence at the expense of others. We know that increased opportunities to control the production and exchange of prestige materials, including metalwork, had important social implications elsewhere during the Early Bronze Age—for example, early metal use in the Wessex area appears to have contributed to a more entrepreneurial form of leadership (Shennan 1982). However, this may not have been true for all insular societies in this period. In the case of south-west Ireland, we must ask whether powerful individuals or groups emerged in the Early Bronze Age whose position was linked to their controlling interest in the supply of metal.

To address this question, we need to understand what metal signified to the population groups in question. In addition to its utilitarian value, metal was widely used in Early Bronze Age Europe as an expression of personal prestige, power and wealth which contributed to increasing social differentiation in this period. This is illustrated by the use of high-quality metalwork in gift exchanges, votive offerings and as grave-goods. The importance of these copper, bronze and gold objects lay not only in their inherent value but also in their cosmological references. The Toormore axehead is a prime example of how a metal object could be symbolically charged through association with a sacred place. Objects like this acquired an important ideological value which may have been significant in the structuring of social relations.

The supply of metal in the Early Bronze Age was to a large extent determined by the way society was organised. While much attention has focused on the role of middlemen and specialist traders, the circulation of raw and finished metal was probably organised within the structure of individual societies. In tribal society, certain individuals or groups may have emerged who had an important managerial role in the production and supply of commodities (O'Brien 1994, 247). This seems possible for the Beaker copper mine at Ross Island, where the scale and duration of mining suggest a higher level of organisation in what appears to have been an entirely different social setting (O'Brien 1995). It is of interest that this mine was worked over a long period (*c.* 2400–1800 BC) by local population groups who do not appear to have built wedge tombs in the general environs of the mine.

The mining of copper by various wedge tomb communities in West Cork may be interpreted differently from the Ross Island production. We have already linked some of these groups to the Mount Gabriel-type operations, an approach to mining which reflects both the limited metal needs of these small communities and their ability to mobilise resources to engage in large-scale enterprises. The supply of metal here was probably structured by the segmentary nature of society, with metal objects exchanged across a cellular tribal network through kin relations and other social ties. Instead of centralised control, metal production may have been in the hands of local descent groups (primary tribal segments) who occasionally collaborated in mining ventures and exchanged metal products and expertise, possibly within wider clan-like affiliations. The circulation of metal was determined in the first instance by social distance and subsequently by a desire to obtain scarce materials like gold, tin and amber through trade exchanges. Tin supply is likely to have been of particular significance from *c.* 2100 BC, as bronze-making groups in south-west Ireland were forced to engage in regional exchange to obtain this raw material.

We have no understanding of how this exchange of metal and other materials was organised at an inter-regional level. These transactions may have been managed by individuals or groups who gained considerable influence as a result. We might expect these social inequalities to be expressed in the consumption of prestige goods and in ostentatious funerary display and monument-building. This is not apparent in the wedge tomb areas of Cork and Kerry, where there are few artefacts or ritual contexts indicative of personal prestige, nor any indication of competitive monument-building. This is reinforced by the limited penetration of Early Bronze Age 'single burial' practice, involving the use of food vessel and cinerary urn ceramics, into this region (Waddell 1990, 58–62, 96). Understanding the social context of Early Bronze Age gold lunulae and discs from the south-west would be of considerable help in this regard (O'Brien 1999, 284–5).

In the case of wedge tombs, the social status of the deceased interred in these monuments continues to pose questions. While some interments may have been sacrificial or dedicatory and otherwise symbolic of group identity, it is more likely that the limited number of interments and the formal architectural setting suggest some degree of hierarchy within these communities. These wedge tombs may have contained the remains of individuals who in life achieved positions of leadership, possibly as respected 'elders', and subsequently went on to gain recognition as 'founding fathers' for their respective communities and lineages. In societies whose membership is defined by kinship, the ancestors have a special significance and may in fact be buried at a special place. How the individuals buried in these monuments achieved these positions of social standing is unknown, as is the important question of whether this was tied to an involvement in metal production and supply.

Participation in the Beaker network of exchanges gave an important impetus to social differentiation in many regions during the Early Bronze Age. In some cases, this led to the emergence of individuals and groups who had a controlling interest in the supply of metal. We do not know whether this happened in the south-west, where any resource control may have been a destabilising element, leading to the aggrandisement of individuals or groups whose power threatened the basic fabric of society. This is not immediately obvious from the archaeological record, where clear expressions of personal prestige are lacking, unless of course we interpret the building of wedge tombs and the use of gold discs in this way. The absence of indicators of personal prestige may be highly significant, supporting Cooney and

Grogan's (1994, 94) argument that the use of wedge tombs into Early Bronze Age times indicates that communal identity was still a dominant feature of society. Finally, we might also consider how control over metal supply contributed to the breakdown of wedge tomb society in south-west Ireland from 1700–1500 BC onwards, and its eventual replacement by a new social order marked by the building of stone circles and related monuments.

CONCLUSIONS

While ritual practice and industrial manufacture belong to two separate spheres of human activity today, this may not have been the case during the Bronze Age, when the making of metal was probably surrounded by much ritual and superstition. For prehistoric people, what today we call the 'economy' was an embedded part of their social existence and cosmological understanding of the world. The wedge tomb was an important sacred site in their spiritual lives, providing a suitable ceremonial setting at different times of the agricultural year and for appropriate offerings to supernatural powers. This may have included investing elements of the natural environment with quasi-human spirits, the deification of the earth itself and fertility symbolism. In this way, the presence of megalithic tombs on good land symbolises a belief in the endurance of the earth and its products. With the Toormore find we can see how the act of metal-making may also have been associated with magical powers, and consequently had to be undertaken in a suitably charged environment.

Wedge tombs may have validated control over the use of natural resources; however, they held a far greater significance for prehistoric communities. They were built by small-scale segmentary groups, for whom membership was determined on the basis of lineage and residence locality, both of which were symbolised in these monuments. The wedge tomb existed primarily as a shrine, sanctified by an association with ancestors and used for periodic offering and sacrifice to supernatural powers. At another level, it was an important symbol of group identity for a local population, contributing to the symbolic construction of their community through the physical expression of a common sense of belonging and ideology. The proliferation of these monuments may reflect a tribal network, founded on these same principles of lineage ties and local residence. Finally, while many studies emphasise the competitive environment in which megalithic tombs were built, it is difficult to identify such tensions among the wedge tomb communities of south-west Ireland. Though functioning as external expressions of identity ('territorial markers'), we should also emphasise the role of these monuments as an internal symbol of community for multi-family groups bound by close lineage relationships which promoted social cohesion.

Like the Cassiterides of Classical sources, Ireland has held a position in Bronze Age studies as a mysterious isle of metal, a remote place which provided much of the copper and gold used during this period in north-western Europe. The noted scholar George Coffey went so far as to describe the island as the 'El Dorado of the western world' (Coffey 1913, 46). This view owes much to the quality of metal-working expertise in the Irish Bronze Age and to the obvious availability of raw material. It is also marked by neo-colonial attitudes which coloured much culture-historical thinking with respect to Ireland's place in Europe.

The importance of metal in the Irish Bronze Age has largely been considered in terms of external inspiration and contacts, with little attention paid to its important local and regional development in indigenous societies. Today, we are slowly moving to an understanding of the contribution which metal made to the internal dynamics of these groups, while also mindful of the doors that this opened to an outside world.

Many of the ideas raised in this paper are developed in greater detail elsewhere (O'Brien 1999). This research stems from fieldwork carried out on early copper mines and megalithic monuments between 1983 and 1990 in the Mizen Peninsula, Co. Cork. In the excavations on Mount Gabriel and at the boulder-burial sites of Cooradarrigan and Ballycommane I was ably assisted by Liz Anderson, in whose memory this paper was written and who will always be missed.

REFERENCES

Blance, B. 1961 Early Bronze Age colonists in Iberia. *Antiquity* **35**, 192–202.

Bradley, R. 1990 *The passage of arms*. Cambridge University Press.

Chapman, R. 1981 The emergence of formal disposal areas and the 'problem' of megalithic tombs in prehistoric Europe. In R. Chapman, I. Kinnes and K. Randsborg (eds), *The archaeology of death*, 71–82. Cambridge University Press.

Chapman, R. 1995 Ten years after: megaliths, mortuary practices and the territorial model. In L.A. Beck (ed.), *Regional approaches to mortuary analysis*, 29–51. London. Plenum Press.

Childe, V.G. 1940 *Prehistoric communities of the British Isles*. London. W.& R. Chambers.

Coffey, G. 1913 *The Bronze Age in Ireland*. Dublin. Hodges Figgis.

Cooney, G. 1983 Megalithic tombs in their environmental setting: a settlement perspective. In T. Reeves-Smyth and F. Hamond (eds), *Landscape archaeology in Ireland*, 179–94. British Archaeological Reports, British Series 116. Oxford.

Cooney, G. and Grogan, E. 1994 *Irish prehistory: a social perspective*. Bray. Wordwell.

Daniel, G. and Renfrew, C. 1988 *The idea of prehistory*. Edinburgh University Press.

de Valera, R. and Ó Nualláin, S. 1982 *Survey of the megalithic tombs of Ireland. Volume IV: Cork, Kerry, Limerick and Tipperary*. Dublin. Stationery Office.

Flanagan, L. 1979 Industrial resources, production and distribution in earlier Bronze Age Ireland. In M. Ryan (ed.), *The origins of metallurgy in Atlantic Europe. Proceedings of the Fifth Atlantic Colloquium*, 145–63. Dublin. Stationery Office.

Macalister, R.A.S. 1935 *Ancient Ireland*. London. Methuen.

Needham, S.P. 1988 Selective deposition in the British Early Bronze Age. *World Archaeology* **20**, 229–48.

O'Brien, W. 1993 Aspects of wedge tomb chronology. In E. Shee-Twohig and M. Ronayne (eds), *Past perceptions: the prehistoric archaeology of south-west Ireland*, 63–74. Cork University Press.

O'Brien, W. 1994 *Mount Gabriel: Bronze Age copper mining in Ireland*. Bronze Age Studies 3. Galway University Press.

O'Brien, W. 1995 Ross Island and the origins of Irish–British metallurgy. In J. Waddell and E. Shee Twohig (eds), *Ireland in the Bronze Age*, 38–48. Dublin. Stationery Office.

O'Brien, W. 1996 *Bronze Age copper mining in Britain and Ireland.* Princes Risborough. Shire Publications.

O'Brien, W. 1999 *Sacred ground. Megalithic tombs in coastal south-west Ireland.* Bronze Age Studies 4. Department of Archaeology, National University of Ireland, Galway.

O'Brien, W., Northover, J.P. and Cameron, E. 1989/90 An Early Bronze Age metal hoard from a wedge tomb at Toormore, Co. Cork. *Journal of Irish Archaeology* **5**, 9–17.

O'Kelly, M.J. 1969 A stone mould for axeheads from Doonour, Bantry, Co. Cork. *Journal of the Royal Society of Antiquaries of Ireland* **99**, 117–24.

O'Kelly, M.J. and Shell, C. 1979 Stone objects and a bronze axe from Newgrange, Co. Meath. In M. Ryan (ed.), *The origins of metallurgy in Atlantic Europe. Proceedings of the Fifth Atlantic Colloquium*, 127–44. Dublin. Stationery Office.

Ó Nualláin, S. 1978 Boulder-burials. *Proceedings of the Royal Irish Academy* **78**C, 75–100.

Ó Nualláin, S. 1984 A survey of stone circles in Cork and Kerry. *Proceedings of the Royal Irish Academy* **84**C, 1–77.

Ó Nualláin, S. 1988 Stone rows in the south of Ireland. *Proceedings of the Royal Irish Academy* **45**C, 83–181.

Patton, M. 1993 *Statements in stone: monuments and society in Neolithic Brittany.* London. Routledge.

Perry, W.J. 1915 The relationship between the geographical distribution of megalithic monuments and ancient mines. *Memoirs and Proceedings of the Manchester Literary and Philosophical Society* **60**, 1–36.

Renfrew, C. 1967 Colonialism and megalithismus. *Antiquity* **41**, 276–88.

Renfrew, C. 1973a *Before civilization.* London. Jonathan Cape.

Renfrew, C. 1973b Monuments, mobilization and social organization in neolithic Wessex. In C. Renfrew (ed.), *The explanation of culture change: models in prehistory*, 539–58. London. Duckworth.

Renfrew, C. 1976 Megaliths, territories and populations. In S. de Laet (ed.), *Acculturation and continuity in Atlantic Europe*, 198–220. Brugge. De Tempel.

Renfrew, C. 1977 Space, time and polity. In J. Friedman and M. Rowlands (eds), *The evolution of social systems*, 89–112. London. Duckworth.

Renfrew, C. 1979 *Investigations in Orkney.* London. Society of Antiquaries London.

Rothenberg, B. and Blanco-Freijeiro, A. 1981 *Studies in ancient mining and metallurgy in south-west Spain.* London. Institute of Archaeo-metallurgical Studies.

Sahlins, M.D. 1961 The segmentary lineage: an organization of predatory expansion. *American Anthropologist* **63**, 322–45.

Service, E.R. 1962 *Primitive social organization.* New York (2nd edn, 1971). Random House.

Shennan, S.E. 1982 From minimal to moderate ranking. In C. Renfrew and S.E. Shennan (eds), *Ranking resource and exchange*, 27–32. Cambridge University Press.

Siret, H. and Siret, L. 1887 *Les premiers âges du métal dans le sud-est de l'Espagne.* Anvers.

Waddell, J. 1990 *The Bronze Age burials of Ireland.* Bronze Age Studies 1. Galway University Press.

DIFFERENT AGES, VARYING PERSPECTIVES: THE PHENOMENON OF HOARDING

Denise Maher and John Sheehan

Had fate taken a different course, Liz Anderson would undoubtedly have set new agendas in Irish prehistory, particularly for the Mesolithic period. Her work on the Mesolithic drew her westwards to the extreme end of the Dingle Peninsula in County Kerry. While there, she often stood entranced by the sight of gannets diving into the sea between Ballyferriter and the Blasket Islands. This image poignantly recalls a Corca Dhuibhne moment in the life of another, very different woman:

> *Shuíos síos ar phort na trá mar a raibh radharc álainn im thimpeall . . . Bíonn sé go hana-dheas nuair a bhíonn an ciúineas ann . . . Do bhíos ag breithniú uaim amach ar na mílte d'éanlaithe mara a bhí ag eiteall thall is abhus ar thóir rud éigin le n-ithe. Bhí ón nguardal do dtí an fiach mara, is ón gcircín trá go dtí an gainéad, is a cheol féin á chanadh ag gach cineál acu . . . do bhí na mílte agus na mílte ann . . .* (Sayers 1936, 209)

This paper is offered in fond memory of Liz, a colleague whose discussions were a constant source of enjoyment to us.

INTRODUCTION

The phenomenon of hoard deposition appears to be particularly associated with two periods of Irish archaeology—the Late Bronze Age and the Viking Age. About the same number of gold and silver hoards of Viking Age date are on record as bronze and gold hoards known from the Dowris Phase of the Late Bronze Age (about 130 examples in each case). At the most basic level these finds appear to represent the same phenomenon—the removal of objects from use or circulation by disposing of them, either temporarily or permanently. Whether one regards this practice as *deposition* or *hoarding* depends, to some extent, on one's interpretation of various aspects of these finds. For instance, one archaeologist might focus largely on the actual content of a find, while another might be more influenced by the location and context of its find-spot. For convenience the phenomenon will be termed 'hoarding' in this paper, despite the fact that it cannot always be demonstrated that 'hoards' were necessarily intended to be recovered.

As archaeologists specialising in the historic period, the authors considered it of interest to gain an overview of how these two chronologically distinct groups of Irish hoards have been studied. Initially they appear to share many characteristics, but when one explores how they have been categorised and interpreted many of the expected similarities tend to become blurred. There are several good reasons for this, the main one concerning the different forms of wealth that the two groups of hoards represent. Viking Age silver hoards are made up of combinations of objects, such as coins, ingots, ornaments and hack-silver, which represent wealth in varying forms of currency. On the other hand, Bronze Age gold hoards comprise objects which did not apparently function as currency, though they may be interpreted as representing wealth or power. Therefore comparing the functional significance of Viking Age hack-silver and Bronze Age scrap hoards, as has been attempted by Bradley (1990, 147–51), is an exercise which appears to be based on a misunderstanding of the significance of forms of wealth and currency. Of course, this does not mean that Viking Age and Bronze Age hoards cannot be compared in general terms, because wealth, whether its significance be commercial or symbolic, equally confers status and power on its possessor.

Two main themes in hoard studies will be explored in this paper: categorisation and interpretation. A basic premise is that when there is a sufficiently large number of recorded hoards that clearly belong to a single period, as is the case in both the Dowris Phase and the Viking Age in Ireland, then the internal composition and structure of the hoards themselves can form a basis for their categorisation. The process and results of categorisation, in turn, should form the basis for at least part of the follow-up procedure—the interpretation of the character of the hoards and the reason, or reasons, for their deposition. In this way the process of interpretation takes formal cognisance of data internal to the hoards as well as of their broader contextual variables. It will be suggested below that archaeologists, whether they are concerned with the prehistoric or historic period, tend occasionally to advance rash interpretations regarding the deposition of hoards which can sometimes be at variance with what the internal character of the finds themselves seems to suggest.

VIKING AGE SILVER HOARDS

Traditionally Viking Age silver hoards have been categorised on the flawed and rather simplistic basis of whether or not they contained coins. Thus, even in current practice, hoards may be categorised as coin hoards, coinless hoards and mixed hoards (hoards which contain both coins and non-numismatic material). It is clear that the basis of this form of categorisation focuses on one characteristic: whether a hoard contains coins or not. The principal reason for this bias is that until recent decades in Scandinavia, as well as in Ireland and Britain, it was numismatists who carried out most research on Viking Age hoards. The legacy of this numismatic perspective on the study of those hoards that also contain non-numismatic material is not entirely negative, though it has sometimes led to seriously skewed interpretations being put forward. For instance, when Viking Age economic issues were being considered, the relevance of a large body of data—the non-numismatic elements within the hoards—often went unappreciated and ignored.

A recategorisation of those Irish Viking Age hoards which contain non-numismatic material has recently been proposed (Sheehan 2000). Rather than grouping them along traditional lines, such as coinless and mixed hoards, this recategorisation focuses on the composition and structure of their non-numismatic contents. In this way the varying degrees of complexity within the hoards become more evident. The basis for the new classification is the presence, absence or association of the three non-numismatic elements that may occur in Viking Age hoards—ornaments, ingots and hack-silver. The presence or absence of coins is not deemed to be particularly significant, as coins were variously regarded as bullion, ornaments or money during the period.

A fivefold classification of hoard structure, in which the shared non-numismatic characteristics are stressed, emerges from this exercise. The composition of the separate classes of hoards is as follows: Class 1, ornaments only; Class 2, ingots only; Class 3, ornaments and ingots; Class 4, ornaments and/or ingots with hack-silver; Class 5, hack-silver only. The five divisions are capable of accommodating further subclassification for the purposes of more detailed analysis. For instance, hoards containing hack-silver (Classes 4 and 5) have twelve potential permutations and combinations, of which nine are actually represented in the Irish hoard data.

The advantage of the proposed classification system is that it transcends the overly segregational nature of the traditional type of categorisation, while also being flexible enough to be superimposed upon it. When this is carried out, the resulting trends serve to emphasise the compositional similarities, rather than differences, between the coinless and mixed hoards. This, of course, further undermines the validity of the traditional categorisation and demonstrates how the numismatically driven approach, being focused upon a single hoard element, has served to separate what are clearly related phenomena.

There must be a meaning and a purpose beyond the actual practice of an empirically defined type of classificatory exercise such as that summarised above. There is, for when the broad contextual information for Ireland's Viking Age hoards, such as chronology, distribution and find location, is added to the proposed hoard classifications, it becomes possible to more readily identify and appreciate the social, as well as the economic, significance of the finds. The five principal hoard categories that emerge from this exercise have particular and reasonably discrete distribution patterns (Sheehan 2000, fig. 9a–f). This indicates that the categories are not archaeological creations and that they reflect some Viking Age reality. It also suggests, despite the imperfect nature of the antiquarian and archaeological record, that when a fairly large body of hoard data is dealt with there is an increased likelihood that the trends which emerge will reflect aspects of past realities.

In summary, a large body of hoard data has been reassessed on the basis of an empirical system of categorisation. The interpretation of the hoards then proceeded on the basis of this categorisation and related contextual information. The results of the exercise challenge some of the generalisations about Viking Age hoards that have been proposed in the past and which have emanated from both archaeologists and numismatists.

PERSPECTIVES ON INTERPRETATION

Archaeologists, whether they specialise in the prehistoric or the historic period, are frequently guilty of simplifying the process of hoard interpretation by focusing most of their attention on one characteristic of hoards or hoarding. One of the most obvious examples of this type

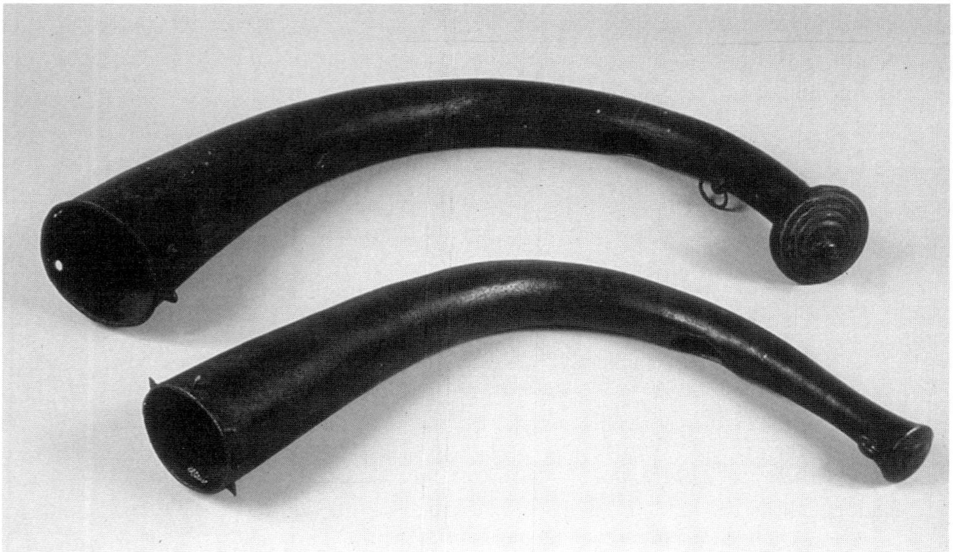

Pl. 1—Two horns from the Dowris Phase hoard from Moyarta barony, Co. Clare (courtesy of the National Museum of Ireland).

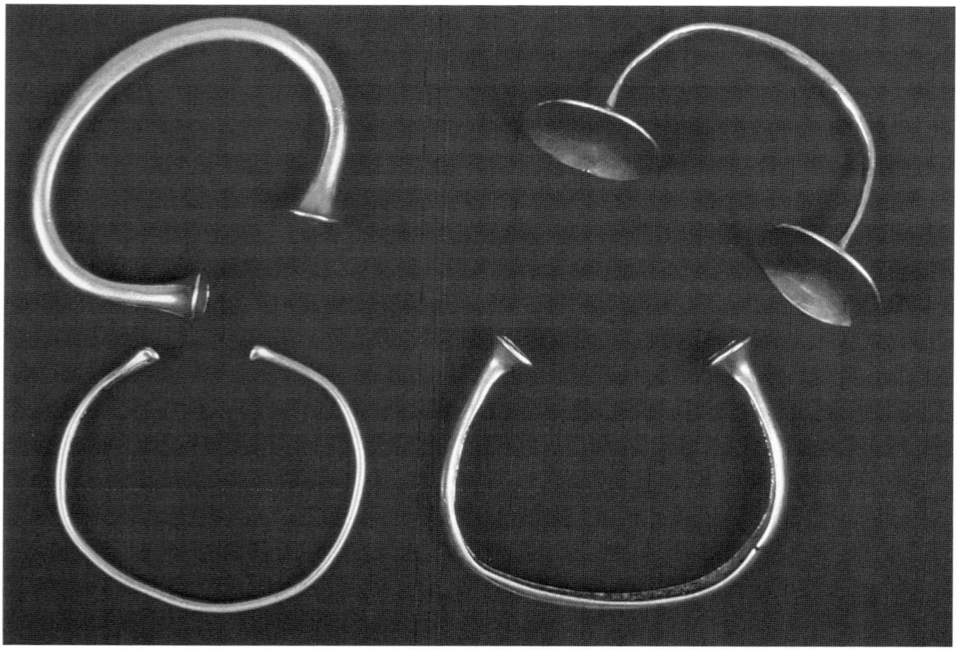

Pl. 2—The Dowris Phase gold hoard from Kilmoyly North, Co. Kerry (courtesy of the National Museum of Ireland).

of approach concerns coin-dated hoards. Some scholars, armed with a deposition date, searched through the documentary sources and attempted to match the date with a historic event. If an 'appropriate' one was found it was then used to form or support the basis of the proposed interpretation of that particular hoard (e.g. Dolley 1962). Naturally, one of the effects of this type of approach was to bolster the general association between hoards and traumatic events, such as battles, raids, etc. It is very likely that some hoards were buried in troubled times, during the prehistoric as well as the historic period, though sometimes one gets the impression that this type of stress was the main motivating factor behind the practice of hoard deposition in the latter period. Grinder-Hansen (1992, 126), in his recent consideration of medieval hoards from Denmark, warns:

> One should bear in mind that it was not necessarily the events of which knowledge has coincidentally survived until today which had the greatest significance at the time, or which were the direct cause of the deposition of the hoard. Over-hasty conclusions of this kind can lead to guess-work or perhaps even to direct manipulation of our knowledge about the historic past.

Grinder-Hansen believes that the majority of Denmark's Viking Age and medieval hoards are to be interpreted as 'savings' rather than 'emergency' hoards and that, accordingly, they should be interpreted commercially. Of course, a savings hoard could also have been kept above ground and only buried in the event of an emergency.

It seems that the correlation of hoard deposition with impending traumatic events is used too readily by historic archaeologists. The equation of deposition with such times of stress appears to be less frequently advanced by prehistorians. Is this simply because these finds are prehistoric and therefore cannot be associated with known events, or is it that prehistorians have a more considered view of the hoarding phenomenon? On the other hand, is this form of interpretation avoided by prehistorians in the interests of emphasising other forms of interpretation instead? If this is the case, is this because the prehistorian's mindset, consciously or unconsciously, opts for ritual explanations for phenomena for which secular explanations might be advanced if they existed in the historic period? Equally, the question may be posed as to why archaeologists who specialise in the historic period only rarely use ritual as a basis for hoard interpretation. There is, for Viking Age hoards at least, some justification for advancing ritual explanations on the basis of the so-called Odin's Law (which is referred to by Snorri Sturluson in *Heimskringla*), which states that men would enjoy in Valhalla the treasures that they had buried in the earth. Yet very few Viking Age hoards are interpreted within a ritual framework.

LATE BRONZE AGE HOARDS

Can an approach like the proposed classification of Irish Viking Age hoards, concentrating on the internal composition and structure of the finds, be applied to the Late Bronze Age material? Attempts have been made to do so in the past, but the results seem to be of secondary concern in the current climate of emphasising the importance of the locational contexts of the hoards (see below). One such attempt (Hodges 1957), which appears to have much merit, is rarely cited nowadays. Hodges's paper deals only with hoards that contain bronze objects, although several also feature items of gold. The hoards are classified into four groups on the basis of whether they contained weapons only, tools only or combinations of these, and are interpreted along traditional lines as founders', merchants' or personal hoards. There was little new or revolutionary in this approach, which was largely based on the schemes proposed by Evans (1881, 457–9) and others during the nineteenth century.

Hodges merely dealt with the categorisation of the hoards, not being overly concerned with the interpretation of their deposition. Nevertheless, his approach is of interest in that it represented an attempt to consider the finds on the basis of their internal structure and composition. His personal hoard category, for instance, which accounted for the clear majority of the material he was concerned with, had three principal subdivisions. It might be suggested that these groupings were predictable and somewhat meaningless, but they do contain a significant degree of internal cohesion. The most striking example of this is that when spearheads occur in his weapons-only category they are all large examples, whereas when they occur in the category comprising associated weapons and tools they tend to be small specimens. This would suggest that Hodges's categorisation scheme actually relates to some prehistoric reality of unclear significance. Clearly, if regularities appear in the data when the composition and structure of hoards are compared with one another, as was the case for the Viking Age hoards, it follows that systematising the material in this way is a valid approach.

If a much broader and more comprehensive approach than Hodges's were undertaken on Bronze Age hoards, based firmly on their internal characteristics, it is likely that new agendas would arise for consideration. This is especially true given the quality of information now published for the large numbers of Late Bronze Age hoards on record (Eogan 1983; 1994). Such agendas could relate to social and economic issues as well as to the ritual ones which currently seem to be pervasive (e.g. Cooney and Grogan 1994, 158–67) and, of course, they could have implications for issues relating to the interpretation of hoard deposition. Broad interpretative overlaps relating to various aspects of hoards and hoarding may emerge if a more holistic approach to their study is adopted. In such an approach the internal trends of the hoards themselves should first be elucidated, before being considered alongside patterns that arise from, for instance, studies of hoard location and distribution. If the interpretations of groups of hoards, defined as particular because of their internal characteristics, overlap with the interpretation of their broader contextual attributes, then the possibility of arriving at valid conclusions is increased.

This seems to be the case with the Irish Late Bronze Age horn hoards (Pl. 1; Coles 1963; Cooney and Grogan 1994, 164–5; Waddell 1998, 234–6). The majority of the 120 or so horns on record, comprising two distinct types with discrete distribution patterns, derive from thirteen Dowris Phase hoards. In terms of their internal structure and composition these hoards form the most exclusive of all the Late Bronze Age examples in that eleven of them seem to have been composed only of horns. The locational contexts of ten of these hoards are on record, and of these nine are from bogs. This is the type of wetland context which is commonly accepted as being indicative of ritual deposition. In addition, the nature of the horns themselves, with their musical capabilities, suggests that they functioned as ceremonial objects. So, in this rather straightforward case-study, ritual and ceremony are clearly attested linking themes: the interpretations of the objects themselves, of the compositions of the hoards in which they occur and of the locations in which they are found all seem to converge.

In the case of the horn hoards, a high degree of compositional consistency and exclusivity is strikingly evident; however, such characteristics are rare in the Irish Late Bronze Age hoards. Frequently these contain a variety of objects of different classes, such as ornaments, weapons and tools, with each class sometimes being represented by different types. In addition, some hoards contain gold and amber as well as bronze objects. The challenge is to identify differences and contrasts, as well as similarities and consistencies, in the structure and composition of these hoards and to recognise that these may be significant. Owing to Eogan's valuable work, the data exist to enable this kind of task to be carried out. The results of a rapid analysis by the current authors indicate that 65 per cent of the Dowris Phase hoards included in his 1983 catalogue are mixed in content, while the remainder feature only one class of object. Each of these two hoard categories is capable of subdivision: in the first a large number of permutations and combinations are possible, but it is likely that particular ones would emerge more strongly than others (as was the case in the Viking Age hoards exercise); in the second category, comprising finds containing only one class of object (weapons, tools, ornaments etc.), subcategories of compositions should also emerge. If a comprehensive exercise of this type was carried out it should become possible to identify the typical categories of Dowris Phase hoards, defined according to their composition and structure. (The Dowris hoard itself, for instance, can hardly be considered as typical of Dowris Phase hoards.) Hodges's interesting concept of the 'ideal' Irish Late Bronze Age hoard (1957, 53–4) may have arisen from a move towards this form of exercise.

It is from this stage that interpretation of the hoards should commence. The internal evidence of the hoards should be considered alongside information on the state of the objects (such as whether they were broken or complete/new or old when they were deposited) and the type of locations in which they were found (such as whether these were wetland or dryland), as well as relevant distribution information. Such a methodical, empirically based approach should lead towards a balanced interpretation, based on all apparently significant aspects of the data.

Archaeologists often seem to rush into generalised interpretation when they are dealing with hoards (and this applies equally to specialists in both the historic and prehistoric periods). This appears to be a particularly valid criticism in the case of those, usually prehistorians, who interpret groups of hoards as ritual, ceremonial or votive deposits. Without doubt a significant number of Irish Late Bronze Age hoards were deposited for non-secular reasons, and perhaps explanations for this practice are contained in Gregory's (1982, 59–61) and Bradley's (1985, 30–3) theories on ritual and votive hoarding. Textbook generalisations, however, seem to push the incidence of prehistoric ritual deposition too high. For example, Waddell, in his recent book on Irish prehistory, wrote about ordinary tools of the Dowris Phase, such as axeheads, sickles, gouges and knives, and stated: 'A series of bronze

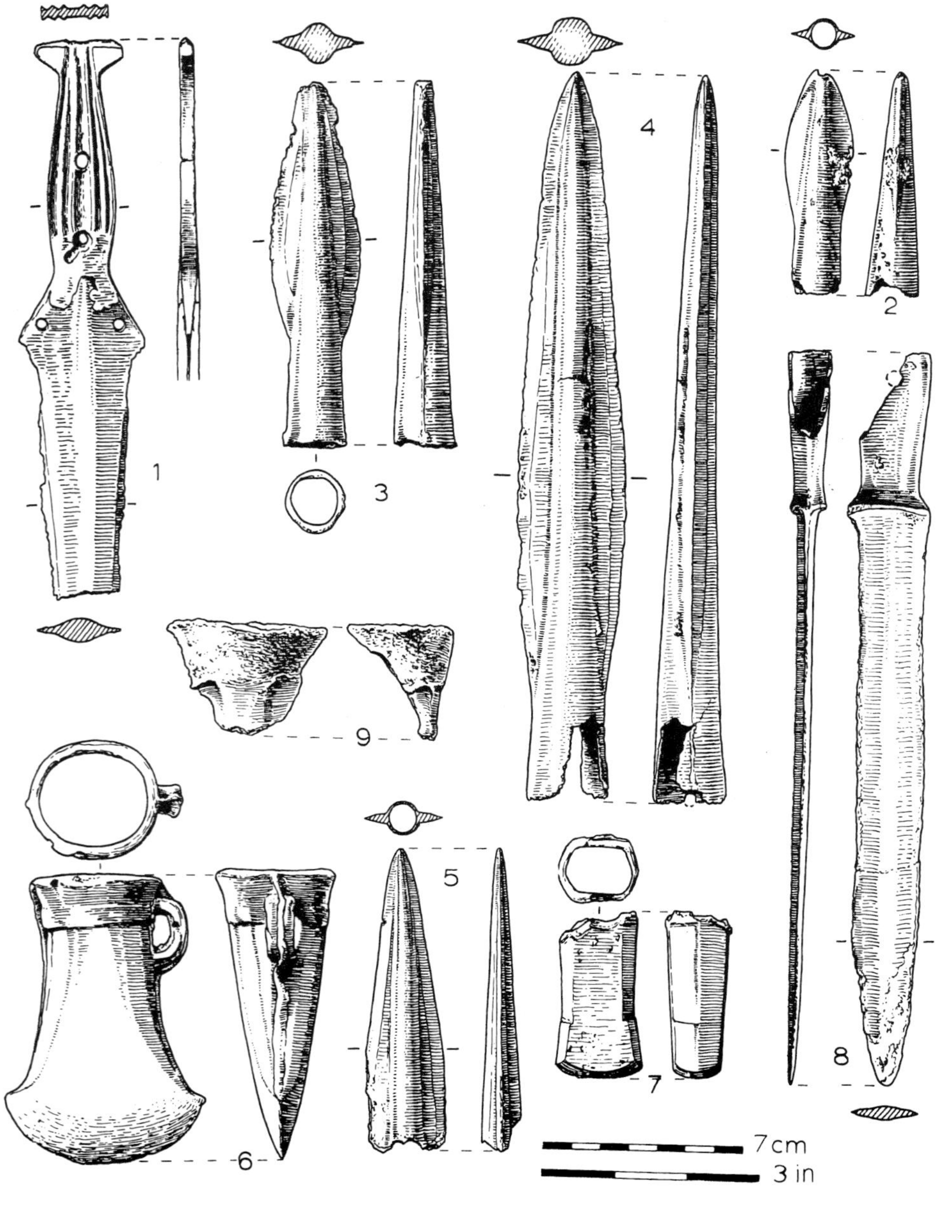

Fig. 1—The Dowris Phase bronze hoard from Dreenan, Co. Fermanagh (after Eogan 1983).

tools and implements had more mundane roles in society though their occasional presence in hoards suggests they may sometimes have been symbols of social position and have had a ceremonial use' (Waddell 1998, 259). Here the implication appears to be that all hoards are ritual in nature. In a later context he writes: 'The presence of tools such as gouges and chisels in a small number of hoards indicates that certain craftsmen had high status and were also entitled to representation in the ceremonial sphere' (*ibid.*, 275). While ethnographic studies have sometimes demonstrated the symbolic roles of otherwise apparently mundane objects, such as the classic Australian example of the axes of the Yir Yoront tribe (Sharp 1964), the background assumption in Waddell's statements seems to be that if something is found in a hoard it is, by implication, of symbolic or ceremonial significance. The subtext appears to be clear: hoards are primarily deposited for ritual or ceremonial purposes.

In many cases, this tendency to promote the ritual interpretation of hoards seems to be largely based on the type of locational contexts in which hoards are often found. Its proponents emphasise the wetland contexts of many Late Bronze Age hoards without necessarily assessing the internal evidence of the hoards themselves. For example, in their recent book, which critically examined the social context of Irish prehistory, Cooney and Grogan (1994, 164) state:

> The hoards of the Dowris Phase may represent a variety of meanings and human intentions but the deliberate, formal deposition of material would appear to have been the major factor. This could have been the case with even apparently utilitarian items and broken or scrap material which has previously been seen solely in an economic light.

This is a general statement and, like most generalisations, it is generally sound. Nevertheless, with a few strokes of the pen the status of those Dowris Phase hoards that could be regarded as 'utilitarian' on the basis of their contents is questioned, and it is suggested that they may have been formally deposited for votive or ritual reasons. From the broad context of this statement it seems that the basis for this viewpoint concerns the wetland locations of the find-spots of the majority of Dowris Phase hoards.

Cooney and Grogan's suggestion about the ritual status of utilitarian and scrap hoards deserves to be examined in greater detail. On the basis of what might constitute such hoards—the presence of significant proportions of fragmented, broken, damaged or unfinished artefacts or items such as waste-pieces, mould-gates and bronze cakes or lumps, etc.—a minimum of fourteen examples may be identified in Eogan's 1983 catalogue.[1] These include: Teernagloghane, Co. Clare, which contains three bronze artefacts (an unfinished axehead, an axehead broken in antiquity and a fragment of a ring); Dreenan, Co. Fermanagh (Fig. 1), which contains various artefacts, all of which are damaged or incomplete, and a lump of bronze; Ballycroghan, Co. Down, which contains two unfinished bronze swords and one finished example, all of which were apparently cast in moulds manufactured from the same model; and Scotstown, Co. Monaghan, which contains two gold 'sleeve-fasteners', fragments of amber beads, five bronze rings and at least twelve portions of bronze rings.

Records exist of the locational contexts of twelve of these fourteen proposed utilitarian hoards. Of these, five (42%) were found in 'wet' contexts while seven (58%) were recovered from 'dry' contexts. Although it is a poor statistical sample, it is interesting to note that this breakdown of find-context type actually represents an exact reversal of the overall 'wet'/'dry' ratio for Dowris Phase hoards noted by Cooney and Grogan (1994, 162, fig. 8:11), who found that 58% of Dowris hoards are from 'wet' contexts while 42% are from 'dry' contexts. This reversal of the trend is significant because on this basis, if one accepts that wetland find-contexts generally equate with the practice of ritual deposition, it can be argued that the deposition of apparently utilitarian hoards is less likely to be ritual in character.

A similar exercise was carried out on the 28 Dowris Phase hoards listed in Eogan's catalogue which were composed exclusively of gold objects.[2] These mostly contain objects like bracelets, 'sleeve-fasteners' and 'dress-fasteners', with a minority containing examples of the more ceremonial or enigmatic objects of the period, such as gorgets, bullae and gold boxes. In fact, no less than nineteen of the 28 hoards exclusively contain objects of the former type, and most of these are small examples containing only two or three individual objects. Typical examples of this type of hoard include those from Kilmoyly North, Co. Kerry (Pl. 2), which features three bracelets and one 'dress-fastener', and Craighilly, Co. Antrim, which contains three 'sleeve-fasteners'. Of those hoards with recorded contexts 62% were found in 'dry' locations. As is the case with the utilitarian hoards, this finding represents a reversal of the overall 'wet'/'dry' trends for Dowris Phase hoards and a concomitant statistical reduction in the likelihood of their ritual deposition. Indeed, given the compositional nature of most of these gold hoards, it is suggested that they could be regarded as personal hoards representative of wealth or power. As such, they may be interpreted in social rather than in ritual terms.

The two cursory exercises on Dowris Phase hoards outlined above demonstrate the dangers of proposing generalisations on the basis of analysing one aspect of the phenomenon of hoarding. In addition, they demonstrate that there exists some potential for matching, in a general way, the find-context information of hoards with their structure and composition. Taken together, the synergy of these two forms of evidence is more likely to produce a sound basis for interpreting hoard deposition than either is individually.

REFERENCES

Bradley, R. 1985 *Consumption, change and the archaeological record: the archaeology of deliberate deposits.* Department of Archaeology Occasional Paper 13. University of Edinburgh.

Bradley, R. 1990 *The passage of arms: an archaeological analysis of prehistoric hoards and votive deposits.* Cambridge University Press.

Coles, J. 1963 Irish Bronze Age horns and their relations with Northern Europe. *Proceedings of the Prehistoric Society* **29**, 326–56.

Cooney, G. and Grogan, E. 1994 *Irish prehistory: a social perspective.* Bray. Wordwell.

Dolley, R.H.M. 1962 The 1843 find of Viking-age silver coins from Co. Tipperary. *Journal of the Cork Historical and Archaeological Society* **57**, 41–7.

Eogan, G. 1983 *Hoards of the Irish Later Bronze Age*. University College Dublin.
Eogan, G. 1994 *The accomplished art: gold and gold-working in Britain and Ireland during the Bronze Age (c. 2300–650 BC)*. Oxford. Oxbow.
Evans, J. 1881 *The ancient bronze implements, weapons and ornaments of Great Britain and Ireland*. London. Longmans.
Gregory, C. 1982 *Gifts and commodities*. London. Academic Press.
Grinder-Hansen, K. 1992 Categories of treasure-hoards and their composition. In J. Steen Jensen, K. Bendixen, N. Liebgott and F. Lindahl (eds), *Danmarks Middelalderlige Skattefund c. 1050–c. 1550*, Vol. 1, 119–26. Copenhagen. Det Kongelige Nordiske Oldskriftselskab.
Hodges, H.W.M. 1957 Studies in the Late Bronze Age in Ireland: 3, the hoards of bronze implements. *Ulster Journal of Archaeology* **20**, 51–63.
Sayers, P. 1936 *Peig: a scéal féin*. Baile Átha Cliath. Clólucht an Talbóidigh.
Sharp, L. 1964 People without politics: the Yir Yoront. In P.B. Hammond (ed.), *Cultural and social anthropology*, 84–94. New York. Macmillan.
Sheehan, J. 2000 Viking Age silver hoards from Ireland: structure and composition. *Acta Archaeologia* **71**, 98–114.
Waddell, J. 1998 *The prehistoric archaeology of Ireland*. Galway University Press.

Endnotes

1 These are (with Eogan's catalogue nos): Ardlow, Co. Cavan, no. 47; Corracanvy, Co. Cavan, no. 51; Boolybrien, Co. Clare, no. 55; Teernagloghane, Co. Clare, no. 60; Ballycroghan, Co. Down, no. 71; Dreenan, Co. Fermanagh, no. 76; Money Lower, Co. Laois, no. 96; Drumany (O'Brien), Co. Leitrim, no. 98; Ballyroe, Co. Limerick, no. 100; Park, Co. Meath, no. 114; Scotstown, Co. Monaghan, no. 116; near Athlone, Co. Roscommon/Westmeath, no. 124; Cooga, Co. Sligo, no. 128; and Ballyvadden, Co. Wexford, no. 152.

2 These are (with Eogan's catalogue nos): Craighilly, Co. Antrim, no. 36; Bailieborough, Co. Cavan, no. 48; Lattoon, Co. Cavan, no. 53; Gorteenreagh, Co. Clare, no. 56; Mooghaun North, Co. Clare, no. 58; County Clare, no. 61; Clonleigh, Co. Donegal, no. 69; Downpatrick, Co. Down, no. 72; County Galway, no. 86; Kilmoyly North, Co. Kerry, no. 89; Askeaton, Co. Limerick, no. 99; County Limerick, no. 104; Counties Louth/Meath, no. 106; Liverourd or Oldcastle, Co. Mayo, no. 109; County Mayo, no. 111; Drissoge, Co. Meath, no. 113; Tara, Co. Meath, no. 115; near Athlone, Co. Roscommon, no. 122; near Athlone, Co. Roscommon/Westmeath, no. 123; Cashel, Co. Tipperary, no. 134; Arboe/Killycolp, Co. Tyrone, no. 138; Killymoon Demesne, Co. Tyrone, no. 140; near New Ross, Co. Waterford, no. 145; near Enniscorthy, Co. Wexford, no. 153; south of Ireland, no. 157; Ireland, no. 159; Ireland, no. 160; and Ireland, no. 161.

AN APPALLING VISTA? THE CELTS AND THE ARCHAEOLOGY OF LATER PREHISTORIC IRELAND

Barra Ó Donnabháin

In Irish archaeology, cultural change during the middle of the first millennium BC has traditionally been explained in terms of the immigration of Celtic peoples from continental Europe and Britain (e.g. Macalister 1928; 1949; J. Raftery 1951; Harbison 1976; 1988; Herity and Eogan 1977; de Paor 1986). This model of Celtic invasions pre-dates the development of Irish archaeology as a discipline (Waddell 1978). Archaeological concepts of the Celts and their migrations originated in eighteenth-century Continental and British scholarship (Chapman 1992). In the following century, these concepts were combined with narratives derived from a series of embryonic disciplines, such as comparative linguistics, history and anthropology, which developed in parallel with archaeology during that century (Chapman 1977; Morash 1998). The Celtic immigration model was the product of the merging of ideas drawn from these various disciplines. To this day, most discussions of the archaeology of the period also refer to historical, linguistic and other lines of evidence (e.g. Mallory 1984; 1993; O'Kelly 1989; Waddell 1991; 1998; Warner 1991). However, the traditional model of a major intrusion of Celtic populations has been qualified somewhat since the appearance of Waddell's (1978) critique of the invasion hypothesis in Irish prehistory. In much of the more recent archaeological literature relating to the Bronze Age/Iron Age transition, the growing corpus of data has been interpreted as reflecting cultural continuity during the period with little evidence of population intrusion (e.g. B. Raftery 1989; 1991; Cooney and Grogan 1991; 1994). The resulting apparent conflict between the archaeological record and the traditional narratives that developed in linguistics and other disciplines has provoked a number of responses among Irish archaeologists. It is interesting that most of these have focused on the roles of élites as engines of social and linguistic change. For example, Waddell (1991; 1992; 1995) has drawn on the concept of 'cumulative Celticity' developed by Hawkes (1972) in the context of Iron Age Britain to argue for a more complex explanation than that provided by invasion. Waddell has suggested a scenario that involved the gradual 'Celticisation' of Ireland through a process of acculturation, particularly at the level of ruling élites. In contrast, Warner (1991) has argued for an intrusion, or sequence of intrusions, of Celtic 'freebooters' who displaced the old ruling élite and thereafter effected radical changes on the indigenous masses who were descended from the Late Bronze Age inhabitants of the island. Raftery also toyed with the idea of a small intrusion at the élite level, but ultimately took a pessimistic approach to the conflicting discourses when he wrote that

> Archaeology presents us with a perplexing picture, one which is largely at variance with that presented by philology, early Irish history, folklore and tradition. It seems

> almost heretical to insist that a Celtic invasion of Ireland never happened. In this regard, however, the archaeologist should be aware of the limitations of his discipline (B. Raftery 1994, 228).

These responses—acculturation, élite-level *coups d'état* or the preference of narratives drawn from other disciplines than archaeology—could be viewed in terms of tinkering with the Celtic paradigm rather than engaging with the assumptions which underlie it. As a result, they all serve to maintain this theory as an explanatory construct in Irish archaeological interpretation. Similarly, strategies for new research continue to be formed within the paradigm. In 1991, the Bronze Age/Iron Age transition was chosen as the initial research focus of the state-funded Discovery Programme so that the 'period and the various transitions and intrusions that took place within it should be better understood, in particular, the emergence of a complex Celtic society' (Anon. 1992, 6).

It is not surprising, then, that the projects that emerged from this initiative have a strong emphasis on field monuments thought to have élite associations, such as Tara, Mooghaun and Dún Aonghasa. However, the Discovery Programme's objectives make for disappointing reading in the light of a growing body of archaeological and anthropological literature that questions the validity of the scholarly tradition underpinning the Celtic paradigm (e.g. Hill 1989; Chapman 1992; Piccini 1996; Collis 1997; James 1998). The Programme's brief does nothing to encourage any engagement with these heterodox notions.

A number of different theoretical perspectives are represented in the literature that questions the validity of traditional ideas of the Celtic, but they are united by the view that the generation and interpretation of archaeological data are profoundly influenced by the cultural milieus of archaeologists themselves. These concepts of archaeology as a socially and politically embedded activity owe much to the ideas of the French philosopher Michel Foucault, who denied that knowledge is a neutral expression of some objective reality. He suggested the opposite: that the production of knowledge is never neutral but rather is an operation inextricably linked with relations of power. Foucault (1980; Yadlon 1997) argued that there is a symbiotic relationship between power, knowledge and discourse, and that it is necessary to analyse the power relations that produce a particular discourse—to examine its historiography. He also argued that it is necessary to examine which set of power relations is bolstered by that knowledge production—in other words, which status quo is maintained by particular discourses.

Foucault's theory of knowledge is a useful perspective from which to view the Celtic paradigm in Irish archaeological discourse. Even a cursory examination of the iconography of the opposing traditions in Northern Ireland would demonstrate that ideas related to the Celtic past, far from being a neutral expression of some objective reality, are deeply embedded in broader political discourses. The historiography of the archaeology of Celts in Ireland also reveals the development of a set of metamorphosing ideas that were intimately related to various political contexts.

Although invasion plays a strong role in medieval Irish pseudo-history, the Celtic paradigm is of relatively recent origin and does not feature in the medieval origin myths of the Irish, which were chiefly concerned with establishing a direct link between Ireland and the Biblical account of human origins and development. *Keltoi* were first mentioned by Classical Greek authors in references to the indigenous peoples of what is now southern France, and the word was later used as a generic term for non-Greeks living to the north and west of metropolitan Greece. The Romans adopted and adapted the Greek term and wrote of the *Galatai* and the *Galli*. To both the Greeks and the Romans, Celts were exotic foreigners to the north, and Classical writings stressed their otherness and difference. With the collapse of the Roman Empire in the west, the term 'Celt' disappeared from western European literature, though it was retained in the Eastern Empire. Until the demise of the Byzantine world in 1453, *Keltoi* was an omnibus term for the inhabitants of the barbarian kingdoms of post-Roman Europe (Chapman 1992).

The term resurfaced in the west in the wake of the Renaissance rediscovery of Classical texts, and one of the earliest applications of the term 'Celtic' in an archaeological context was by the English antiquarian William Stukeley (1687–1765), who used it to describe all prehistoric material culture in Britain. (Stone and metal cutting implements dating from all periods of the past were still being described as 'celts' well into the first half of the twentieth century.) Stukeley and his contemporaries were products of an education system that relied heavily on Classical texts and their use of the term 'Celtic' was equally invested with connotations of otherness and difference (Piccini 1996). An opposition was established between the primitive and barbaric past and the civilised present. In Britain, these ideas were further developed in the eighteenth and nineteenth centuries in the context of an increasingly powerful and expanding imperial state with colonial adventures that were also infused with notions of a binary opposition between civilised people and the primitive or barbaric peoples of the present (Saïd 1994). The oldest of these adventures were in Wales and Ireland. By the mid-nineteenth century the merging of ideas from the series of discourses mentioned at the outset (archaeology, history and comparative linguistics, but also, crucially, ideas drawn from biology and emerging theories of race) had produced an explanatory construct that accounted for the difference between the coloniser and the colonised and also served to legitimise the set of relations between these groups. This was the dichotomy or structural opposition between Celts and other European 'races' (Sims-Williams 1986). In particular, this opposition was expressed in relation to the Anglo-Saxon 'race'.

The tradition of Anglo-Saxon racialism had its roots in the post-Reformation antiquarian movement, but flourished in mid-nineteenth-century England with the importation of ideas derived from evolutionary biology (Stocking 1987). It was part of 'a broader tradition of European thought that validated national, religious or class interests by linking them with specific populations of the early medieval period' (*ibid.*, 62). This validation process was rooted in the past, retrospectively creating the myth of the timelessness of modern social realities through this 'invention of tradition' (Hobsbawm and Ranger 1983). Archaeology, comparative linguistics and folklore studies were used to stress the Germanic roots of the Anglo-Saxons. By the middle of the century, what had begun primarily as a linguistic identity was fused with ideas from ethnology and biology and was explicitly expressed in terms of ethnicity and 'race' (Curtis 1968; Stocking 1987). The racial binary opposition of Celt and Saxon permeates Victorian literature and is the foundation on which ideas such as a Celtic national character are constructed.

The racial paradigm was central to the work of Matthew Arnold (1822–88), an influential English Celtophile who moulded the British popular image of things Celtic (Chapman 1977). Like many of the Anglo-Saxonists, Arnold contrasted the enterprising, self-reliant, self-controlled and libertarian Saxon with the impulsive, imaginative, child-like and mystical Celt. He wrote of the Germanic genius of steadiness, science and orderly government, and contrasted it with the Celtic genius of language, muse and spiritualism. These oppositions were often expressed in gendered terms, the masculine steadiness of the Saxon contrasted with the feminine idiosyncrasy of the Celt. Arnold's exoticisation, feminisation and infantilisation of the Celtic have clear antecedents in earlier concepts of the Celts and have direct parallels in European imperialist encounters with other 'exotic' peoples. This included the notion that such peoples were best dealt with by keeping a firm hand. 'They' understood coercion best because 'they' were not like 'us', and for that reason deserved to be ruled (Saïd 1994).

Arnold's construction of the Celtic had a major influence on the late nineteenth-century Celtic Revival movement in Ireland, which was dominated by the Anglo-Irish ruling élite. This social group also dominated the nineteenth-century antiquarian studies from which Irish archaeology emerged. Ideas about the Celtic past already had a long history when archaeology was called on as a means of further exploration. Irish archaeological discourse in the nineteenth and early twentieth centuries served to corroborate these concepts and thereby validate the social and political status quo. Ideas of intrusive élites dominating and radically changing 'lumpenised' indigenous populations have an ignoble history in Ireland.

Edward Saïd (1994) has written that 'more than any other of its colonies, Britain's Ireland was subjected to innumerable metamorphoses'. Among these metamorphoses we can count the paradox that ideas of a Celtic past were readily embraced and internalised by nineteenth-century Irish nationalism and were to become central tenets of the separatist cause. Concepts that were 'largely the construction of the English, the metropolitan ruling power itself' (Piccini 1996, 7), were to become tools in efforts that sought the de-Anglicisation of Ireland. This was not the only such paradox in operation at the time. By the late nineteenth century, Irish nationalism was largely an anglophone movement. It had aspirations to island-wide political unity, something that had not existed in the past. From the time of the earliest written records, Ireland was characterised by a multiplicity of internal frontiers and consisted of a mosaic of political identities. Political and administrative unity in the modern sense were, ironically, imposed by the British colonial regime in the seventeenth and eighteenth centuries. Notions of past socio-cultural unity would have had an obvious appeal in this context.

As Leersen (1996) has pointed out, the process of identity formation in nineteenth-century Ireland was shaped by the colonial experience, defined in oppositional terms and located in the past. This process was intensified in the decades after 1922. In the early years of the independent Irish state, policies related to such disparate phenomena as education, civil service recruitment, language revival and cultural development were all intricately interwoven (O'Leary 1994; Woodman 1995). A shared Celtic past helped to bolster the social and economic status quo in the new state by providing a common heritage which masked deep internal divisions in Irish society.

The ideational framework whose pedigree is briefly outlined here has had a profound influence on the praxis of the archaeology of the later prehistoric period. It influences the questions that are asked and the way in which archaeological research is carried out. Yet this is rarely acknowledged. For example, when viewed in the context of the colonial exoticisation and 'othering' of the population of Ireland, the 1991 issue of the journal *Emania*, which was devoted to the Bronze Age/Iron Age transition and the 'problem' of Irish origins, takes on a distinctly neo-colonial hue. Yet only one paper, that by Cooney and Grogan (1991), gently suggested that perhaps the question of 'Where did the Irish come from?' might be anachronistic and irrelevant to discussions of the later prehistoric period.

It is argued here that the Celtic paradigm is being sustained by a lack of debate on the rarely questioned assumptions that underlie it. This is not to suggest that the archaeology of the later prehistoric period in Ireland is moribund. There have been many interesting efforts at more lateral thinking. Despite the stated objectives of the Discovery Programme and the choice of fieldwork locations, the publications that have resulted from this initiative have avoided appeals to Celticism (e.g. Newman 1997). However, the paradigm has proven to be a resilient one that has, for the most part, constrained efforts to construct alternative perspectives. This is particularly evident at the level of popular culture, where the qualifications and reservations that have emerged in archaeological discourse have not been communicated to a wider audience. In the dominant public narrative of the Irish past, the Celts and the construction of the Celtic have played an important role in identity formation. This narrative is perceived to be rooted in 'real' events in the past, with archaeology providing a window to those events. The term 'Celtic' is frequently employed as a synonym for 'Irish' and is used to describe diverse phenomena, ranging from the art of the Early Christian church through émigré soccer teams to less tangible but perhaps more potent constructs such as the 'national character' of the inhabitants of Ireland.

I have suggested above that this particular construct has its origins in a racially motivated dialectic of imperialist intent. Yet archaeologists have played an active role in popularising this construct. This is perhaps best illustrated by a quote from Etienne Rynne that appeared in an article entitled 'The Celts' in the *National Geographic* magazine in 1977. In response to the question as to whether there was anything in twentieth-century Ireland that could be recognised as Celtic, Professor Rynne was quoted as having replied:

> A lot. The folklore. The pagan survivals. The fairies, or good people . . . We're often still considered drunk with words. We love to exaggerate, to boast, to argue, to show off, much as did the ancient Celts . . . (quoted in Chapman 1992)

In the title of this paper, I paraphrase Lord Denning's response to a case concerning police brutality. He argued that allegations that police officers were lying under oath must be rejected because to accept them presented the 'appalling vista' of a criminal justice system that was fundamentally flawed. My thesis in this paper is that the archaeology of later prehistoric Ireland is afflicted with a similar malaise in the form of a fatally flawed Celtic paradigm. Stripping away the parts of a familiar Celtic past would leave us with many casualties and the appalling vista of the unfamiliar. At a broader level, it is easier to take an empirical approach to archaeologically generated data than to tackle a key element of Irish identity construction. This has been demonstrated by the contentious debate generated by Simon James's book *The Atlantic Celts: ancient people or modern invention?* (James 1999a), which was published during the interval between the conference at which this paper was delivered (February 1999) and the publication of the conference proceedings. The ideas propounded by James (*ibid.*) parallel many of those expressed here. James's book has generated considerable controversy, not because of his views about how we conceptualise later prehistory but because of the implications of his arguments for identity construction in the present. James (1999b) says that he has been accused of intellectual terrorism for trying to deny modern people their Celtic heritage. Clearly, ideas related to the Celtic past are solidly imbricated in modern conceptions of group identities in Ireland, Britain and elsewhere. The tremendous academic, political and, perhaps more influentially, emotional investment in the Celtic past has proved to be a formidable barrier to its reassessment, and—as predicted by Foucault—acts to preserve the status quo.

Friedman (1992, 846) has written that the 'authentically constituted past is always about the transition from today to tomorrow'. In this light, examining the historiography and, if necessary, questioning the validity of ideas that are central to self-definition today is surely a duty rather than an act of subversion.

The theme of this volume is 'New agendas in Irish prehistory'. I suggest that the most appropriate new agenda would be to recognise the social context of archaeological praxis. This would present the history of human interactions on this island as a dynamic phenomenon rather than one ossified in some safe, familiar 'Heroic Age', where noble warrior Celts ruled over a docile peasantry unworthy of our investigation. Acknowledging the underlying assumptions of archaeology would allow for the creation of multi-dimensional views of the past. In our own social and political context, that in which we practise archaeology here in Ireland at the beginning of the twenty-first century, we are faced with the challenges of rapid social change and the task of reworking Irish identities along more pluralist and inclusive lines. A question such as 'Can Irish archaeology contemplate an Iron Age without Celts?' has a direct relevance to where we find ourselves. Is there space within the borders of Irish identities to allow us to pose this question, or would it conjure up the terrifying prospect of a state without a nation? I suggest that archaeology can facilitate the creation of such space by communicating the diversity and dynamism of human interactions on this island in the past and, by modifying an idea from the linguist David Greene (1964, 20), that modern Ireland is a product of the sum of all the influences—genetic, linguistic and social—that have touched this island over the last 9000 years.

ACKNOWLEDGEMENTS

I wish to thank the following people for commenting on various drafts of this paper: Diarmaid Ó Donnabháin, Curriculum Development Centre, Shannon; Mary O'Donnell, Archaeological Services Unit, UCC; Orla O'Donovan, Department of Applied Social Studies, UCC; Catherine O'Donovan, Shannon; Michelle O Riordan, Dublin Institute for Advanced Studies; and Jerry O'Sullivan, Edinburgh. I bear sole responsibility for any opinions or misunderstandings expressed in this paper.

REFERENCES

Anon. 1992 *The Discovery Programme: strategies and questions.* Dublin. The Discovery Programme.

Chapman, M. 1977 What science is saying about the Celts. *Journal of the Anthropological Society of Oxford* **8** (2), 84–94.

Chapman, M. 1992 *The Celts: the construction of a myth.* New York. St Martin's Press.

Collis, J. 1997 Celtic myths. *Antiquity* **71**, 195–201.

Cooney, G. and Grogan, E. 1991 An archaeological solution to the 'Irish' problem. *Emania* **9**, 33–43.

Cooney, G. and Grogan, E. 1994 *Irish prehistory: a social perspective.* Bray. Wordwell.

Curtis, L.P. 1968 *Anglo-Saxons and Celts: a study of anti-Irish prejudice in Victorian England.* Bridgeport, Connecticut. University of Bridgeport.

de Paor, L. 1986 *The peoples of Ireland: from prehistory to modern times.* London. Hutchinson.

Foucault, M. 1980 *Power/knowledge: selected interviews and other writings 1972–1977.* Brighton. Harvester.

Friedman, J. 1992 The past in the future: history and the politics of identity. *American Anthropologist* **94** (4), 837–59.

Greene, D. 1964 The Celtic languages. In J. Raftery (ed.), *The Celts*, 9–21. Cork. Mercier.

Harbison, P. 1976 *The archaeology of Ireland.* London. Bodley Head.

Harbison, P. 1988 *Pre-Christian Ireland: from the first settlers to the early Celts.* London. Thames and Hudson.

Hawkes, C.F.C. 1972 Cumulative Celticity in pre-Roman Britain. *Études Celtiques* **13**, 607–28.

Herity, M. and Eogan, G. 1977 *Ireland in prehistory.* London. Routledge and Kegan Paul.

Hill, J.D. 1989 Re-thinking the Iron Age. *Scottish Archaeological Review* **6**, 16–24.

Hobsbawm, E. and Ranger, T. (eds) 1983 *The invention of tradition.* Cambridge University Press.

James, S. 1998 Celts, politics and motivation in archaeology. *Antiquity* **72**, 200–9.

James, S. 1999a *The Atlantic Celts: ancient people or modern invention?* London. British Museum Press.

James, S. 1999b A lost civilisation? *The Times Higher Education Supplement*, 4 June 1999, 19. London.

Leersen, J. 1996 *Remembrance and imagination: patterns in the historical and literary representation of Ireland in the nineteenth century.* Cork University Press.

Macalister, R.A.S. 1928 *The archaeology of Ireland* (1st edn). London. Methuen.

Macalister, R.A.S. 1949 *The archaeology of Ireland* (2nd edn). London. Methuen.

Mallory, J.P. 1984 The origins of the Irish. *Journal of Irish Archaeology* **2**, 65–9.

Mallory, J.P. 1993 The archaeology of Irish dreamtime. *Proceedings of the Harvard Celtic Colloquium* **13**, 1–24.

Morash, C. 1998 Celticism: between race and nation. In T. Foley and S. Ryder (eds), *Ideology and Ireland in the nineteenth century*, 206–13. Dublin. Four Courts Press.

Newman, C. 1997 *Tara: an archaeological survey.* Dublin. Royal Irish Academy.
O'Kelly, M.J. 1989 *Early Ireland: an introduction to Irish prehistory.* Cambridge University Press.
O'Leary, P. 1994 At the cow's rump or in the National Theatre?: issues in Gaelic drama, 1922–1939. *Proceedings of the Harvard Celtic Colloquium* **14**, 132–61.
Piccini, A. 1996 Filming through the mists of time: Celtic constructions and the documentary. *Current Anthropology* **37** (Supplement), 1–45.
Raftery, B. 1989 Barbarians to the west. In J.C. Barrett, A.P. Fitzpatrick and L. Macinnes (eds), *Barbarians and Romans in northwest Europe,* 117–52. British Archaeological Reports, International Series 471. Oxford.
Raftery, B. 1991 The island Celts. In S. Moscati, O.H. Frey, V. Kruta, B. Raftery and M. Szabó (eds), *The Celts,* 555–71. London. Thames and Hudson.
Raftery, B. 1994 *Pagan Celtic Ireland: the enigma of the Irish Iron Age.* London. Thames and Hudson.
Raftery, J. 1951 *Prehistoric Ireland.* London. Batsford.
Saïd, E.W. 1994 *Culture and imperialism.* London. Vintage.
Sims-Williams, P. 1986 The visionary Celt: the construction of an ethnic preconception. *Cambridge Medieval Celtic Studies* **11**, 71–96.
Stocking, G.W. 1987 *Victorian anthropology.* New York. The Free Press.
Waddell, J. 1978 The invasion hypothesis in Irish prehistory. *Antiquity* **52**, 121–8.
Waddell, J. 1991 The question of the celticization of Ireland. *Emania* **9**, 5–16.
Waddell, J. 1992 The Irish Sea in prehistory. *Journal of Irish Archaeology* **6**, 29–40.
Waddell, J. 1995 Celts, celticisation and the Irish Bronze Age. In J. Waddell and E. Shee Twohig (eds), *Ireland in the Bronze Age,* 158–69. Dublin. Stationery Office.
Waddell, J. 1998 *The prehistoric archaeology of Ireland*. Galway University Press.
Warner, R. 1991 Cultural intrusions in the Early Iron Age: some notes. *Emania* **9**, 44–52.
Woodman, P.C. 1995 Who possesses Tara? Politics in archaeology in Ireland. In P.J. Ucko (ed.), *Theory in archaeology: a world perspective,* 278–97. London. Routledge.
Yadlon, S. 1997 Skinny women and good mothers: the rhetoric of risk, control, and culpability in the production of knowledge about breast cancer. *Feminist Studies* **23** (3), 645–77.

ARCHAEOLOGICAL SURVEY IN CORK AND ELSEWHERE: AN UPDATE

Denis Power

Amongst her many talents Liz Anderson was an excellent typist, and for many years she inputted much of the data for the Cork Archaeological Survey. Like the story of the elves and the shoemaker, we would leave a pile of hand-written pages beside the computer in the evenings and the next morning, as if by magic, the whole thing had been neatly and correctly typed into the machine. Liz was a joy to work with, ever willing and always reliable. This paper is offered, with deep respect, in her memory.

INTRODUCTION

The practice of Irish archaeology has undergone dramatic change in recent years, most obviously indicated by the increased number of licensed excavations (Fig. 1).[1] One of the main reasons for this phenomenal growth is the rise in economic activity allied to a far greater archaeological input into the planning process. Since 1994 the section dealing exclusively with planning matters in the National Monuments and Historic Properties Service (NMHPS)[2] has grown from one contract archaeologist to a unit of five contract archaeologists under the supervision of a senior archaeologist, and three administrative staff. Also allied to this unit are a number of contract archaeologists working, in liaison with

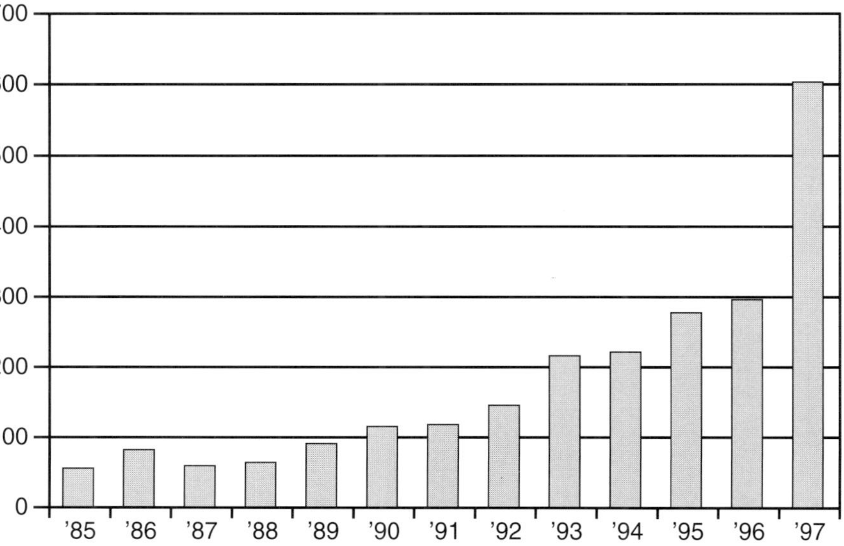

Fig. 1—Number of licensed excavations in Ireland, 1985–97.

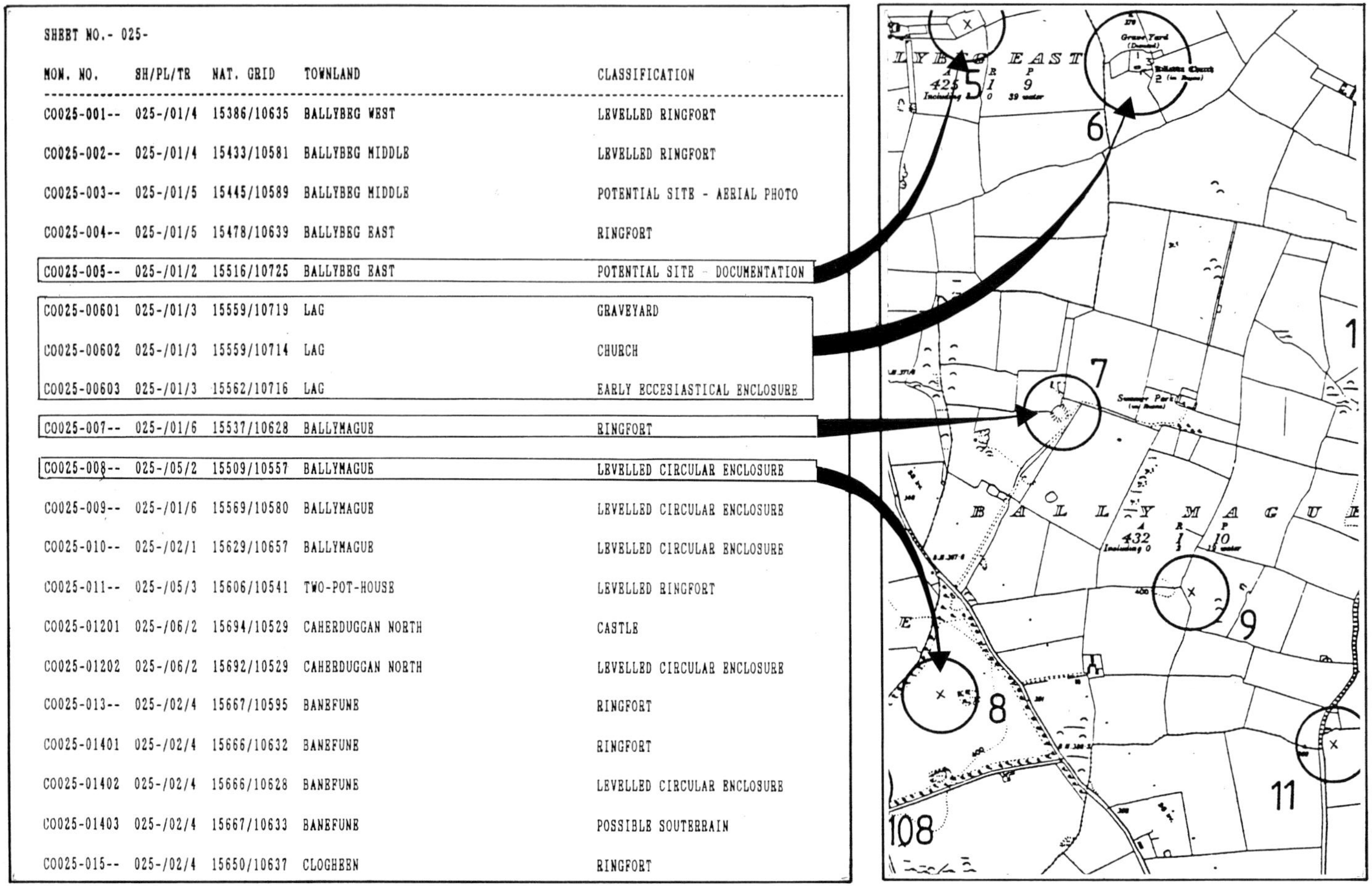

SHEET NO.- 025-

MON. NO.	SH/PL/TR	NAT. GRID	TOWNLAND	CLASSIFICATION
CO025-001--	025-/01/4	15386/10635	BALLYBEG WEST	LEVELLED RINGFORT
CO025-002--	025-/01/4	15433/10581	BALLYBEG MIDDLE	LEVELLED RINGFORT
CO025-003--	025-/01/5	15445/10589	BALLYBEG MIDDLE	POTENTIAL SITE - AERIAL PHOTO
CO025-004--	025-/01/5	15478/10639	BALLYBEG EAST	RINGFORT
CO025-005--	025-/01/2	15516/10725	BALLYBEG EAST	POTENTIAL SITE - DOCUMENTATION
CO025-00601	025-/01/3	15559/10719	LAG	GRAVEYARD
CO025-00602	025-/01/3	15559/10714	LAG	CHURCH
CO025-00603	025-/01/3	15562/10716	LAG	EARLY ECCESIASTICAL ENCLOSURE
CO025-007--	025-/01/6	15537/10628	BALLYMAGUE	RINGFORT
CO025-008--	025-/05/2	15509/10557	BALLYMAGUE	LEVELLED CIRCULAR ENCLOSURE
CO025-009--	025-/01/6	15569/10580	BALLYMAGUE	LEVELLED CIRCULAR ENCLOSURE
CO025-010--	025-/02/1	15629/10657	BALLYMAGUE	LEVELLED CIRCULAR ENCLOSURE
CO025-011--	025-/05/3	15606/10541	TWO-POT-HOUSE	LEVELLED RINGFORT
CO025-01201	025-/06/2	15694/10529	CAHERDUGGAN NORTH	CASTLE
CO025-01202	025-/06/2	15692/10529	CAHERDUGGAN NORTH	LEVELLED CIRCULAR ENCLOSURE
CO025-013--	025-/02/4	15667/10595	BANEFUNE	RINGFORT
CO025-01401	025-/02/4	15666/10632	BANEFUNE	RINGFORT
CO025-01402	025-/02/4	15666/10628	BANEFUNE	LEVELLED CIRCULAR ENCLOSURE
CO025-01403	025-/02/4	15667/10633	BANEFUNE	POSSIBLE SOUTERRAIN
CO025-015--	025-/02/4	15650/10637	CLOGHEEN	RINGFORT

Fig. 2—Extract from SMR listing and constraint map.

NMHPS, within local authority planning departments. In the south-west we now have archaeologists attached to Cork and Limerick city corporations, and to Cork, Limerick and Kerry county councils.[3] As more planning conditions include archaeological constraints (whether excavation, test-trenching, monitoring or watching briefs), so the need for private archaeologists to do this work has grown—full membership of the Irish Association of Professional Archaeologists has risen from 72 in 1984 to over 250 in 1998. Inevitably, with all this activity, the amount of new archaeological information coming on stream is having an impact, e.g. the 'boom in Neolithic houses' reported in a recent edition of *Archaeology Ireland* (Cooney 1999).

THE ARCHAEOLOGICAL SURVEYS

This input into the planning process is largely structured around the Sites and Monuments Record (SMR) and its successor, the Record of Monuments and Places (RMP). The SMR consists of annotated Ordnance Survey (OS) six-inch maps showing the location of all known and suspected archaeological sites, with an accompanying list, derived from a computerised database, giving site classification and locational information (Fig. 2). As with the OS map series, the SMR is organised on a county-by-county basis. The SMR programme was initiated in 1982 and was completed for all 26 counties in 1992. The RMP, which is essentially an update of the SMR, was completed in 1998. Under section 12 of the 1994 National Monuments (Amendment) Act, all sites listed in the RMP have statutory protection from the date of issue of the RMP for the relevant county. With the placement of the SMR, and latterly the RMP, in local authority planning offices and other relevant agencies, the number of referrals to NMHPS has grown dramatically, thus necessitating the planning team mentioned above.

Most of the issued SMRs were based on a 'paper survey', with annotated constraint maps compiled from 'desk' sources alone.[4] This was necessitated by the urgency caused by a rising threat to archaeological monuments, but a fieldwork programme was also initiated in 1982, in conjunction with SMR production. Thus the SMR for County Cork, issued in 1988, was fieldwork-based, as was the 1987 SMR for County Galway, amongst others. As well as producing constraint maps, the SMR 'paper survey' units also prepared a file for each site, on which the subsequent fieldwork is based.

Like the SMRs, the fieldwork is organised on a county-by-county basis, and is being carried out by the Archaeological Survey of Ireland (ASI), a section within NMHPS. It was decided at an early stage that the fieldwork should be rapid and extensive in nature, so that all known sites could be visited and inspected within a brief time-scale. In order to create a focus for this work, and to make its results as widely available as possible, the 'inventory' series was initiated. These are published volumes (for a county or part of a county) in which each field monument is briefly described, with a short summary of any relevant published material. Each volume includes location maps, indexes and a bibliography. This series is now well advanced (Fig. 3) and, provided that current funding is maintained, will be completed and fully published before 2010.

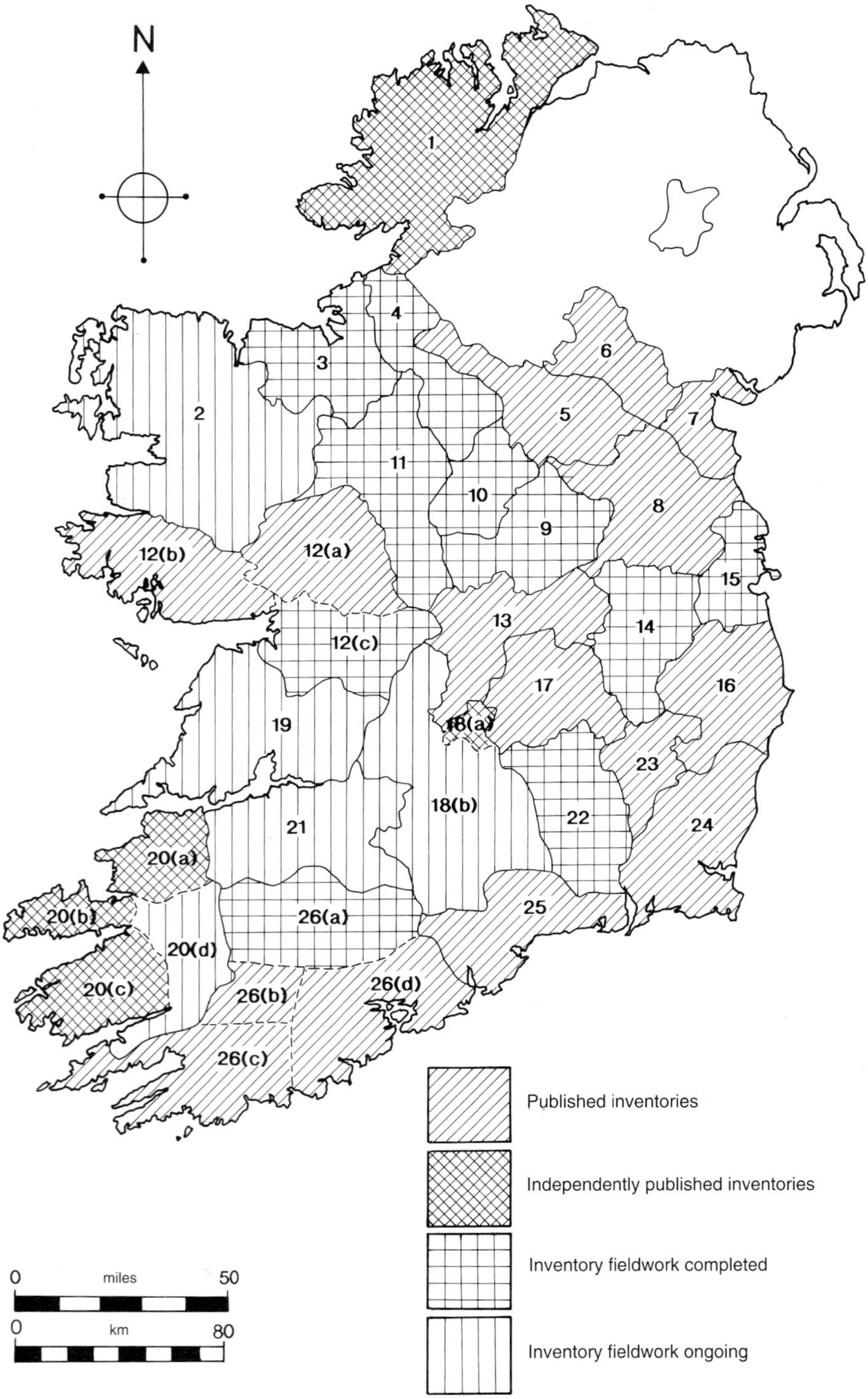
N
1
2
3
4
5
6
7
8
9
10
11
12(a)
12(b)
12(c)
13
14
15
16
17
18(a)
18(b)
19
20(a)
20(b)
20(c)
20(d)
21
22
23
24
25
26(a)
26(b)
26(c)
26(d)
Published inventories
Independently published inventories
Inventory fieldwork completed
Inventory fieldwork ongoing
0 miles 50
0 km 80

It should be remembered that the bulk of the fieldwork in the inventory programme is being undertaken by contract archaeologists, working on their own, with quotas of numbers of sites-per-week to visit. The aim is to compile a basic inspection record rather than a Royal Commission-type 'full survey', and it would be unfair to judge the inventories by that standard. In summary, the SMR/RMP/inventory programme is primarily a response by the State to its legislative responsibilities to record and protect all known or suspected archaeological sites.

Over time the nature of the SMR has changed (see Fig. 3). Initially the process was self-contained, with the 'paper survey' and fieldwork directed solely at the production of constraint maps (both SMR and latterly RMP) and the county inventory series. But this has now developed into a more interactive system, with the SMR files/database being used internally, by the planning unit and other sections of NMHPS, and externally, by independent archaeologists working on projects like Environmental Impact Statements and by students as a resource for field studies and theses. In this way the term Sites and Monuments Record is now being used with reference to the database/archive rather than simply the constraint maps; this is in line with the use of this term elsewhere (Land 1992). Such a model requires that the SMR be continually updated to keep pace with archaeological research and be in line with the latest technological advances. A recent policy document from the Department states that 'the Record of Monuments and Places will be updated so as to take account of future results of the Archaeological Survey of Ireland' (Anon. 1999, 38)—but what is the future for the ASI once the 'inventory' programme is completed?

Muiris de Buitléir (pers. comm.), who deals with computer matters in NMHPS, is currently putting the SMR database on CD, which will also include the Marine Database and the Excavation Register, as well as the listing of Heritage Sites and Natural Heritage Areas. This will be available shortly, on single CDs, to anyone with a genuine interest—at most there will be a nominal charge. At the moment it is not possible to set up an interactive Geographical Information System (GIS) Internet site because of the difficulty of accessing OS maps in digital form. Instead, NMHPS are going to set up a File Transfer Protocol (FTP) Internet site, from which the SMR database and the other items listed above can be downloaded.

Fig. 3—Archaeological inventories produced to date.
Key to counties: (1) Donegal (Lacey et al. *1983), (2) Mayo, (3) Sligo, (4) Leitrim, (5) Cavan (O'Donovan 1995), (6) Monaghan (Brindley 1986), (7) Louth (Buckley 1986), (8) Meath (Moore 1987), (9) Westmeath, (10) Longford, (11) Roscommon, (12a) North Galway (Alcock* et al. *1999), (12b) West Galway (Gosling 1993), (12c) South Galway, (13) Offaly (O'Brien and Sweetman 1997), (14) Kildare, (15) Dublin, (16) Wicklow (Grogan and Kilfeather 1997), (17) Laois (Sweetman* et al. *1995), (18a) Ikerrin (Stout 1984), (18b) Tipperary, (19) Clare, (20a) North Kerry (Toal 1995), (20b) Dingle Peninsula (Cuppage 1986), (20c) Iveragh Peninsula (O'Sullivan and Sheehan 1996), (20d) Kerry (areas not already covered), (21) Limerick, (22) Kilkenny, (23) Carlow (Brindley and Kilfeather 1993), (24) Wexford (Moore 1996), (25) Waterford (Moore 1999), (26a) North Cork, (26b) Mid-Cork (Power* et al. *1997), (26c) West Cork (Power* et al. *1992), (26d) East and South Cork (Power* et al. *1994).*

THE DEVELOPMENT OF FIELD SURVEYING IN COUNTY CORK

The 1983 monograph *Landscape archaeology in Ireland* (Reeves-Smyth and Hamond 1983) reflects the perception of field survey in Ireland in the early 1980s. The editors, in the concluding chapter, stated that 'Ireland, unlike Britain, has no real tradition of fieldsurvey... apart from the work of the Ordnance Survey in the last century, and a few notable pioneers such as de Valera, Ó Nualláin, Orpen, Knowles and Westropp' (*ibid.*, 382). It has been noted that the first-edition OS maps 'brought an ordered and sustained effort to bear on the study of field antiquities on a countrywide scale' (Herity and Eogan 1977, 8). The subsequent revision of these maps maintained their position as an essential research tool. For example, in County Cork the 1930s revision included many new sites (notably *fulachta fiadh*)[5] and could be taken at the time as an up-to-date statement of field monument distribution. However, the absence of a revision of these maps since the 1930s has created a 'visibility gap' in this respect. In many other ways the 1930s mark a turning-point in Irish archaeology, with the waning of the antiquarian tradition and the failure to establish a viable State survey under the 1930 National Monuments Act (Power 1993, 137). Thereafter, archaeological fieldwork concentrated on excavation carried out by professional archaeologists. One consequence of this 'visibility gap' was that when mechanised farming began to develop in Ireland in the 1970s many thousands of field monuments were levelled or removed without the State's, or the archaeological fraternity's, knowledge.

The Ordnance Survey did maintain its interest in antiquities with the work of the Megalithic Survey of Ireland, whose first volume appeared in 1961 (de Valera and Ó Nualláin 1961). That work, and the subsequent extension of the range to include stone circles, boulder burials, stone rows and pairs, etc. (Ó Nualláin 1978; 1984a; 1984b; 1988), represents an important achievement in the development of Irish archaeology. Now, sadly, we are seeing the end of this tradition, with the transferral in 1999 of the two remaining archaeologists[6] with the OS to NMHPS.

Thus the establishment of the SMRs created a mechanism whereby the 'archaeological landscape' became visible as an entity for the first time since the 1930s. For example, when the Cork Archaeological Survey (CAS) began work in the county in 1982 the total number of sites to be visited was estimated at about 8000. This was based primarily on site counts from the three editions of the OS six-inch maps: 1842, *c.* 1900 and *c.* 1938—the last six-inch maps for Cork were published in 1940. The SMR, issued in 1988, listed 14,608 sites, whilst the current (July 1999) number of sites in the database is 17,705.[7] These new sites have come from a variety of sources—aerial reconnaissance, documentary research, independent studies, the inclusion of post-medieval sites, etc.—but the vast majority were discovered by CAS survey teams in the course of regular fieldwork. They achieved this by their own observations and by tapping into local knowledge, asking landowners if they knew of particular features, giving talks to historical groups, schools, etc. This type of approach is often undervalued by comparison with the more 'high-tech' methods of site discovery using remote sensing. It also emphasises the under-representation of field monuments on the OS maps.

To illustrate this growth in the 'visible archaeology' of County Cork, Table 1, based on

Class	**Total 1999**	**Shown on 6" OS map**	**Published by S. Ó Nualláin**	**Extra sites**
Wedge tombs	103	48	59	44
Boulder burials	79	19	45	34
Stone rows	68	58	59	9
Stone pairs	92	67	68	24
Multiple stone circles	40	33	37	3
Five stone circles	52	41	43	9
Radial stone cairns	11	3	6	5
Radial stone enclosures	10	2	3	7
TOTAL	455	271	320	135

Table 1—Additional sites identified by CAS since Ó Nualláin 1978; 1984a; 1984b; 1988; and de Valera and Ó Nualláin 1982.

site types published by Ó Nualláin (1978; 1984a; 1984b; 1988), shows how these numbers have increased since the CAS began its work. If we take these site types as representing the most thoroughly catalogued site types in the south-west, then the impact of the SMR programme on the wider distribution of known archaeological sites can be gauged. Not only are new dots being added to the map but entirely new maps are being created. The recognition of archaeological landscapes in Ireland has advanced considerably since 1983, when the Behy–Glenulra field system represented a unique example of a relict prehistoric landscape (Caulfield 1983). In County Cork the most notable discovery of such a landscape is that identified by Connie Murphy on the Beara Peninsula (Murphy 1997). This work was not directly part of the CAS, though many of the sites were published for the first time in the West Cork inventory (Power *et al.* 1992). Elsewhere, the work by Michael Moore on Monavullagh, Co. Waterford (Moore 1995), and by Chris Corlett on Kilgeever, Co. Mayo (Corlett 1997), show the kind of critical work on prehistoric landscapes beginning to emerge from the ASI.[8] Another recent publication which shows the scope of work possible using the SMR database is *Archaeology and forestry in Ireland* (Johnson 1998). This forms a comprehensive insight into the ongoing interaction between archaeology and forestry development in Ireland, using information mainly collated by the CAS. One important point emphasised by Johnson (*ibid.*, 19) is the over-reliance on SMRs as representing the totality of field monuments in a given area. This is especially the case in 'upland' areas, where mapping by the OS, including the marking of antiquities, is likely to have been very sketchy. It is not, however, within the brief of the inventory surveys to extensively field-walk these areas.

Since 1982 archaeological field survey in Ireland has undergone something of a renaissance. Outside the work of NMHPS, as outlined above, many other important projects with a survey element are now under way. Of particular note are those being carried out by the Discovery Programme. Their landmark publication *Tara: an archaeological survey* (Newman 1997)[9] deserves special mention. This is the first study published in Ireland of a prehistoric landscape which incorporates the broad range of non-intrusive remote-sensing

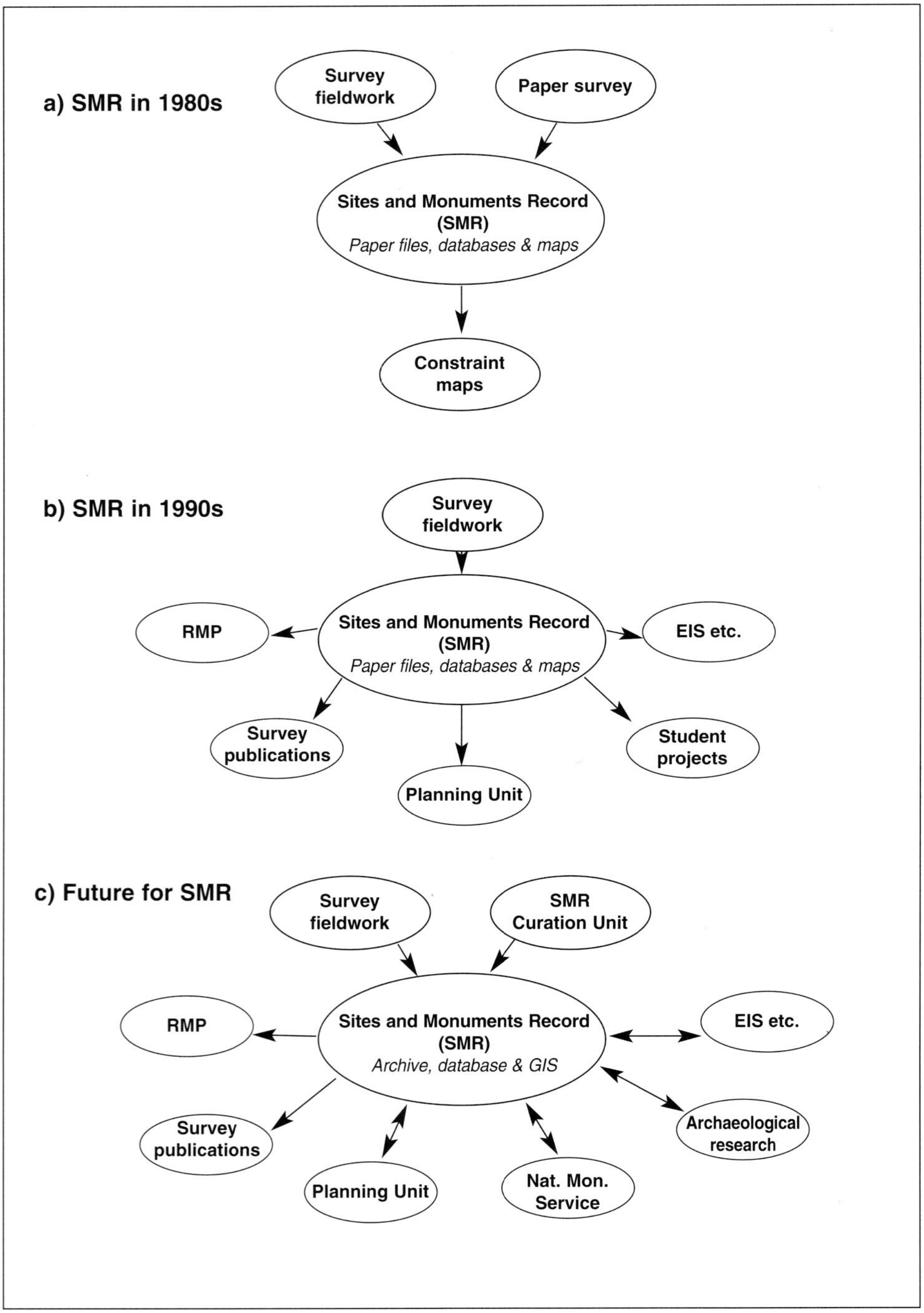

Fig. 4—Model for development of the SMR.

techniques, as well as more conventional survey methods.[10] It demonstrates the potential for non-intrusive archaeological investigation, and with the ever-increasing availability and refinement of geophysical prospecting techniques, the relationship between survey and excavation is likely to alter profoundly.

In 1983 (Reeves-Smyth and Hamond 1983, 386–7) it was observed that

> Much data is accumulated for no purpose other than its description and cataloguing . . . Even quite simple, yet basic questions go unanswered. Why are sites located where they are? Are any regularities in site location apparent? In what way do such settlement patterns change through time? Why do they change in such a fashion?

Indeed, survey work is sometimes seen as 'little more than the systematic ordering of existing information', which at best 'codifies the present state of our knowledge' (Bradley 1993, 151). It is easy to see how the inventories might give this impression: page after page of ringfort or *fulacht fiadh* descriptions would seem to contribute little by way of enhancing our 'understanding' of the past. The ubiquitous nature of many of our field monuments perhaps lends itself to this interpretation. But surely our knowledge that a particular site is a ringfort, ringwork or moated site, rather than a pattern of hachures on an OS map, is a significant qualitative advance in what we know?

Furthermore, Bradley suggests that for the archaeologist fieldwork should be 'a consequence of theory-building, and not the starting point of his research' (*ibid.*). One can appreciate the point that Bradley is making: fieldwork, whether excavation or survey, is often the first resource of an archaeological endeavour, with little regard to its ultimate aims. Fowler (1980) has amply demonstrated how this approach typified field survey in Britain during the 1960s and 1970s. But the relationship between data collection and theory must surely be dialectic rather than unidirectional. For example, if the SMR remains primarily a tool of planning control, then the occasional foray by a research student may indeed result in more frustration than enlightenment. And yet it is only by attempting to use the SMR for research purposes, and through the feedback from this, that its academic potential can be realised. Again the process needs to be two-way—as well as taking information from the SMR, the researchers must be able (and must feel the need) to feed their results back into the process. This model for the development of the SMR (Fig. 4) will require the State to go somewhat beyond its statutory obligations, but it will also require potential users to engage with the system at its development stage and to understand its functions.

The SMR/inventory programme is clear in its primary objectives: to visit and briefly record all known field monuments in the 26 counties of the State; to order this information using a computerised database; and to make this available for general use in an appropriate form. This seemed like a vain hope in 1975 (Haworth 1975), but its impact will probably not be fully appreciated until the project is completed and little-known areas like 'forgotten Munster' (Monk and Sheehan 1998, 6) are finally put on record. This objective is now within reach.

REFERENCES

Alcock, O., de hÓra, K. and Gosling, P. 1999 *Archaeological inventory of County Galway: volume 2.* Dublin. Stationery Office.

Anon. 1999 *Framework and principles for the protection of the archaeological heritage.* Dublin. Department of Arts, Heritage, Gaeltacht and the Islands.

Bennett, I. (ed.) 1988–97 *Excavations bulletin.* Bray. Wordwell.

Bradley, R. 1993 'For I would ask a question of them all': reflections on the prehistory of south-west Ireland. In E. Shee Twohig and M. Ronayne (eds), *Past perceptions: the prehistoric archaeology of south-west Ireland,* 151–4. Cork University Press.

Brindley, A.J. 1986 *Archaeological inventory of County Monaghan.* Dublin. Stationery Office.

Brindley, A.[J.] and Kilfeather, A. 1993 *Archaeological inventory of County Carlow.* Dublin. Stationery Office.

Buckley, V.M. 1986 *Archaeological inventory of County Louth.* Dublin. Stationery Office.

Caulfield, S. 1983 The Neolithic settlement of north Connaught. In T. Reeves-Smyth and F. Hamond (eds), *Landscape archaeology in Ireland,* 195–215. British Archaeological Reports, British Series 116. Oxford.

Cooney, G. 1999 A boom in Neolithic houses. *Archaeology Ireland* **47**, 13–14.

Corlett, C. 1997 The prehistoric archaeology of the parish of Kilgeever, south-west Mayo. *Journal of the Royal Society of Antiquaries of Ireland* **49**, 65–103.

Cotter, C. (ed.) 1985–7 *Excavations Bulletin.* Dublin. Wordwell.

Cuppage, J. 1986 *Archaeological survey of the Dingle Peninsula.* Ballyferriter. Oidhreacht Chorca Dhuibhne.

de Valera, R. and Ó Nualláin, S. 1961 *Survey of the megalithic tombs of Ireland, vol.1: County Clare.* Dublin. Stationery Office.

de Valera, R. and Ó Nualláin, S. 1982 *Survey of the megalithic tombs of Ireland, vol. 4: Counties Cork, Kerry, Limerick, Tipperary.* Dublin. Stationery Office.

Fitzpatrick, E. and O'Brien, C. 1998 *The medieval churches of County Offaly.* Dublin. Government of Ireland.

Fowler, P.J. 1980 Tradition and objectives in British field archaeology, 1953–78. *Archaeology Journal* **137**, 1–12.

Gosling, P. 1993 *Archaeological inventory of County Galway, volume 1: west Galway.* Dublin. Stationery Office.

Grogan, E. and Kilfeather, A. 1997 *Archaeological inventory of County Wicklow.* Dublin. Stationery Office.

Haworth, R. 1975 Archaeological field survey in Ireland—past, present and future. *Irish Archaeological Research Forum* **2**, 7–19.

Herity, M. and Eogan, G. 1977 *Ireland in prehistory.* London. Routledge and Kegan Paul.

Johnson, G. 1998 *Archaeology and forestry in Ireland.* Kilkenny. Heritage Council.

Lacey, B. *et al.* 1983 *The archaeological survey of County Donegal.* Lifford. Donegal County Council.

Land, N.A.R. 1992 Sites and monuments records in Great Britain. In C.U. Larsen (ed.), *Sites and monuments: national archaeological records,* 171–81. Copenhagen. National Museum

of Denmark DKC.
Monk, M.A. and Sheehan, J. 1998 Research and early medieval Munster: agenda or vacuum. In M.A. Monk and J. Sheehan (eds), *Early medieval Munster: archaeology, history and society*, 1–8. Cork University Press.
Moore, M.J. 1987 *Archaeological inventory of County Meath*. Dublin. Stationery Office.
Moore, M.J. 1995 A Bronze Age settlement and ritual centre in the Monavullagh Mountains, County Waterford, Ireland. *Proceedings of the Prehistoric Society* **61**, 191–243.
Moore, M.J. 1996 *Archaeological inventory of County Wexford*. Dublin. Stationery Office.
Moore, M.[J.] 1999 *Archaeological inventory of County Waterford*. Dublin. Stationery Office.
Murphy, C.J. 1997 The prehistoric archaeology of the Beara Peninsula, Co. Cork. Unpublished MA thesis, University College Cork.
Newman, C. 1997 *Tara: an archaeological survey*. Discovery Programme Monograph 2. Dublin. Royal Irish Academy.
O'Brien, C. and Sweetman, P.D. 1997 *Archaeological inventory of County Offaly*. Dublin. Stationery Office.
O'Donovan, P. 1995 *Archaeological inventory of County Cavan*. Dublin. Stationery Office.
Ó Nualláin, S. 1978 Boulder-burials. *Proceedings of the Royal Irish Academy* **78**C, 75–114.
Ó Nualláin, S. 1984a A survey of stone circles in Cork and Kerry. *Proceedings of the Royal Irish Academy* **84**C, 1–77.
Ó Nualláin, S. 1984b Grouped standing stones, radial-stone cairns and enclosures in the south of Ireland. *Journal of the Royal Society of Antiquaries of Ireland* **114**, 63–79.
Ó Nualláin, S. 1988 Stone rows in the south of Ireland. *Proceedings of the Royal Irish Academy* **88**C, 179–256.
O'Sullivan, A. and Sheehan, J. 1996 *The Iveragh Peninsula: an archaeological survey of south Kerry*. Cork University Press.
Power, D. 1993 Archaeological survey in the Republic of Ireland and the Cork experience. In E. Shee Twohig and M. Ronayne (eds), *Past perceptions: the prehistoric archaeology of south-west Ireland*, 137–9. Cork University Press.
Power, D., Byrne, E., Egan, U., Lane, S. and Sleeman, M. 1992 *Archaeological inventory of County Cork, vol. 1: West Cork*. Dublin. Stationery Office.
Power, D., Byrne, E., Egan, U., Lane, S. and Sleeman, M. 1994 *Archaeological inventory of County Cork, vol. 2: East and South Cork*. Dublin. Stationery Office.
Power, D., Byrne, E., Egan, U., Lane, S. and Sleeman, M. 1997 *Archaeological inventory of County Cork, vol. 3: Mid Cork*. Dublin. Stationery Office.
Reeves-Smyth, T. and Hamond, F. (eds) 1983 *Landscape archaeology in Ireland*. British Archaeological Reports, British Series 116. Oxford.
Stout, G.T. 1984 *Archaeological survey of the barony of Ikerrin*. Roscrea Heritage Society.
Sweetman, P.D., Alcock, A. and Moran, B. 1995 *Archaeological inventory of County Laois*. Dublin. Stationery Office.
Toal, C. 1995 *North Kerry archaeological survey*. Dingle. Brandon.

Endnotes

1 Figures derived from Cotter 1985–7 and Bennett 1988–97.

2 NMHPS is part of *Dúchas* The Heritage Service, a section of the Department of Arts, Heritage, Gaeltacht and the Islands.

3 Respectively: Maurice Hurley, Celie O'Rahilly, Catryn Power, Sarah McCutcheon and Michael Connolly.

4 The 'paper survey' was compiled by two teams of contract archaeologists working in Dublin under the direction of Geraldine Stout and Michael Gibbons; contracts for counties Limerick and Clare were placed with UCC, under the direction of Seán Kirwan. A separate Urban Archaeological Survey dealt exclusively with medieval boroughs.

5 This information was supplied by antiquarian referees such as Canon Power and Michael Bowman.

6 Paul Walsh and Eamon Coady.

7 The total number of site records in the national SMR database in 1998 was 111,000.

8 Though the first research monograph to emerge under the imprint of ASI is a study of the medieval churches of County Offaly (Fitzpatrick and O'Brien 1998)!

9 The other aspects of the Discovery Programme all incorporate an element of field survey, but their chief focus is on excavation.

10 Excepting the work by Burenhult at Carrowmore, Co. Sligo.

ADVENTURERS IN HYPERSPACE: INTERNET PUBLICATION, A STEEP LEARNING CURVE

Caroline Wickham-Jones

INTRODUCTION

This is a very personal paper, but then this is a very personal volume. It describes my experiences when writing up an excavation report for publication on the Internet. Internet publication is something that we are only just beginning to think about. I was certainly very naive, and perhaps reading about my experience will benefit others.

Background

In the summer of 1996, during a watching brief for the construction of a golf-course, Headland Archaeology Ltd discovered a small archaeological site just to the north of Crail, on the coast of Fife, Scotland (Fig. 1). As the artefacts suggested that the site was Mesolithic I was called in, and though I did not participate in the excavation I was involved from then on.

Fife Ness was a particularly small site (3.5m by 2.5m), lying about 15m above present sea-level, 8m from the coast. Since most Mesolithic sites in Scotland are considerably larger (Wickham-Jones and Dalland 1998a; 1998b), Fife Ness was initially thought to be unusual because of its small size (Pl. 1). It had, however, other unusual elements of interest and importance. First of all, the 1500 lithic artefacts were all of flint, which is exceptional in Mesolithic Scotland, where flint is generally supplemented by other materials. Secondly, while the assemblage contained the usual run-of-the-mill scrapers and edge-retouched pieces, the microliths were dominated by crescents (Fig. 2), and this is not at all common. It is not unusual for microlithic assemblages to be dominated by one particular type of artefact, but crescent-dominated assemblages are very rare. Of almost equal interest was the complete absence of some of the Scottish Mesolithic's most common microlith types, such as the scalene triangle.

In addition, the radiocarbon dating produced an unexpected result. Fourteen samples were selected for dating to investigate the contemporaneity of the different features and to test whether a short period of activity had been involved. The results were all statistically overlapping, making it very likely that the features were indeed contemporary, and that they covered a short space of time (Fig. 3). What had not been expected was that these samples would provide some of the earliest dates for human activity in Scotland, in the early ninth millennium, almost at the same time as the settlement on Rum on the west coast of Scotland (Wickham-Jones and Dalland 1998a, ill. 10).

It was clear, therefore, that the site was important and merited publication to as wide an audience as possible. The initial plans for funding had provided for publication in the *Tayside and Fife Archaeological Journal*, and this would of course go ahead, but perhaps wider

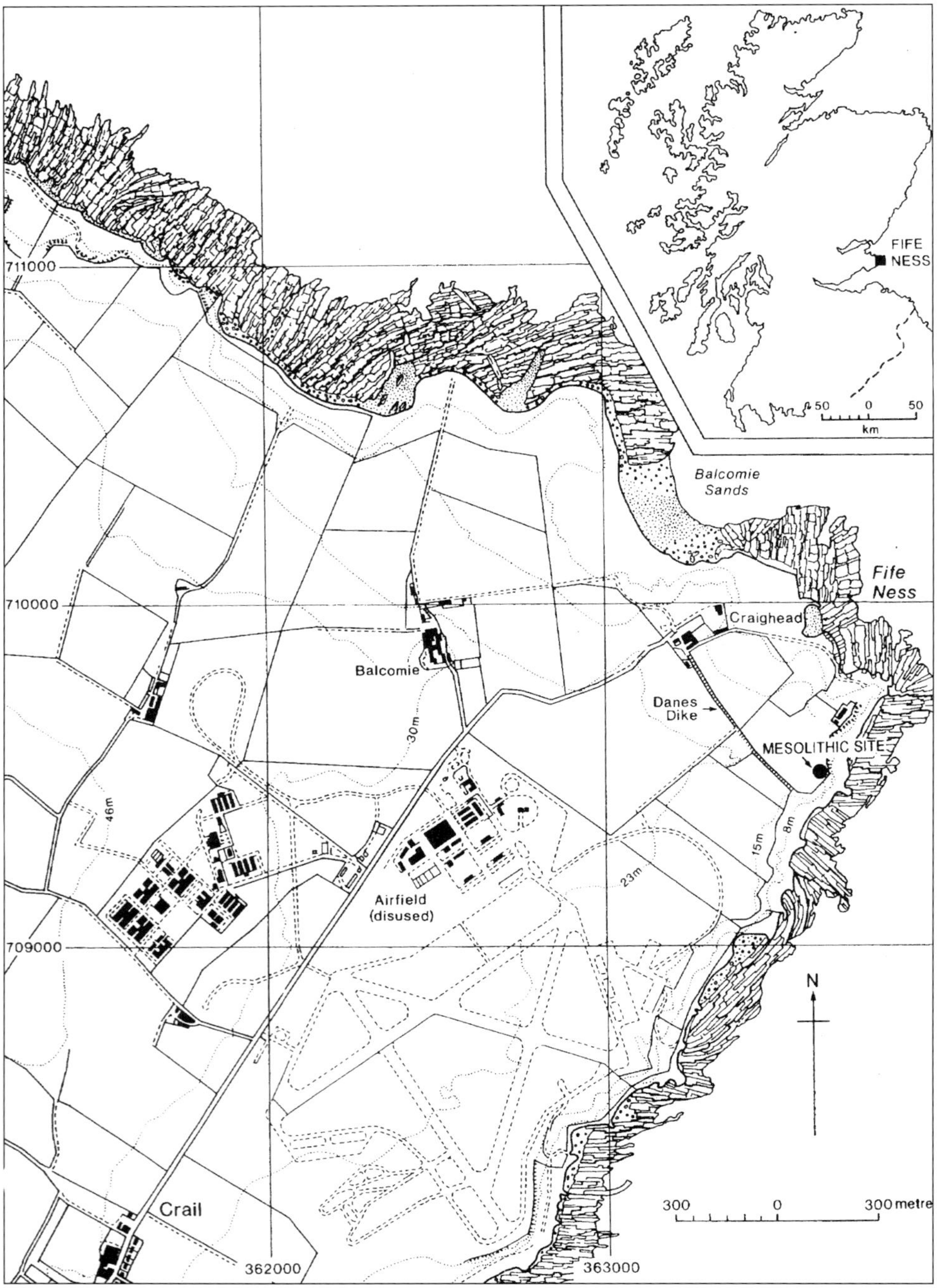

Fig. 1—Fife Ness: site location map.

Pl. 1—Fife Ness: general view of the site from the south-west.

circulation could also be arranged. Having recently seen *Internet Archaeology* on the Web, I suggested that we approach its editors to see whether they might be interested. Naively, I thought that Web publication was much the same as paper publication: all we would have to do was produce the word-processed text as for our paper publication, modify it slightly, stick in a few hypertext links for key words, and there you were. Well, the principle was there but the practice was quite different, and over the next few months I did have rather a lot to learn!

INITIAL APPROACHES

Initially we got in touch with the editors of *Internet Archaeology* by e-mail. They were interested in the possibility of publication and we arranged to meet with the editor, Alan Vince. Together we went through the report and site archive with a fine-tooth comb.

The existing report was to be used as a basis for publication, and Alan Vince explained clearly what would be involved in preparing it for publication on the Internet. I have it all written down in my notebook, but I realise now that most of what he said went over my

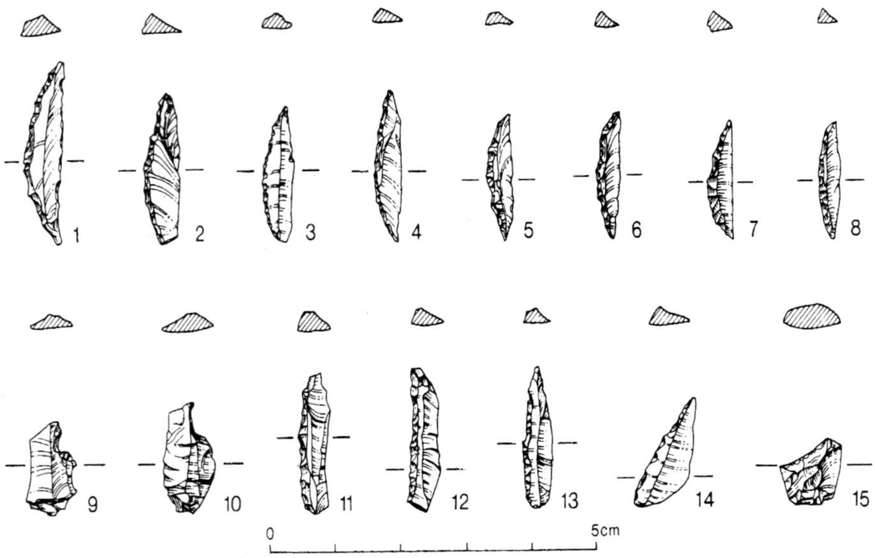

Fig. 2—Fife Ness: microliths.

head. For example, I just didn't know what was involved in putting in the source code in order to make up the sections into *Internet Archaeology* format. Alan made everything sound very simple and straightforward (which it is if you know what you are doing), and so we blithely agreed to his estimate of the time involved and discussed how best to proceed.

The next step was to obtain funding for editing and preparing the report. Gordon Barclay and Olly Owen at Historic Scotland were both very keen and helpful. They were interested in the project and pleased to use a small site like Fife Ness as a trial for Internet publication.

THE FIRST STAGE OF WORK

An Internet Assistant package for Microsoft Word was my first necessity, and I was pleased to find that it downloaded smoothly without crashing my computer, as so often happens when I try to be adventurous in hyperspace.

I then had to sit down with the text and insert all the possible hyperlinks that I could think of, in order to provide the reader with the means of jumping to different, but related, parts of the paper. While trying to be helpful and provide useful connections I also had to be cautious because the blue links (indicating hyperlinks) are distracting and I did not want too many on any one screen. Nor did I want to link to text that lay only a few lines away from the reader's position. Once I had grasped exactly what I had to type in, the hyperlinks were relatively simple, although they did tell on my right hand—never had I clicked the mouse so often in such a short space of time, and I began to see how people get repetitive strain injury!

At the same time, I was preparing the lithics catalogue for integration into the paper. I work with Access and therefore I had to provide a version without any queries, forms or reports. Alan Vince then scrutinised the data for errors and omissions, totals that didn't add up, and general misunderstandings. I have been working on lithic material for over twenty years, but none of my catalogues has ever been taken apart in such detail. Luckily for me he found only a couple of minor points to question, and soon he was able to begin formatting the material for readers to query on-line.

There were no other finds from the site, and because the stratigraphy was very simple we did not consider adding this information into the Internet publication. With hindsight I think that perhaps we should have done so for completeness.

Preparing the visual material

We included all of the line drawings that had been prepared for the paper publication, and supplemented these with photographs of selected flint artefacts. Although many of the lithics were very small and difficult to photograph, the images seemed to be satisfactory and Magnar Dalland began to scan them for digital reproduction. This was more complicated than anticipated, however, mainly because our photographs were not as good as we had thought. A digital camera and/or professional help would be in order next time to help reproduction, especially of small pieces like the microliths. The finished product in the Internet paper is not 100% satisfactory.

Scanning of the line drawings was easier, though the end result could also have been improved with experience.

Finalising the paper

The next step was to divide the major sections of the paper into separate files and to summarise each for the table of contents. This was a relatively simple task, though it meant that some of the hyperlinks had to be rewritten. Again with hindsight, it would be preferable to separate the paper into files first and then set up the hyperlinks. Subdivision meant that instead of having one paper to deal with, there were suddenly several shorter files, and keeping track of them all became quite complex. There were 24 files in all for Fife Ness. (Full HTML editors now have site management facilities that make this task easier.)

The files were all interlinked so that the reader can jump between them and revisit them in any order. I suddenly realised that this meant the paper no longer had a beginning, a middle and an end like a conventional paper publication, and that in many ways it was a disadvantage to work from an existing text. Had I started to write from scratch, I could have produced something that was more tailored to the circular approach that Internet publication offers.

I then had the tricky task of editing the HTML code so that the paper would conform to the *Internet Archaeology* house style. Of course this had to be done separately for each file and, though I got very clear instructions from the editors, this was the point at which I began to flounder. No matter what I tried, I could not get rid of some rogue italics from my screen, and in the end the task was taken over by *Internet Archaeology* themselves. Though it would undoubtedly be useful for archaeologists to have this skill, I cannot help feeling that it is better left to those who have devised the house style. They are the most practised and experienced at it, and only in that way can they be certain that their own house style is

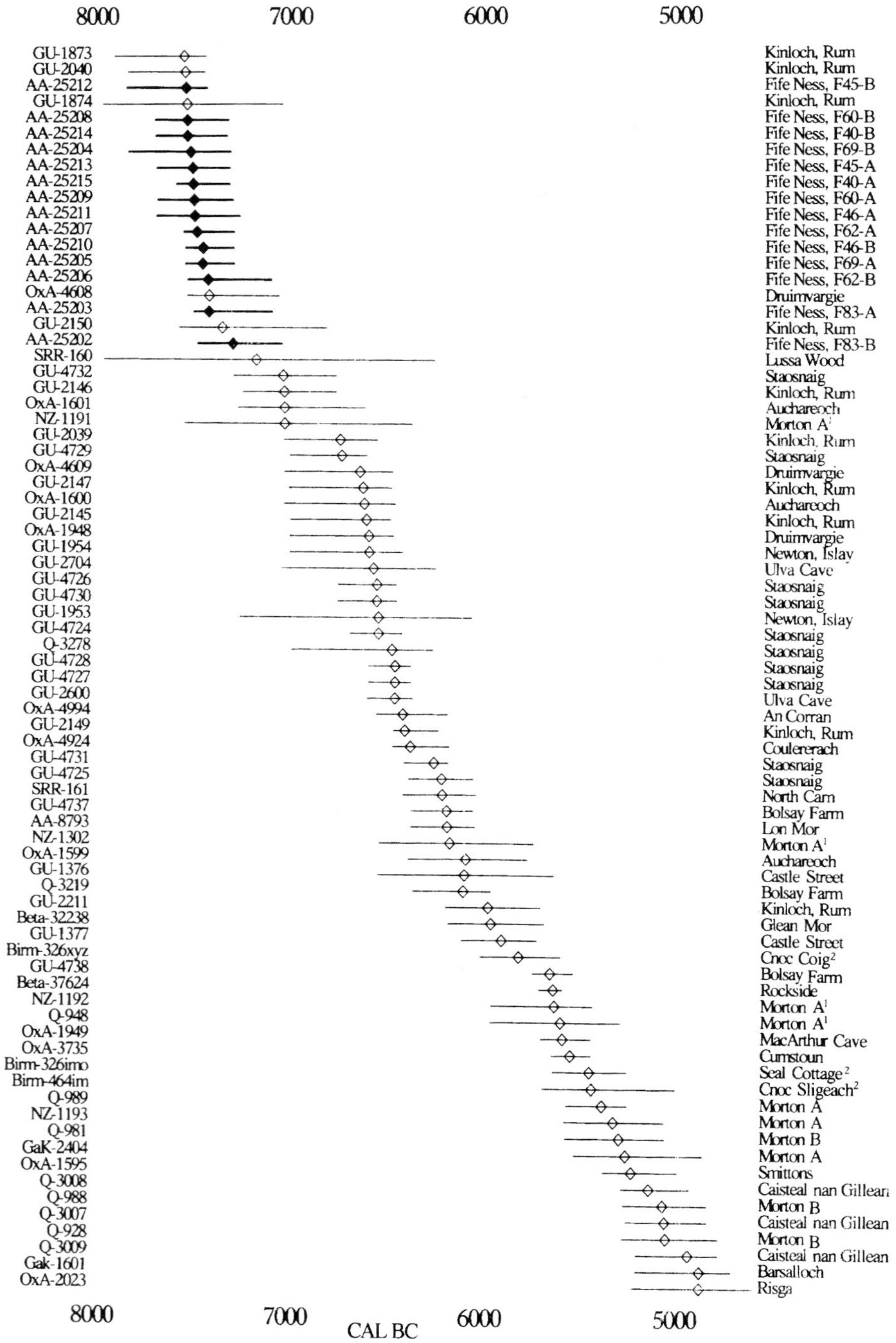

[1]The dated material is a mixture deriving from several different contexts

[2]Combination of individual dates derived from separate samples of the same shell

Fig. 3—Radiocarbon dates for the early Mesolithic in Scotland as of August 1998.

consistently applied. The use of templates or style-sheets should make this easier in future.

MAPPING THE MESOLITHIC

When we first thought of Internet publication we had the brilliant idea that we could animate our distribution map of related sites in order to show how the sites occurred through time. That is to say, we thought that someone else would be keen to do it for us. We found our someone else in Rob Sands, and he set to work writing a programme that would incorporate the radiocarbon dates and provide an animated map. Meanwhile Magnar Dalland worked on the dates themselves.

We wanted to take account of the fact that any one radiocarbon determination deals with the probability of the date falling within a certain range of time. We also had to take into account the fact that each of the sites in which we were interested had not one but several determinations. Magnar therefore had to manipulate the data in order to provide one average determination for each site, as well as providing the different probability readings over the duration of the time-range specific to that site.

Each date was calibrated, using the OxCal calibration programme, and divided into a series of four-year probabilities. These were then added up into 20-year intervals (Fig. 4) in order to reduce the resolution of the data, and 100-year intervals at the centre of every 20-year block were calculated. All the dates from a single site could then be plotted on to one graph and divided into five different classes of probability (Fig. 5). In this way each site could be allocated various levels of colour according to the probability of its having been occupied at any one time. Sites therefore not only light up but also change colour. This takes some getting used to and, like any distribution map, it can only reflect archaeological work carried out, but the result is interesting nonetheless.

Making the animated map was a slow and arduous process because we were all learning as we went along and some elements were refined over and over again. The map was produced using the Java programming language. One of the main problems encountered was that this field is developing so fast that the structure of the map was out of date almost as soon as it had been completed. The basic work has been done, however, and the programme can be run on any set of data. (New versions of the programme would, no doubt, be more sophisticated.)

As not everyone will have a browser that can support the animation, a static version of the map was also produced. This can be accessed more easily and provides the same information without the time-depth variation. The lack of suitable browsers is a problem that will be overcome as people upgrade their equipment. In the meantime, links to sites where patches to upgrade a browser can be obtained were also included.

This highlights a more general problem in Internet publication: namely, that authors will always be keen to use the most sophisticated software to show off their data, while individual readers may not be able to upgrade so frequently (though the two key browsers are free and 'easily' set up). Problems like this do not arise in paper publication where the publisher, in effect, provides the browser.

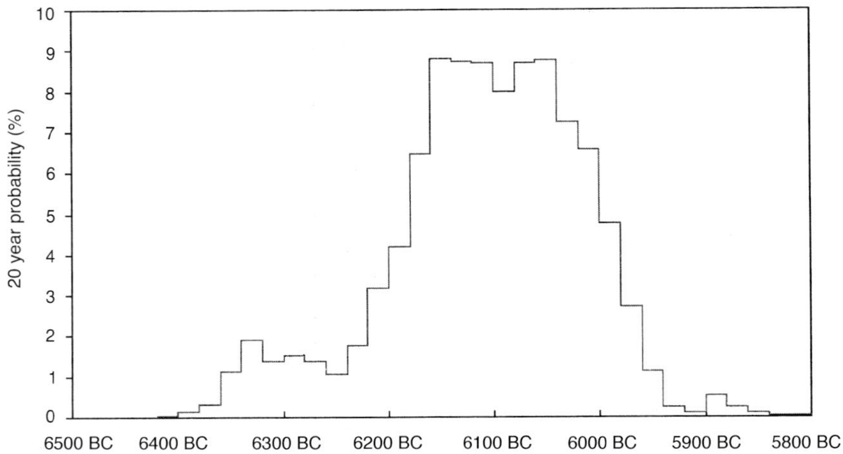

Fig. 4—Radiocarbon determination OxA-1599: example of a calibrated probability distribution at 20-year intervals.

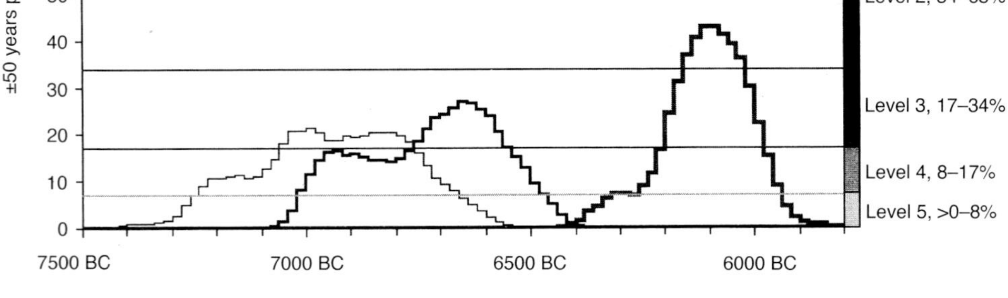

Fig. 5—The five levels of probability for the three dates from Auchareoch.

Reaching out to related sites
One feature of the Internet is that it is not a static entity and there are few boundaries. Thus it was possible to provide links from the sites located on the map to information about those sites recorded by the Royal Commission on the Ancient and Historical Monuments of Scotland (RCAHMS). In this way a simple distribution map related to one site could become a major resource of information about associated sites.

Each site location was made active so that extra details of the dating information related to that site could be brought up on screen. From this extra information, individual links were made to Canmore, the RCAHMS computerised, searchable database. These links take readers to the relevant record in the Canmore database. Clearly, this adds to the utility of the Fife Ness paper, but it was not without its problems.

Not surprisingly, permission was needed in order to make use of the Canmore pages. This was just as you would expect with regard to the reproduction of photographic or other illustrative material. RCAHMS had not, however, received many requests for permission to make use of their Web material, and so it took some time for a suitable licence to be arranged. At first they could only offer a yearly, renewable licence, which was not suitable, but after some negotiation an agreement was reached. In future this sort of problem should be eased as people become more familiar with the requirements of Internet reproduction.

Those who have read the paper in detail will also realise that the Canmore information is essentially unedited and very variable in content. Thus some sites have several pages of information, while others are restricted to a couple of paragraphs. In general, however, all entries have useful information on dates, fieldwork and further references.

Another problem was deciding at which point to stop. We were afraid that the tail was beginning to wag the dog. It would have been possible to follow up the information provided for the related sites in more detail. However, this was essentially a report on a small, if interesting, site in Fife. It did not seem appropriate that there should be more information about general aspects of the Mesolithic than of the site under consideration. These could be kept for a wider-ranging discussion paper (into which future site reports could be linked).

As they stand, the Canmore pages accessed from the Fife Ness paper provide a wonderful database of the Scottish Early Mesolithic as it was understood at the time of writing. Together with the map they will, of course, go out of date quickly—in fact they are already out of date as this discussion paper is being written. Canmore will, however, be continually worked on and updated, and readers can also access the rest of Canmore from the paper. The map programme has now been written and can be upgraded and used as the basis for any set of information. In this respect new Mesolithic reports can provide updated information in the time-honoured tradition of paper publication.

THE FINAL TOUCHES

All of the usual additions of a paper publication appear in the Fife Ness paper—acknowledgements, references and so on—but there are also one or two extras. Because it may well be read by people who are not familiar with the Mesolithic and lithic technology,

Region	Number of users
Africa	2
Asia	5
Australasia	12
Europe	46
North America	85
South America	3
UK	146
Rest of world	2
Blank	124
Total	**425**

Table 1—Recorded users at 30 September 1998.

Type	Number of users
Academic	96
Student	65
Public	39
Private	76
Other	34
Blank	115
Total	**425**

Table 2—User profile at 30 September 1998.

Part of paper accessed	Number of hits
Open access areas, e.g. table of contents	2346
Main text and images	4664
Lithic catalogue	433
Calmap	3711
Canmore links	110
Total	**11,264**

Table 3—Breakdown of access to paper at 30 September 1998.

Region	Number of hits
Africa	12
Asia	58
Australasia	252
Europe	1698
North America	2013
South America	107
UK	7909
Rest of world	14
Blank	258
Total	**12,321**

Table 4—Number of hits to 20 November 1998.

we decided to include a glossary. In future this may become unnecessary as new papers can link back to glossaries in earlier publications. The development of a European electronic archaeological glossary, with which RCAHMS is involved, may also render individual glossaries redundant.

Links were also added to related Web pages that dealt with Mesolithic material. Thus readers of Fife Ness can access directly other Mesolithic papers in electronic publications like *Assemblage*, and they can visit museums with related displays such as the Kilmartin House Museum. Links were provided to Canmore and other Scottish archaeological institutions.

Finally, a version of the text was provided to be downloaded. This takes some time, but it means that readers can print out their own copy of the paper (albeit without some of the electronic wizardry like the consultable catalogue and the animated map). Hard copy is clearly very important if people wish to make use of a publication over and over again. No one wants to have to access the Internet every time they wish to check a minor point. Thus the Fife Ness paper can also fill a space on a bookshelf and be passed to friends, even where the *Tayside and Fife Archaeological Journal* is not available.

THE PROOF OF THE PUDDING

The Fife Ness paper was published on 20 August 1998, and within a week of going live it had recorded over 3000 hits (that is, accessed pages) from 425 users around the world and was within the top six *Internet Archaeology* papers. I would guess that few of my previous publications have reached as wide an audience (Table 1). By the end of September there had been over 11,000 hits to the different parts of the paper (Table 3).

By late November there had been little change in the overall readership (Table 4). The initial surge of interest had settled down to between two and five readers a day, and a total of 572 readers had been recorded by 21 November 1998. There was no sign of any real fall-off in the use of the paper.

Statistics are one thing—interpreting them is another. The recorded hits for the Fife Ness paper may be impressive, but did each user read it? No! We can be certain of that because many users never went further than the table of contents. It is a feature of electronic publication that every time a page is accessed it is recorded, and *Internet Archaeology* compiles an impressive set of records relating to the precise use that is made of its papers. Thus it is possible to see which sections of the report are more popular. Not surprisingly, more people access the beginning sections of any chapter and then figures tail off for the later pages. By the beginning of October there had been 189 hits for the description at the start of the structural section and 148 for the initial part of the lithics chapter. Hits for the lithics material tailed off to 43 by the end of the chapter and there were 53 hits for the last section of the structural chapter. We can see that there were 38 hits for additional information on the site at Morton and 33 for the site at An Corran. We can also see that there were ten queries to the catalogue regarding information on the microliths and four regarding platform cores. People were certainly interested in the paper, but it is impossible to know why—were they just idly browsing, curious medievalists wondering what an electronic excavation report looks like, or were they avid Mesolithic specialists devouring every word? We don't know (Table 2).

Of course the same caveats must apply to a paper publication. You can send out all of your offprints, but you can never be sure whether people will read and digest them, or use them to level up the corner of their keyboard. Nevertheless, the electronic publication has undoubtedly reached a far wider audience than a similar paper publication.

THE BENEFIT OF HINDSIGHT

With the benefit of hindsight it is obvious that we were actually working on a completely new product that would be used in quite a different way to the paper publication. It would certainly have been better to have started from scratch with the report-writing and to write the Internet publication independently of the paper version.

When writing for the Internet it is, in many ways, easiest to start with the conclusions. The different elements that have gone into reaching those conclusions can then be expanded in their own sections and subsections as the reader is led deeper and deeper into the maze of information. The writer provides the information and has a duty to make it accessible, though it no longer has to be curtailed in the way that it once did on paper. The data storage possibilities of the Internet are apparently limitless. It is the reader, however, who designs the path through this information—they make the maze, as they follow leads into areas that interest them. No two readers will read the report in the same way, and they are unlikely even to read it the same way themselves if they go back to it more than once. It is worth pointing out, however, that no reader will thank the writer for providing superfluous information. Electronic publication may make it possible to publish larger quantities of data, but it is still important to edit work carefully.

At times during the writing we were criticised for the apparent cost and work necessary for the publication. As I do not generally deal with the financial side of excavation report production, I cannot comment on the comparative cost of Internet and paper publications. However, this is not a valid comparison anyway. It is like saying that because cars cost more than bicycles we should only use bicycles.

An Internet publication and a paper publication serve related needs, but they do not serve the same need. Both provide information for an interested audience; however, the Internet publication not only reaches a much wider audience with no barriers of geographical location, but it can also provide the audience with different levels of information to suit their own particular needs. At its most detailed level, raw data about site stratigraphy, finds and so on can be integrated within a report for specialist readers to manipulate as they wish. Less keen (or less crazy) readers can read the results of the analysis provided by the team of specialists. Those who are interested in the site but not in its particulars can stick with the summary information that sets it in a general context. This is an over-simplification, but I hope that it gets the general idea across. The paper publication, on the other hand, is constrained by factors of space and size and can usually only approach one level of information successfully. For this reason most journals have a target audience, and conflicts

Fig. 6—Fife Ness: artist's reconstruction.

arise as to whether the material within any one publication should be more, or less, detailed. Many people will remember the anguished debates about the use of microfiche for specialist data: those are a thing of the past with the use of electronic publication.

As I was finalising this paper, an interesting briefing appeared in the journal *Nature*: 'The writing is on the web for science journals in print' (Butler 1999). With an examination of the world of scientific publishing, where electronic journals are now well established, and the fact that some libraries are starting to phase out paper altogether, it concludes that: 'A journal without a web version is now rare, and probably endangered' (*ibid.*). How many archaeological journals have started to think seriously about this issue? There are many elements that need to be addressed, such as refereeing, and even open on-line refereeing, as well as an examination of copyright and the possibility of the parallel electronic and paper publication of an article (something that has even been an issue with this paper). Some scientific journals now post manuscripts on the web as they come in, as an electronic peer-review and communication process. I particularly like the idea of a software robot that can carry out many of the processes of editing and publication. The scientific world is clearly well down the road of electronic publication, and I hope that archaeologists will not take long to follow.

Caveat

I hope that this has not appeared to be too negative a paper. Internet publication has much to recommend it and I hope that I shall be able to put some of my new-found experience to work on further publications. It is an exciting thought. I have identified the negative aspects of our work in the hope that they might be minimised for others working on new papers, but it was not my intention to emphasise this side of things.

Whatever we thought, we must have got some things right: *Internet Archaeology* was awarded a Special Mention in the Charlesworth Group Award for Electronic Journals 1998. Overall design, ease of use and innovative use of electronic publishing are all taken into consideration for the award, and in this case *Internet Archaeology* was commended for its use of innovative features in Issue 5, such as the division of the text into readable segments, the hypertext bibliography and glossary, and the interactive maps as found in the Wickham-Jones and Dalland paper. Somebody liked it!

BACK TO THE FUTURE

So, we have dipped our toes into Internet publication, and we now have to decide where to go from here. The Internet offers the possibility of a completely new style of publication. It is a publication with apparently endless flexibility, but it is one that may be harder to compile (I have deliberately not used the word 'write' here). We shall have to open up our innermost data for scrutiny by all and sundry, and we shall have to get off the fence and say what we think it all means (Fig. 6). Personally, I hope that we will take up the challenge and make the most of these exciting new possibilities.

The possibilities of Internet publication benefit not only the archaeological community, who want to make use of increasing amounts of comparative information, but also the general public, who wish to know more about a subject that interests them and touches their own background. Despite the proliferation of sub-ologies in the profession of archaeology we have seen our relationship with the general public grow over the last few years, and anything that makes us closer, while at the same time assisting our own work, must surely be a good thing.

ACKNOWLEDGEMENTS

First and foremost I have to thank Magnar Dalland and Rob Sands, who were very patient and understanding fellow team members. All of the staff at *Internet Archaeology*—Alan Vince, Sandra Garside-Neville and Judith Winters—put up with my many e-mail interruptions and cries for help with great forbearance (and they were cries from time to time, believe me). Judith and Alan in particular have been very helpful in reading through this paper and providing the statistics regarding readership. Gordon Barclay, Olly Owen and Patrick Ashmore at Historic Scotland have all helped on different aspects of the project. Figure 6 was drawn by Mary Kemp Clarke, and Figs 1 and 2 were drawn by Sylvia Stevenson. Magnar Dalland produced Figs 3 and 4. Finally, thanks to the readers whose comments on the paper and use of Internet publications can only help us to go forward.

REFERENCES

Butler, D. 1999 The writing is on the web for science journals in print. *Nature* **397**, 195–200. **http://www.nature.com**

Wickham-Jones, C.R. and Dalland, M. 1998a A small Mesolithic site at Fife Ness, Crail, Scotland. *Tayside and Fife Archaeological Journal* **4**, 1–19.

Wickham-Jones, C.R. and Dalland, M. 1998b A small Mesolithic site at Fife Ness, Crail, Scotland. *Internet Archaeology* **5**. **http://intarch.ac.uk/journal/issue5/index.html**

For those of you who are not attracted to the Mesolithic (shame on you), other *Internet Archaeology* papers may be found at: **http://intarch.ac.uk**

Happy browsing!

PREHISTORIC ARCHAEOLOGY IN IRELAND: REFLECTIONS AND RESPONSES

John Coles

This conference was an enquiry into and commentary on where we are in Irish prehistoric archaeology, and a celebration of the archaeological life of Liz Anderson. Although I did not know Liz personally, the many references to her by speakers at the conference showed the high regard in which she was held, and I have benefited from reading some of her papers. In this closing paper, which I hope will be a more reasoned assessment than the spoken summation, I will confine myself to those aspects of prehistoric archaeology that seem to me, in 1999, to demand attention, while begging the forgiveness of my many Irish colleagues for stating the obvious and overlooking or misunderstanding aspects that I should know better.

One way to approach such a reflective undertaking is to examine how prehistoric studies in Ireland have been viewed from without as well as from within. Of the literature on European prehistory written in the last 40 years or so, only Grahame Clark in his *Prehistoric Europe: the economic basis* (1952) seriously trawled the Irish sources and exposed a large and varied range of evidence that owed much to organic preservation as well as to a number of nineteenth-century excavations. Stuart Piggott in his *Neolithic cultures of the British Isles* (1954) concentrated on megalithic tombs, stone axe factories and Lough Gur, a rather serious demerit being his consistent use of the term 'British Neolithic'. He did better in his *Ancient Europe* (Piggott 1965), and the Irish tombs, house plans, artefacts and Celts all figured in his magisterial treatment of European prehistory. The global stage, with Clark's *World prehistory* (1977), had only a bit part for Ireland, and that was concerned with Clark's deep interest in prestige objects, both objects and monuments that spoke of status and thereby stratified societies. In more modern books, it has been somewhat disappointing to see that Irish prehistory is reduced to a few sites—Mount Sandel, Newgrange and Knowth in the main. There is a wide disregard of Ireland as an island and as a unique place within north-west Europe that might be considered as a model for particular enquiries (Champion *et al.* 1984; Cunliffe 1994; Whittle 1996); this matter is referred to below.

Of course, these books could not be expected to press for new concepts aimed at any particular area, and they are for us mere reportage, although cleverly constructed and useful in glancing at the wide stage. More relevant, then, are the books that are specifically aimed at Ireland, at the presentation of the prehistoric past and at the development of research themes and new approaches. Such books, written within the past two decades or so, should reflect the concerns of their contemporary archaeology and they might acknowledge the new directions that were being promulgated during the 1970s and 1980s. In the main, they tend to avoid such matters for which there was little enthusiasm, and they press home the interests of the authors (no bad thing). The books (Herity and Eogan 1977; O'Kelly 1989; Cooney and Grogan 1994; Waddell 1998) are useful quarries, of course, for the literature on Irish prehistory, but there is an imbalance in presentation. The treatment of the Irish Mesolithic, for example, is very uneven and there seems to be a lack of real enquiring interest in the period; in contrast, the Late Bronze Age has throughout claimed a very sizeable proportion of the texts. Since there has been as much innovative and more pioneering research into the Mesolithic than into the Late Bronze Age within the past 20 years, the textual result is surprising.

But more disappointing has been the lack of enthusiasm for examining, accepting, rejecting or modifying the theoretical concepts that were being offered throughout the periods of production of these books. One exception, in part, to this is Cooney and Grogan's 1994 book, which faced up to the difficult episodes in our archaeology of transitions between the traditional periods that prehistorians use. (That such periodisation has hampered rather than helped prehistoric studies is now clear, but there is no sense trying to persuade anyone or everyone to abandon the system; others have tried and failed.) But, more importantly, none of the books seriously attempted to apply the many concepts and stances that were offered to us over recent decades; Irish prehistorians are not alone in this deliberate shuttering, and their texts may thereby be the more useful to the many but the less stimulating to the few. In passing, it is worth noting here that the more recent of these books have very extensive bibliographies; Cooney and Grogan (1994) list over 500 references, many of them recent publications, a good reflection of the amount of work under way; Waddell (1998) in his massive treatment of prehistory lists over 1000 references.

Some of Liz Anderson's writings appear in these bibliographies, and I think that her paper on fishing (Anderson 1993) would have met with the approval of Grahame Clark, especially for her closing remark on seeking out 'those areas that will provide the best potential for the preservation of the environmental and organic assemblages' of the past. She was an active worker in many archaeological matters and her expertise is reflected in her short specialist reports. Many of today's graduates in archaeology find work if they seriously seek it, but many are offered minimal opportunities to utilise their talents and their training beyond the most basic levels in rescue and development archaeology. I would see one of the agendas for Irish archaeology as ensuring that young workers are offered responsibilities on sites and surveys, and in processing the results, so that experience is gained and, equally important, potential revealed. It is quite clearly what Liz had, and Irish archaeology has benefited from it.

My own involvement with Irish archaeology started in 1956 when I began to study the Bronze Age of Scotland, and came to Dublin for comparative work. Here I met two people who would become major players in Irish archaeology, George Eogan (then a research student) and Etienne Rynne (then at the National Museum). Since 1956 my visits have been many and varied, as a participant in conferences and excursions, as External Examiner, and as research worker (no capitals here; I don't deserve them). Throughout these visits, and by observing the flow of publications from Ireland, I can claim to have some familiarity with prehistoric studies, even if my knowledge is uneven. There have been a number of very useful developments in the past two decades and these will need no detailed listing; the important comment to make is that they are widely respected, and in particular cases widely envied. The Discovery Programme, which has to date concentrated its efforts on later prehistoric studies (North Munster, the Western Stone Forts, the Ballyhoura Hills, Tara) but is now moving into new areas of research, has already attracted much attention in western European archaeology. Its continued financial support and critical assessments should ensure that it will achieve a model status in national archaeologies; the key lies in its academic base and proactive approach.

I would also single out the various surveys that have been conducted in recent years, the Cork Archaeological Survey among them in its fundamental work of recognition, recording and extensive publication. The several gas pipeline surveys seem to me to have been particularly valuable in the exposure of new kinds of evidence rather than more of the same, and in the opportunity to begin to identify the intensity of settlement and activity in Ireland through an archaeologically random landscape. In contrast to these surveys, the continued research into a few major monuments, such as Knowth or the northern Irish forts, and into specific themes, such as the south-west copper mines, have augmented and refined previous ideas about these sites and introduced new concepts about prehistoric activity in Ireland. It is also worth a thought that, in national terms, some major high-profile surveys and excavations are always needed to maintain public interest and to attract the attention of a wider archaeological community. This may not appeal to the purists among us, but it is a fact of life.

The public's involvement in Irish archaeology can only be achieved and maintained through a serious effort to maintain a rate of publication of results, whether that be by traditional methods of monographic or periodic papers or by the more innovative use of new technology—both are needed. As already noted, the fact that Waddell's 1998 book contains over 1000 references, a majority of these referring to work published since 1980, indicates two things: the quite remarkable rate of presentation of results, and the need to maintain adequate outlets, both journals and monographs. At a different level of publication I single out the success of *Archaeology Ireland* as contributing both to early notice of work done and to wide public and international awareness of work in a variety of fields of enquiry. It may also serve to put some pressure on those whose discoveries appear in the pages of the magazine and who might otherwise have allowed their potential scholarly reports to lapse into the obscurity that so often overwhelms research. It might behove all Irish archaeologists to skim back through *Archaeology Ireland* from time to time to remind ourselves of what still remains to be put into the full record.

The following remarks about work for the future arise from my reading of the literature and from my presence at the conference. It was refreshing to hear the speakers address some of the particular themes that I had brought in my intellectual baggage, and their presentation of these was based on an understanding of Irish prehistory far greater than I possess. They also disabused me of certain of my ill-founded opinions.

One rather fundamental aspect has always puzzled me—although we all know Ireland to be an island, there appear to be few prehistorians who actively acknowledge this and seek to explore it in their research. This island has an enormously long and varied, attractive and forbidding, economically wealthy, and often accessible coastland. Rather few archaeologists, other than those studying the Mesolithic, seem to retain this fact in their minds as they seek to identify and explain the appearance and development of ancient communities. Small islands sometimes receive the treatment that they deserve, as do peninsulas here and there, but the big picture, Ireland as an island, somehow seems to evade recognition. Island archaeology is important; it excludes by definition some of the difficulties that a place like, for instance, Hungary has with its uneven and seemingly illogical bombardment from all sides, through drift as well as directed action. Environment, animal and plant life, trade, innovations in the record, the chronology of development, are interesting to us all, but an island archaeology starts off with the advantage of isolation; it helps the identification and dating of innovation, whether internal or introduced, and also the rates of change and evolution. This is nowhere more clear than for one of Europe's most pressing archaeological questions—the inception of the Neolithic, with the interaction of Mesolithic and Neolithic agencies (traditionally defined), if indeed they were separate, and if so by how much and for how long. These are questions that could be isolated here and examined in a variety of ways. In these conference proceedings, Monk's paper has got to grips with the environmental and economic evidence in a suitably critical way. And the important questions about Mesolithic involvement with the island landscapes are being addressed by Woodman in both directions, back in time towards a first colonisation and forwards to the merging of traditions of activities within a Neolithic period, however defined.

Not being much of a megalithic person, it seems to me that many of the big Irish tombs have been studied to death as objects themselves. More can always be done, of course, but they have had a tremendously good press. Failing any discoveries of untouched tombs with stratified internal deposits and immaculate preservation, maybe they could be considered at greater length as objects within their own landscapes, with their own positions as places of undoubted power, and be seen more as focal points for the societies whose intimate lives are not at all well known. Pre-eminent must be the great endeavours at and around Knowth, where the complex of monuments is only comprehensible by consideration of its place over wide space and a long time. At a different and equally important level, O'Brien's territorial assessments appear to me to be the only sensible approach to take for the tombs of the south-west. In passing, I think a neglected study is the place of these massive monuments within the ideological systems of much later, historic, times. Of course, the quite astounding megalithic art attached to the large tombs will continue to attract research, and here the realities of the art, now being exposed by Shee Twohig, should surely be pursued by the few who can be objective about them, to the detriment of the subjective maunderings of the many.

I have been asked to be critical, and so I venture to express the personal opinion that Irish later prehistoric metalwork, admirably and enticingly suited for study, has been drawn, typologised, analysed and interpreted enough for the moment. The gaps in knowledge are not to be filled from the bronzes themselves, but from their contexts within their immediate surrounds as well as within the wider social tensions and relationships of the first millennium BC. We do not know how a large number of these objects got into their watery graves, who put them in, from what place the operation was directed, how they came to be assembled in their various combinations, what the presumed effects on the manipulators and the observers of the actions were, and for how long this seemingly wasteful activity went on. The paper by Maher and Sheehan opened the debate and exposed some of the complexities of the record. We need new discoveries and assessments of place and circumstance rather than the objects themselves, because the work of assembling and internal analysis has been done so comprehensively and well.

We know relatively little about the later prehistoric landscapes of Ireland, the effects of minor climatic changes and environmental alterations, aspects like the manipulation and aligning of the land, or the smaller settlements and their internal structures. The assembly of the evidence on houses by Doody makes a useful start, but there is surely a vast amount of work to be done. Places of prestige and power like the big forts and stone circles always command attention and there is nothing wrong with that, but it is time, I think, for a look at and search for the little people. The Discovery Programme has directed attention towards these problems, and McCarthy's paper exposed to me the slenderness of the evidence for utilisation of wildlife, which we must suspect to have been far greater than the survivals indicate. But how to augment the evidence?

A real achievement, I believe, is the growing involvement of a number of archaeologists in regional studies. There can be no substitute for landscape assessments of particular areas (the smaller the better, in some respects), where intimacy can permit a reconstruction and a prediction that far outweighs global models in terms of understanding. The south-west of Ireland has been a testbed for much of this, with the pipelines helping to forge new lines of approach. But a better focus on chronology, on the detail of environmental change, and on predictions of population density are needed, and the current developments in archaeological science and modelling should permit matters to move on. A great advantage of small-scale landscape surveys is the ability to involve local people in the work, as well as the opportunity to test theories about early societies, the rate of change in economic or industrial practices, the impacts of new technologies and fashions, and the movement of people. This last, however, is to my mind grossly over-used and is no substitute for real confrontation with the problems of the record. We really cannot continue to assert that 'people were on the move' without much more critical assessment of the evidence.

One advantage to the reader rather than to the listener is that the former can shut the book while the latter may be trapped in the lecture hall. The story is told about the opening lecture given by Henri Breuil at the Madrid Congress about 50 years ago. Breuil was 77 years old, and his keynote lecture was attended by various dignitaries who began to fidget and groan as the Abbé droned on and on. At last, the Congress Past-President, Emil Vogt, sought to silence him by tugging his coat-tails; Breuil wrenched himself free with the lively vigour of the polychrome bison of Altamira that he was at that point describing to a dwindling audience. I have no such reason to resist the action of readers who may wish to give up at this point, if indeed anyone has got this far.

The theme of the conference was new agendas, and I will not be drawn into producing a list of raw subjects that might be pursued; others will know them better than I do. Indeed, the 1993 book *Past perceptions* (Shee Twohig and Ronayne 1993) has foreshadowed much of my own thinking, so that what follows may well seem to be as old-fashioned as some of us are. But different things interest different folk, and among the former are, for me, a constant desire to come closer to the individual in prehistory, those who to us must remain in nameless anonymity but who pursued their individuality during their brief lives. We glimpse a few of them through the individualising of the deposition ceremonies for the dead, but we are almost wholly uninformed about the majority, the unrecovered, the unmarked, the unknown. The ordinary people, those whose lives were not distinguished by death and are at present almost invisible, must surely become a focus for us. We may be able to identify them, as a group, by patterning of the record, but that will require a greater effort to move away from the concept of site as definition and towards the idea of social landscapes, in an off-site archaeology that still lacks a real theoretical base.

Of other generalised thoughts, I only mention a few.

Our hard evidence, the material culture upon which many of us expend our energies, has become too rigid and has come to define our research rather than to serve as accessories to our studies. It is time to create research themes that seek to enlarge our understanding and to look beyond what we can hold in our hands. Fossils we dig up, but our ideas must not be shaped by their unyielding forms.

The big picture, if not global archaeology then all-Ireland archaeology, must not overwhelm and outweigh the small intimate scenes that enliven our comprehension of the past. Small is certainly beautiful; we need smallness to refine the bigness that otherwise will mask the details of life. Of course, we need both viewpoints, but most of us seek to model behavioural patterns on a maxi-scale.

The gaps in our archaeological record are well known and the conference papers faced up to some of them. We need to produce ways and means to identify the seemingly unidentifiable, to acknowledge that perhaps we have unconsciously ignored, because we cannot classify, particular kinds of evidence, or that we have inadequate techniques of recovery, or that perhaps those gaps did not exist in past realities. The Celts?

A concern that troubles me, at all levels, is the reliability of the record. Our models are constructed upon the records that we have accumulated over the past decades, and new evidence is sometimes made to fit into the old patterns. Our records are always going to be inadequate, some as good as possible, some mediocre because incomplete, some downright wrong and misleading. How to weed out the last, to avoid its distorting influence, is a real problem. Once lodged within an official record, it becomes in a way part of the past and must influence our perceptions of that past; it might just be the wrong past.

Much of this last point might be resolved by a recognition that landscapes and sites will in their turn yield only what can be preserved by the natural factors at work, altered by what we have done to that environment, and distorted by our priorities in recovery. If we start with badly preserved evidence, we can hardly do more than our best, and the record will still be poor. If we begin our enquiries with evidence that is, or seems to be, well preserved, then we have a chance to augment the record and expose new possibilities for interpretation. Such conditions need not be wet, although that often helps, but they may merely be less disturbed than usual and thereby unique within their particular sphere. Recovery techniques, with all that is now analytically possible, must evolve by experimentation and the development of scientific work at all levels.

Listening to the papers, considering their implications for future research, and trying to see how new sets of evidence and new concepts can reframe Irish prehistoric studies, it is easy to see within them some of the ideas and concerns of Liz Anderson. She was interested in coastlands as resource and as opportunity, in the intimacy of landscapes, in the exploitation of resources, and in the mobility of populations. I dare say that the last will prove to be one theme that will come to dominate some of our research in the future, and doubtless her other ideas will also be pursued. The current active research now under way in Ireland to my mind augurs well for the future that Liz sought to promote during her all-too-brief archaeological life.

REFERENCES

Anderson, E. 1993 The Mesolithic in Munster: fishing for answers. In E. Shee Twohig and M. Ronayne (eds), *Past perceptions: the prehistoric archaeology of south-west Ireland*, 16–24. Cork University Press.

Champion, T., Gamble, C., Shennan, S. and Whittle, A. 1984 *Prehistoric Europe.* London. Academic Press.

Clark, J.G.D. 1952 *Prehistoric Europe: the economic basis.* London. Methuen.

Clark, [J.] G. [D.] 1977 *World prehistory.* Cambridge University Press.

Cooney, G. and Grogan, E. 1994 *Irish prehistory: a social perspective.* Bray. Wordwell.

Cunliffe, B. (ed.) 1994 *The Oxford illustrated prehistory of Europe.* Oxford University Press.

Herity, M. and Eogan, G. 1977 *Ireland in prehistory.* London. Routledge and Kegan Paul.

O'Kelly, M.J. 1989 *Early Ireland: an introduction to Irish prehistory.* Cambridge University Press.

Piggott, S. 1954 *The Neolithic cultures of the British Isles.* Cambridge University Press.

Piggott, S. 1965 *Ancient Europe.* Edinburgh University Press.

Shee Twohig, E. and Ronayne, M. (eds) 1993 *Past perceptions: the prehistoric archaeology of south-west Ireland.* Cork University Press.

Waddell, J. 1998 *The prehistoric archaeology of Ireland.* Galway University Press.

Whittle, A. 1996 *Europe in the Neolithic: the creation of new worlds.* Cambridge University Press.